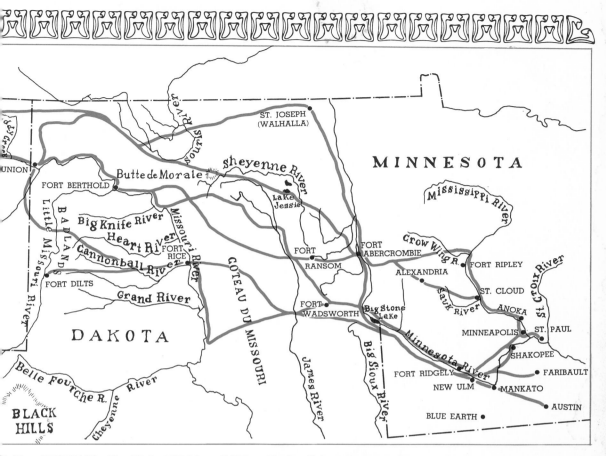

ST. JOSEPH
(WALHALLA)

MINNESOTA

FORT UNION

FORT BERTHOLD

Butte de Morale

Lake Jessie

sheyenne River

Souris River

Mississippi River

Big Knife River

Heart River

FORT RICE

Cannonball River

FORT DILTS

Grand River

BADLANDS

Little Missouri River

Missouri River

COTEAU DU MISSOURI

DAKOTA

Belle Fourche R.

Cheyenne River

BLACK HILLS

James River

Big Sioux River

FORT RANSOM

FORT WADSWORTH

Big Stone Lake

FORT ABERCROMBIE

Crow Wing R.

ALEXANDRIA

Sauk River

FORT RIPLEY

ST. CLOUD

ANOKA

MINNEAPOLIS

St. Croix River

ST. PAUL

SHAKOPEE

FARIBAULT

Minnesota River

FORT RIDGELY

NEW ULM

MANKATO

BLUE EARTH

AUSTIN

LD FIELDS IN THE YEARS 1862-1867

978   White
c. /   Ho! for the gold fields

Publications of the

MINNESOTA HISTORICAL SOCIETY

RUSSELL W. FRIDLEY

Editor and Director

JUNE DRENNING HOLMQUIST

Associate Editor

HO! FOR THE

Northern

MINNESOTA HISTORICAL SOCIETY

GOLD FIELDS

Overland Wagon Trains

of the 1860s

HELEN McCANN WHITE, *Editor*

ST. PAUL, 1966

Preface

THIS BOOK has a long history. In the early 1930s the Alvord Memorial Commission of the Mississippi Valley Historical Association became interested in publishing a volume of documents relating to the James L. Fisk expeditions which went from Minnesota to the Montana gold fields in the 1860s. The editors of the planned book were to be Theodore C. Blegen, superintendent of the Minnesota Historical Society, and Charles J. Ritchey, then professor of history in Macalester College, St. Paul. Dr. Blegen, his predecessor, Solon J. Buck, and two curators of manuscripts on the Minnesota Historical Society's staff — Miss Ethel B. Virtue and Dr. Grace Lee Nute — had instituted a search for documents that would shed light on the little-known Fisk expeditions. Two of the manuscripts they found, the diaries of Dr. William D. Dibb, are included in these pages.

Continuing the search, Professor Ritchey located other pertinent documents in Montana. Among them were the diaries of Andrew J. and Robert E. Fisk reproduced in the 1866 section of this book. Additional research turned up newspaper accounts of the James A. Sawyers trains, which went from Iowa to Montana in the 1860s, and further information on trains led by Peter B. Davy and Thomas A. Holmes, including Luther Brown's account which is represented here. In the years that followed the editors expanded the scope of their work to cover all of these trains. They also drafted introductions to the documents they selected for inclusion, but other professional commitments prevented them from completing the project.

In 1944 Dr. Nute, who was then chairman of the Alvord Commission, asked me to take over the task of preparing the volume for publication. In beginning the project anew, my study of early Minnesota newspapers revealed the significance of the wagon train migrations to the dreams of Minnesota expansionists. After extensive research I reluctantly dropped the section on the Iowa trains and decided to focus the book on the eight Minnesota expeditions. With newly discovered source materials, I then annotated all the documents and wrote introductions to tell the story of the Minnesota expeditions. Research in Montana and in Washington, D.C., provided much new information on Fisk as well as data on many of the emigrants. The latter was used to compile the rosters which constitute the appendix of this volume.

The documents included in this book are in private hands and in the collections of three institutions. The manuscript diaries of Dr. Dibb remain in the hands of his descendants, and I am indebted to Mr. Gerald E. Fitzgerald of St. Paul for permission to publish them. The Minnesota Historical Society has the newspapers that contain most of the accounts of the Holmes and Davy trains, as well as the journal of Robert Fisk for which publication rights were generously granted by its donor Mrs. Agnes Train Janssen. The Historical Society of Montana — which has the only extant copy of Gilbert Benedict's diary as well as newspapers containing other source materials on the Davy train — granted permission for their use in this book, while Bruce M. Fisk of Seattle, Washington, who gave the Andrew Fisk papers to the Montana society, graciously allowed the publication here of a part of his grandfather's diary. James Fisk's report of 1864 and the Andrew Osland letter of the Davy expedition are reproduced from the holdings of the National Archives. James Fisk's brief report on the 1862 expedition is reprinted from a government publication.

My selection of the documents in the book was governed by a number of considerations. Whenever possible I chose letters and diaries that had not been previously published or, if published, were not readily available. I also tried to preserve a reasonable balance in the amount of space devoted to each of the wagon trains and to present documents which offer maximum information within this space. Finally, I have included source materials which tell something of emigrant life in the gold region at the conclusion of the overland journey.

In editing the letters and diaries here presented I wished to preserve the unique flavor of each document, with its idiosyncracies of language, spelling, and punctuation, while at the same time meeting the requirements of clarity and readability. To do so, only a few changes were made in the manuscript form: (1) Raised letters were omitted in date entries and either omitted or placed flush with the lines elsewhere in the documents. (2) The intent of the author was respected in deletions and insertions in the documents, and occasional words repeated in error were dropped from the text. (3) Bracketed letters were inserted to correct a misspelled word the first time it occurred, and later, where the meaning would be confusing without such corrections. If an author frequently misspelled a word in a variety of ways, his most characteristic spelling was followed. Misspelled proper names are followed the first time used by the correct name in brackets if it is known. Existing recognizable place names have not been changed, but obsolete names or those grossly misspelled are followed by bracketed present-day names in the form recommended by the United States Geographic Board. Only a few other bracketed insertions appear where they seemed necessary to an understanding of the text. (4) A few changes have been made in punctuation. Colons, dashes, and hyphens terminating sentences have been converted to periods. If no punctuation marks appeared at the end of a sentence either a period has been added or extra space left in the text. (5) In the interests of economy and readability, some short paragraphs were combined and some long ones divided. (6) Unusual editorial problems relating to individual documents are noted in footnotes to the text. In several of the journals, entries beyond the overland journey and the scope of this volume were omitted, and this fact is recorded in textual footnotes.

Funds from four organizations have aided this project over the years. Initially the Alvord Commission provided money for typing assistance, for a preliminary check of selected newspaper sources in the Minnesota Historical Society's collection, for copies of some of the pictures reproduced here, and for two maps prepared for an early version of the manuscript. When the Alvord Commission was disbanded in the 1950s, its funds were transferred to the Minnesota Historical Society to be used for the publication of this book. In 1955 the Minnesota Historical Society granted me additional financial aid. Nine years later I received the society's annual McKnight Foundation grant, which enabled me to go to Montana in search of information which appears in the rosters. In 1965 a grant-in-aid from the American Association for State and Local History allowed me to secure needed photocopies and make a trip to Minnesota to work with the society's editors.

Many people, literally around the world, have helped me with this project. Because of my husband's government service, we have lived, during the years I have been engaged in the preparation of this book, in five states (Minnesota, Utah, California, Colorado, and Virginia) and in three foreign countries (Japan, the Philippines, and France). Research and writing were interrupted frequently for long periods by family duties and official and community responsibilities, but librarians in these and many other places helped me find useful reference materials.

Special thinks are due the grandchildren of James L. Fisk — Mrs. Thomas W. Fountain, Mrs. Margaret Zastrow, and Mr. Charles Frisbie — who permitted me to use, copy, and quote from manuscripts in their possession dealing with the Fisk family and Fisk's expeditions. Present and former staff members of the Historical Society of Montana have aided me over all the years I have worked on this project. I am especially grateful to Mrs. Anne McDonnell, Miss Virginia Walton, Miss Mary Dempsey, Mr. Michael Kennedy, Miss Bernice Boone, Mrs. Harriet Meloy, and Mr. Michael Fleming. Other Montanans who have helped me include Miss M. Catherine White of the University of Montana Library, Missoula, Dr. Stanley R. Davison of Dillon, and Mr. and Mrs. Charles Bovey of Great Falls and Virginia City.

Among the present and former staff members of the Minnesota Historical Society not already mentioned who have assisted me, I am especially grateful to Russell W. Fridley, director of the society, and to Miss Lois M. Fawcett, Miss Lucile M. Kane, Messrs. Willoughby M. Babcock, G. Hubert Smith, Michael Brook, and Alan R. Woolworth. I owe a special debt to the members of the society's publications department and especially to patient and capable editor Mrs. Anne A. Hage, and talented editor and friend Mrs. June D. Holmquist, without whose advice and encouragement I would never have completed this book. I also wish to record my appreciation of the help I received from present and former staff members of the National Archives: Mrs. Sarah Jackson, Mr. Albert Blair, Mr. Milton Chamberlain, and Dr. Frank Burch.

Other persons who aided me in various ways were Mrs. Jack Vezina, Mrs. Margaret LaRue, Miss Irene McCourt, and Mr. Walter Dahl of St. Croix Falls, Wisconsin; Mrs. Robert Morreim, Mr. Carlton Eckberg, and Mr. John Pattison of St. Cloud, Minnesota; Mrs. Amy Handschuh Sjostrom, Redwood City, California; Mr. Roger Williams, St. Paul; Mr. Herman Chilson, Webster, South Dakota; Mrs. Ruth Davidson and Mrs. Elden Billings, Washington, D.C.; Mr. S. Barlow, Nuneaton, England; Dr. J. Porter Graham of Spokane, Washington; and the late Dr. Charles S. Kingston of Cheney, Washington. Mr. Hartwell Bowsfield drew my attention to the diary of William Johnstone in the collections of the Provincial Library of Manitoba in Winnipeg, Canada, and Mrs. J. W. Glenwright of Toronto kindly gave me permission to quote from it.

Alan Ominsky of the Minnesota Historical Society staff prepared the maps in this volume, and Mrs. Marjorie Kreidberg is responsible for the handsome hand lettering on the end sheets. Unless otherwise credited the pictures reproduced in these pages are in the collections of the Minnesota Historical Society, and the able curator of the picture department, Eugene D. Becker, provided high-quality photographic copies of many of them.

My three children, Barbara, Timothy, and Bruce, have each in turn grown into the job of helping to check newspapers, city directories, census schedules, and military and pension records used in the preparation of the rosters. My sister-in-law Mrs. Philip White, my mother Mrs. Edward McCann, and my brother Edward R. McCann have also provided invaluable aid at critical stages in the preparation of this book. To these members of my family and to all other persons and organizations that helped me I express my sincere appreciation. Most of all, however, I thank my husband for his encouragement, enthusiasm, and financial support of this project over twenty-two years.

St. Paul, Minnesota   Helen M. White
September 13, 1966

Contents

Maps

❀❀❀❀❀❀❀❀❀❀❀❀❀❀❀❀❀❀❀❀❀❀❀❀❀❀❀❀❀

HO! FOR THE GOLD FIELDS

General Introduction

EARLY ON A SUMMER DAY IN THE 1860s, when new grass had turned the prairies green, a Minnesota wagon train uncurled from its rendezvous corral and rolled out on the Dakota plains. Guides and scouts on horseback rode ahead to search for a trail, watching for signs of Indians, locating easy river crossings, and spotting suitable campgrounds. Then came an armed escort, followed by a rumbling mule-drawn wagon carrying a mountain howitzer, and next the light wagon of the expedition leader with its American flag floating proudly in the prairie breeze. Behind them rolled the wagons and carts of a hundred or more emigrants, each in its assigned place in the order of march. As the wagons turned into the deepening trail, wheels and ox yokes squeaked, pans rattled, men shouted orders, children called, dogs barked, chickens cackled. Canvas wagon tops gleamed in the sunlight and crudely painted slogans proclaimed the train's destination: "Ho! for Montana!" "Ho! for the Gold Fields!" [1]

Eight such trains set out across the northern plains between 1862 and 1867, carrying emigrants from Minnesota to newly discovered gold fields in that area of rapidly changing boundaries which eventually became the state of Montana. Flushed with the same gold fever that had lured them to California in 1849, restless Americans were again hitching their wagons to a golden star. At the beginning of the 1860s they could reach the new gold fields by traveling over the central plains toward California and Oregon and then following one of the cutoff trails to the northern Rockies. Or, if they wished to travel light and fast, they could take the more expensive steamboat journey from St. Louis up the Missouri River. Minnesota frontiersmen, however, chose instead to open new and shorter trails directly west across the northern plains. Between Minnesota and the Montana El Dorados lay more than a thousand miles of unmapped wilderness, inhabited

[1] For additional background on the material discussed here and below, see Helen M. White, "Minnesota, Montana, and Manifest Destiny," in *Minnesota History*, 38:53–62 (June, 1962).

In the interests of brevity the following abbreviations have been used throughout this volume: MiHS — Minnesota Historical Society; MoHS — Montana Historical Society; *SMP Register* — James U. Sanders, ed., *Society of Montana Pioneers Register* ([Helena], 1899); WRR — United States War Department, *The War of the Rebellion: A Compilation of the Official Records of the Union and Confederate Armies*, series 1. The *St. Paul Press* is cited throughout as *Press;* the *St. Paul Pioneer and Democrat* and its successor after September, 1862, the *St. Paul Pioneer,* are both cited as *Pioneer.* Unless otherwise noted, daily editions of newspapers have been used.

1

by Indians and dotted by only a few widely scattered fur trading posts and military forts.

This volume attempts to explain why Minnesota frontiersmen ventured across an unsettled and little-known region. It tells the story of the fourteen hundred or so emigrants who traveled the northern overland route from Minnesota to Montana in the 1860s and undertakes to answer these questions: Who were these emigrants? Where did they come from? Where were their trails, and what was the significance of their migration for Minnesota, the Dakotas, and Montana? The story is told in the emigrants' own words in letters, diaries, and newspaper accounts relating their day-to-day experiences on the trail. Introductions and explanatory notes provide background and describe the plans and schemes of farsighted Minnesotans who saw in the gold fields the first substance of an old dream of empire. That dream was to have important implications for a developing nation, and it is an integral part of the historical fabric of Minnesota and the northern plains states.

Minnesota promoters encouraged emigration to the gold fields because they believed that each emigrant who traveled over the northern plains served the long-range good of the state. They saw immediate profits to be made from outfitting the emigrants and the army troops who would inevitably be sent to protect them. Beyond the plains, burgeoning towns in the gold fields offered a trading area that would look to Minnesota for supplies and capital. Sensitive to the promise of this expanding empire, boosters urged emigrants to go west and button Minnesota to the sleeve of the gold region.

Some Minnesotans had an even broader view. They saw the gold fields as mere way stations on a broad road to a vast economic empire. They believed that Minnesota, because of its geographical location, was destined to lie on important lines of communication across the North American continent. The trails of the emigrant, they thought, would inevitably become the pathways of commerce between the Atlantic and the Pacific, the arteries of trade through which would flow the products of European civilization and the wealth of the Orient. To men with this vision each emigrant who traveled through Minnesota to the gold fields hastened the day of destiny, and the destiny was manifest — as clear as the waters of Lake Superior or the springs that fed the sources of the Mississippi. A few facts of geography, treated with boundless imagination, and a decade of projects had brought the leaders of the territory and state to this view.

The vision did not develop overnight. It was born in the 1850s when certain Minnesotans came to believe that the territory's greatest resource was its unique geographical position at the heart of the North American continent. Its capital city, St. Paul, was located on the forty-fifth parallel, halfway between the equator and the North Pole — a circumstance which assumed symbolic and almost mystical meaning. At the head of Lake Superior, Minnesota stood at the terminus of an interior waterway which dreamers even then believed would bring ocean vessels from the Atlantic into the center of the continent. Within the state's borders lay the headwaters of the Mississippi River, the nation's great inland waterway. To the north Minnesota shared a boundary with the British possessions and commanded the sources of the Red River of the North, a navigable stream leading to Winnipeg and the waters flowing into Hudson Bay. Thus situated on natural avenues of commerce to the east, south, and north, Minnesota needed only a connection with the Pacific to place it in easy communication with all of the Northern Hemisphere.

Climate became an important consideration in this global vision. In the mid-nineteenth century it was widely believed that the severe weather of the northern country would not support settlement. Since it was undeniably true that winters were cold and waterways were frozen half the year, it was better to speak of averages rather than extremes. Dreamers turned attention from latitudes to isotherms and reasoned away the bugbears of snow and ice with the help of two scientist-dreamers, Alexander von Humboldt and Lorin Blodget. Pointing out that the climate of a region is influenced by humidity, prevailing winds, configuration of the land, and altitude, as well as distance from the equator and the poles, Humboldt developed the concept of isothermal lines connecting points of equal average temperatures. Maps drawn by Blodget indicated that Minnesota and much of the northern plains lay in an isothermal zone of moderate temperatures which extended around the globe in the Northern Hemisphere. Because this zone also embraced the great population centers of the world in regions having a high degree of civilization, it was asserted that the climate there was particularly conducive to the health and happiness of the human race. The exhilarating conclusion to be drawn from such reasoning was that human enterprise would inevitably expand and flourish in Minnesota and in the unsettled areas to the west.[2]

Around the world in the Northern Hemisphere, Minnesota's global dreamers foresaw a growth of settlement and lines of communication which they felt supported their vision of Minnesota's destiny. Russia was expanding into an unsettled area much like the northern plains in terrain and climate, and Minnesota newspapers reported Russian plans to extend postal, telegraph, and railroad lines across the continent to settlements on the Amur River. The opening of Japan to trade following the expedition of Commodore Matthew C. Perry in 1852–54 was greeted by the *St. Paul Pioneer* of June 28, 1854, as "one of the great achievements of the nineteenth century." The results of Perry's trip seemed even more promising after the publication of scientific information on the Japan Current. This led to speculation about the advantages of a shorter, great-circle sailing route from the Orient across the Pacific to Puget Sound and caused one Minnesota booster to rhapsodize that "even the broad currents of the Pacific enter into the conspiracy of natural and human agencies for building up this great Northern Highway to the Indes."[3]

The premature opening in 1858 of the Atlantic cable — a joint British-American venture — occasioned a large public celebration in St. Paul hailing it as a major stride toward linking the markets of Europe and America. Lines of communication with the eastern United States had been strengthened in 1854 by the com-

[2] Alexander von Humboldt, *Cosmos: A Sketch of a Physical Description of the Universe*, 2:317–335 (New York, 1850); Lorin Blodget, *Climatology of the United States and of the Temperate Latitudes of the North American Continent*, 529–534, charts op. 210, 308 (Philadelphia, 1857). For evidence that Minnesota promoters made use of the isothermal concept, see *Minnesota Democrat* (St. Paul), June 22, 1853; *Pioneer*, July 3, 14, December 10, 1858, January 28, April 5, May 22, November 13, 1859.
[3] *Pioneer*, September 18, 1858.

pletion of a rail line to the Mississippi River at Rock Island, Illinois; in the next year the opening of the Sault Ste. Marie Canal between Lakes Superior and Huron eliminated a costly portage which had blocked direct ship passage to the head of the Great Lakes. Communication with the East was further improved in 1860 when telegraph service reached St. Paul.

As for the North, during the 1850s a thriving trade grew up between Minnesota and the Canadian Red River settlements. Toward the close of the decade the British showed a fresh interest in the development of their North American possessions, and the prospect of settlement in the fertile prairie areas stimulated the hope of Minnesotans that central Canada could be tied economically, if not politically, to the United States.[4]

Thus by the 1860s only the West remained to be conquered. Hopes were fired as early as 1853 when the federal government authorized the exploration of several possible routes for a Pacific railroad, one of which lay between the forty-seventh and forty-ninth parallels. Isaac I. Stevens, newly appointed governor of Washington Territory, was chosen to survey the northernmost route. He outfitted in St. Paul and hired Pierre Bottineau, a competent Red River guide well known in the Minnesota capital, to lead him to the upper Missouri. Reports of the Stevens survey appeared that summer and fall in the *Minnesota Democrat.* An outgrowth of his work was the opening in the early 1860s of a military wagon road built by Lieutenant John Mullan over the Rocky Mountains between Fort Benton on the Missouri and Fort Walla Walla on the Columbia.[5]

The Mullan Road was the only immediate and tangible outcome of the Stevens survey. Nearly two thousand miles of wilderness remained to be spanned, and there was little possibility of railway construction in an area too sparsely settled to support a road. But it had already occurred to the dreamers that any form of communication over any route between Minnesota and the Pacific might encourage the settlements which would eventually make a railroad possible. Thus these men bent their efforts toward opening emigrant wagon routes, which they hoped would serve as entering wedges for the iron horse. As a St. Paul newspaper remarked in 1856, "an emigrant road becomes of far greater importance to the people of Minnesota, than attaches to it merely as a wagon road through our territory to the Pacific."[6]

For a time it seemed as though the course of destiny would be directed over a road from Minnesota to California. William H. Nobles, a settler of territorial Minnesota and a veteran of the California gold rush, became a prime mover in this project. Nobles had discovered a pass through the Sierras which still bears

    [4] Henry C. Klassen, "The Red River Settlement and the St. Paul Route, 1859–1870," p. 19, 23, 37 (master's thesis, 1963, University of Manitoba, photocopy in MiHS).

    [5] For Stevens' description of his journey, see *Narrative and Final Report of Explorations for a Route for a Pacific Railroad, near the Forty-seventh and Forty-ninth Parallels of North Latitude, from St. Paul to Puget Sound,* in 36 Congress, 1 session, *House Executive Documents,* no. 56 (serial 1054). Stevens' maps are in 33 Congress, 2 session, *Senate Executive Documents,* no. 78 (serial 768).

    For reports of his expedition, see *Minnesota Democrat,* April 20, May 11, 18, June 8, 22, September 14, 1853. For the Mullan Road, see John Mullan, *Report on the Construction of a Military Road from Fort Walla-Walla to Fort Benton* (37 Congress, 3 session, *Senate Executive Documents,* no. 43 — serial 1149).

    [6] *Pioneer,* December 17, 1856.

his name, and for several years after he returned from the West in 1853 he worked with great energy to enlist local and governmental support for a northern wagon road. In 1856 Nobles and a group of influential speculators succeeded in obtaining a congressional appropriation of fifty thousand dollars for a road which would begin at Fort Ridgely in central Minnesota, cross the Missouri east of the Black Hills, and join the central overland roads at South Pass in present-day Wyoming. Nobles was put in charge of the construction. Late in the fall of 1856 he made a preliminary reconnaissance of part of the route; during the following year he marked the roadbed from Fort Ridgely to the Missouri with mounds of earth, graded the riverbanks, and put in permanent fords — at least one of which could still be seen almost a hundred years later. Work on the project was halted in 1858 by political and financial difficulties.[7]

Destiny pointed a new direction in 1858 when rich gold deposits were discovered on the Fraser River in British Columbia. "The interest which the discoveries of gold in that locality has excited, has revived to the verge of practical solution the favorite Minnesota project of a northern emigrant route to the Pacific," wrote the editor of the *St. Paul Pioneer and Democrat* on July 9, 1858. St. Paul businessmen took the lead in an effort to open a line of communication with western Canada and the Fraser River. In 1858 and 1859 mass meetings were held, and the St. Paul city council and the Minnesota legislature sent resolutions to Washington on behalf of a wagon road to the gold fields. The state House of Representatives ordered the printing of a report on the gold mines and on a route through Minnesota to them. The army in 1858 established a new military post — Fort Abercrombie — on the Red River. These events prepared the way for the organization of an expedition to explore a northwestern emigrant route from St. Paul to the Fraser River, which it was hoped would not only gather detailed information about the country but also eventually help to extend Minnesota's sphere of influence and trade into the Canadian West. Nobles actively promoted this project, and in 1859 he led a group of gold seekers, explorers, and newspapermen as far as Fort Ellice on the Assiniboine River, in what is now Manitoba, where the expedition disbanded. Although small parties of men passed that way for some years, the wished-for wagon road did not materialize.[8]

In the early 1860s prospectors found rich deposits of gold in the Cariboo Lake district of British Columbia and in the Salmon River region of present-day Idaho. A flood of gold seekers bound for the Canadian mines traveled across Minnesota, and many more began to think of going to the new El Dorado on the American side of the border. Congress, spurred to action by the great interest in the new

[7] Information about Nobles and the road is summarized in W. Turrentine Jackson, *Wagon Roads West*, 168–170, 175, 179–190 (Berkeley, 1952), but see also S. S. Judy and Will G. Robinson, "Sanborn County History," in *South Dakota Historical Collections*, 26:3 (Pierre, 1953); *Minnesota Democrat*, February 22, 1854; and *Pioneer*, March 6, 1856.

[8] For a discussion of gold discoveries in the northern Rockies, see William J. Trimble, *The Mining Advance into the Inland Empire* (University of Wisconsin, *Bulletins*, no. 638 — Madison, 1914). Minnesota reactions are described in Alvin C. Gluek, Jr., *Minnesota and the Manifest Destiny of the Canadian Northwest: A Study in Canadian-American Relations*, 133–140 (Toronto, 1965). See also Willoughby M. Babcock, "Gateway to the Northwest: St. Paul and the Nobles Expedition of 1859," in *Minnesota History*, 35:249–262 (June, 1957), and Minnesota Legislature, *Report from a Select Committee of the House of Representatives, on the Overland Emigration Route from Minnesota to British Oregon* (St. Paul, 1858).

American discoveries and the need for increased gold supplies to finance the
Civil War, appropriated funds in 1861 and 1862 for the protection of emigrants
on overland routes to California and the Northwest.

A number of Minnesotans in strategic positions in the Lincoln administration
moved immediately to see that five thousand dollars of the 1862 appropriation
was allocated for the protection of a northern route which would follow Stevens'
path from Fort Abercrombie to the northern Rockies. This action marked the
launching of the full-scale campaign of the 1860s to open direct lines of communication with the Pacific Coast. Using the methods and techniques of the 1850s and
leaning heavily on the now familiar logic of manifest destiny, Minnesotans again
schemed for both private and government support to help realize their dream. At
the same time they actively recruited gold-field emigrants, attaching great importance to the number of persons who could be induced to travel over northern
trails. In their view each emigrant who swelled the gold-field population increased
the need for economic ties with the settled regions, and each emigrant was a potential voice in the chorus advertising the virtues of route and region.

In order to obtain federal funds and military assistance during the Civil War
years, it was necessary to demonstrate that the development of new travel routes
was in the national interest and did not constitute a diversion of resources more
urgently needed in the war effort. Promoters of the northern trails pointed not
only to the augmenting of the nation's gold reserves, but also to the importance of
tying the western areas more closely to the Union cause, deterring British en-
croachment into the Northwest, and discouraging the alliance of hostile plains
Indians with British Canadians to the north or Confederate forces to the south.
After the uprising of the Minnesota Sioux in 1862 they also emphasized the necessity for a strong military force to check further Indian attacks.[9]

During the 1860s members of Minnesota's congressional delegation — Senators
Henry M. Rice, Morton S. Wilkinson, and Alexander Ramsey, and Representatives Cyrus W. Aldrich, William Windom, and Ignatius Donnelly — supported
bills to aid northern routes, protect overland emigration, build wagon roads, and
extend post and express routes. In these years only one bill for a northern wagon
road was enacted into law; Congress authorized a road from Niobrara (Nebraska) to Virginia City (Montana) in 1865, but it proved to be of little value to
Minnesota. Congressional acts for the protection of emigration, passed in 1862,
1863, and 1864, were most useful to the Minnesota campaign. Under the terms of
this legislation, the army appointed superintendents who organized and escorted
emigrant trains along specified routes across the plains. Army units on duty in
the region extended additional military protection to both government-sponsored
and privately organized trains and assisted them in other ways. The extent of
this support varied from year to year, but all the northern overland trains except
the first one in 1862 received some assistance from the army. Most often the
help took the form of military escort between posts on the trail; indeed, a number of forts were specifically located in 1864 to guard the route of expected gold-
field emigration.

Although some promoters felt that the keystone of their program was financial

[9] See, for example, the *Winona Republican*, March 7, 1864; *Faribault Central Republican*,
March 16, October 5, 26, 1864.

support from the federal government, the campaign for the northern route was actually a broader one in which federal and state government, business organizations, citizen groups, and individuals participated. Each at one time or another played an effective role, and the results of each season's campaign grew out of the interplay of all these forces.

A typical campaign of the 1860s began in the middle of winter, when Minnesota newspapers printed dispatches from the most recently discovered gold fields. A lecturer — perhaps a returned emigrant or an expedition leader — addressed boards of trade, library associations, or mass meetings of citizens interested in the gold fields. He described the mining region, the northern routes, and the organization of a wagon train. Some veteran of other gold fields might offer advice on what the gold seeker should take with him to the mines. The meeting would then adopt resolutions and memorials for transmittal to the legislature, Congress, cabinet officers, army generals, or perhaps even the President, asking financial and military support for a northern route. Newspapers printed reports of these meetings, and a flurry of letters to the editor supported, criticized, and amended the information published.

The immediate benefits to be expected in the form of increased commerce and trade with the gold-field settlements were described in great detail, and the long-range significance of communication with the Pacific Coast was emphasized again and again. Local businessmen's organizations pledged financial support, and merchants planned to send wagonloads of goods over the trails for sale at the mines.

As the campaign gathered momentum, handbills, circulars, and maps were issued describing the gold fields and the routes to them and announcing the time and place of rendezvous for wagon trains. Such literature was an important feature of the campaign because few guidebooks for western travelers contained information about the northern region or its routes. Randall H. Hewitt, who traveled to Montana and the Pacific Coast in 1862, recalled that the maps available "proved more or less inaccurate," and the guidebooks "only served to make confusion worse confounded."[10] The most useful information for any prospective emigrant planning to cross the northern plains could be found in Isaac Stevens' report with its superb descriptions of the land, the rivers, the Indians, and the wildlife, but it is unlikely that many emigrants had seen this report, much less obtained a personal copy.

Minnesota newspapers both reflected and fired enthusiasm for the campaign to open northern routes. They publicized each new gold discovery, reprinted useful items from other newspapers in the East and West, published informative letters from emigrants on the trail and at the mines, reported the comings and goings of emigrants and promoters, and carried announcements of the time and place of rendezvous for wagon trains. The papers also frequently gave editorial support to the route they believed would be most beneficial to their city and trade area, often with a narrow partisanship that fostered jealous rivalries. On the other hand, they published healthy criticism of special schemes which they felt would enrich individual promoters rather than benefit the northern routes.

The St. Paul Press carried a dozen or more articles by James Wickes Taylor,

[10] *Across the Plains and Over the Divide*, 71 (New York, 1906).

perhaps the best informed and most skillful spokesman for Minnesota expansionism. Taylor was a lawyer who had settled in Minnesota in the mid-1850s. He was a close friend of Salmon P. Chase, Lincoln's secretary of the treasury, and during the 1860s he acted as a special agent of the treasury department. In this capacity he was charged, among other duties, with investigating mining operations in the West and commercial relations with Canada. Taylor brought to the task of disseminating information and ideas about the northern plains his varied talents as a lecturer, politician, and writer, and many an article filled with useful information for gold-field emigrants was published over his signature in Minnesota newspapers.[11]

The most energetic and widely known promoter of northern overland emigration was the pre-eminent expedition leader and propagandist, James Liberty Fisk. Because of their potential usefulness to emigrants, the official reports of his first two expeditions in the 1860s were published by the government. Fisk was also the author of *Idaho: Her Gold Fields, and the Routes to Them*, the first guide to the northern route, published in New York in 1863. His other propaganda efforts included maps, prospectuses, numerous speeches, conferences with chambers of commerce, military leaders, members of Congress, and even, in 1864, a well-publicized visit with President Lincoln at the White House. In preparation for his last expedition in 1866, Fisk set up information and recruiting offices in various cities in the East, and from his headquarters in St. Paul carried on an immense correspondence with people interested in traveling the northern route to the Rockies. Fewer than half the people who went to the gold fields from Minnesota actually traveled with Fisk, but most of them took the northern trail either directly or indirectly as a result of his campaigns.

James Fisk conducted four overland expeditions during the 1860s — three of them under the sponsorship of the federal government and one which he organized privately. Two other men also led wagon trains from Minnesota to the Rocky Mountains. Thomas A. Holmes, a modest, grizzled frontiersman of long experience, took three trains across the prairies. Peter B. Davy, a short dapper Civil War veteran, organized the last train to the gold fields in 1867.

To many of the gold seekers who set out on these journeys, the region of the northern plains was, as one emigrant put it in 1862, "almost *terra incognita*." They thought of the plains as primarily wide, open reaches of semiarid land. Fisk and other promoters took pains to assure them that the area was not a trackless waste and that water and grass were more plentiful than on the central route. Men with some experience in western travel or those who had read Stevens' report knew, however, that serious geographical obstacles to wagon travel lay across the route. Perhaps the most formidable was the Coteau du Missouri, a glacier-roughened upland plateau in eastern Dakota — fifteen to twenty-five miles wide, pocked with alkali ponds and strewn with boulders. Across the Missouri rose the mountain island of the Black Hills and the fantastically eroded Badlands of the White,

[11] Theodore C. Blegen, "James Wickes Taylor: A Biographical Sketch," in *Minnesota History Bulletin*, 1:153–195 (November, 1915). For examples of Taylor's articles, see *Press*, March 25, May 18, 30, June 18, September 3, 1862; January 15, August 29–September 12, 1863.

Cheyenne, and Little Missouri rivers. Also to be avoided if possible were the often difficult crossings of such rivers as the James, Sheyenne, Missouri, and Yellowstone.[12]

The ideal route, recommended by Stevens for a northern Pacific railroad, followed the height of land between the James and Sheyenne rivers and, avoiding all major river crossings, moved in a long, northwesterly sweep to the Missouri at its great bend in northern Dakota. Stevens' trail had the advantages of skirting the coteau and of following as far as possible a prairie area which offered adequate supplies of wood, water, and grass. In the vicinity of the Dakota-Montana border, the trail came at last to the arid, short-grass region of the high plains and followed a natural highway through the valleys of the Missouri and Milk rivers to a spot near present-day Havre, Montana. There it turned south into the foothills of the Rockies.

Although interest focused on the general route Stevens had surveyed, there was in fact no single route or trail. Each year emigrants followed a somewhat different path according to the experience of leaders and guides, the amount of water and grass available during the season, the threat of Indian attack, or the military strategy adopted by the army that year. In 1864 a combination of circumstances persuaded Fisk and others to employ a more southern route, close to the mystic forty-fifth parallel, but Indian attacks and a difficult passage through the Badlands discouraged emigrants from going that way again. If no one train followed the so-called Stevens route all the way from Minnesota to Montana, some part of it was used by most of the wagon trains of the 1860s.

Fur trade posts and army forts served as important landmarks for the overland emigrants. The largest and most imposing of the fur establishments was Fort Union on the upper Missouri with its sixteen-foot-high palisade of cottonwood timbers. Fort Benton, a sturdy adobe fur post strategically located at the head of navigation on the Missouri, provided a major port of entry to the gold fields during the 1860s. After 1864 Fort Berthold, the American Fur Company's post in east-central Dakota, was occupied by army troops and became a way station for emigrant trains.[13]

The small military establishment of Fort Abercrombie on Minnesota's western border was an important rendezvous for the overland trains, but the emigrants also used Fort Ripley on the Mississippi and Fort Ridgely on the Minnesota River as gathering points. Other forts — Wadsworth, Rice, Ransom, Stevenson, and Shaw — were established by the military in the 1860s, at least partly to furnish protection for emigrant trains. On the Washington frontier Fort Walla Walla marked the end of the Mullan Road.

At these posts along the routes, the travelers stopped to replenish supplies, exchange news with other white men, send and receive mail, and secure informa-

[12] The quotation is from Samuel R. Bond, "Journal of Expedition sent by Government to protect emigrants to Gold regions on Washington and Oregon frontiers by the Northern Overland Route," July 5, 1862, typescript in MiHS, original in the Ipswich (Massachusetts) Historical Society. Helpful sources for the geography of the region are Nevin M. Fenneman, *Physiography of Western United States* (New York, 1931), and Walter P. Webb, *The Great Plains,* 3–9 (Boston, 1931).

[13] Francis Paul Prucha, *A Guide to the Military Forts of the United States,* 55, 100–109, 114 (Madison, 1964).

tion about conditions on the trail ahead. Members of the Fisk expedition who visited Fort Union in 1862 bought moccasins, calico, molasses, and gunpowder, and the leaders of the train were entertained at a dinner that featured roast pig, buffalo meat, and dried-apple pie. In 1864 William L. Larned obtained from the commissary at Fort Rice a quantity of hardtack which he regarded as a luxurious addition to his diet. The average emigrant, however, considered provisions expensive at the army posts, and one of them remarked in 1866 that "only in case of emergency would it be wise to purchase . . . at their extravagant prices."[14]

The vast stretches of wilderness between these tiny enclaves of civilization were Indian country, and the possibility of trouble with the red man loomed large in the mind of the emigrant. A dozen or so roving tribes camped and hunted in the region — Chippewa and Sioux in Minnesota and Dakota; the Plains Assiniboin, Gros Ventres, and Crow in northern Dakota and Montana. Farther west in Montana emigrants crossed the lands of the Blackfeet, Piegan, and Bloods. Where the trails ended in southwestern Montana, travelers encountered the Snake and Bannock tribes. Beyond Montana they met the Pend d'Oreilles and the Coeur d'Alenes.

The emigrants had reason to be apprehensive. By the 1860s expanding frontiers had forced Indians from other areas onto the hunting grounds of the northern plains tribes. Abrogated treaties, Indian raids, and the ensuing punitive army expeditions contributed to steadily worsening relations. The movement of emigrant trains across Indian lands was itself a disturbing factor. As it turned out, only the 1864 expeditions suffered serious attack, but the threat was always present. Armed escorts, vigilance, and frontier expertise saved emigrants from more serious encounters, but the stealing of horses and mules was a common occurrence.

Generally the emigrant viewed the Indian as an indolent, filthy, half-naked creature, very likely inclined to treachery and undeniably a thief. Some travelers saw him as an object of pity, a challenge to the energies of Christianity and civilization. Others thought that force and annihilation were the only ways to deal with the red man. Few emigrants of the 1860s viewed the Indians as noble savages, but many were curious about their way of life. The emigrant letters and diaries in this volume record a variety of observations about dress, ceremonies, and burial customs.

Gold seekers bound for Montana gathered in Minnesota frontier towns during the months of March, April, and May. Most of them came from the northern tier of states — New England, New York, Pennsylvania, Ohio, Indiana, Illinois, and Wisconsin. Some resided briefly in Minnesota before they moved on again. A few were immigrants from the countries of northern Europe. Although all ages were represented, the average migrant was in his middle thirties. More family groups accompanied the trains in the last two years; before that the migrant was likely to be a bachelor, or a married man who had left his family behind while he went to try his luck in the gold fields. Among the emigrants were men trained in a variety of professions and trades — medicine, law, carpentry, printing, shoemaking,

[14] Bond, "Journal," August 11; William L. Larned Diary, August 22, 1864, typescript in MiHS (original last known to be in the possession of Horatio Larned, Lansing, Michigan); William Johnstone Diary, June 14, 1866, photocopy in MiHS (original owned by Mrs. J. W. Glenwright, Toronto, Canada).

brewing, farming. There were draft-dodgers and former soldiers, substantial men and fugitives from justice.[15]

Whatever their status or occupation, a great many of them seem to have ignored James Fisk's firm caution: "None who have *homes* and a reasonable means of livelihood should be incited by big stories, however true they may be, to emigrate to far off territories after a phantom fortune." The dream of gold brought them together and lured them west.[16]

Before assembling at the rendezvous points on the edge of the plains, the migrants paused in such frontier towns as St. Paul, St. Cloud, or Mankato to complete the outfit needed for their three-month journey. The key item in the emigrant's outfit, and one of the costliest, was his wagon. If he did not already own a suitable vehicle, he bought one from a farmer or a local wagonmaker. Most serviceable on the northern plains were narrow-track, thimble-skein, canvas-topped wagons capable of carrying two or three thousand pounds. A wise emigrant acquired a watertight wagon box which would keep the load dry during river crossings.[17]

Some frontiersmen on the northern expeditions preferred Red River carts, pulled by ponies or oxen. Originally used by half-breeds in the fur trade of the Red River region, these carts were durable all-wood vehicles with a capacity of about a thousand pounds. In 1864 William Larned purchased both carts and a wagon for his outfit. A cart, complete with canvas cover and ox chain, cost Larned about forty-six dollars. The price of the wagon was ninety dollars.[18]

Draft animals represented another sizable investment. Larned bought six yoke of oxen at prices ranging from sixty to over a hundred dollars a pair. Under normal conditions two yoke of oxen were required to pull a light wagon, but it often took as many as four or five teams to get up the steeper hills. Experience demonstrated the advisability of taking extra oxen to prevent delay when the regular teams became fatigued or suffered from "foot-ail," a hoof infection of cattle. It was usual to bring along a few cows for milk and for use in yoke with the oxen.

Although wagons were sometimes drawn by mules or horses, oxen were preferred for a number of reasons. The initial expense was less, and oxen could be used for food or as draft animals at the mines. They could be driven with a wooden yoke and chain, while a more complicated harness was necessary for horses. In addition, oxen subsisted better than horses on short or sparse grass, and it was easier to find good grazing for them along the trail. Horses required supplementary rations of grain, which had to be carried in the wagons. Moreover, raiding Indians prized horses and frequently tried to steal them, but usually did not bother oxen.

Another important item in the emigrant's outfit was his gun, useful both for hunting game and for protection against Indians. Several new and efficient types of firearms were carried on the northern plains in the 1860s. Fisk had a Ballard

[15] Rosters listing known members of the eight expeditions in the 1860s may be found in the Appendix.
[16] *Idaho*, 22.
[17] The thimble-skein, which came into common use at this time, was a conical metal sheath that protected the wooden spindle of the axle. Advertisements may be found in the *Chicago Tribune*, April 10, 1865, and T. G. and C. E. Turner, *Turner's Guide From the Lakes to the Rocky Mountains*, 4 (Chicago, 1868).
[18] The introductory pages of William Larned's diary list his outfit and the hardware stock he planned to sell at the mines, with the price he paid for each item.

globe-sight rifle, a type noted for its accuracy. Many emigrants used breech-loading rifles and repeaters. Their letters and diaries mention Remington, Spencer, and Winchester rifles, Henry and Sharps' carbines, and Wesson seven-shooters. The weapons issued to soldiers and expedition guards in this period, however, were often Enfield and old-style Springfield muzzle-loading rifles. The Fisk expeditions also carried an army mountain howitzer, which was of more psychological than real value.

Food supplies, representing a substantial part of the contents of the wagon, were usually stowed near the front within easy reach. The emigrant was advised to take enough staple provisions for a year, although the actual journey required only three to four months. Food was scarce and expensive at the mines, and a desire to profit from the sale of extra foodstuffs, as well as to have an ample supply to carry their families through the winter, caused many emigrants to take more than they would need on the trail.[19]

Flour, dry beans and peas, corn meal, oatmeal, hominy, rice, and other cereals were commonly included in the food stocks, as were crackers, zwieback, sugar, salt, pepper, saleratus (baking soda), lard, tea, and coffee. Bacon, ham, salt pork, and cheese were popular. Some emigrants took crates of live chickens and a pig or two for butchering on the trail. Dried apples, peaches, raisins, pumpkins, and sweet corn were frequently included, as were onions, potatoes, turnips, and other root vegetables. Thrifty housewives placed jars of preserved fruits and vegetables in barrels of flour to keep them from breaking. One woman baked quantities of zwieback and cookies and placed them in large socks; unfortunately the cookies were soon jolted to bits and the family thereafter breakfasted on cooky crumbs and milk.

The hunters of the expedition supplemented these food supplies with a variety of wild meat, fish, and fowl. Berries growing in the woods, along streams, and in the mountains also furnished tempting fresh dishes. At least one expedition carried bags of pemmican — dried buffalo meat mixed with tallow — but the men did not care for it, and most of it remained in the wagons at the end of the journey.

In addition to food, the family wagon carried a variety of furnishings necessary for life on the trail and in a new home at the mines. A sheet-iron cookstove was useful for baking bread and for cooking on rainy days. Other household equipment, stowed inside the wagon or dangling from the wooden sideboards, might include lanterns, candles, frying pans, a Dutch oven, a wash tub, and a clothesline. A ten-gallon pail or barrel was used for water, and a bucket held tar to grease the wagon wheels or to rub on the hoofs of animals suffering from foot-ail.

The emigrant's outfit usually contained picks, shovels, pans, and other mining implements. Frequently it also included plows, tools for blacksmithing, shoemaking, and carpentering, and implements for repairing harnesses and wagons. Many men were wise enough to know that where people mined for gold other services would be required, and not all the gold would be obtained by digging.

Inside the wagon, too, were often a tent, trunks or chests of clothing, bedding, and perhaps a precious piece of furniture, although emigrants were cautioned not

[19] Interesting details of an emigrant outfit are in Arthur J. Dickson, *Covered Wagon Days,* 41, 44 (Cleveland, 1929), and "Biography of Mary Anna Geyermann Weydert," a manuscript in the MoHS.

to lug along bedsteads, bureaus, or chairs. They were advised to use the space for extra stores of tobacco, ammunition, or boots and shoes, on which they might make an estimated profit of 500 per cent at the mines. Tucked away in odd corners might be a clock, a few books and medicines, stores of whisky — medicinal or otherwise — soap, seasonings and herbs, seeds and plant cuttings, or perhaps a window sash for the new home in the West.

Not all overland travelers went west in their own wagons. After the Civil War wagon train promoters offered a new service for single persons, designed to appeal especially to the restless veteran with discharge pay in his pocket. For a hundred dollars or so, a traveler could buy a ticket which entitled him to provisions and the protection of the group during the journey. Personal baggage was transported in a wagon; the emigrant usually supplied his own horse or walked his way west with the train.

After an emigrant gathered his outfit he moved on to the rendezvous. The time and place of assembly were determined by the expedition leader, by military authorities, or by agreement among the emigrants. A suitable location commanded enough water and fuel for camps of from sixty to several hundred people with their numerous animals. The ideal spot, safe from Indian attack, was located either well within the line of settlement or close to a military post. It lay far enough along the line of march to give travelers time to break in their animals and try out their equipment, yet close enough to an outfitting town so that unsatisfactory equipment could be replaced and supplies replenished. Because it was difficult to find a rendezvous combining all these attributes, emigrants of the 1860s gathered not once but several times, their ranks swelling at successive rendezvous as they lumbered across Minnesota. At the final staging area on the frontier — near Forts Ridgely, Abercrombie, or Wadsworth — the wagon train roster was at last completed.

Most of the people who traveled in the northern overland trains knew that the hazards of the journey would be minimized if they worked together. The necessity for organization, learned earlier on the central plains, was also a recognized fact of frontier life. Most emigrants accepted it and were willing to delegate authority to captains of their own choosing or to accept the officers appointed by the government. Plains-seasoned leaders and guides chose the route from day to day, selected campgrounds, assigned guard duty, and meted out punishment to those who disobeyed regulations.

The form of organization varied from group to group. Trains led by Thomas Holmes were characterized by spontaneity and informality. The emigrants organized into companies, each with an elected captain. Holmes, the captains, and such other officers as wagon master, chaplain, and Indian interpreter, formed the train's governing body.

The remaining expeditions — four led by Fisk and one by Peter Davy — were organized in a more authoritarian manner. Fisk conducted his expeditions of 1862, 1863, and 1864 under the sponsorship of the federal government. Acting under instructions from the secretary of war and with federal funds at his disposal, he hired his own staff and employed a protective corps of forty to fifty men. He also drew up regulations for the conduct of the trains.

Emigrants tended to interpret the obligations of the train leadership broadly.

At the least they looked for protection against Indian attack. At the most they expected to be supplied with a full range of services from wagon-repair shops to commissary and medical departments. A train society attempted to safeguard its unlucky, careless, or improvident members, but the leader faced a difficult problem when a decision to help an individual might jeopardize the safety of all. The entire group was endangered if the train halted in Indian country while one man repaired a broken wagon or others searched for an emigrant who had wandered off on the prairie.

Whatever their decisions, the leaders were subject to criticism, and the wagon train organization never entirely coped with dissident members. Many men who had agreed to abide by the decisions of the leaders jealously guarded their right to object and complain. Only rarely were individuals sufficiently dissatisfied to leave the train, but groups of dissidents occasionally split off and continued the journey under new leaders.

Beginning in 1864 the army, fearful of the results of the reciprocal antagonism between Indians and white men, ordered all overland travelers to go west in groups that were carefully organized, well armed, and large enough to discourage Indian attack. Although some travelers ignored the military regulations and struck out by themselves, most emigrants sought the protection and assistance of regularly constituted expeditions.

The wagons usually traveled on the trail in single file. The wheels of each successive vehicle deepened the ruts in the sod, marking the way for those who came after, a week, a month, or a year later. Emigrants were urged to maintain close formation because wagons strung out for miles along the route were vulnerable to Indian attack. In times of danger the expedition could travel more safely if the wagons moved four or five abreast. Such a formation was possible on the broad plains, but in rough, hilly, or mountainous country they traveled singly and more slowly. Most wagons were equipped with locks and chains for the wheels, but few had brakes, and much caution was necessary to prevent them from crashing into one another going down steep slopes.

Rivers sometimes offered formidable obstacles to wagon trains, and devising ways to cross them required considerable ingenuity. While the Stevens route generally avoided crossings of the larger rivers, there were many smaller streams and coulees to get over. Shallow streams with firm beds of rock or sand could be easily forded, but it was often necessary to cut down the steep sides of coulees or to fill and grade soft riverbanks. To cross one marshy stream, the Fisk expedition of 1862 cut quantities of rushes and spread them thickly on the shallow water. If wood was available, temporary log bridges were built across deep streams. Sometimes the emigrants made a bridge of wagons and carried their supplies across it, floating the other wagons and letting the stock swim. In other cases the wagon boxes were blocked up to clear the water or removed from the wheels entirely and used as flatboats.

The trains ordinarily traveled fifteen to eighteen miles a day, the distance being imperfectly measured by an odometer mounted on the wheel of a wagon. A bugle sounded reveille at daybreak, the guard took the oxen out to graze, and the emigrants prepared breakfast. At a second call the animals were hitched up and the day's journey began. A train usually covered from seven to twelve miles in the morning and then stopped for an hour or so while the emigrants ate lunch and the cattle grazed. In extremely hot dry weather it was sometimes necessary to travel after dark in order to reach adequate water and grass, but ordinarily the expedition leader tried to make camp several hours before nightfall. An ideal campsite offered fresh water, good grass, and a nearby supply of wood or buffalo chips for fuel. It was located in an open, treeless spot where it could be guarded against Indian ambush.

When the train reached its campsite, the wagons formed a large circle or corral. One after another they pulled into position, with the back wheels of each wagon overlapping the front wheels of the next, and the tongues turned toward the center. The oxen were put out to graze while the emigrants set up a ring of tents outside the corral and built fires to cook their evening meals. On a typical expedition a bugle call about half-past eight was the signal to drive the oxen inside the corral. Mules and horses were picketed near the tents. Taps sounded about nine, guards were posted for night duty, and the emigrants went to bed in their tents or under their wagons.

Day and night, members of the overland expeditions lived on intimate terms with the weather. When temperatures rose into the upper nineties and hot winds blew, the grass became parched, lakes and rivers dried up, and thick clouds of dust enveloped the moving train. One emigrant reported: "our eyes ran with tears, our noses sympathized . . . our mouths become parched and our lips bled with soarness." If a hot day ended in a camp with no water, the emigrants went to bed thirsty, and the cattle bellowed uneasily all night. After days of such weather the animals became weak from hunger and thirst, and jangling discord enveloped the train.[20]

In wet years grass and water were plentiful, but they harbored swarms of ferocious mosquitoes. Wagons made their tortuous way through mudholes and swollen streams. With little warning, tremendous storms of rain and hail struck the unsheltered trains. Equipment was soaked in the downpour, tents and wagon tops were tossed about by whipping winds, and crashing thunder and egg-sized hailstones stampeded the animals.

Most emigrants were resigned to the weather. A far greater threat to their peace of mind was the fear of being lost on the plains. Hardly a wagon train went west without losing at least for a time someone who had gone out to hunt game, search for a strayed animal, or scout a trail. Emigrant diaries testify that being lost on a vast, level plain without a landmark in sight was a frightful experience.

Expedition leaders customarily made every effort to locate a missing person. They sent out search parties, fired guns and rockets, and even halted the train for an entire day to hunt for a lost member. When William Johnstone became separated from the Holmes train of 1866, he crawled through the darkness on his hands and knees and located the trail by feeling for the flattened grass which marked the passage of the wagons. A tenderfoot member of the Fisk expedition of 1863 nearly died of thirst before he was found, and the following year three men on a reconnaissance broke their compass and lived on little more than berries for four

---

[20] The quotation is from the Johnstone Diary, July 5.

days. Luckily they and all the others lost from the northern overland trains safely rejoined their companions.

Disease and injury seem to have been minor problems, and only a few people died on the trail. Most of the expeditions apparently included physicians among their members. On occasion the doctors were called upon to deliver babies or to treat the victims of accidents. More often their professional work consisted of prescribing remedies for a disease variously described as chronic diarrhea, bilious sickness, or dysentery accompanied by boils — the most common ailment of the journey. This illness was thought to be caused by eating large quantities of fresh meat, by drinking the alkali water of the plains, or by both in combination with the sudden change in the habits of people accustomed to a more sedentary life. Frontiersmen believed that the ailment resulted from eating fresh buffalo meat and called it *le mal de vache*. Remedies included eating rice, crackers, or chokecherries and using evacuants. One overland adventurer (not a medical man) claimed that the only way to cure dysentery was to drink nothing but whisky, or at least to follow every other drink with a whisky chaser.[21]

The lurching, joggling, monotonous routine of the trail was occasionally broken by a day's layover in camp. If a party had been traveling over rough country, it was often necessary to stop for wagon repairs. William Larned's diary of August 19, 1864, noted: "Our camp is a Very Wagon shop, nearly every Wagon is undergoing a repairing of some kind. Mostly legging up wheels, & setting the tires." Three of the Fisk expeditions enjoyed extra time in camp when babies were born and the train stopped over so that the mother could rest.

Although overland parties frequently halted on Sunday, the day was far from restful for the emigrants. On Saturday night the women put their soiled clothes to soak and set salt-rising bread. Early Sunday morning they washed clothes and laid them out to dry. Then there was mending, churning, breadmaking, and other cooking to be done. Men cleaned their guns, overhauled and greased wagons, tightened wheels, and treated the necks of oxen where yokes had rubbed them sore. If the camp were near an outcropping of coal, blacksmiths of the party could burn a coal pit, set up their forges, and mend iron wagon tires or shoe the horses and oxen. On the Fisk expedition of 1862 an Episcopal deacon conducted religious services, and the Holmes emigrants of 1866 joined together in hymn singing.

On Sunday, or on any day spent in camp, emigrants found time for reading books, writing letters, bringing diaries up to date, or sitting in the shade of any object that offered protection from the sun. Occasionally men organized target-shooting matches, horse races, fist fights, or hunting expeditions. Others spent the hours in the congenial company of friends and bottles of tangle-leg (whisky). Now and then a musician brought out his violin or concertina and the emigrants enjoyed a concert or square dance under the stars. Sometimes people sat quietly by the evening fires, telling stories and making buffalo-horn finger rings, camp-stools, or plains-style leather pants.

Even after a hard day on the rough trail, some travelers at least were not too weary to be thrilled by the clear, wide view of the sky at night. Samuel R. Bond, a member of the 1862 Fisk expedition, witnessed a magnificent midnight display

---

[21] Charles Larpenteur, *Forty Years a Fur Trader*, 1:21 (New York, 1898); Andrew J. Fisk Diary, October 6, 1864, in MoHS (typescript MiHS).

of aurora borealis on July 23 while on guard duty. The scene so impressed him that he described it at some length in his journal. "First appeared in the east a luminous body much resembling a large comet with the nucleus near the horizon and the tail in a direct line towards the zenith," he wrote. "Then appeared a precisely similar light in the west, and soon their tails met and blended so as to form a complete arch from the eastern to the western horizon directly across the zenith." The display lasted about an hour before it dimmed and gradually disappeared.

Van H. Fisk, who accompanied his brother on the expedition of 1864, described one of the tantalizing mirages that bemused plains travelers. He and others with him saw a beautiful lake with tall, waving grass and weeds along its shores. They rode toward it for three hours, but "just as the last rays of the setting sun left the plain . . . our beautiful lake, with all of its inviting water disappeared also." This mirage was so real that the horses whinnied when they saw it.[22]

Emigrants were often appalled by the landscape of the West. Describing the Missouri coteau region, one traveler wrote that there was "not a land mark to guide nor a bush or shrub upon which the eye could rest." Travelers were amazed by the desolate Badlands with their grotesque peaks rising steeply above dry gullies. William Larned first saw the Cannonball River Badlands in 1864 and called the area a "perfect desert, not a leaf of *Green* vegetation, except wild wormwood, and that was *blue*." It was, said another emigrant, a region "never explored by white man and avoided by other portions of creation."[23]

Traveling through northern Montana in the valley of the Milk River, the overland emigrants had their first glimpse of mountains when the peaks of the Little Rockies and the Bearpaw loomed up in the distance. They welcomed the mountain country with its clear streams and cool, misty mornings, even though the nights were so cold that ice crusted in the water pails.

Once in the mountain region the emigrants were nearing the end of their journey. Most of the wagon trains disbanded at Fort Benton. Although some emigrants went on to Fort Walla Walla or the Pacific Coast, many more moved out to search for gold in the mountain valleys adjacent to the Mullan Road.

In their search along Montana's streams, Minnesota prospectors joined other "Pilgrims" from the East and South, "Tother Siders" from Oregon, "Pikes Peakers" from Colorado, and "Forty Niners" from California. During the 1860s Montana prospectors gravitated to three centers of mining development — Bannack, Virginia City, and Helena.[24]

In 1862 members of the Fisk and Holmes trains stopped off to prospect in the valley of the Prickly Pear and on Gold Creek near Deer Lodge. Finding little gold in these areas, they straggled on to Bannack, a raw village springing up around

[22] Alva J. Noyes, "Lost on the Plains, A Story of Van Haden Fisk of Sixty Four," 8, manuscript in MoHS.

[23] Johnstone Diary, June 24; William Larned Diary, August 24; Gilbert Benedict, "Trip to Montana," 8, prose reminiscence in MoHS.

[24] Merrill G. Burlingame, *The Montana Frontier*, 78–94 (Helena, 1942), describes gold discoveries in the 1860s. For a vivid account of life in the mining region in 1867, see Alexander K. McClure, *Three Thousand Miles Through the Rocky Mountains*, especially p. 242, 284–289, 292–296, 342–353 (Philadelphia, 1869).

rich placers discovered on Grasshopper Creek that very summer. Minnesotans settled on the east side of the creek and laid out a townsite which they called Yankee Flats. Considerable mining was done in the Bannack area in 1862, and it became the destination of the wagon train which left Minnesota in 1863.

In that summer gold was found seventy miles to the east on Alder Gulch. When news of the strike reached Bannack, people from the Minnesota trains joined the general exodus to the Alder Gulch area. A number of settlements sprang up there; the largest was Virginia City, a rip-roaring town which boasted a population of more than ten thousand during its heyday. Nearly twenty miles in length, Alder Gulch was one of the longest and richest placers ever worked in Montana, and probably in the world. Between 1863 and 1866 it produced an estimated thirty million dollars' worth of gold.

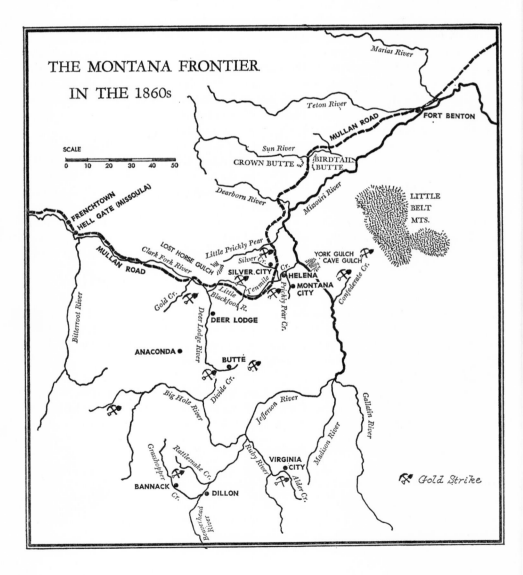

In 1864 the fickle and impatient prospector was again drawn to rich new strikes, this time in Last Chance Gulch on Prickly Pear Creek. The original discovery at Last Chance was made by a party which included one of the Fisk emigrants of 1863. There in the fall of 1864 the city of Helena was founded and named for a small town in Minnesota. Emigrants of 1864, 1866, and 1867 ranged out from Helena to join the throngs who prospected at such places as Grizzly, Oro Fino, Trinity, New York, and Lost Horse gulches.

The new diggings in Bannack, Virginia City, and Helena were much alike, consisting at first of little more than a few tents and wickiups — rude shanties made by laying cross poles on four upright posts and covering them with brush. A larger village might have two rows of log cabins, perhaps an eighth of a mile long, with houses and stores set next to pigpens and stables. The historian H. H. Bancroft described these early mining camps as collections of "ophir holes, gopher holes, and loafer holes."[25]

Some of the camps grew rapidly. As townsites were laid out and frame buildings put up, the little settlements mushroomed into cities with a population of thousands. The mining towns were crowded from morning to night with men, teams, and wagons. Particularly on Sundays prospectors from nearby gulches poured into town to find a square meal, go on a spree, and buy supplies for the next week's work. Street-corner auctioneers sold everything from needles to freight wagons. Handbills offered rewards for the capture of murderers and highwaymen who terrorized the settlements during the early 1860s. In saloons, dance halls, and gambling houses, poker and monte games rivaled the charms of dancing girls and whisky in separating the miners from their dust. While some diggings matured into thriving towns, others were left crumbling and empty after the first easy gold had been mined, a monument both to those who had made a pile and to those who, "having seen the elephant," went away with empty pockets.

The Montana placers which the miners first exploited lay close to running water and were known as poor men's mines because a prospector could wash out the gold with inexpensive equipment and limited technical knowledge. Amateur pick-and-pan miners skimmed off half the placer gold in Montana within a few years.

As long as new placers were being discovered, the call of the poor men's mines was loud and compelling. But prospectors also found rich lodes of gold-bearing quartz and placer deposits far removed from streams. These discoveries could be exploited only by the installation of expensive machinery and the construction of ditches and tunnels to bring water to dry gulches. The heavy investment required for this kind of mining made it necessary to consolidate many small claims under one management. As pick and pan gave way to stamp mill and arrastra, the day of extensive migration to the Montana gold fields ended.

Of the fourteen hundred emigrants who went to Montana across the northern plains, only a few seem to have struck it rich in the mines. Most searched for gold at first, but soon turned to other occupations. Some left the territory within a short time. Others joined the ranks of the highwaymen, died young and violently, and were forgotten. Still others practiced trades or professions, holding their claims for sale or spare-time mining. They set up sawmills, built coffins, opened boarding-

[25] *Washington, Idaho, and Montana, 1845–1889,* 777 (San Francisco, 1890).

houses, made shoes, operated stage lines, raised vegetables, or hung out a lawyer's shingle. An ingenious few fenced off a portion of the road to a new mine and charged tolls. Many settled on farms or ranches near the mining towns. An emigrant of 1866 served in Congress; a number held office in state and local government. One and all, they played a role in building the territory and state of Montana.

The story of the northern overland wagon trains is one of small and large dreams — private dreams of quick fortunes in El Dorado and public dreams of commercial empire and national greatness. Promoters envisioned an economic empire on the northern plains as soon as a northern railroad should link the center of the continent to the Pacific Ocean. They looked on emigrant wagon trails as essential to the achievement of their dreams. Businessmen, newspapers, propagandists, and government all worked to open trails and attract emigrants. Although their attempts did not immediately bear fruit and the wagon trails lay neglected, the railroads came at last. Nearly twenty years after the Montana gold rush, the Northern Pacific Railroad was completed. In 1883 a final gold spike was driven at Gold Creek near Deer Lodge where members of the first northern overland train had prospected in the fall of 1862. Another ten years saw the completion of the Great Northern Railway, and in 1909 the Chicago, Milwaukee, and St. Paul extended its line to Puget Sound.

The present-day traveler who crosses the plains on these railroads comes close to the northern emigrant trails at many points. The Great Northern and Northern Pacific follow portions of the trail between Fort Abercrombie and Fort Union in North Dakota. The line of the Northern Pacific follows closely the route of the 1864 Holmes train through the Badlands — between present-day Dickinson, North Dakota, and the Montana border — and down the Yellowstone Valley to the vicinity of Fort Union. The Milwaukee Road on its line between Rhame and Marmarth, North Dakota, passes not far from the spot, now known as Fort Dilts, where the Fisk expedition of 1864 was attacked by Indians. In Montana the route of the Great Northern from Bainville to Havre and south to Box Elder lies near the Fort Benton trail used by many emigrants.

Faint ruts left by the wagon trains may still be seen on the plains, and a few written records of the human experience on the trail have survived as well. The letters, diaries, and journals printed in the following pages tell the emigrants' own stories of the northern overland wagon trains of the 1860s.

1862

THE HOLMES AND FISK TRAINS

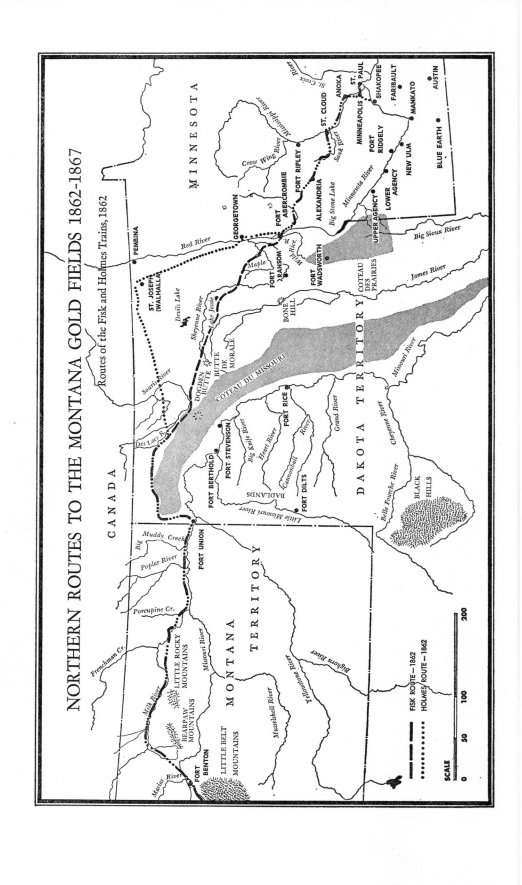

NORTHERN ROUTES TO THE MONTANA GOLD FIELDS 1862-1867

Routes of the Fisk and Holmes Trains, 1862

CANADA

MINNESOTA

DAKOTA TERRITORY

MONTANA TERRITORY

PEMBINA

ST. JOSEPH (WALHALLA)

GEORGETOWN

FORT ABERCROMBIE

FORT RIPLEY

ST. CLOUD

ALEXANDRIA

ANOKA

ST. PAUL

MINNEAPOLIS

SHAKOPEE

FARIBAULT

AUSTIN

MANKATO

BLUE EARTH

NEW ULM

FORT RIDGELY

LOWER AGENCY

UPPER AGENCY

FORT RANSOM

FORT WADSWORTH

COTEAU DES PRAIRIES

BONE HILL

DOGDEN BUTTE

BUTTE DE MORALE

COTEAU DU MISSOURI

FORT RICE

FORT STEVENSON

FORT BERTHOLD

FORT DILTS

BADLANDS

FORT UNION

FORT BENTON

LITTLE BELT MOUNTAINS

BEARPAW MOUNTAINS

LITTLE ROCKY MOUNTAINS

BLACK HILLS

Red River

Mississippi River

Crow Wing River

Sauk River

St. Croix River

Minnesota River

Big Stone Lake

Big Sioux River

James River

Maple R.

Wild Rice R.

Devils Lake

Lake Jessie

Sheyenne River

Souris River

Des Lacs R.

Missouri River

Little Missouri River

Big Knife River

Heart River

Cannonball River

Grand River

Cheyenne River

Belle Fourche River

Muddy Creek

Big Poplar River

Porcupine Cr.

Frenchman Cr.

Milk River

Marias River

Musselshell River

Missouri River

Yellowstone River

Bighorn River

SCALE

0   50   100   200

FISK ROUTE – 1862

HOLMES ROUTE – 1862

1862 ✸✸✸✸✸✸✸✸✸✸✸✸✸✸✸✸✸

The Holmes and Fisk Trains

IN APRIL, 1862, A WEEK AFTER THE ICE went out of the Mississippi River, gold seekers from as far away as London began to gather in St. Paul, Minnesota. From eastern points they had traveled by train to La Crosse, Wisconsin, the northernmost port on the Mississippi then accessible by rail, and there they boarded packet boats for the eighteen-hour trip upriver to the Minnesota capital. At St. Paul the travelers disembarked on wharves piled high with merchandise and sought accommodations in such frontier hostelries as the Merchants or the City Hotel, which provided board and lodging for fifty cents a day. They tramped plank sidewalks slushy with melting snow to reach outfitters' stores where they could buy supplies for the journey to the mines.[1]

These people gathered in St. Paul, a thriving metropolis on the edge of a virtually unsettled country that stretched westward to the Rockies, because it was the logical gateway to the northern plains. By the 1860s St. Paul boasted a population of more than ten thousand persons. The Mississippi at its doorstep connected the Minnesota capital with railroads to the east and with St. Louis and New Orleans to the south. As an entrepot for the fur trade of a large territory, the city at the head of Mississippi River navigation had long been the terminus of various trails which ran northwest to the Red River and settlements in what is now central Canada. These "Red River Trails," as they were called, became the basis for the state's early stage roads. In 1859 transportation to the Red River improved when the Hudson's Bay Company found it advantageous to transport supplies to its mid-continent posts via Chicago and St. Paul, rather than by the northern route through Hudson Bay. A stage-freight line between St. Paul and the Red River settlements went into operation, with steamboat connections at the head of navigation on the Red River. Thus by 1862 St. Paul provided a convenient outfitting point for the gold seekers headed for the Cariboo mines of what is now western Canada or for the newly opened Salmon River gold fields of present-day Idaho.[2]

[1] *Press*, April 22, 24, 29, May 10, 25, 30, 1862; *Pioneer*, April 18, May 1, 2, 7, 10, 13, 15, 18, 1862.
[2] J. Fletcher Williams, *A History of the City of Saint Paul, and of the County of Ramsey, Minnesota*, 395 (*Minnesota Historical Collections*, vol. 4, 1876); Russell Blakeley, "Opening of the Red River of the North to Commerce and Civilization," in *Minnesota Historical Collections*, 8:45–66 (St. Paul, 1898); Gluek, *Minnesota and the Manifest Destiny of the Canadian Northwest*, 96–100, 140–150.

Some of the prospectors bought complete outfits in St. Paul — wagons, tents, animals, food, clothing, guns, ammunition, and tools. Campbell's on Third Street, for example, offered the prospective miner "everything in the Furnishing Line," including rubber blankets, leggings, tent cloth, and gray, blue, and red shirts. Other migrants to the Cariboo fields, wishing to travel light and fast, purchased only a few portable items and boarded the stagecoaches which left at 4:00 A.M. three mornings a week. The stage lines ran north along the Mississippi to St. Cloud and then west through a string of settlements to Fort Abercrombie and George-town, a Hudson's Bay Company depot on the Red River. From Georgetown a little steamer took passengers and trade goods to Fort Garry (now Winnipeg) and other British settlements north of the border, where additional outfitting supplies could be procured for the trip to Cariboo.[3]

Hundreds of prospectors undertook the journey through Minnesota and over the plains to the gold fields in 1862, and as they trooped through the state many a Minnesotan, his imagination fired, dropped whatever he was doing and hustled onto the trail. This chapter tells the story of two wagon trains, comprising about two hundred people, which steered for the Salmon River fields on the American side of the border.

The first train — later to be known by the name of its guiding spirit, Thomas Holmes — was made up of several groups of gold seekers who got together in rather haphazard fashion. Early in May a number of St. Paul men chartered a steamboat to take them down the Mississippi to St. Louis and up the Missouri to Fort Benton. A few days later they abandoned this plan and on May 14 left St. Paul in oxcarts. Some wanted to go to Cariboo; others favored traveling south of the border.[4]

About the same time two other groups outfitted in the Minnesota River Valley and started off for Cariboo. The first of these, which came from Shakopee and included Holmes, camped near Fort Abercrombie at the end of May. The second group overtook the St. Paul party along the way and traveled with it, reaching the fort on May 30. Their numbers were further augmented by small parties from the Minnesota towns of Red Wing and St. Cloud. At Abercrombie the three groups, totaling about forty men, decided to combine forces and travel the rest of the way together. After some discussion they abandoned plans to go to Cariboo and decided to head for the Salmon River fields. These gold seekers — together with a fourth group of about thirty people who later overtook them on the Dakota plains — formed the first northern overland wagon train of 1862.

Some seventy-odd persons were members of the Holmes train. Most were residents of Minnesota. Among them were two lawyers, a doctor, a dentist, several carpenters, at least two lumbermen, and farmers from various parts of the state. A Negro named Tom accompanied a St. Paul building contractor and acted as his cook.[5]

---

[3] *Pioneer,* May 4, 10, 1862; *Press,* April 22, 24, 29, May 10, 1862.

[4] *Pioneer,* May 3, 7, 10, 15, 1862; *Shakopee Argus,* May 17, 1862; *St. Cloud Democrat,* May 8, 15, June 5, 1862. Other information in this paragraph has been taken from the documents printed herein. Throughout it has not ordinarily been thought necessary to provide citations to the documents included in this volume.

[5] For names of the emigrants, see William Cuthbert, "Notes on Trip from St. Paul to Fort Benton, 1862," a two-page reminiscence based on a diary now lost, in MoHS, and the newspaper

Although Holmes was not the titular leader of the train — that honor went to a Shakopee man named Salter — he seems to have been its leader *de facto* because of his experience and reputation as a frontiersman. Born in Pennsylvania in 1804, Thomas Holmes had for nearly sixty years moved from one frontier to another, driven, as one of his contemporaries said, by a *"demon of unrest."* During the 1830s and part of the 1840s he lived in Wisconsin, where he engaged in the fur trade and undertook various land promotion projects. He was an early settler of Milwaukee and one of the founders of Janesville.[6]

For most of his life he was the victim of an acute case of townsite mania; he participated in the founding of such Minnesota towns as Jordan, Chaska, Shakopee, Itasca, Holmes City, and Sauk Rapids. In 1849 he lived at Sauk Rapids and sat in the territorial legislature. During the 1850s he ranged over the Minnesota River Valley, trading with the Indians and developing towns. He was not unfamiliar with the Red River country, and he had gone with a group of Shakopee men to the Fraser River in 1858. Holmes was highly respected among early Minnesotans for his intimate knowledge of Indians and frontier ways. James W. Taylor referred to him in 1862 as "the noted Tom Holmes" and called him a "representative man of the Northwestern frontier." Holmes once appraised his own talents by saying, "While I can only just about write my name now, *I can skin a musk-rat quicker than an Indian."*[7]

Although he seems to have been an ineffective organizer and at times a poor guide, emigrants gathered eagerly to travel with him and placed great confidence in his ability to take them safely across the plains. He led expeditions to the gold fields in 1862, 1864, and 1866.

Three members of the first Holmes train — John F. Hoyt, Mark D. Ledbeater, and Vallencourt H. Cady — wrote letters during the journey and sent them back for publication in Minnesota newspapers. Hoyt, age thirty-two and a lawyer, was associated with his father in the real estate business in St. Paul. Described as "one of the most sociable of men, free, frank, with a fine sprinkling of fun," he had served as probate judge in Ramsey County and was to sit on the bench in Montana during his brief stay there. Ledbeater, who had been born in England, was also in his early thirties. In Minnesota he was for a time a frontier postmaster and a hotelkeeper. Little is known of Cady, the third correspondent. He was born in Vermont in 1810 and before his departure for Montana had been in the real estate business in Shakopee. The letters of these men, which are printed in this text, are the only known contemporary records left by the Holmes emigrants of 1862.[8]

accounts cited in note 3, above. A roster of known members of the train appears in the Appendix, below.

[6] Julius A. Coller, *The Shakopee Story*, 24, 566 (Shakopee, 1960); La Fayette H. Bunnell, *Winona and its Environs on the Mississippi in Ancient and Modern Days*, 217–224, 239 (Winona, 1897). The quotation is from Bunnell, page 218.

[7] Coller, *Shakopee Story*, 24, 25, 32, 566–568; Warren Upham, *Minnesota Geographic Names*, 177, 508, 519 (*Minnesota Historical Collections*, vol. 17, 1920); *Pioneer*, July 25, 1858. For the quotations, see *Press*, May 30, 1862 (Taylor), and Bunnell, *Winona*, 224 (Holmes).

[8] For biographical information on Hoyt, see Thomas S. Newson, *Pen Pictures of St. Paul, Minnesota and Biographical Sketches of Old Settlers*, 92–94 (St. Paul, 1886); Nathaniel P. Langford, *Vigilante Days and Ways*, 1:262, 267 (Boston, 1890). For Ledbeater, see *SMP Register*, 106; United States Manuscript Census Schedules, 1860, Stearns County, Minnesota, p. 437; *Press*,

About forty men and some seventy head of cattle left Fort Abercrombie on June 1 and traveled north along the Red River to Georgetown. There, before crossing the river into Dakota Territory, the train was formally organized and officers were elected. Holmes was designated military captain and Indian interpreter. In Dakota the emigrants, apprehensive of Indian attack, followed a trail used two years before by fur trader Charles Larpenteur, who had swung his supply carts far north of his usual route to the Missouri in order to avoid the Sioux. The train crossed the rolling prairie to the fur post at St. Joseph, where it waited several days for a group of about thirty people to catch up.[9]

From St. Joseph, Larpenteur's route traced a line close to the Canadian border before moving southward toward the Coteau du Missouri. The Holmes emigrants, now seventy strong, crossed the Souris River in the vicinity of present-day Minot, North Dakota, and then wandered for several days among the rough, rolling hummocks and valleys of the coteau. Their route is not clear; the guide deserted and Indians stole the odometer, so the emigrants were not sure where or how far they traveled. Farther west, in what is now Montana, the train was guided by Blackfeet Indians along the Milk River and the general route of the Stevens railroad survey to Fort Benton. From there the Mullan Road took them safely to the Deer Lodge Valley. Some of them found the prospecting good and decided to stay, others went on to gold fields farther west. Probably few, if any, reached the Salmon River.

While members of the Holmes train were gathering at their outfitting towns and moving out onto the prairie, events in Washington, D.C., led to the organization of a second train, a government-sponsored expedition which was later given the name of its leader, James Fisk. In January Congress had approved the expenditure of twenty-five thousand dollars for the protection of emigration to California, Oregon, and Washington.[10] Influential Minnesotans sought to obtain a share of the grant for a northern overland route which would begin in their state.

Congressman Cyrus Aldrich, who had given special attention to a northern Pacific railroad, appears to have been a prime mover in the undertaking. Early in 1862 Aldrich's interest in obtaining military protection for the northern route was stimulated by Joseph P. Wilson, a Minneapolis merchant who wanted to organize a wagon train for the Salmon River fields. William P. Snider, a St. Paul lawyer employed in the Department of the Interior, was said to have "used his best exertions" to advance the project. During the spring of 1862, James Taylor, the articulate spokesman for Minnesota expansionism, published a number of articles in Minnesota newspapers on the Cariboo and Salmon River gold discoveries. He also consulted Aldrich and other members of the Minnesota congressional delegation about plans for opening a northern route.[11]

March 27, 1861; *Pioneer*, June 5, 1856. Cady is listed in Census Schedules, 1860, Scott County, p. 172. Federal manuscript census schedules for Minnesota were consulted in the MiHS.

[9] Larpenteur's route is described briefly in Charles H. Lee, *The Long Ago*, 47, 55 (Walhalla, North Dakota, 1899); "Red River Trails," in *The Valley Lutheran*, 2:10 (September, 1950); and Larpenteur, *Forty Years a Fur Trader*, 2:310–316, 330.

[10] United States, *Statutes at Large*, 12:333.

[11] Aldrich's name is signed to "Pacific Railroad, Minority Report," 36 Congress, 1 session,

These activities bore fruit early in April. Aldrich, accompanied by Oregon Senator James Nesmith, called on Edwin M. Stanton, secretary of war, and asked him to earmark part of the appropriated funds for a northern route. Stanton did so, designating for protection the route of the Stevens railroad survey between Fort Abercrombie and Fort Benton. On May 2 Aldrich's telegram announcing this success appeared in the *St. Paul Press.*

The next step was the appointment of an official to superintend emigration over the designated route, and Minnesota politicians also secured this plum. On May 19 James Fisk, a twenty-six-year-old private who was serving with the Third Minnesota Infantry near Columbia, Tennessee, was summoned to the capital for a new assignment. Fisk arrived in Washington about May 29 and in short order was notified that he had been appointed superintendent of emigration on a route between Fort Abercrombie and Fort Walla Walla, Washington.

James Fisk possessed a variety of qualifications for what was to become an unusual career as a superintendent of emigration. Born in Royalton, New York, on September 12, 1835 — the second eldest of six brothers — he had spent his early years within sound of Niagara Falls. His mother had been a schoolteacher; his father was a lawyer. His father's brother, John H. Fisk, was a man of imagination who apparently greatly influenced his nephew; in the 1850s the uncle was interested in railroad building, in the construction of the first suspension bridge at Niagara Falls, and in the first "Maid of the Mist" tourist steamboat to sail below the falls. When James was only eleven, the illness of his father forced him to become a wage earner. He worked for a time at a seed garden in Fredonia, New York, and later learned the trade of wagon- and carriage-making. He also made several rafting trips on the Allegheny and Ohio rivers.[12]

The family lived at various times in New York, Ohio, and Indiana. In Lafayette, Indiana, Fisk worked for the *Daily Courier* and acquired some training in the newspaper craft. (A taste for journalism was seemingly a family trait, for four of Fisk's brothers also took up the profession.) Although James was only a "humble associate" on the *Courier*, as he later put it, nevertheless he gained invaluable experience in many aspects of frontier journalism, and his fascination for the West was nurtured in the *Courier* office. During leisure moments he "rummaged" through congressional reports of expeditions into the West and "formed a fixed resolution to know more of that vast and novel region." Fisk was far too active to remain long in an editor's chair, and perhaps too prolix to be a disciplined writer, but he found the profession attractive. Some years later when he enlisted in the army

House Executive Documents, no. 428 (serial 1069). See also Wilson to J. G. Smith, August 22, 1869, in the Joseph P. Wilson Papers, MiHS; *Press,* March 10, 1866; Warren Upham and Rose B. Dunlap, *Minnesota Biographies, 1655–1912,* 868 (*Minnesota Historical Collections,* vol. 14, 1912). On Snider, see Bond, "Journal," July 19; United States Manuscript Census Schedules 1860, Ramsey County, Minnesota, p. 60; *Pioneer,* May 31, 1862. Taylor's letters appeared in the *Press,* May 18, 30, 1862.

[12] "Briefly Biographical: Col. Jas. L. Fisk" and James Fisk, "Record of Original and Selected Miscellany," 29, photocopies in the James L. Fisk and Family Papers, MiHS; *Helena Weekly Herald,* January 15, 1891; *St. Paul Dispatch,* February 5, 1877.

The James Fisk Papers in the MiHS include originals and copies of documents relating to Fisk and his brothers. Items for which the society has photocopies are, unless otherwise indicated, owned by Fisk's grandchildren, Mrs. Margaret Zastrow, Mr. Charles G. Frisbie, and Mrs. Catherine Fountain. The copies were obtained by the author through the courtesy of Mrs. Fountain.

he gave his occupation as editor. His facility with words, his flair for finding, exploiting, or making the newsworthy event, and his easy familiarity with men of the craft were later to be among his most valuable assets.[13]

In the spring of 1857 Fisk moved to Minnesota. Impulsive, generous, and proud, he hoped to rebuild the family's fortunes, but he was careless with money, squandering his earnings on the needs of the moment and the dreams, great and small, that fired his imagination. He married, bought land near White Bear Lake, not far from St. Paul, which he farmed sporadically, and wrote occasionally for a St. Paul newspaper. Soon after his arrival in Minnesota he and one of his brothers became associated with the Dakota Land Company, a St. Paul-based group of speculators interested in properties in southern Minnesota and Dakota. Fisk also joined William Nobles' expedition to build a wagon road from Fort Ridgely to South Pass during the summer of 1857. These two projects, aimed at extending Minnesota's influence into the West, took him out on the plains and brought him into contact with some of the new state's prominent men. Fisk's frontier experiences and associates were almost certainly responsible for his summons to Washington in 1862.[14]

In the West he became a hardy sportsman, a fancier of good horses, and a dead shot with rifle or pistol. Openhanded, loyal to his friends, and capable of small kindnesses which often disarmed his critics, Fisk at twenty-six possessed the useful skills and attributes of a frontier man of action as well as a gift of gab and the talent and training of a journalist. And he had fallen in love with the plains of "fair Dakota."

By the time Private Fisk left his regiment in Tennessee and reached the capital, the season was well advanced; the Holmes train was already moving out onto the plains, and other emigrants were waiting to travel with the government expedition. Representative Aldrich hurried his protégé through the intricacies of official routine. Fisk recalled later that the congressman "took me by the shoulder on my arrival at Washington, had me appointed, confirmed, commissioned, mustered out and mustered in, my bonds satisfactorily filed, the appropriation transferred, my instructions furnished me, all in twenty-four hours after my arrival." Fisk was commissioned a captain in the quartermaster corps. He took his oath of office and executed a performance bond for ten thousand dollars. Among the bond's cosigners were William Nobles and the three Minnesota congressmen who had recommended him for the job, Senator Morton Wilkinson and Representatives Aldrich and William Windom.[15]

[13] *Press*, March 10, 1866 (quotes); Mrs. Marguerite H. Anderson to Theodore C. Blegen, September 24, 1934, in the author's files; Helen M. White, "Fisk Genealogy," in the James Fisk Papers; Compiled Service Record of James L. Fisk, Company B, Third Minnesota Infantry, Office of the Adjutant General, Record Group 94 in the National Archives. Hereafter records in the National Archives are indicated by the symbol NA, followed by the record group (RG) number.

[14] James to Robert E. Fisk, August 16, 1859, April 25, May 14, October 23, 1860, in the Robert Fisk Papers, MoHS; Charles A. Smith to Helen M. White, March 25, 1945, in the author's files; Fisk, "Record of Miscellany," 4. Fisk mentions his earlier experience on the plains in *Expedition of Captain Fisk to the Rocky Mountains*, 34 (38 Congress, 1 session, *House Executive Documents*, no. 45 — serial 1189), and in his report on the 1864 expedition, p. 136, below.

[15] *Press*, March 10, 1866 (quote); Fisk to Lorenzo Thomas, May 31, 1862, F231 Commission Branch 1864, and Wilkinson, Aldrich, and Windom to Stanton, April 30, 1862, file 163F 1862, both in NARG 94. Fisk's bond is in records of the Bureau of Accounts (Treasury), NARG 39.

Five thousand dollars were placed to Fisk's account in the United States treasury and the secretary of war instructed him to organize and outfit a corps of men for the protection of emigrants "not only against hostile Indians but against all dangers including starvation, losses, accidents, and the like." He was ordered to hire such assistants as secretary, guide, Indian interpreter, physician, and wagon master, as well as teamsters, herders, and cooks. He was further advised to set a time for rendezvous at Fort Abercrombie and arrange for the wide advertising of his plans. His responsibility for emigrant protection ended at Fort Benton, the eastern terminus of the Mullan Road. Because army crews were still at work on the road and because the Indians of the far Northwest had been peaceable for some years, the War Department no doubt felt that emigrants were safe beyond Fort Benton. Fisk was additionally instructed, however, to proceed over the Mullan Road to Fort Walla Walla, sell his government property, and return home by way of Panama.[16]

The assignment posed a number of practical problems. Fisk's instructions were a hasty revision of those prepared for another superintendent with a much larger budget on a different route and were not well tailored to fit his circumstances.[17] He was, for example, authorized to recruit men for an estimated four months' journey at salaries and wages well over his total appropriation. He was told to outfit the expedition "in the most complete manner," to secure guns, ammunition, gifts for the Indians, and emergency supplies of food and medicine. At the end of the journey he was expected to auction the travel-worn wagons and animals and any other surplus government property and realize enough money to pay all outstanding bills. Given these conditions and Fisk's temperament, his subsequent financial problems were inevitable. He consistently spent more than his allotted funds and did not succeed in finally settling his expedition accounts until years after he had left the army.[18]

Fisk was on detached service under assignment from the secretary of war, held a commission in the quartermaster corps, and reported to the adjutant general, but had no immediate superior who was at all concerned with what he was doing. Furthermore, he was a frontier citizen-soldier, unschooled in military ways and interested in the spirit rather than the letter of his instructions. It was fortunate for Fisk that his was a political appointment, and that the Minnesotans who supported him cared more about what he did for western emigration than how he observed the regulations of the War Department.

The new superintendent managed to complete his business in Washington in two days; then he hurried to Minnesota, reaching St. Paul on June 3. The lateness of the season left him little time for elaborate preparations, and his limited funds precluded any but the sketchiest outfit. He made his first announcement to prospective emigrants in the pages of the *St. Paul Pioneer* on June 7, and nine days later he was ready to leave for the rendezvous. He was able to hurry preparations

[16] Stanton to Fisk, May 29, 1862, photocopy in James Fisk Papers. For conditions on the Mullan Road, see *St. Paul Weekly Press*, May 8, 1862.

[17] A draft of a letter from Stanton to Medorem Crawford, April 26, 1862 (in T360 Volunteer Service 1862, NARG 94) was altered in pencil to apply to Fisk.

[18] Abstracts of Fisk's accounts and a record of their final settlement are in records of the third auditor, General Accounting Office, NARG 217.

by recruiting his protective corps from the emigrants and by finding staff members among his friends and their acquaintances.

As his second assistant in charge of commissary, Fisk chose Nathaniel P. Langford, the brother-in-law of James Taylor. Langford had written Fisk offering his services for some position of importance, suggesting that his presence on the expedition would ensure Taylor's interest and co-operation.[19]

Samuel Robert Bond, a friend of William Snider, was appointed secretary-journalist of the expedition. He was thirty and was described by a contemporary as "a little, short man, a lawyer, and one of those men who carried the world upon his back." A graduate of Dartmouth College, Bond had served a term as city attorney of St. Paul. He was interested in many community affairs and was said to have inspired the first series of public lectures in the city. The journal kept by Bond became in shortened form the official report of the Fisk expedition of 1862.[20]

Fisk appointed his friend Dr. William Denton Dibb as the expedition's physician. Dibb was a slight, quiet, modest-appearing man of thirty-five. Born in England, he had studied medicine for three years and had been admitted to the Royal College of Physicians and Surgeons in 1846. He emigrated to America with his parents in the early 1850s, settling first in Illinois and later moving to Minnesota. He practiced medicine in St. Anthony (now part of Minneapolis) and joined a St. Paul militia company. Like his father, who had brought his prized English hunting dogs with him to America, Dibb was an ardent sportsman. He often visited Fisk at White Bear Lake and may have been on hunting excursions with him before 1862. Dibb was to accompany three of the Fisk expeditions and two of his diaries are published in this text. Dibb's mementos of the journeys — a quill-embroidered buffalo robe, shells from Mexico, a piece of petrified wood from Dakota, and his journals — have been cherished in his family for many years.[21]

Pierre Bottineau, another friend, was recruited by Fisk as the expedition's guide. Already famous on the frontier, Bottineau had guided Stevens in 1853 and Nobles in 1859 and had been associated with other expeditions and enterprises. His reputation as a guide was very high. A newspaper correspondent wrote of him in 1863: "If there is any rock, hill, creek, ford, or clump of bushes in the whole territory of Dakotah that he is not acquainted with, I should like to hear of it." Bottineau was forty-five in 1862 and was described by an early St. Paul settler as a large man, with a prominent head, swarthy complexion, and piercing eyes. In odd contrast to these features was the "exceeding pleasant smile which nearly always radiates his face. He has the characteristics of the bear and the gentleness of the woman." His fifteen-year-old son Daniel accompanied him on the expedition.[22]

[19] Langford to Fisk, May 20, 1862, photocopy in James Fisk Papers.

[20] The quotation is from Newson, *Pen Pictures*, 715. See also *American Biographical Dictionary for the District of Columbia*, 45 (Washington, 1908). The official report, *Expedition from Fort Abercrombie to Fort Benton*, was published in 37 Congress, 3 session, *House Executive Documents*, no. 80 (serial 1164).

[21] Biographical information about Dibb was gathered from the *Minnesota Republican* (St. Anthony), July 16, 1857; United States Manuscript Census Schedules, 1860, Hennepin County, Minnesota, p. 337, and 1870, p. 753; and interviews with Mrs. Katherine Dibb Fitzgerald and Thomas Dibb, August, 1944.

[22] The quotations are from the *Springfield Weekly Republican* (Massachusetts), September 5, 1863 (typescript in MiHS), and Newson, *Pen Pictures*, 22. See also Margareth Jorgenson, "Life

The other officers included the first assistant, Elihu H. Burritt, a lawyer and former deputy clerk of the Minnesota Supreme Court, and the expedition's surveyor, David W. Charlton, a civil engineer from Minneapolis. Robert C. Knox, the wagon master, who was more than six feet tall and "as genial" in nature as he was "large in stature," had been a pioneer commission merchant in St. Paul, active in city affairs since 1851. George Raymond Noyes, a blacksmith and former shipbuilder, served as the officers' cook. Noyes left his family behind; when he sent for them four years later, they joined the Fisk party of 1866.[23]

Fisk and some of his staff set out from St. Paul on June 16, 1862. The group, joined by others on the way, numbered thirteen wagons when it reached St. Cloud on Saturday, June 21. This frontier town of about a thousand persons boasted a four-story brick business block, four churches, sawmills, saloons, boardinghouses, and the headquarters of Burbank and Company, a wholesale and transportation firm. Samuel Bond, the staff journalist, commented that the town wore "more of an air of life and business than any other place that I have seen in Minnesota." Here the party camped over the weekend and picked up additional travelers, including a number of the officers who came by stage from St. Paul. Members of the expedition purchased more supplies and equipment for the journey and visited friends. On Sunday a local minister conducted religious services in the camp. The next day the company moved on through the Sauk River Valley, probably following much the same route taken by part of the Holmes train.[24]

The men pushed forward rapidly in order to reach Fort Abercrombie by July 4. There the emigrants spent three days merrily celebrating the holiday and making final preparations for the plains journey. With the addition of a group of gold seekers who had been waiting at the fort for Fisk, the expedition was said by Bond to number 117 men, 13 women, and 53 wagons. Like the Holmes train, the Fisk party of 1862 was made up largely of Minnesotans, nearly two-thirds of them from the Minneapolis and St. Paul areas. Among them were merchants, hotelkeepers, farmers, three butchers, a steamboat captain, a millwright, and a tinsmith, as well as clerks and laborers. Unlike the Holmes group, the Fisk party included a number of women. Besides several wives who accompanied their husbands, there were Mrs. Catherine A. Durgan, a widow from St. Anthony who was in her late thirties, and two or three young single women traveling with their families.[25]

On July 7, a fair summer day, the Fisk expedition set out from Fort Abercrombie. Some of the emigrants were fearful of Indians and wanted to go north to the Larpenteur trail, which they thought would be safer. But Fisk was determined to

of Pierre Bottineau," a term paper, and Isaac I. Stevens to Pierre Bottineau, August 7, 1853 (typescript), both in MiHS; United States Manuscript Census Schedules, 1860, Hennepin County, Minnesota, p. 114; *Pioneer*, June 11, 1862.

[23] For biographical data on Burritt, see *Pioneer*, December 23, 1862; *Press*, January 31, 1863; *Stillwater Messenger*, February 3, 1863. On Charlton, see United States Manuscript Census Schedules, 1857, Hennepin County, Minnesota, p. 64 (photocopy); *Minneapolis City Directory* 1859–60. On Knox, see Michael A. Leeson, ed., *History of Montana, 1739–1885*, 1341 (Chicago, 1885), and Newson, *Pen Pictures*, 249. On Noyes, see Alva J. Noyes, *The Story of Ajax; Life in the Big Hole Basin*, 3 (Helena, 1914), and Leeson, ed., *Montana*, 1347.

[24] Bond, "Journal," June 21–23; Henrietta L. Memler, "A History of St. Cloud, Minnesota, 1861–65," a term paper in MiHS; *Pioneer*, June 25, 1862.

[25] For the names of members of the 1862 Fisk expedition, see *Press*, July 19, 1862; Bond, "Journal," July 10, September 22, 1862; and Appendix, below.

follow the Stevens route, and he had Bottineau to show him the way.[26] The captain had encouraged the fainthearted by obtaining an army howitzer from the fort, little knowing that two months later, during the Sioux Uprising, the post would have far more use for the cannon than he had.

At the head of the coteau the expedition followed the trail of the Holmes party for a few days, unaware that Holmes's guide had deserted. At Fort Union Bottineau decided to return to Minnesota, and Fisk hired Robert Meldrum, a fur trader, to guide the train to Fort Benton. Meldrum, or "Round Iron," had come to the plains some thirty years before to trade with the Crow Indians. Possessed of a mild disposition, superior intelligence, and great courage, he was described as "one of the most remarkable men ever employed in the service of the American Fur Company."[27]

The Fisk emigrants reached Fort Benton in mid-September without serious mishap and camped for several days, utilizing the services of the post's blacksmiths to shoe their oxen. When members of the party visited the fort, they encountered the famous frontiersman Dr. Monroe G. Atkinson, whom Bond described as "the most complete specimen of a mountaineer, as my imagination had pictured one, that I ever met. He dresses in a full buck-skin suit, has two or three pack-horses, and his commissary stores consist chiefly of dried Buffalo meat and flour, while his faithful rifle is relied upon to afford game." Atkinson is a mysterious figure in early Montana history. Reportedly he had discovered gold in many places, but, as Bond put it, "he seems to have been constantly impelled, as if by mania, to keep traveling on, and . . . has never stopped to enrich himself. He said he would not work at mining unless he could make $100 per day."[28]

At Fort Benton Fisk's official responsibility for the emigrants ended. The Mullan Road, which gave access to the gold fields, was clearly marked and safe from Indian attack. However, since Fisk had to follow the road to Fort Walla Walla, where he was instructed to sell his equipment, the emigrants petitioned to travel with him on an informal basis. Therefore the expedition continued much as it had until it reached the valley of the Prickly Pear Creek, near present-day Helena. There a small party of gold seekers turned off to prospect. The specimens they found persuaded most of the emigrants to try their luck at Prickly Pear instead of going on to the Salmon River.

The departure of Fisk and the rest of the party on September 22 was marked by several small ceremonies. Mrs. Durgan entertained the officers of the expedition at a table "decked with a fine white tablecloth and snowy napkins" and "loaded with viands." As Fisk prepared to leave, the emigrants gathered around the flag wagon and presented a testimonial, signed by members of the train, expressing their appreciation for his services in guiding them safely across the plains. After

[26] Fisk's party apparently carried with it a copy of Stevens' report, and from time to time Bottineau indicated places where the railroad survey party had camped. See Bond, "Journal," July 22, 23, 31, August 13.

[27] On Meldrum, see the following articles in *Montana Historical Contributions:* "Journal of James H. Bradley," 2:201 (Helena, 1896); "Affairs at Fort Benton From 1831 to 1869," 3:254–256 (Helena, 1900); and "Original Journal of James H. Chambers, Fort Sarpy," 10:284 (Helena, 1941). The quotation is in 3:255.

[28] *Press*, March 19, 1863.

hearty cheers, general handshaking, and kissing of the ladies, Fisk and his small group moved on, leaving some eighty-two emigrants at Prickly Pear.[29]

On a cold, rainy morning a few days later, when snow fell thickly on the tops of nearby mountains, the wagons of the Fisk party crossed the Deer Lodge Valley toward American Fork, a settlement near the junction of the Deer Lodge and Clark Fork rivers. Some of the officers set off on horseback to visit a miners' camp on Gold Creek at Pikes Peak Gulch. There in a narrow ravine lined with willows and cottonwoods they met a group of ten fellow Minnesotans from the Holmes train. The men had purchased a claim for a hundred and fifty dollars and were living on it in a shelter made of posts and boughs. The "Minnesota Company," as they called themselves, entertained the Fisk men at a dinner of fried bread, pork, and coffee. Two days later the Holmes men returned the visit and ate a sumptuous dinner prepared by Noyes which included beef liver, canned peaches, blackberry pie, and cake.[30]

At this point in the Deer Lodge Valley the last of the Minnesota emigrants left the Fisk party to seek their fortunes in the mining region that within two years would become Montana Territory. With three wagons and thirteen men, Fisk completed the final leg of the journey to Walla Walla by the end of October. Encamped on a creek near the settlement, the men gathered around a comfortable fire to read letters from home and to peruse a bundle of St. Paul newspapers in which they learned of the Sioux Uprising in Minnesota.[31]

At Walla Walla Fisk sold the expedition's equipment and compared experiences with Captain Medorem Crawford, who had been superintendent of emigration for the central plains route. Then on November 8 Fisk, Bond, Dibb, Burritt, and Charlton took the stage for Wallula on the Columbia River. From there they traveled to Portland, Oregon, where they obtained steamboat passage to San Francisco. Eventually they made their way to New York via Panama. Nine members of the Fisk company remained in Walla Walla, where they secured work until the return of warm weather made gold hunting possible.

Many of the gold seekers who traveled west with Holmes and Fisk became pioneer settlers of Montana. Mark Ledbeater took up farming near Manhattan, Montana. John Potter, a farmer from Long Prairie, Minnesota, became a merchant in Helena and Hamilton. Potter's earlier political experience in Maine and Minnesota served as preparation for similar activities in Montana, where he took part in Republican politics and was chosen Helena's first postmaster. David E. Folsom, a member of the Fisk expedition who had been a schoolteacher in St. Paul, settled at White Sulphur Springs and became a stock raiser, banker, and member of the state legislature. In 1869 he accompanied an exploring expedition to the headwaters of the Yellowstone to investigate the strange natural phenomena of which he had heard rumors. His careful account of the marvels he saw was one of the first published reports on the region that later became Yellowstone Park. Fisk's commissary assistant, Nathaniel Langford, was to become widely known as a

[29] Bond, "Journal," September 22.

[30] Bond, "Journal," September 26, 28. See also Paul C. Phillips, ed., *Forty Years on the Frontier, the Journals and Reminiscences of Granville Stuart,* 1:224 (Cleveland, 1925).

[31] For information here and below, see Bond, "Journal," October 30, November 8.

Montana pioneer, writer, explorer, and the first superintendent of Yellowstone Park.[32]

Robert C. Knox, Fisk's wagon master, helped frame the first laws of Montana Territory; years later he became a probate judge at Butte. Charles St. Clair, a St. Paul clerk born in England, served as secretary to one of Montana's early territorial governors. Another Englishman, Robert Halliday, gained some fame in Montana for his sketches and paintings of the frontier scene.[33]

Cornelius Bray, an Irish tinsmith from St. Paul who enrolled in Fisk's protective corps, took up ranching at Red Rock. Ard Godfrey, in association with Bray and Langford, built the earliest sawmill in Montana; a millwright from Maine, Godfrey had already constructed in Minnesota the first commercial sawmill on the site of the future city of Minneapolis. Other members of the Fisk expedition included Henry C. Harrison, who settled on a ranch at Harrison, Montana, and William F. Bartlett, who went into the mercantile and hotel business at Butte. Mrs. Catherine Durgan operated a frontier hostelry at Tenmile Creek near Helena. John M. Castner, a St. Paul grocer and former coroner of Ramsey County, was elected mayor of Virginia City, where he operated a saloon and boardinghouse. Albert Egnell, a Swedish hotel clerk from Ramsey County, established a stage line at Helena. John T. Mannheim, a German brewer from Chatfield, Minnesota, was said to have made some of the first beer in Montana, using as ingredients wheat, Utah sorghum, and the tops of spruce trees.[34]

One of the more colorful Fisk emigrants was Giles S. Olin, a blacksmith and machinist from St. Anthony. Olin and his teen-age son opened a blacksmith shop in Deer Lodge where they made and repaired mining tools. On a stampede to new gold fields in the winter of 1865, Olin's feet were so badly frozen that they had to be amputated. He then made himself a pair of artificial feet, so skillfully fitted that he was able to continue his blacksmith business. Olin also contrived a handy cart drawn by a pair of Newfoundland dogs with which he traveled on wheels or runners as far as Butte and Helena.[35]

Perhaps the best known member of the Fisk train of 1862 was James Fergus. Born in Scotland in 1813, Fergus had been a millwright and a manufacturer of machinery in Illinois before he moved to Minnesota Territory, where he engaged in townsite speculation and became a proprietor of Little Falls. Fergus joined

[32] On Ledbeater, see *SMP Register*, 106. On Potter, Leeson, ed., *Montana*, 1153. On Folsom, *Progressive Men of the State of Montana*, 2:1480–1482 (Chicago, [190?]), and David E. Folsom, *The Folsom-Cook Exploration of the Upper Yellowstone in the year 1869* (St. Paul, 1894). On Langford, *Dictionary of American Biography*, 10:592 (New York, 1933).

[33] On Knox, see Leeson, ed., *Montana*, 1341; *New North West* (Deer Lodge), June 8, 1888. On St. Clair, see *Montanian* (Virginia City), September 25, 1873; *Helena Herald*, September 24, 1873. At least one of Halliday's sketches, depicting the cabins of several Minnesota miners at Bannack, is in the collections of the Montana Historical Society. It is reproduced in this book.

[34] On Bray, see *SMP Register*, 46. On Godfrey, see Upham and Dunlap, *Minnesota Biographies*, 262; notes by Harriet Godfrey in the Ard Godfrey Family Papers, MiHS; Thomas J. Dimsdale, *The Vigilantes of Montana*, 31, 203 (Helena, 1915). On Harrison, Leeson, ed., *Montana*, 1269. On Bartlett, *SMP Register*, 225. On Mrs. Durgan, *Helena Weekly Herald*, September 13, 1888. On Castner, Newson, *Pen Pictures*, 720; *Press*, May 10, 1862; *Avant Courier* (Bozeman), April 28, 1876. On Egnell, United States Manuscript Census Schedules, 1860, Ramsey County, Minnesota, p. 82; "Helena," in Nathaniel P. Langford Papers, MiHS. On Mannheim, Census Schedules, 1860, Fillmore County, Minnesota, p. 217; Dimsdale, *Vigilantes of Montana*, 265.

[35] *Helena Herald*, June 30, 1877; "Giles S. Olin," in Kate Fogarty, "Butte in the Sixties," typescript in MoHS.

the expedition on a sudden impulse, with only two days' preparation. He gathered some bedding and food, hitched four oxen to a wagon, bade his wife good-by, and overtook Fisk at Fort Abercrombie. In Montana Fergus became famous as a hospitable rancher, as a director of the first bank in Helena, and as a member of both the territorial legislature and the constitutional convention. He wrote frequently for Montana papers and was an avid reader and an independent thinker in politics and religion. In 1884 he was named "the most typical and distinguished" of Montana pioneers.[36]

Some years after the journey Fergus wrote that his companions on the trail had included "broken down lumbermen . . . broken down merchants, and scalawags of all sorts." Another emigrant, in a letter published during the autumn of 1862, described the organization of the train as a "lamentable farce." The officers lacked experience, the writer complained, and the emigrants were required to serve guard duty. By the spring of 1863 many other reports from both the Fisk and Holmes parties appeared in Minnesota newspapers. The *St. Paul Press* of March 19 took a more positive view of the 1862 emigration, characterizing the gold seekers as a "victorious army . . . sent forth by Minnesota to clear the path of emigration and commerce to the Pacific."[37]

As a result of the journey Fisk himself became convinced of the importance of the northern route for Minnesota, the gold fields, and the country as a whole. From this time on, he considered his duties as army officer and superintendent of emigration secondary to his role as explorer and promoter. He was imbued with the desire "on any occasion or at any time" to demonstrate to the people of Minnesota and to the government the incalculable benefits of the northern route. As he recalled a few years later, he even hoped that he might become the medium for securing a permanent road over the northern plains. To these ends he devoted himself for the next four years.

[36] *Minneapolis Journal*, March 15, 1902; David Hilger, "James Fergus, 1812–1902," a memorandum in the Fergus Papers, MoHS (quote).

[37] Fergus to William Butler, March 20, 1875, in Fergus Papers; *St. Cloud Democrat*, October 2, 1862. Other letters from the gold fields appeared in *St. Cloud Democrat*, January 1, 15; *Pioneer*, January 13, March 24; *Press*, January 27; *St. Peter Tribune*, April 4 — all in 1863. Fisk's recollections quoted below are in *Press*, March 10, 1866.

1862 ✸✸✸✸✸✸✸✸✸✸✸✸✸✸✸✸✸✸✸✸

Letters from the Holmes Train

VALLENCOURT H. CADY TO J. L. MACDONALD[1]

Campbells Station on Red River, June 1st, 1862

DEAR MAC: — Agreeable to request I now embrace the opportunity of dropping a few rambling sketches by the wayside, to inform you of our whereabouts, and the progress of our trip thus far toward the destined El Dorado of the West.

As you will recollect, we left Shakopee on the morning of the 16th, and camped within 3 miles of Minneapolis. On the 2nd morning we yoked up our cows and put them in our team and have worked them every day that we have travelled since. They have given us no trouble at all but have been of great service to us in hauling as well as furnishing us with plenty of milk. As a matter of economy many of the poor farmers of Minnesota who find themselves unable to keep both oxen and cows will find the latter a good substitute for the former, by working them moderately in getting in their crops and doing general farm work.

On the 2nd day after leaving Minneapolis we overtook Mr. [Franklin] Chase, who was also using cows for one half of his team.[2] We have thus far made greater progress in our trip than we expected. Passed through St. Cloud on the 21st, and arrived at Fort Abercrombie on the evening of the 30th, thus performing the trip in fifteen days; distance 280 miles. Overtook the St. Paul train on the 24th and have kept together since. We also came up with our old friend Tom Holmes and party on the evening of the 30th, they had camped within about a mile of the Fort and were waiting for us. All are in good health and spirits. Our party now number about 40 men, and will be increased in a day or two to 50, so that we apprehend no danger from hostile Indians. We have not yet organized but shall when we reach Georgetown.

We expect to go as far north as St. Jo before striking out in a westerly course.[3]

[1] The letter was written to the editor of the *Shakopee Argus*. It appeared in that newspaper on June 14, 1862. Campbell's Station was a stage stop on the Minnesota side of the river about a dozen miles north of Fort Abercrombie. See Samuel H. Scudder, *The Winnipeg Country*, 16 and map (Boston, 1886).

[2] Little is known of Chase, who came from Shakopee and was accompanied by a nephew. See Cuthbert, "Notes on Trip from St. Paul to Fort Benton, 1862."

[3] The fur trading settlement and Hudson's Bay Company post of St. Joseph stood on the site of present-day Walhalla, North Dakota. See Lee, *The Long Ago*, 18.

From Fort Abercrombie to Georgetown the distance is 47 miles, and from Georgetown to St. Jo we expect to go through in 12 days; from St. Jo to Fort Union we expect to travel in 20 days. From Fort Union to Fort Benton the reputed distance is 440 miles. From Fort Benton to Bitter Root Valley the distance is computed at 115 miles, this will take us through or over the Rocky Mountains. We have in our train 13 cows and 5 horses or ponies, most of which are worked.

For the last fifty miles we have seen numerous relics of buffalo. In fact the bones of these wild roamers of the western prairies are found on about every quarter section that we have passed over in the last named distance. The numerous antlers of the elk give ample testimony of their having been slain in great numbers to furnish sport for the hunter or food for the Indians. A party of half breed Indians camped with us last night. They are mostly freighted with pemmican and dried buffalo meat bound for St. Paul or a market.

Many an Englishman and Frenchman are *en route* for the Cariboo mines; some take the stage from St. Paul, others carts, while some have even started on ponies, and I have seen some who have gone down the Red River on rafts, so great is the excitement and anxiety to reach the mines. I was told by an Englishman to-day that there was a party of 500 that would embark for the Cariboo mines on the 17th of this month, and they had engaged a passage through in forty days at a cost of forty Guineas per head. This looks like an earnestness of their expectations in reaching the mines this fall. We have yet heard of no such fabulous reports of the great draughts of gold found in Washington Territory as are given of the Cariboo mines, yet we hope to do well should we be fortunate enough to reach the mines safely with our outfit.

I may write to you again on reaching St. Jo should we spend any time there. We were in hopes to have received mail matter at Fort Abercrombie but were disappointed. We shall not now expect to hear from home until we reach Fort Benton in Washington Territory. Should our friends think proper to write us there they will please direct them to Fort Benton, Washington Territory *via* St. Louis Mo., where we are in hopes to receive them on reaching there. Please send us a bundle of papers of a proper date, to reach us about the middle of August or from the 1st to the middle of that month.

While writing this I am surrounded by a crowd of men who are almost boisterous in their conversation, therefore should you find any omissions or tautology, please make the necessary corrections. I have stood the trip thus far better than I was fearful I should, not having rode five miles since I started.

My feet give more trouble than any other part of the body, but they are improving, and I hope will safely carry me through. This being Sunday, many of the party are writing, so that you will probably hear from others by the same mail. I have yet spare room on my sheet, but know of nothing more that will interest you, therefore will close. Respectfully Yours

V. H. CADY

JOHN F. HOYT TO THE EDITOR OF THE ST. PAUL PRESS[4]

Camp Twelve Miles Below Fort Abercrombie, June 1st, 1862

To the Editor of the St. Paul Press. Arriving at the Fort Friday evening, we found the Shakopee company, consisting of fifteen men with five teams waiting for us.

There are now, in what is known as the St. Paul company, twenty-one men with seven wagons, twenty yoke of oxen, five cows and five ponies. We expect six or seven teams to overtake us within a week, which will make the whole party number about fifty men.

Yesterday morning we had a long discussion as to the route we should take. A few were for the route surveyed by Gov. Stevens. But the great majority of the party insisted on what is known as the Larpenteur's route, and this we take. We will cross the Red River at Georgetown, go thence to St. Joseph, a settlement thirty miles west of Pembina, thence directly west to Fort Benton on the Missouri River. The road to St. Joseph is good. And from St. Joseph to Fort Benton we expect no difficulty from any source.

At Fort Abercrombie Capt. Vanderhoof [John Vander Horck], in command there, treated us very kindly. Many of our party will remember his as the last table perhaps we may sit down to for months.

From St. Cloud thus far we have had plenty of game and fish. Last Sunday (this party intend to keep the Sabbath) three or four men took from a lake near which we camped, not less than fifty fine wall-eyed pike. Nothing prevents our living well. Our milk is a luxury. Last evening we all had "mush and milk," as good, too, as we ever got at home.

A party from the Red River Settlement camped near us last night. We had as a guest an English gentleman, who gave us, seated around our camp fire on the banks of the Red River of the North, sweet music from his concertinie, while from the camps of the half breeds came the more lively music of the violin.

The people along the way tell us we have the best teams and the best outfits they have ever seen on the road. Our cattle are improving. Not a lame or a sick ox yet. We will make about one hundred miles per week, stopping always Sundays.

We have not effected any organization yet — don't know that it is necessary. Tom Holmes is the acknowledged head of the Shakopee company, while we St. Paul boys rather look up to the practical, good natured, fat W[ilson] C. Morrison.[5]

We are all in the best of spirits, and send greeting to all the friends at home. Truly and respectfully,

J. F. H.

[4] The letter appeared in the *Press*, June 10, 1862.
[5] Bond and Dibb refer to the Holmes train as the Morrison party. See Bond, "Journal," August 25, September 23, and page 60, below.

MARK D. LEDBEATER TO WILLIAM B. MITCHELL [6]

Rush Lake, on Red River Trail, June 10th, 1862

FRIEND WILL. — As the mail carrier stays with us to-night, I will drop you a line. Our party consists of forty-two good, able bodied men, seventy-six head of cattle (thirteen cows included) and five ponies. We have our officers elected — one captain of the train and one quartermaster, and one military captain and one lieutenant. All the men obey orders, and everything works to a charm. Roads good — cattle all in good order — feed excellent — no Indians to be seen. It is getting dark — candles are scarce — I will write you again from St. Joseph. Truly Yours.

MARK D. LEDBEATER

CADY TO MACDONALD [7]

St Jo, Dakota Territory, June 16th, 1862

DEAR MAC: — In my last letter to you I was at Campbells Station, some 12 or 13 miles above Fort Abercrombie. The next point of any importance was Georgetown, situated on Red River. This at present, is the highest point that the steamboat reaches, and is principally owned by the Hudson Bay Company. There is at this time some 30 soldiers stationed there as a protection against hostile Indians. A Mission is also established there. It [i]s embarkation for land carriage by the numerous [oxcart] trains that annually make their trips to St. Paul. There are some twenty or thirty houses, including a good hotel, post office several stores, private dwellings, &c. The steamboat that runs to this place will vie with many of the Mississippi boats, in point of tonnage, finish, &c., and will pay well for the investment. Much danger is apprehended from the Indians down the river, as they have threatened to burn the boat if the company do not pay them an exhorbitant price for wood used to run it. At the time we reached there, a large company of Canadians was waiting to take passage to Fort Gar[r]y, in transitee to the Cariboo mines. Amongst the lot were several Catholic Priests, Sisters of Charity, &c., to look after the spiritual comforts of their followers. A steam saw-mill was erected there last fall. In looking through it, our old friend and fellow traveller, Thomas Holmes, Esq., recognized his engine, it having been brought from Holmes City without the consent of its original owner. We found it somewhat difficult to ferry at this point, as there was no ferry-boat short of taking the one used to ferry across Buffalo river.

Our Shakopee company crossed over Red River with our wagon bodies and got every thing over safe. The St. Paul company took the Buffalo ferry boat some five or six miles down the river, and managed to cross with that.

On the 1st of June, we took up our line of embarkation for this point. For the

[6] The letter appeared in the *St. Cloud Democrat*, June 19, 1862. William B. Mitchell was assistant editor of the *Democrat*, owned and edited by his aunt, Jane Grey Swisshelm. See Upham and Dunlap, *Minnesota Biographies*, 515. Rush Lake, four days' travel north of Georgetown, was probably located in southern Nelson County, North Dakota.

[7] The letter appeared in the *Shakopee Argus*, July 12, 1862.

first two or three days we found wood and water very scarce, having to carry wood in our wagons or go without hot coffee, after a long days drive. Ever since we left the Fort, we found plenty of grass for our stock, and a good smooth prairie to travel over. To this, however, we found some exceptions, particularly in crossing some small streams, with deep, muddy bottoms. A few miles below this is a long marsh of some two miles, which in wet weather, is almost impossible to cross. We managed to get over, however, without any great delay or trouble. A large portion of our route from Georgetown, was over a dead level prairie, and for days not a vestige of timber was to be seen, or a stick of brushwood large enough to makes a mosquito *smudge.*

Before leaving Georgetown, we organized our company by electing Mr. Salter our train Captain, and a Mr. Voder [James C. Vaiter] of St. Paul, our Wagon Master. We also elected Thomas A. Holmes, Esq., Military Captain, and Mr. Morrison of St. Paul, 1st Lieutenant. Under their guidance and protection, we have no fear of our success in crossing to the Rocky Mountains, particularly if we take a guide from this place, as we now contemplate doing. We are pretty well satisfied now that we would have saved about 200 miles travel if we had procured a guide at Fort Abercrombie, and taken a direct course to Fort Benton. Should emigration set westward another year for the mines, I hope some party will cross at this point, and test its practicability.

We have reached here just in time to see the embarkation of the Buffalo hunters, some 400 or 600 in number, with nearly as many carts to procure their annual stock of pemican and dried meat.[8] The party consists of half-breed Chippewas and Rees, and when they all get under way will form a cavalcade of two or three miles in length. Their course is toward Devil's Lake [North Dakota] and its vicinity. In going out on this hunt they take their entire families, and all make themselves more or less useful in the hunt.

St. Jo is situated on the Pembina river, and if the country hereabouts belonged to the white population, it would at no distant day, be the most charming location of all the northwest. In fact it is the only point that I have seen within the last 300 miles that I would be willing to locate on. It stands on a deep valley that stretches as far as the vision of the eye can sweep, and is interspersed with timber and prairie. But a small portion of this country is under cultivation; the natives or "half-breeds," subsisting almost entirely on pemican and dried Buffalo meat, without bread, potatoes, or in fact any kind of vegetables. Some few have cows, and almost all of them horses. Dogs compose a part of the family. These are of the wolf species, and not less than half breeds like themselves. Very few of the natives speak the English language, so that we found it difficult to make ourselves understood. We shall remain here some 4 days, waiting for a party of thirty persons who wish to join us from below. When these reach us we shall number 72 persons, a force sufficient to stand our hand against a small tribe of hostile Indians, should they think proper to encounter us. Without the last augmentation named, we have upward of 80 head of cattle, and 5 horses. We are promised, in the event of hiring a guide here, all the fresh Buffalo meat we want on the trip, besides any quantity to dry.

[8] Bond said that he had seen ten distinct trails made by "at least 2000 Red River Carts" which probably belonged to this train. "Journal," July 22, 25.

Since leaving Fort Abercrombie, we have heard that a Mr. Fisk had been appointed by government, to raise a company to guard or escort us across the plains.[9] Under the appropriation made for that purpose, if such is the fact, he can be of no service to us on this trip, and the appropriation properly, should be given to us, should we safely cross to the Rocky Mountains, as we will in all probability be the first train that ever crossed through Uncle Sam's dominions so far north. Let Mr. Fisk remain at home, and give us the appropriation, and we will be of as much service to our dear Uncle, as if his tardy agent was along. Can't you give us a lift on this score, Mac?

Not a day's sickness has visited a single member of our company since we left home, and we have not had but three days of hot weather. Yesterday the weather was unpleasantly cold, attended with a drizzling rain. Today it is warmer, yet cold enough for April, and still rainy. It is the first rain of any importance since we left home. I hope you have been more favored in Minnesota.

We were much disappointed in not receiving any letters or papers, on reaching the Fort or Georgetown, but hope all will be made up in arriving at Fort Benton.[10] We are not certain that there is any provision made for transmitting the mails to that point, but hope there is; at all events we cannot at present see any other chance of getting news except through that channel.

I do not think that we will reach Fort Benton in less than forty days, which will take us until the 25th of July, and perhaps longer.

Our townsman, Mr. Chase, has lamed one of his oxen, and had to take him out of his team yesterday, and set his young man to lead him behind the train. On reaching camp and waiting some three hours, he did not come up, and Mr. Chase returned back some six miles to see what was the matter. He found the ox, but no one with him. After hunting some hours, he returned to camp without finding him, nor did his nephew reach camp last night. This morning a party have gone out to hunt him and had not returned when I left. If they do not find him before we leave here, I will inform you by letter.[11]

I know of nothing more that will interest you at present. This is the last point that I shall write at before crossing the prairie, so until then adieu. Respectfully yours,

V. H. Cady

LEDBEATER TO MITCHELL [12]

In Camp Near St. Joseph, June 17th, 1862

Friend Will. — We arrived at St. Joe day before yesterday — had a good trip — the roads in good order with the exception of a few bad sloughs, and one marsh about a half mile long. We had no difficulty in crossing, however, as our teams were in good condition, and plenty of them. We have waited several days for a

[9] The *Press* of June 18, 1862, reported that the Holmes party would be informed at Georgetown of Fisk's appointment.

[10] According to the *Pioneer*, July 15, 1862, a half-breed delivered letters and newspapers to the St. Paul members of the train four days out of Georgetown.

[11] No further reference was made to Chase's nephew, and it is presumed that he was found.

[12] The letter appeared in the *St. Cloud Democrat*, July 10, 1862.

party of fifteen or twenty to come up, and I hear that they will be at St. Joe to-night (we are camped five miles from there.) We have had some difficulty in getting a guide — have made bargains with several who backed out, but I think the matter is now settled.[13]

The half-breed train left on Monday for the hunt. It has been estimated that fifteen hundred carts will go in the train. They start from different points and meet somewhere on the Plains. This I have from parties in St. Joe. I saw about three hundred in this last named place.

St. Joseph is a lovely site for a town. There are, I should judge, about seventy-five houses and one church. By-the-way, six half-breeds were married before starting on the hunt, taking their better halves with them to help dry the meat and make the pemmican. The corn and vegetables look well — full as early as any I have seen. The wheat also looks well and thrifty. The people are very attentive to church matters, nearly all attend. I heard some excellent singing. I saw but one American in the place, the rest having gone off somewhere, perhaps to St. Paul to buy goods.

18th. — The rest of the party arrived here today. They have an arrangement on the wheel to measure the distance, and so when I write I shall give the distances traveled each day, &c., &c. I shall write you from Fort Benton. Truly Yours.

Mark D. Ledbeater

LEDBEATER TO MITCHELL[14]

Fort Benton, August 10th, 1862

Dear Will. — We arrived here yesterday, safe and sound, after a tedious trip of fifty-three days from St. Joe, out of which we laid over eleven days. It would be useless for me to give you an account of the trip in detail, as each day would amount to the same thing.

Before leaving St. Joe, we hired a guide to bring us here, paying him two hundred dollars — one hundred "down," and the balance when at Fort Benton. All went on well until the 11th of July, when we fell in with a party of Sioux and Stony Lake Indians, about eighty in all. Our guides advised us to hold council with them. We did so, and gave them flour, tobacco, &c. When we first saw them coming down the hills, we thought they intended to attack us, as they came yelling and firing off their guns in grand style. They formed themselves in line and dismounting, shook hands with us. We prepared ourselves for a council in our "correll," and after several speeches were made by a chief, we gave them our presents and started on our journey. Our guides were very much afraid of the Indians, and these knew it. So, the next day (12th) our guides very treacherously left us to ourselves, and returned to a party of half-breed hunters that we had passed two

[13] Bond stated that Antoine Osier guided the Holmes train, while William Cuthbert named "Michelle" and "Baptiste" as guides. Bond, "Journal," July 31, August 10; Cuthbert, "Notes on Trip from St. Paul to Fort Benton, 1862."

[14] According to the editor, the printed letter consisted of extracts from the original. It appeared in the *St. Cloud Democrat*, October 2, 1862.

days before. The same day, or in the evening, an Indian came to our camp to guide us to Fort Union. He said he was going to the Fort and would show us the way. We believed him to be a horse thief, (which he proved to be) but took him along. For two days we watched him night and day, but at last he beat us by stealing a horse and running away in daylight. It was a good joke on us, but the company paid for the horse.[15]

We were now within a short distance of the Missouri river. On the 15th, two of our party went to Fort Union, finding it to be not more than twelve miles from our camp. On the 16th we fell in with another party of Indians, to whom we gave presents. They camped with us at night. On the 23d we fell in with a large party of Grossventrees [Gros Ventres] (pronounced Grovonts) Indians. They were a very fine body of Indians, well mounted, had but few guns, were "dressed to kill," and withal very friendly. They must have had five hundred horses at their camp, not a few of which would bring $150 at St. Paul, at the present prices.

At night when we camped they brought their wives and daughters, and offered them to the men. They thought it would be honorable in us to accept, or at least they wanted to make us believe it; but in fact they wanted to make a good thing out of us and get all they could by offering their wives and daughters and so get provisions and ammunition in exchange for their honor. All the next day part of them brought their women along, but we made them leave, the thing was becoming too disgusting, but before they left they stole our Odometer from the wheel which was a sad loss to us. It would have been useless to return to their camp in search of it.

We did not go to Fort Union on account of its being several miles out of our way. We offered to board a Blackfoot half-breed, his wife and another half-breed woman and daughter to Fort Benton if he would guide us there. He accepted, and we brought them along. The Blackfeet and Grossventrees are at war, and have been for the past year, so that when the women saw the latter coming, they got in the wagon and covered themselves, hid themselves and remained so for two days.[16] The half breed was as badly frightened as the women. A few days after, we fell in with a small party of Blackfeet Indians, who kept with us until we arrived here. The road all along from Georgetown to Fort Benton was in excellent order.

We made the distance to Mouse [Souris] River from St. Joe, 145 miles, in eight days four days to second crossing of Mouse River 60¾ miles; ten days' travel to within twelve miles of Fort Union, 167½ miles twenty-two days from Fort Union to Fort Benton, distance 460 miles. The country from St. Joe to Fort Union, as a general thing, is very poor — all prairie, poor water and scarcely any wood. We were nearly twelve days after leaving Mouse River without wood, and half the time with but poor water. Feed for cattle was pretty good. For description of country between Ft. Union and Fort Benton, I refer you to Stephens' [Stevens'] Report, for we traveled on his trail.[17]

[15] Ledbeater probably meant that the cost of the stolen horse was borne by the whole group.
[16] For information on the warfare, see John C. Ewers, *The Blackfeet: Raiders on the Northwestern Plains*, 242 (Norman, Oklahoma, 1958).
[17] Stevens, *Narrative and Final Report*, 88–99.

After we crossed Mouse River we saw lots of buffalo, and killed all we wanted. When we got to the Missouri, we had buffalo, black tail deer, elk and antelope. Every morning two or three hundred pounds of fresh meat would be thrown. One of the Blackfoot Indians went to a drove of buffalo, three miles off, and selecting a fat cow drove it to within ten rods of our camp and shot it. He gave it to us and said he would drive more if we needed them. The Blackfeet are very peaceable — they do not beg as other Indians. We saw thousands of buffalo in one herd.

We saw a natural curiosity — a dog with three legs. It has always been so, and is just as smart as one with four legs. There have been four boats at Fort Benton this spring, and they expect another in a few days.[18]

Several persons have returned from the gold fields to Fort Benton — some tell one thing and some another, but all think there is gold there.

At this point there are 600 bbls. of flour, and other stuff in proportion. The next boat will bring 400 more bbls. flour. This article is selling at $30 per bbl., with other things more reasonable. We start to-morrow; so, good by. Yours in haste,

M. D. LEDBEATER

The address of any of this party is, Care of Worden & Co., Hell Gate, via Fort Walla Walla.[19]

LEDBEATER TO MITCHELL[20]

Pikes Peak Gulch, Near Deer Lodge Valley, August 31st, 1862

FRIEND WILL. — As a party will leave here tomorrow for Iowa *via* Ft. Benton, I embrace the opportunity to send you word how our company is getting along. I wrote you from the summit of the Rocky Mountains, which letter I hope you have received. We arrived at Deer Lodge Valley all safe and sound, a few days ago. We heard of this place and started for it. Here I saw a young man by the name of Mike Harkins, with whom I was acquainted at St. Cloud, who showed me some claims. So, twelve of us made claims on the 28th and to-morrow will commence work. We intend to form a company and work together this fall. [C. C.] Vandenburg, the two Hoyts and myself are in the company, the balance from Sauk Valley.

The claims above us are paying from $5 to $12 per day, and those below from $4 to $6 per day. We cannot tell how ours will turn out. We will have to work hard for two weeks before we can get our sluices up. We may make a good thing

[18] The boats at the fort were the "Spread Eagle" and the "Key West" operated by Pierre Chouteau, Jr., and Company, and the "Shreveport" and the "Emilie" owned by La Barge, Harkness, and Company. See *Montana Historical Contributions*, 3:280; Hiram M. Chittenden, *History of Early Steamboat Navigation on the Missouri River*, 2:287–297 (New York, 1903).

[19] In 1860 F. L. Worden and C. P. Higgins, associates in Worden and Company, built a small log house which became the nucleus of the village of Hell's Gate near Missoula. See F. H. Woody, "A Sketch of the Early History of Western Montana," in *Montana Historical Contributions*, 2:99.

[20] This letter appeared in the *St. Cloud Democrat*, November 27, 1862. The letter Ledbeater mentioned below has not been found. It was probably written on August 20 or 23, when members of the Holmes train inscribed their names on the summit milepost of the Mullan Road. See Bond, "Journal," September 23.

out of it, and perhaps not make our board. Some of the St. Paul company are further up the Valley, but three-fourths of the whole party will start for Oregon on the first of September. When they saw what work was to be performed to get the gold, they concluded to go to Oregon, where they thought they could get money with less work.

The other day one man was shot, another hung and another sentenced to be hung. The three had stolen some horses from Bitter Root Valley, one hundred miles from here. They were taken four miles from this place. The trio was taking it very easy in the shade, playing cards, when the Sheriff came up and told them that they were his prisoners. One started on the run and the Sheriff shot him dead. When he started he had a pack of cards in his hand, and when shot clasped the cards so hard, that they remained in his hand after he was dead, and he was buried with them in his hand. The one that was hung jumped off of the wagon as soon as the rope was put around his neck. The other has since been released. Such is the way they deal with thieves in this country.[21]

Provisions are very reasonable — flour, $40 per barrel; pork, 35 cts per lb; fresh beef 15 cts for choice pieces and such beef as you don't get every day. The cattle as a general thing, are too fat to eat. One man by the name of [John F.] Grant has 1000 head of cattle in Deer Lodge prairie.[22] The boys sold cattle to him for $60 to $75 per yoke. Wagons sold for $20 to $35.

I have just heard of some very rich diggings one hundred miles from here. Our party will send out a man to prospect it; but the miners will lie so about such diggings, that a man has to go and see for himself.

I would not advise any one to come, except those who want to go to Oregon. They might go through this way to see for themselves. Perhaps the next thing you will hear, is, that I am bound for Cariboo. I would advise those who cross the Plains to come in strong parties, as the Indians are getting woke up. On the Southern routes we hear that they are killing the whites.

The report here is that McClellan and forty thousand men were taken prisoners near Richmond. I have not seen a letter or paper since we left St. Joseph. There are a great many seceshers in this country. I will write again soon. Yours Truly,

MARK

P.S. — I send you a specimen of gold which I have just panned out — my first panning. Direct, Deer Lodge Valley, *via* Walla Walla and Hell Gate.

[21] For an account of this affair, see Langford, *Vigilante Days and Ways,* 1:218. Langford called the episode the "first expression of Vigilante justice in . . . Montana."

[22] Grant had herds of cattle and horses which he purchased from emigrants, winterfed, and then often drove back along the overland trails to sell to other emigrants. See Phillips, ed., *Forty Years on the Frontier,* 1:126; 2:97.

LEDBEATER TO MITCHELL

Pike's Peak Gulch, October 26th, 1862

DEAR WILL. — Once more I write you, altho' I have not received a letter from Minnesota since I left. I think I have written four or five to you, but I suppose I must have several letters on the way. * * * [23] I have just heard from Grasshopper, or better known as "Beaver Head" a little over one hundred miles from here. There are about five hundred men at work; they are getting from five to fifty dollars per day, and some are making as high as one hundred dollars per day. But you must remember this is done by hired labor. The man who has a claim, and can make ten dollars per day, will hire twelve men and pay them four dollars per day, and make, of course, six dollars per day off each man, consequently big wages for himself. Now I am well satisfied that if we had plenty of water that we could make from ten to twelve dollars per day. We have very heavy stripping to take off before we get to our "pay dirt." This is from three to four feet deep — the stripping is from three to six feet deep. Two men with plenty of water can strip more land in one day than twelve can do with shovels. Another advantage we gain is, that we get rid of all the surface dirt. This we intend doing in the Spring.

Last week we (two men) took out fifty dollars in one day, and the next fifty-three dollars. This is a new streak; very likely we cannot work it this fall. The stripping is too deep to shovel off — it has to be done with water, and as our old friend, Mr. [Charles T.] Stearns, would say, we have to "rig a purchase" to get it off.[24]

Mining is very hard work. Those who leave Minnesota to make money in the mines, will find that it is no child's play, I can assure them. I had to laugh at some of the last train from Minnesota. When they saw us up to our knees in mud and water, they exclaimed, "My God, is that the way you get gold?" One said, "Well, I'm sure I shall not dig for gold unless I can get it easier than that." About one half of both teams, have left for Walla Walla and points of Oregon without trying to get gold by digging. No, they preferred to get gold by living on what they could borrow from their friends.

(Mr. L. here speaks of having just heard the Indian news from Minnesota.)

At Beaver Head the Indians are very numerous. It is their Winter quarters — that is, for the Snake and Bannock tribes. They have given the miners more trouble than all the other Indians combined. They are a bloody set of *Varmints.* Many a poor fellow has bit the dust this Summer in crossing through their country. They will have to keep pretty cool this Winter, or they will be "cleaned out" by the miners, who are very numerous in that place. The Indians (Snakes and Bannocks) are brave, well-armed with rifles, double-barrel shot-guns, and all kinds of revolvers, with any amount of money — which they have taken from emigrants on their way to Pike's Peak and this country. The other tribes are very peaceable.

---

[23] This letter is reprinted exactly as it appeared in the *Democrat* of January 15, 1863. This deletion and the note in the fourth paragraph appeared in the newspaper. Grasshopper Creek, where Bannack was founded, is a tributary of the Beaverhead River.

[24] Stearns, for whom a county in Minnesota was named, was an early St. Cloud settler and the father-in-law of Dr. Freeborn F. Hoyt, a member of the Holmes train. See Upham and Dunlap, *Minnesota Biographies,* 736.

They are controlled by Catholic priests. There are now several hundred Indians encamped within four or five miles of us. They are on their way to their hunting-grounds at the head of the Yellow Stone, and are very peaceable. There are four distinct tribes — the Ness Perce [Nez Percé], Ponderrays [Pend d' Oreilles], Flat-Heads, and the other name I have forgotten. They have to go in large parties for protection, as the Black-feet, Snakes, Bannocks and other Indians are at war with them. They offered to furnish us with 150 men and all the horses we wanted if we would go up and "clean out" the Snakes and Bannocks. We did not take them up, for as long as the Indians will let us alone, we shall not meddle with them.

Provisions are up. Flour is to-day selling at $35 per sack, and other things in proportion. Tobacco $5 per pound; 80-rod whiskey $2 per drink. My respects to all. Ever the same,

MARK D. LEDBEATER

Oct. 31st. — We got to-day a nugget weighed 16.30 [ounces].

1862 ✸✸✸✸✸✸✸✸✸✸✸✸✸✸✸✸✸✸

Two Reports from the Fisk Expedition

JAMES L. FISK TO LORENZO THOMAS [1]

[Washington, D.C. February, 1863]

Sir: Under instructions of the Secretary of War, I was despatched from this place, on the 3d [first?] day of June last, to proceed at once to organize, equip, and conduct an escort to [an] emigrant train from Fort Abercrombie, across the plains of the north, to Fort Benton, Dakota Territory; thence across the mountains, *via* Captain Mullan's government wagon road, to Walla-Walla — there dispose of the expedition property, and return *via* Oregon and San Francisco.

The fact that most of the route designated for my trip was entirely new, (except as surveyed by the late lamented General Stevens, in 1853,) and that the season was so far advanced before orders reached me at my regiment in Central Tennessee, together with the limited means placed at my disposal, led me to doubt much whether I could accomplish the objects of this commission. Having entered upon the work, however, and done the best in my power under the circumstances, I am pleased to be able to report at this date the experience and general results of the expedition.

Samuel R. Bond, esq., who accompanied me as clerk and journalist, respectfully submits a summary of his notes, and which is a fair statement of principal incidents of trip, topography of country, &c.

In the proper place will be found the brief report of Dr. Dibb, physician and surgeon of party; and I likewise offer for your consideration, as supplementary to the general report required, an itinerary of each day's travel, with accompanying chart of route from Fort Abercrombie to Fort Benton.

I need hardly assure you, in this connexion, of my personal regards and esteem

---

[1] Thomas was the adjutant general of the United States Army. This letter appears in 37 Congress, 3 session, *House Executive Documents*, no. 80, p. 1–3 (serial 1164). The document also includes an abbreviated version of Bond's journal, the medical report of Dr. Dibb, and an itinerary prepared by David Charlton. Charlton's map of the route may be found in file 163F 1862, NARG 94 (photocopy MiHS); it was published in Fisk, *Idaho.*

48

for those gentlemen, one and all, who accompanied me as assistants — part of them the entire journey. Always true, and never found wanting in the discharge of duty, I can but commend them for those good qualities which fit men for public service.

The importance at present attached to this route, and which will very much increase as the new gold fields opened up by it come into note, constrains me to believe it justifiable in extending my report so as to cover all the chief points of interest, and to believe that the itinerary and map furnished will prove of great utility if published.

That our little expedition, being wholly an experiment, succeeded beyond the most sanguine expectations is attributable to several facts, viz: Nearly if not quite all of the men of the escort and emigrants had seen more or less of frontier life, were not afraid to encounter hardships, and knew how to surmount impediments in whatever shape occurring. The season was most wonderfully favorable, plenty of grazing and water for our purpose, and yet not sufficient rain at any time to swell the streams or soften the basins of the prairie country.

Our organization was complete, not only of the fifty (50) men of the escort, but of the emigrants also, in case of an emergency. No violation of rules occurred from first to last; every order was promptly and cheerfully obeyed. We moved, halted, camped, corralled on the march, rallied, mounted guard, &c., by bugle calls.

We had no serious difficulties with Indians, though we met numerous bands and tribes, and were not aware, until met in the mountains by an express from Walla-Walla, giving news how narrowly we had escaped the terrible raid of the Sioux on the border of Minnesota, even laying siege to the very post which we had shortly previous started from.

The Assineboines [Assiniboin] were "saucy," which with them is preliminary to mischief. Their conduct convinced me that they were knowing to the raid of the Sioux Indians, and that they themselves were becoming infected with a desire for plunder.

It required more nerve to *refrain* from punishing them for their insolence than to have done it. The traders along the Missouri besought me to urge upon the [war] department the necessity of establishing one or more military posts along that river, between Forts Berthold and Benton. From what I could see and learn, I do not hesitate to say that the presence of troops is absolutely necessary to insure the safe occupancy and transit of that upper country by the whites.

The severe chastisement of the hostile Sioux the coming season would intimidate the Missouri river and mountain tribes; and the distribution of an infantry or cavalry regiment along the Missouri, from Fort Berthold to Benton, with headquarters in the mountain district at the head of that river, where there are most people scattered about, mining, would insure safety in travel, exploration and development of a rich mineral country.

Pierre Chouteau, jr., & Co. take occasion to inform me by letter that they "will most cheerfully give all the accommodations necessary for quartering troops and storing supplies in either or all of their trading posts on the Upper Missouri."[2] These *forts*, as they are called, are not undeserving the name, for they are most

[2] On Pierre Chouteau, Jr., a leading fur trader of St. Louis, see Hiram M. Chittenden, *The American Fur Trade of the Far West*, 1:381–383 (New York, 1935).

admirably adapted as quarters for troops, *militaire* in appearance, and entirely defensible.

After emerging from the Côteau du Missouri on the west side, opposite to the nearest point to the river *Des Lacs*, I was desirous of heading straight for Fort Benton, coming down to Milk river at last crossing, instead of making that circuitous route by Fort Union.[3] But not finding any of my party ready to try the experiment, I moved southward to a camp on the Missouri fifteen (15) miles above Fort Union. On our journey to Fort Benton we were joined by two French half-breed *voyageurs*, from whom I learned that the line of travel from the Coteau to Fort Benton, which I had proposed trying, was in every way practicable for a wagon road, and *"ten days shorter."*

My loss of stock between Abercrombie and Benton were two (2) oxen and one (1) mule. Between Benton and Walla-Walla, one (1) team-horse and one (1) saddle-horse. In the wilderness of St. Regis de Borgia [St. Regis River], at the eastern base of the Coeur d'Alène mountains, I found Major [Charles] Hutchins, Indian agent, in distress, from having lost part of his pack animals while on his journey to relieve Major [John] Owen, agent of the Flathead Indians.[4] In the emergency of his case I felt obliged to relieve him, so far as I could give him anything available for transporting his supplies, and fitted him out with a span of animals and good wagon.

From this point to Walla-Walla I hauled only the howitzer and flag-wagon, and every animal I had was unmarketable, because so very thin in flesh. If I could have had the usual allowance of extra work animals upon the start, such would have been the condition of the whole as to bring, at public sale, at the close of the journey, all they would cost in fitting out.

Captain Mullan's road, from Fort Benton to Walla-Walla, is passable, and there has been performed upon it an immense amount of labor, but it will have to be worked, materially improved in places, or it will very soon become useless as a wagon road.

On leaving St. Paul on the 16th (sixteenth) of June, I had unfurled, from a staff lashed to the front of the express wagon, which led the train, the national colors; and I am proud to say, that it every day floated to the breeze from the Mississippi to the Columbia, and no man insulted it.

At Portland, Oregon, I was glad to meet Captain Medorum [Medorem] Crawford, who had just closed his expedition on the central overland route. We spent a day together in comparing notes. Captain Crawford did not hesitate to congratulate me on having discovered a most desirable route, and one that must soon attract a large emigration over it. I am under obligations to this gentleman for courtesies which he extended to me while there, and for pecuniary favor in my need.[5]

Under dates of December 14 and 27, I am in receipt of letters from very reliable

[3] Fisk probably refers to the Milk River crossing near present-day Havre, Montana. He attempted to follow the shorter route in 1863, but reached the Milk River farther to the east.
[4] On Hutchins and Owen, see Seymour Dunbar and Paul C. Phillips, eds., *The Journals and Letters of Major John Owen*, 2:279–284 (New York, 1927).
[5] Crawford's comparison of the central and northern overland routes may be found in Fisk, *Idaho*, 23. For Crawford's official report, see 37 Congress, 3 session, *Senate Executive Documents*, no. 17 (serial 1149).

men, who went out with me and are now mining at "Grasshopper diggins," (the *Grasshopper* being a small tributary of the Jefferson fork of the Missouri, and at which place there are now about one thousand (1,000) persons,) stating their general success beyond all expectations, and that "claims are yielding from fifty dollars ($50) to one hundred and fifty dollars ($150) per day to the man."

Reaching this city, on my return, about the 1st of the present month, I hastened to prepare this report, which I now have the honor to submit.

With very great respect, I am, sir, your most obedient servant,

JAMES L. FISK
Captain, A.Q.M., Commanding Expedition

DIARY OF DR. WILLIAM D. DIBB, 1862 [1]

THE RENDEZVOUS FOR THE EMIGRANTS was Fort Abercrombie, but some joined us at St. Cloud.

The following officers were appointed

First Assistant,	E. H. Burritt	Physician,	W. D. Dibb M D
Second Assistant,	N. P. Langford	Wagon Master,	R. C. Knox
Surveyor,	David Charlton	Guide	Pierre Bottineau
Secretary,	S. R. Bond	Sioux Interpreter,	George Giere [Gere]

The Capt with his own supplies left St Paul on June 16. for Ft Abercrombie via St Cloud. I joined the train here. After purchasing some necessary things we left on June 23 & camped on Sauk River Crossing 4 miles from St Cloud.

June 24. Fine morning — got a good start and passed thro' St Joseph, a small German village (Catholic) having a Church, school &c.[2] A good farming country & grain looks well. Plenty of water from small streams crossing the road. We camped on a pleasant Knoll, some 2 miles from Richmond. Travelled 19 miles.

25. Rise at 4 A.M. Cattle all right. Walked on ahead to Richmond — (2 stores and one Catholic Church) A good farming country around. Water every 3 or 4 miles. Passed New Munich (a village just starting). I called to see the Slattery's on their farm & had supper with them — then walked with M[ichael] & P[hilip] to the camp on Getchell's creek.[3] Rigged up my saddle & bridle. Traded my pony for a smart little Bl[ac]kfoot pony which I named Peter. Good Camp. Travelled 20 miles.

26. Had a severe thunderstorm last night, & rain continued until 10 A.M. Started at 10, & lunched at the second Crossing of Sauk River. The afternoon was very hot; travelled slowly as our cattle suffered. The land not so good as yesterday but a fine country. Camp at the 3rd crossing of the Sauk. Visited a child at [George R.] Stewart's, over the river, & opened an abscess of the ankle.[4]

---

[1] Dibb's diary, in the possession of Mr. Gerald E. Fitzgerald of St. Paul, is reproduced with permission of the owners. The MiHS has typewritten and photostatic copies of Dibb's diaries for 1862, 1863, and 1864.

[2] St. Joseph in Stearns County, Minnesota, should not be confused with the St. Joseph in Dakota Territory (now Walhalla, North Dakota), described in letters from the Holmes train.

[3] Michael, Philip, and John Slat[t]ery are listed as farmers in United States Manuscript Census Schedules, 1860, Stearns County, Minnesota, p. 485.

[4] Stewart's Crossing of the Sauk River is shown in A. T. Andreas, *Illustrated Historical Atlas of the State of Minnesota*, 154 (Chicago, 1874).

27. Rise at 4:30. Misty. Start at 7 A.M. Continued misty until noon, when it came out hot. Passed over fine prairie. Crossed Sauk R. for the 4th time, then struck into rolling prairie for 6 or 8 miles & camp on Lake Osakis (Lake Terror, or Scare) which is a fine large lake, nearly round, & is some 4 or 5 miles in diameter. This lake is the head or source of Sauk River. Travel 18 miles.

28. Rise at 5. Morning fine. Went as far as the Alexandria Woods, and lunched.[5] Then started to pass thro' the terror of this route — the roads were bad indeed for 6 miles, then we reach a lake (or two lakes [Geneva and Victoria] with a creek between [)]. Went on to Alex[andri]a which is 4 miles from this lake. A[lexandri]a is composed of one house, & one store or grocery. Mr [Charles] Cook & family (English, from London) occupy the house — they paid a visit to our camp, & appear to be very pleasant people. We had a swarming [of bees?] this evening. B [Pierre Bottineau?] went for a light & made some half a dozen blow out.

29. A.M. 4:30 — fine morning. Botu [Bottineau] & I let the train go ahead, while we visited Mr Cook. We then took a short cut — dined at a Canadians — Then caught the train at supper, camped near Eagens [Evans].[6]

30. A.M. 4:30. fine morning. After the train started some of us struck off & had a hunt. Killed some ducks & plover. caught the train at lunch on Pelican Lake. After lunch we again struck off, getting a few more ducks & met the train at the Crossing of the "Pomme de Terre" River. Here we left the old trail & made a short cut across the prairie. Camped on a small lake, which we called "Lake Curlew" [Horseshoe Lake].[7]

July 1. A.M. 4:30. Started from Lake Curlew & after 3 miles struck the old trail. B[ond] with 3 or 4 of us went hunting. Got 2 cranes, 1 goose, & about 20 ducks. Reach "Otter tail" or Red River, & camp on the bank.[8] This is a very rapid river, & runs contrary to all we have as yet seen. No trees or brush on the banks.

2. A.M. 4:15. Some cattle had strayed back, & delayed us for 2 or 3 hours. We got them, & crossed the river by ferry. Pleasant day, with strong wind — reached Breckenridge by a little after noon. B. is made of one Hotel (empty) & a saw mill. Camped on the river 4 miles from Be. A buffalo was seen near the train by some of the teamsters. Good Camp.

3. A.M. 4. Warm & pleasant. Reach Fort Abercrombie by noon. Cross the river by ferry & camp near the grave-yard. Officers at the Ft very pleasant & obliging. Great talk of the coming 4th. We are invited to join in the celebration.

4. A.M. 3. Fire a salute of small arms in response to the big guns at the Ft. At 9 A.M. join with the military at the Fort & have a grand procession; ending with a general "Beer Salute." Bond gave a very good oration. Every one feels gay. Attend a ball at the Officer's Qrs and have a good time generally.

[5] Dibb is referring to a heavily wooded region of deciduous trees, known as the Big Woods, which covered much of central Minnesota. Alexandria was on the western edge of this belt.

[6] The camp was between the present-day towns of Brandon and Evansville, probably near the cabin of a mail carrier named Evans. See Upham, *Minnesota Geographic Names*, 176; Bond, "Journal," June 29.

[7] The "old trail," followed by the expedition from St. Cloud to Fort Abercrombie, was one of the Red River Trails used by traders between St. Paul and Canadian fur trade posts. See maps of Upper B Trail, Works Progress Administration, Red River Trails, in MiHS.

[8] Although this river is properly the Red, the part from its source to the bend at Breckenridge is known as the Otter Tail. Upham, *Minnesota Geographic Names*, 390. The crossing was made south of present-day Fergus Falls, where the river flows in a southerly direction.

This Fort, or post rather, is not sufficiently compact to repel Indians in force — the buildings are scattered — & the timber is allowed to stand near & surround some of them giving excellent shelter to indians. It is in a good position — plenty of water, & good grazing for miles around.

Saturday 5. Pleasant day. All busy in getting things we need from the fort. The Officers visit us in Camp, & we have a good time — a little 4th.

Sunday 6. Preparing to start tomorrow. Some 30 or 40 teams are here waiting for the escort. A good many are timid about crossing direct from here to the Missouri — they would rather go by way of Pembina & St Joseph — altho' this would be 250 or 300 miles out of the course — but with the preparation they see made, & from our obtaining a 12 lb Howitzer from the fort — their fears are allayed — & we start tomorrow. We have prayers read (Episcopal) — most of the officers attend.

Monday 7. Up early — all busy preparing for the start into the wilderness. Leave the Fort at 11 A.M. — accompanied by a good number of the officers as far as the "Wild Rice River" which we had to bridge — this river is from 6 to 10 ft in width, & 2 or 3 in depth. All pass well, & camp on the prairie by 6 p. m. Good feed. Travelled 4 miles.[9]

Tuesday 8. A.M. 4. cloudy — 5 a.m. rains heavily 8. clear. Make a start, but the rain again commences, & lasts for 2 hours. Travel across level prairie towards the "Sheyenne River," which we reach by 6 p.m.[10] Prairie level & grass good — we camp on the east bank, & prepare to build a bridge tomorrow. The river is from 6 to 10 ft deep & 60 or 70 wide. There is water after leaving wild rice [river] at 3 miles (bend of W. R.) & at 10 miles at a small pond. 15:50 N.W.

Wednesday 9. Fine morning — get to work on the bridge — plenty of timber. Bob. [Knox] Dan. [Bottineau] Geo. G[ere] & I cross the river to hunt — but did not see either Buffalo or Elk. Saw signs of the latter in the sandy bluffs, or ridges. On our return for supper — find the bridge built, & teams over, about a mile from the river. The water in the river is good. found some springs on the banks. There are signs of an overflow in the spring freshets, to such an extent as to make it difficult to bridge it so as to stand.

Thursday 10. 4 A.M. fine day. Cross a fine prairie as level as a floor. We must travel 18 miles without water — day warm, but cattle do well. ground dry & good for travelling. Reach "Maple River" by 4 p.m. which we ford tomorrow. Maple R. is a small stream, emptying into the Sheyenne, some 25 ft. wide & 2 to 6 deep — at the ford about 2 ft deep. This river shews signs of being 20 to 30 ft deep — & very wide in spring freshets. 18. miles W.N.W.[11]

Friday 11. Up at 4:30 a. m. Fix the crossing & get over in good order. Today

[9] The emigrants crossed the Wild Rice River, a tributary of the Red, in Richland County, North Dakota. See Dana Wright, "Military Trails in Dakota: The Fort Totten-Abercrombie Trail," in *North Dakota History*, 13:110 (July, 1946).

[10] This river, a tributary of the Red, should be distinguished from the Cheyenne, which is a tributary of the Missouri. The crossing was probably made at a place later known as Nolan's in Richland County or between that point and the Great Northern Railway crossing south of Kindred, North Dakota. See Wright, in *North Dakota History*, 13:107–110.

[11] The Maple River crossing was probably made southeast of present-day Chaffee, North Dakota, at a place later known as Watson's Crossing. See Wright, in *North Dakota History*, 13:106, 110.

we pass over dry, tolerably level prairie — grass poor except in sloughs, & around ponds. Find water about 8 miles in a small creek running into Maple River. We cross this & camp on a bend of same creek one mile beyond crossing. 9 miles. N.W.

Saturday 12. Cool night & all rest well — up at 5. a. m. Good day for travel. Strike E. branch of Maple R. 10 miles from camp & lunch. This branch is in places 8 to 10 ft deep. We cross in shallow water & fill in by cutting rushes. Geo. Dan. & I followed the branch, & got 1 goose & some ducks.

When we returned to the train found all excited — four Buffaloes had been seen at some distance to the left of the train. Capt. [Fisk] & Botu had given chase — & while looking to see if we could make out how matters went — we saw a black object crossing a ravine. (Those with telescopes proclaimed it a buffalo.[)] I threw off some extra traps & started for him — keeping out of sight until I could get near enough — he had seen some of our people & started. I cut across to try to head — but in crossing a long narrow slough Peter mired (my pony). I got off & with some trouble got him out, as he had sunk to his head. As soon as I mounted I rounded the slough, & met one of our men returning — he had only a navy revolver & had emptied that & given him up — but I persuaded him to go back with me.

After riding some time easily we espied the old fellow drinking in a small pond — he saw us directly & giving himself a shake he started, apparently as well as ever. The ground was rolling but after a run of 2 miles, we began to overhaul him rapidly & Peter seeing [him] cheered up, & ran like a hound, watching him as [he] passed over ridge & hollow. We were getting so near that I was changing my gun to the front so as to be ready when poor Peter, more intent upon watching the old bull, than the ground he was going over, put both his forefeet in a wolf-hole & turned a complete somersault. My gun was laid in my left arm, with my thumb in the trigger guard which was a good deal sprained by my falling on & twisting the gun — but I mounted as quickly as I could & again we started.

The old fellow had crossed the next ridge, & not seeing us follow, was taking it easily walking along with his tongue out — but when he heard us coming — he steamed up, & ran for about a quarter of a mile quite briskly — but this could not last — he flagged, & we neared him fast. I ran alongside (but at a very respectful distance) as the nearer we got to him the more terrible was his appearance. I tried a shot with the big bullet (my gun was a rifle & shot[gun] [12] — the shot barrel carried a 1⅛ ball) while running — which had the effect of stopping, with out hitting him — he wheeled about & stood ready. I stopped, & took a steady pull with the rifle. This time I heard the bullet "thug" as it struck him.

I had expected to see him reel or stagger — but instead of either the bullet appeared to have put fresh life into him — for giving a short, deep bellow he charged at me. I wheeled and did my very best at running from him, & continued this for over a quarter of a mile before daring to look back. When I did I found

[12] Dr. Dibb probably had a double-barreled cap-lock firearm. One barrel was rifled and used a lead ball of about .50 caliber or larger. The smoothbore barrel, probably about the diameter of a modern 12-guage shotgun, could have used either shot or the lead ball mentioned by Dibb. The barrels may have been side by side or "over and under," with the rifle beneath the smoothbore barrel. Alan R. Woolworth to the author, October 29, 1964.

he had not run more than 40 or 50 rods & had again stopped. I loaded & went back to him — he continued to move round in a short circle — but when I came near him he presented a bold front & even as I shifted round to get a shot at his side, he would turn & still present his front.

At last I got the other man to come up & take his attention. Then as he turned to face him I got a good chance & gave him both bullets in his ribs. Again he charged, & I ran, but not so far — & loaded up — on returning I found him evidently suffering — the blood streaming from his nose & mouth. I tried him again with both barrels, this time he did not charge — but shivered from head to tail. Then turning round 3 or 4 times, staggering, he fell. Then we raised such lusty cheers as must have astonished any other buffalo which may have been within hearing.

Now we had the opportunity to examine his powerful frame — his high, heavy shoulders — & his shaggy, ugly head. We now proceeded to take his tongue, but how to get it was the question. We were both green at the business — but we got the most of it by opening his mouth & propping open with a rock, putting our hands in, & cutting away in the dark. Then cutting his tail off as a trophy. Forgive us ye buffalo hunters! This was the first wild buffalo that either of us had seen. Now that the excitement was abated we began to think seriously of our return to camp, as it was some time after sunset. We made up our minds as to the direction to take, & after a ride of some 5 or 6 miles came in sight of the white tents & covers. We were received with cheers & after supper, we hunters recited our deeds of the chase to greedy ears. 15.50 N.W.

Sunday 13. A.M. 5:30. Rest well after the fatigues of the chase. Breakfast on buffalo-Steak which all like very much   is juicy, & tender. We are camped near a pond of good water, plenty of feed. No wood. We use the "buffalo chips" which make a very good fire.[13] We have a good rest today, as we do not travel on Sundays.

Monday 14. Rise at 4 A.M. Misty & Cool. Pass over rolling prairie. See plenty of buffalo in every direction. I do not run today, but shot at one with my rifle at 200 yards, he dropped before going 10 rods. Water plenty in ponds, & feed good all thro'. Struck the Sheyenne, forded it, & camp on the other [west] side. 21.50 N.W.[14]

Tuesday 15. The river here has a rocky, hard bottom 60 ft wide & 1 to 2 ft deep with good timber on the banks. The banks are steep from the prairie to the river valley. We had a wedding last night among the emigrants, Langford was the Parson, was quite a rural affair.[15] Today we pass over a rolling prairie which in a wet season would have to be travelled by winding along the ridges. Water plenty in ponds & small lakes, no wood. I killed 3 buffalo today. They are

[13] Fisk, in *Idaho,* page 42, described buffalo-chip fuel: "It burns like peat; lights easily, and answers so well the purpose of wood that we used it for many days rather than load our wagons more heavily by carrying wood along with us."

[14] This crossing, known as Le Traverse Blanc, was about half a mile north of the mouth of the Baldhill Creek in Barnes County, North Dakota, southwest of present-day Pillsbury. See Wright, in *North Dakota History,* 13:91 (January–April, 1946).

[15] Joseph H. Tyler, a lumberman from St. Anthony, was married to Caroline Abbott, a young woman from New Hampshire who was traveling with her brother-in-law and sister, the Josephus Starks. Details of the wedding are in Bond, "Journal," July 14, and Matilda D. Thibadeau, "History of a Montana Pioneer," a reminiscence in MoHS.

seen in large herds all around. Camp on a nice lake [Lake Johnston]. 16 miles W. of N.W.[16]

Wednesday 16. Start by 6 a.m. Strong wind. Same kind of country as yesterday. Lunch on a nice lake 9 miles from camp. See plenty of buffalo, in fact we live on buffalo meat. Travelling good. 18.50 W.N.W.

Thursday 17. We camped last night on "Lake Jessie" or between this and one we named "Lake Lydia" [Lake Addie] in honor of the Capt's wife. The water is brackish in both these lakes but found a good spring. Today we pass a slough 4 miles from Lake Jessie, which is generally bad, but in this dry season we have no trouble.[17] After lunch we killed 6 or 8 buffalo — & sent one herd along the train, when the boys opened on them in style, it was like the rapid firing of a company of skirmishers. Water is plentiful in ponds & good. We carry wood from lake Jessie for 4 days. 19 miles. W.

Friday 18. Fine morning. Some buffalo paid us a visit in camp this morning. They had seen our cattle feeding, & were inquisitive about our piebald buffalo; we have to be careful, as our cattle are very much excited when they get wind of them, & might get up a stampede. Prairie rolling up to noon. This afternoon it is more level. Camp at 6 p. m. on open prairie. Good water. The wolves give us a grand serenade this evening. Buffalo are scattered all over the prairie. 20 miles. W. or S. of W.[18]

Saturday 19. Rise early & start by 6:30. Very warm. See some Antelope, one of which [David E.] Folsom shot at 300 yds. distance. F. shot at a buffalo lying down, did not hurt him much. I chased 5 or 6 miles — but he escaped by swimming the River Jaques [James] — wh[ich] River we strike some 5 miles from camp. I had a good bath in the river. In catching up with the train, saw some more antelope & wolves. We camp on a Knoll. 19 miles. W.[19]

Sunday 20. Day of rest. We mend up and wash our clothes — clean guns &c prepare generally for the next weeks travel. Thunder shower at noon.

Monday 21. Rise early for a good start. This was a day of slaughter among the buffalo — 10 or 12 being killed. I killed 2. Botu was badly hurt by his horse falling while picking out a fat cow from a large herd. He was stunned, but nothing broken. Langford & I went on a large mound to the N. & E. of our trail & which was named "Langford's Mound" from his getting lost while chasing buffalo & regaining the train by steering for this mound. 19 miles W. or S. of W.[20]

22. Last night we camped near some ponds — with plenty of feed. Today, at noon we pass the "Butte de Morale," and travel W. towards the basswood, or whitewood Island. We found a splendid pass thro' the rough broken country here which lead us near some lakes [White Wood Lakes], but the water was

[16] The camp was probably in the vicinity of Hannaford, North Dakota, on the route of the Great Northern Railway. See Dana Wright, "The Sibley Trail of 1863," in *North Dakota History*, 29:294 (October, 1962).

[17] The spring was at the northwest end of Lake Jessie; see *North Dakota History*, 29:285. The slough was the "very severe slough" mentioned by Stevens in *Narrative and Final Report*, page 60, and by Dibb in his entry for July 23, 1863, page 87, below.

[18] The camp was probably near Grace City, North Dakota, on the James River.

[19] The camp was probably near New Rockford, North Dakota, on the present-day routes of both the Northern Pacific and the Great Northern railroads.

[20] Langford's Mound may be present-day Black Hammer Hill between New Rockford and Heimdal, North Dakota.

saline so we hunted & found a good spring of fresh water with good feed.[21] An old bull charged thro' the train this afternoon. 21 miles. W. or S. of W.

Wednesday 23. Had a very cool night & still cool this morning. Had to pass around some saline ponds before we could get on our true course. 5 or 6 of us catch an old bull asleep — half circle him & give him a warm reception on getting [out] of bed. The wind was blowing strong & he was fast asleep in some tall grass. We whistled after taking our position, but still he slept. We then whooped, & he started to his feet, giving a look of perfect astonishment & dismay he turned to run just when half a dozen bullets spatted his ribs, which no doubt increased his trouble. He ran for about 300 yards then toppled over. We lunch on a nice lake, after passing a stream nearly dry. Here the pass is short, hills rocky feed in the sloughs pretty good. We camp on a pond of fresh water. 15.50 miles. W.

Thursday 24. Still cool. Reach "Wintering River" about 5 miles from camp, & occupy 4 hours in crossing. This river, a branch of Mouse [Souris] River, is from 100 to 250 ft wide & from 3 to 5 ft deep. Scarcely any current bad clay bottom — & filled with bull-rushes. We had to mow rushes & make a road-bed then haul the wagons with a long cable by hand. Drove the cattle over loose. Lost one mule which would neither cross nor come back. Botu went 6 or 8 miles down the river & found a good crossing, hard gravelly bottom, water 2 ft deep (just opposite a bluff in a line S.W. with "Maison du Chien" [Dogden Butte].)[22] After passing we travelled 3 miles on a slough, with good feed, no wood. Appear to [have] had more rain here. 11 miles. W.

Friday 25. Today we come in sight of "Mouse River" but keep well E. to avoid crossing so many Coulées, which run from the prairie towards the river.[23] Geo. G. & I went to the river, crossed it. I killed an old bull while drinking in the river. The water is good — about 100 ft wide & 2 to 3 deep. The valley is very well timbered, & the land rich. Camp on good water & grass. 17.50 miles. W.

Saturday 26. Pleasant day. Keep off 4 or 5 miles from the river. After 11 miles of travelling we come to the head of a large Coulée, & intend to camp here over tomorrow, as we have timber & water in abundance. Started after an old bull for tomorrow's feed — got him — but he proved *too* old — would have taken a week to eat him. 11 miles. W.

Sunday 27. Day of general tinkering — cleaning — casting bullets, saying prayers &c.

Monday 28. Get a good start & keep a little W.S.W. While Burritt & I were hunting we saw Botu chasing something which was running towards the next coulée. We ran to head him — did so. When he hid in some short brush near a creek — we thought to poke him out — when Botu coming up called to us "beware he is a grizzly & wounded." One crossed the creek above — when he

[21] Butte de Morale, in the vicinity of Wellsburg, North Dakota, was named for a half-breed who was killed there. The White Wood Lakes, no longer clearly identifiable, are mentioned by Stevens. See *Narrative and Final Report,* 68. The Basswood or Whitewood Island was a high plateau surrounded by level prairie.

[22] Dogden Butte is four miles west of Butte, North Dakota.

[23] The expedition's course from a point near Bergen, North Dakota, to the vicinity of present-day Minot followed a route paralleling the Souris River four or five miles south of the line of the Minneapolis, St. Paul, and Sault Ste. Marie Railroad.

again started — but it took 10 or 12 shots to kill him.[24] Danl B. had seen him coming thro' some tall grass, & thought it was only a cub, got off his horse to try to catch him — but luckily he did not get near to him. Two more were seen but got away. The country is pretty rolling near the coulées. 16.50 Miles. W.

Tuesday 29. Travelled slowly. Had to cross a good many coulées. Lunch at 7 or 8 miles from camp. Chased some buffalo, but only got one. The rest got into the côteau du Missouri. Country dry this afternoon but find a good pond & camp. 16 miles. W.N.W.

Wednesday 30. Saw the train start. Then Burritt[,] Bond & I went hunting on the côteau. After being out some time, we got separated. I was alone, & in hedging for the train, I saw 3 or 4 white [whooping?] cranes on the edge of a pond. I had to make a considerable circle to get near them. When getting near I left my pony & crawled up a ridge. When I saw them about 100 yards from me — waited until two would get together. I got a rifle shot — the bullet going thro' one & wingin[g *ms. torn*] the other. I tried to get this fellow alive, after chasing him some time afoot, gave that up, & went back for my pony. I tried him again, but after repeated trials to get him alive — had to shoot him with my revolver. They were fine large birds & of beautiful plumage. After securing my birds, i.e., by tying them together, & slinging [them] across my saddle — & leading the pony, for I thought it would be too much to carry us all, as the cranes weighed from 25 to 30 lbs. each.

We then struck across the coteau so as to see the train or the trail — but [in *ms. torn*] the crane chace I had strayed away m[ore] than I at first thought. We travelled S[outh *ms. torn*] & night was closing in. To make it worse a heavy thundershower was coming up which made night close in still earlier. We plodded along until it got so dusky that I was afraid I might cross the trail & not see it — so I made up my mind to stop for the night. First picketing my horse to my saddle — commenced gathering buffalo chips before it got too dark. It [*sic*] had been 2 or [3] heavy showers making the dead grass wet as well as the chips — found some tolerably d[ry *ms. torn*] grass, & not having matches with me — tore some old lining out of my clothes, rubbed gunpowder in — drew my shot, & fired the powder into it — putting this in the dry grass & whirli[ng] it about, I started my fire. Then I had to prepare supper by plucking & broiling [*ms. torn*] one of the Cranes & made a hearty supper. Peter fed around a small pond near, but when it came in dark, he came & fed round the fire until satisfied. It was a miserable, cold, wet night — showers coming over about every hour. I had wrapped my gun in my saddle blanket to be ready if needed — but by taking the large wings of the cranes, hanging two in front — two behind, & sitting up to the fire managed [to] make things a little better. But still it was a long, miserable night — raining, blowing, & wolves howling all night — prevented me from sleeping much. The wolves (I suppose 50 of them at least) were all round me, & sometimes would come near enough to see their eyes glisten in the firelight but as I moved to unroll my gun they slunk off. I did not care for the wolves, but I was fidgetty lest some straggling Sioux, seeing my fire, might pay me a visit out of sheer curiosity.

[24] Bond noted that the grizzly was a female weighing between 350 and 400 pounds. He thought the meat superior to any he had ever eaten. "Journal," July 28.

ↄ Thursday 31. The long night passed at last & I hailed with joy the first grey tint of coming day. Peter saw it too & got up to feed around the fire until it was light enough to go to his old feeding ground near the pond. After having a good wash to clear the smoke out of my eyes — prepared breakfast — cut the breasts off both the cranes, & left the rest. As soon as I began to shake out the saddle blanket Peter came up snickering to be saddled he too was tired of "baching" it alone — fastening the crane breasts to my saddle, we started out in the same direction, as when we travelled last night & in one mile & a half, we struck the wagon trail & followed it — Peter being quite willing to canter. After about 2 hours travel I saw some moving objects on a ridge of the Côteau — made them out to be horsemen but as I did not want to run into a band of indians I rode in a ravine that ran paralel with the trail — riding some time & nearing them I took another observation, & was pleased to find that they were white men & probably of our party. I got out on the trail again, when they saw me, & made towards me. We soon met — gave me a general salute with firearms & another with bread, buffalo tongue, &c, &c. from every haversack — & water, whiskey & water, whiskey & milk, & whiskey pure, from every canteen. After this "slight repast" we rode to overtake the train, which had moved on at 8 o'clk. I was taken before the Capt. as a captured deserter, & punished — sentence, "pint of whiskey, pork & beans."

At noon we struck into the Côteau, on a trail, made by a party of emigrants from Mouse R. to Ft Union.[25] Country rolling & gravelly, ponds of brackish & saline water very numerous — feed very short & scanty on the ridges — tolerable in the valleys — find some small fresh water ponds. Yesterday travelled 20.50 miles. Today travelled 16. miles.

August 1. In travelling today we zigzag about in every direction. Buffalo in every direction & out of all count. Burritt & I were out. I shot a fat cow which had a very young calf, and which stayed by us while taking the tenderloin & when we started for camp he was bound to follow, & went to camp with us. Some of the party put him to a cow — after getting his supper he appeared perfectly contented — & became "one of ours." I killed the largest bull I have yet seen out of a herd of 7 or 800 which slowly filed past at some 80 or 100 yds distance. Saw today the first prairie dogs. There was quite a village of them. Feed very much eaten up. 18 miles W.

Saturday 2. A.M. 6:30 started. Country not so hard to travel as yesterday. By noon we get thro' this part of Côteau, coming out, at what the indians call "the last timber." Plenty of water & feed, besides the timber. Intend to stay over Sunday here. Camp on an old Assiniboine Camp — plenty of fruit in ye Coulées. 10.50 miles.

Sunday 3. Rainy day — do nothing in particular — but a little of everything generally. A horse broke away & got among some buffalo & has not come in yet.

Monday 4. Start in a N.W. direction alongside the Côteau. At noon we strike out W — pass the "White Earth" [River] branches (white from the light colored clay) Water here generally saline. Found petrifications of large timber & some

²⁵ This was the trail of the Holmes train. The Fisk expedition decided to follow it, according to Bond, because "Bottineau says he knows their guide, Antoine Osier, a Chippewa half-breed from Red River . . . and thinks his route will be well selected." Not until later did Fisk learn that Holmes's guide had deserted. Bond, "Journal," July 21, 31, August 10.

coal along the streams forming the White earth river. Grass poor — country barren. We can see timber along the edge of the Côteau. Camp on a lake. 18.50 miles W.

Tuesday 5. The country this morning like that of yesterday. A little before noon we met with a band of Assiniboines — "Broken Arm" their Chief.[26] Gave him some medicine, & some for his young men. Some 30 or 40 came up at lunch — the war chief made a speech which excited the others. Wanted us to turn back — said we scared away buffalo &c. Some were disposed to be saucy, threatened & tried to bully us but finding that did not pay, cooled down & at last begged. Botu & Indians killed 11 buffalo. I killed one. 20.50 miles W.

Wednesday 6. Pass thro' open prairie this morning. At noon we strike the Côteau again, & pass thro' a rolling, rocky, barren country — some feed and water in ravines. Today killed 4 buffalo, 3 bulls, & a young Cow. We begin to [go] S. a little — & travel late to get water & grass. 22.25 miles S.W.

Thursday 7. Country rolling & barren. At noon had a call to see Mrs [Mary J.] Stark who was confined of a son at 11:30 p. m. & doing well.[27] The train rested well from noon on this account. A good camping place. 11 miles S.W.

Friday 8. Started late — had to fix my patient in a spring wagon — she does well — boy hearty. Lunch on a small creek. Camp on a small pond in sight of the bluffs on the Missouri. Pretty good wheeling today. 17.50 S.

Saturday 9. Today we travel something E of S. following the trail of the other guide (Morrison's Party) We get in sight of the Missouri River (about 5 miles off) but do not see anything of Ft Union. Opinions vary as to our whereabouts. Intend to send out a scouting party tomorrow. Camp on a stream, tributary to E. branch of "Little Muddy" [Creek]. 19 miles S. or S.S.E.[28]

Sunday 10. Wet day. Capt. & Sturgiss [William Sturgis] went out towards the Missouri, returning in the evening. They went about 15 miles & found Ft Union. We mended up — & helped Botu to pack up, as he intends returning from Union. We are invited to dine at the Fort tomorrow.

Monday 11. Botu, Dan. & Geo. left the train this morning. B. shook hands with all, & was much affected at the regret all evinced on his leaving. We (Offs) went to the Ft to dinner with Mr [Robert] Meldrum. Did some trading. Took leave here of Botu, with all manner of good wishes for his safety. Geo. takes my Peter, & I take his mule "Fanny." Prescribed for a Mexican h[al]f breed at the fort, who presented me with a splendid buffalo robe, which had belonged to a chief of the crows (Knife) who was killed in a fight with the Sioux 10 days previous.[29] Got back to camp at sundown.

[26] On Broken Arm, see Larpenteur, *Forty Years a Fur Trader,* 1:189, 194; 2:232.

[27] Josephus Stark of Manchester, New Hampshire, had served with the army on the plains between 1857 and 1860. He and his wife went to Minnesota in 1862 shortly before joining the Fisk expedition, intending to go to the Salmon River fields. Stark later became a hotelkeeper at Twin Bridges, Montana. The son was named Julian Fisk. See Bond, "Journal," August 7; *Madison County Monitor* (Twin Bridges), January 6, 1905, p. 1; *Madisonian* (Virginia City), March 31, 1950, p. 1.

[28] It is likely that the camp was near the Dakota-Montana border on a branch of the Little Muddy Creek in Roosevelt County, Montana.

[29] Bond said that the Indian chief was an Assiniboin and that he and the Mexican half-breed had been pursuing Sioux marauders. "Journal," August 11.

Tuesday 12. All ready to start again. Mr Meldrum from the Fort goes with us to Ft Benton (takes his young Squaw along). Start at 9 A.M. and travel W along the valley, from 2 to 5 miles from the Missouri. Lunch at a pond 13 miles from Camp. Move on 2 miles to grass & water on a creek, & camp. 15 miles W.

Wednesday 13. Had a windy night which blew over some tents. Travel today along a valley between high bluffs — good road — country on either side looks bare. Water scarce, only to be found in creeks & gulleys. Reach the "Big Muddy" [Creek] & camp on the bank. 15.25 miles W.[30]

Thursday 14. Cross the "Big Muddy" by making a bridge of wagons — by taking off the covers — and running them up close together across the stream, & pack the goods over & replace them in the wagons on the W. side. All there by noon. The river here is 70 to 80 ft wide, & from 3 to 5 ft deep, with a muddy loose bottom. Reach "Ft Kipp" [Moffat] by 2 p. m. & camp. A few indians & their squaws around here. Bad camp ground & stinks like a slaughter yard. 5 miles W.[31]

Friday 15. Leave Ft Kipp. Day very warm. Keep along the river bottom — grass good in patches along the bottom. Lunch near the river poor water & poor grass. Rest ½ an hour & start for better feed. Camp on the River — feed not good — water from Missouri warm & muddy. 15 miles W.

Saturday 16. Keep along the Missouri generally on dry bottoms. Water scarce— ground parched. Travel late to find water & grass. About noon crossed the "Quaking Aspen" or poplar river — small but water good, flowing over a gravelly bed. Lunch here. Afternoon we travel to a pond of poor water — grass good. 23.50 miles W.

Sunday 17. Have to travel today to find better feed. Lunch at a spring (9 miles.) Push on to "Wolf Point" [Montana], which is a good camping place. The feed & water all along the Missouri is scarce & poor. We still keep in the valley touching the river from point to point. 12.25 miles W.

Monday 18. Again a warm day — pass thro' a like country as yesterday. Lunch at "Lone tree" creek 9 miles from camp — on a spring — feed poor. Reach "Porcupine River" [Little Porcupine Creek] for the night camp. Wounded & ran an old bull into the mud in Porcupine R. just at its entrance into the Miss[our]i The mud here was as soft as batter, & some 8 or 10 ft deep — the old fellow was out of sight some time after the first plunge. Pass thro' a village of prairie dogs. 17 miles W.

Tuesday 19. Leave the Porcupine at 8 a.m. Lunch on a creek with water in holes. Same afternoon we see the banks of "Milk River" which we reach at 3 p. m. Camp on the River 5 or 6 miles from its mouth — river low — water good, but warm — plenty of driftwood. 14.50 miles W.

Wednesday 20. Rest here until noon to shoe up the cattle. Visited by indians — Crows and Gros Ventres. "Rotten-tail" is the Crow Chief "Squaw that Sits" first chief of the Gros Ventres. "Star Robe" second chief. 2 or 300 came to see us in

[30] Bond noted on this day that the party passed a sandstone formation described by Stevens (*Narrative and Final Report*, 89) and noticed on a "perpendicular front" the names of the members of the Holmes train.

[31] The fort, named for fur trader James Kipp, was located on the Missouri River between the mouth of the Big Muddy and present-day Brockton, Montana. Its name was changed to Moffat in 1862. See Larpenteur, *Forty Years a Fur Trader*, 2:316; Bond, "Journal," August 14.

the course of the day. Dr Clarke [J. R. C. Clark] (who is vaccinating) stayed with us last night. We started at noon, & crossed the "Little Porcupine" [Porcupine Creek] and camp on Milk R. Water good, scarce of feed. 10 miles W.[32]

Thursday 21. The country here is very dry — the feed improves a little — have plenty of indian company with us — who trade ponies, robes, &c for sugar, flour &c with our party. This course of the River (upwards) bears to the N.W. Camp on the R. bank — feed better. Indians camp near us & are very orderly & quiet. I visited "Rotten-tail" last night — who presented me with a pair of moccasins. Bond had a celebration of his own.[33] 20 miles N.W.

Friday 22. Another warm day. Country very dry — feed still scanty — water plenty from the Milk R. We keep along the river from point to point. Plenty of dry cottonwood all along the river. We camp on the bank. Indians are still with us — trading as usual. 17.50 miles W.

Saturday 23. Start early & strike the river at the Crossing, & breakfast there — feed pretty good — wood plenty.[34] Fix the river for crossing by putting in willows. Intend to make a good march this evening. Cross at 4 p. m. After traveling some 6 miles a thunder storm came up, which made it very dark. Great commotion at the hind end of the train   a report comes to the head that indians are cutting off the last wagons. On going back could not at first find the indians — but at last got sight of some 5 or 6 indians to one side of the track, seemingly as much alarmed & astonished as some of our folks. We took them along & kept them until morning. 11.50 miles W.

Sunday 24. We did not put up our tents in the storm last night — but slept under wagons. Start this morning at day-break, & strike the bend of the river at 9 A.M. — feed thin, but there is a good quantity of wild flax, the seed is ripe. Today I shot 2 "Sage Birds" [sage hens] — they are made like a grouse, but much larger, & fly like an English pheasant. We Stay over today here. Got a mail here from Ft Chambers [Fort Charles] — none for me.[35] 9 miles W.

Monday 25. Very warm & dusty — feed becomes better. Cross Milk R. again today. 19.75 W.[36]

Tuesday 26. Warm & clear. Keep in the valley. See buffalo plenty. I go afoot,

[32] For the Crow and Gros Ventres chiefs respectively, see "Original Journal of James H. Chambers," in *Montana Historical Contributions*, 10:114, 159, 287; and "Fort Benton Journal," in *Montana Historical Contributions*, 10:59, 61, 274. Dr. Clark was assigned to vaccinate the Indians by the Office of Indian Affairs. See correspondence for June, 1860, in files C562, C569, Letters Received, Central Superintendency, Bureau of Indian Affairs, NARG 75. Bond describes him in "Journal," August 19, 20.

[33] Dibb probably refers to the fact that Bond, who also visited Rotten Tail, tried to enter some other lodges but was stopped by the Indians. See Bond, "Journal," August 20. Dibb made further observations about the Gros Ventres in his medical report (serial 1164). See also "Report of Dr. Dibb," January 9, 1863, in file F163 AGO 1862, NARG 94, for some unpublished comments.

[34] This first crossing of the Milk River was probably made in the vicinity of Hinsdale, Montana. The expedition then traveled on the south and west side of the Milk, cutting across a large bend of the river, until August 25, when it crossed to the north side again.

[35] On Fort Charles, a fur post, see Bond, "Journal," August 20, 27, and Larpenteur, *Forty Years a Fur Trader*, 2:333, 342.

[36] This crossing of the Milk River appears to have been between present-day Malta, Montana, and the mouth of Assiniboine Creek. The trail apparently came close to the route of the Great Northern Railway near present-day Wagner on August 26 and followed the north side of the Milk River until September 1, when it crossed the river a few miles northwest of present-day Havre.

cripple 5 & get 2, leave the others as it is very hot walking. Meet some returning men from Salmon R. — give rather a hard account of doings out there. 15.25 miles W.[37]

Wednesday 27. We stop over today to let the Emigrants get buffalo to dry. 2 or 3 of us went afoot. I shot 2 antelope. Burritt shot a splendid old buck. Saw a white tailed deer but did not get it.

Thursday 28. This is a good morning for travel. Lunch on a lake near the river (9.75.) I miss a good old deer. Camp on the river. 21.75 miles W.

Friday 29. Pretty good start — lunch on the river — still in the valley — feed better — more water. Saw two deer. Burritt wounded one but we did not get her. Another party got 2 antelope & one deer — feed keeps improving. 19.50 miles S.W.

Saturday 30. Morning pleasant — some dew last night, which we have not had for 30 days before. Before noon we crossed a tributary to the Milk which we named "O-mut-pa-pasha" or Meldrum river — & at 3 p. m. another, the "Two lances" (after Meldrum's wife) — these were nearly dry.[38] Camp on a point of the river with good grass, wood, & water from holes in the river. This is quite a model of a camping place — a clear space in the Cottonwood grove large enough for our Corral — at the bottom open enough for a breeze & shady enough to protect us from the sun. 17.75 miles W. or S.W.

Sunday 31. Day of rest. I smoke my skin coat & pants. See signs of indians on the river.

September 1. Start at 7 A.M. — travel fast & lunch on the river (13 miles). This [day] see two large "Medicine Lodges" across the river, which we visit. One is 100 ft in diameter — the other 75 or 80, & about 35 or 40 ft high. Offerings, or Sacrifices were left here, recently by Indians, of Robes, blankets, Hides (dressed), guns, &c, &c, — these were taken by our hfbreeds. A pony was caught, while at lunch, which had been "offered" by them — he had been pricked all over. We heard at Ft Benton that indians had had a kind of treaty here — there were Blk-feet, Piegans, Blood, Crows, & Gros Ventres. In all there were some 10,000, having with them some 12 or 15,000 ponies. 18.50 miles W.[39]

Tuesday 2. Last night, after crossing the river for the last time, we camped on the right bank. This morning we are nearing the "Bearpaw Mounts." A party of us go hunting — but are satisfied with black, & white currants — &c. Gooseberries were too ripe. Cross the "Beaver Creek" & push along for the "Box Alder" [Box Elder Creek]. Good travelling — found good springs. 19.50 miles S.S.W.

Wednesday 3. Got a beaver last night in the creek (Box Alder). Start this morning at 7 a.m. Burritt & I hunt along the creek. Saw the fresh track of a

[37] Bond wrote on this date: "They report rich mines at Salmon river but the claims mostly taken up — report but little gold at Deer Lodge or Bitter Root Valley, provisions cheap, flour and pork at 15 and 20 cts per lb. and cattle, except for beef in no demand."

[38] Meldrum and Two Lances creeks are shown on Walter W. DeLacy's "Map of the Territory of Montana with Portions of the Adjoining Territories" in the approximate locations of present-day Battle and Lodge creeks. DeLacy's 1865 map was consulted in the Bancroft Library of the University of California at Berkeley.

[39] Bond noted on September 1 that 3,000 or 4,000 Indians must have camped on the spot. They had probably assembled for the purposes of killing buffalo and making a medicine lodge, according to *Report of the Secretary of the Interior*, 1862, p. 323 (37 Congress, 3 session, *House Executive Documents*, no. 1, part 2 — serial 1157).

Grizzly — the creek is crooked with brush & stunted timber at the points. We tried these without success — & as we got up the creek the timber gave out — leaving nothing but small brush & willows. We wanted to cross at one of these places, where the bottom was good — & were pushing thro' the willows to see, when up rose the old fellow, with a tremendous growl, not 10 ft from us — he made for us — by [but] my mule & Bs horse took the hint in a moment, wheeled & dashed out of the willows, with old bruin hard after us, but our terrified steeds soon left him behind — when he turned for the creek again. As soon as we could check up, we followed him — & saw him climbing the opposite bank. We tried to cross — got mired, & had to pull out again — tried another place & crossed — but the old rascal had made for some of the heavily timbered points & we could not rouse him out. 4 or 5 more were seen by others but none killed. We stopped near the Bearpaw, on a creek [Big Sandy] (9.75) & rested here until evening — as we intend to go to a spring, some 20 miles off in the night as it will be cooler for the cattle. Start out at 5 p.m.   good road & the cattle travel like horses. We reach the creek or Spring at 12:30 p. m. & camp down until morning. 29.75 miles S.S.W.

Thursday 4. We started at 7:30 for the "Maria's [Marias] River" which we reach by noon — just getting a peep at the Missouri down a Côulee. We stay here for the day. Some 3 or 4 go on to Ft Benton (11 or 12 miles). The "Maria's" is a very pretty river flowing rapidly over a gravelly bed. The descent from the plateau of the prairie down to the river is very steep — but fortunately it is sandy. 13 miles. S.S.W.

Friday 5. Start this morning for a camp, near Ft Benton. We cross the "Teton River" 4 times. Camp at the last crossing, some 4 miles from the Fort. Capt. & I ride in. The fort is on a nice level prairie — a square building, something like Ft Union — inside there is the same dirt, indians, hf breeds, & their children — dogs, pigs, & bugs. We hear various reports about the mines. A great number of indians have just left here. 9 miles. S.S.W.

Saturday 6. Overhauling the goods, & fixing up. Go over to the fort — see an indian child who was shot above the knee — the femur badly splintered longitudinally — doubtful whether the limb can be saved — take a very long time if it can. Some young men, leaving the fort, in passing a tepee belonging to another tribe, in the dusk of evening, fired 5 or 6 shots into it, then left; — they killed one squaw, wounded two others, of which was this one.

Sunday 7. Intended to go to the fort, but did not feel well — bilious, with headache &c.

Monday 8. Expect we shall move again tomorrow. We are getting some necessary supplies from the fort. Among other good things we get a "Sibley tent," so when the evenings get colder we can have a fire, & another good thing it will stand a good wind in the mountains without blowing over.[40]

Tuesday 9. We start this morning at 10 a.m. Pass over a good prairie between the Missouri & Teton. Camp on the "Big Coulee." Charlton & I killed 3 sage birds, & a large rattlesnake. 14.25 miles S.W.[41]

[40] The Sibley tent, named for its inventor, Major Henry Hopkins Sibley, was patterned after the Indian tepee but required only one tent pole and was designed to accommodate a stove. It was large enough to shelter twelve men and was used at this time by the army. See Augustus Meyers, "Dakota in the Fifties," in *South Dakota Historical Collections*, 10:174 (Pierre, 1920).

[41] Beyond Fort Benton the expedition traveled on the Mullan Road. The big coulee and other landmarks mentioned later by Dibb were familiar points on the road and are described in more

Wednesday 10. Rainy morning — roads good. We make the spring by 2 p.m., rest 2 hours — then pull out for the pond [Benton Lake?], which we reach a little after sundown — good grass — water scarce & muddy — no wood. Night cool & frosty for the first time — having no wood we have a shivery camp. Meet some return[ing] miners who are going home disgusted.

from camp to Spring 17.50

"   Spring to Camp   7.50

25.

Thursday 11. Cold morning — had a keen frost last night. Start early for "Sun River" which we reach by 1:30 p.m., crossing the Muddy River [Creek] 1.50 miles before striking Sun R. "Sun River" is a pretty stream about 200 ft wide. Some timber all along, elm, & cottonwood. Some trout are caught this evening. Good feed & splendid water. 15.25 miles. S.W.

Friday 12. Started at 7:30. Cloudy. I crossed the river, & hunted, — no game. We camp 1.50 miles below the agency, on Sun River. Went to see the farm — (intended to teach the indians agriculture). Saw some wheat — not cut — Corn which we might use for feed if we could [find] it among the weeds. They have 15 or 20 acres under plow. Saw two ladies at the farm house (first we have seen for 3 months). 7.25 miles. S.W.[42]

Saturday 13. Camp here for the day, & prepare for the mountains. Considerable trading done among the Blk-feet indians, for ponies &c. "Little Dog" the Blk-feet Chief is with us, on a visit, with 8 or 10 of his warriors — they stay [to] dinner.[43] Little Dog is a good looking indian & pretty well dressed in white man's clothes. Burritt & a party left with Dr [Monroe G.] Atkinson for a trip in the mountains, kind of prospecting tour. We intend travelling tomorrow.

Sunday 14. Cloudy morning, & inclined to rain, but we start at 7 a. m. Clear by 9 a. m. We Cross the Sun River & strike Crown Butte creek, & go down it 2 or 3 miles & camp. Camp in site of Bird-tail Rock [Birdtail Butte]. Today we get some idea of the mountains. Saw an Elk, but did not get a shot. Saw plenty of antelope — but wild. The road is good — food grass & water — no wood. 13 miles. W. or S.W.

Monday 15. Some cattle astray. Start at 8 a. m. Pass "Birdtail rock," & continue on good road to "Beaver [Flat] Creek" (13.) Lunch & reach "Dearborn" [River] for night camp — fine river, 80 or 100 ft wide, with good feed, & water. Caught a doz. very nice fish. 17.50 miles S.W.

Tuesday 16. Dull with showers. 8 a. m. start — roads at first bad on account of the rain — good feed & water all along. Bond & I struck off, & had some real mountain travel; — struck a creek [Rock Creek] some 3 or 4 miles above camp & came down it. Abundant signs of grizzly among the cherry bushes in the valleys A party on horseback go on ahead to the Prickly-pear River [Creek]. 13 miles S. or S.E.

detail in John Mullan, *Miners and Travelers' Guide to Oregon, Washington, Idaho, Montana, Wyoming, and Colorado,* 16 (New York, 1865).

[42] Dibb forgot, for the moment, the women on the expedition. For the Sun River government agency and James H. Vail, the government farmer, see Bond, "Journal," September 12; *Report of the Secretary of the Interior,* 1862, p. 325; Dunbar and Phillips, eds., *Journals and Letters of Major John Owen,* 1:263.

[43] For information on Little Dog, chief of the Piegan, see Ewers, *The Blackfeet,* 235, 237, 240–243; Bond, "Journal," September 12.

Wednesday 17. The creek we camped on last night runs into the Missouri 3 miles from camp. After going 4 miles we strike the "Little Prickly Pear," & we cross this some 20 times today, then cross a spur of mountains. (a very steep grade) travel some 5 miles & strike the river again cross it, & camp in the valley. The travel today was slow, so many crossings, & the long hill compelled us to double teams. We get plenty of the Uva Ursi leaves (Indian Kinnic Kinnic). 11.75 miles S.[44]

Thursday 18. Cattle astray. Started late. Cross the river 5 times — then go along a creek running into the river, & up a long steep hill (Medicine Hill) — have to double teams — then wind down into the valley of the river, & camp at the last crossing in a pleasant valley — had *plenty of water* for 2 days, — good grass — splendid pine on the mountain sides. 5.50 miles. S.

Friday 19. Start at 8 a. m. follow up a ravine on an easy grade for 4 or 5 miles — pass over the divide. On W side struck a creek formed by a spring, follow this creek down a gentle slope, to a branch of the Big Prickly [Silver Creek] — here we camp. And here meet the prospectors who went on ahead. They report well — found the "color." 13 miles. S.W.[45]

Saturday 20. Train started at 8 a. m., & moved on to the next creek [Tenmile Creek], where those who intend to try the "Prickly Pear Diggings" turn off. Folsom & I went afoot to the valley of the Big Prickly. Started a deer but did not get a shot. In the valley I got a double shot at 2 buck antelopes, wounded the first badly with buckshot, but did not follow him. Knocked the other over with the rifle — bled & cleaned him — tied my neck-kerchief over him, & left him to go back to the train, as I see they intend to camp on a branch of the main river. 15 miles. S.

Sunday 21. We start for the diggings, which we reach by noon. Capt. & I go for my antelope — find him all right — tho' there was a circle of wolves crows, ravens, & magpies around him. We try our luck at "panning," & every one gets his pile. We go to bed early, tired. This is a very pretty valley, with an abundance of everything for stopping over the winter.

Monday 22. We talk over a plan for a town for the gold-seekers. Received a host of messages, letters &c for the folks at home — took dinner with the widow [Mrs. Catherine A. Durgan], & prepared to start for our train & camp (wh[ich] we left at the "turnoff"). An address was presented to the Capt. & Officers, thanking them for their attention &c. &c. Then we left. We drove a good jog to our camp. Saw any quantity of game as we went along. Sundown by the time we reach camp.

Tuesday 23. This morning we start for "Deer-lodge," with our reduced train. Crossed a large creek at noon — lunched on another. Then we ascend the "Summit Ridge" of the Main range, — a very easy ascent. On the summit we fired the howitzer, & had some splendid echoes. Go down the other side of ridge, and camp

---

[44] Kinnikinnick was a mixture of dried leaves and bark used by Indians for smoking. The exact recipe for the mixture varied among different Indians in different localities. *Uva ursa,* used by the mountain Indians of this region, is a small oval-leafed evergreen. See *Expedition of Captain Fisk*, 24.

[45] This was the party that left the train on September 16. ". . . and later they gave us private information which determined Captain Fisk and I that later on we would do some prospecting on our own account." The quoted words, appended to the last sentence of the entry, are the first of a series of additions to the original Dibb Diary which are found in the so-called Robert Strong version. For a fuller discussion, see page 118, below.

on Summit Creek [North Fork of the Little Blackfoot?] — good feed & water. Two men from the "Diggins" had started early to overtake us, were stopped some time on the track by an old panther & 3 cubs — they did not disturb her, & she passed slowly away. 16 miles. S.W.

Wednesday 24. Last night I killed an otter, & might have got 3 more, but fooled away the chance. We are on a down grade today — passing along the Summit River until it runs into the "Blk foot River" [Little Blackfoot] on which we lunch. We followed down the Blk-foot, & crossed a tributary, on which we camped. 19 miles. S.W.

Thursday 25. Today we horsemen take an indian trail to Deer-lodge, & reached it by noon. We there met Burritt, Dr Atkinson & Knox — found the camp on "Deer Creek" [Clark Fork]. 16 miles. S.W.[46]

Friday 26. This morning we go down Deer Creek to the "American Forks," & as we have some shoeing to do, we camp near the settlement. 13.75 miles S.W.

Saturday 27. Go around the village to see the sights it consists of some 15 houses, small log houses covered with poles, & earth — rather a hard looking place — 2 stores — 2 saloons — 2 Smith shops.

Sunday 28. Today we are visited by some men from the "Pikes Peak Gulch." Dr [Freeborn F.] Hoyt & brother [John F. Hoyt], with 10 or 12 others I did not know. They are doing well, & seem in good spirits — stay dinner.

Monday 29. We are getting ready to start by noon. Our train now consists of 3 wagons (mule & Horses) the Howitzer, & 30 or 40 pack horses.

The "Deer lodge Valley" is splendid for grazing cattle. One man "Johnny Grant" has 3 or 4,000 head, besides horses, & mules — he does not winter feed, but lets them graze thro' the winter — & we never saw larger, better, or fatter cattle anywhere than he had. They do not farm much — but what we did see looked well — the settlers live by trading & stock raising.

We start at 1 p.m. & go down the "Hell Gate River" [Clark Fork] (formed by the junction of the Blk foot and Deer lodge Rivers, or creeks).[47] We camp on this stream passing along a pleasant valley — good grass and plenty of wood. 9 miles W.

Tuesday 30. Prairie travel, rolling, & good roads. Cross Streams of good water. Can see the mountain tops covered with snow. Overshot an antelope at 300 yds. Saw a Grizzly but could not get a shot at him. 24 miles W. or N.W.

October 1. Follow down the "Hell Gate," sometimes in valleys, & sometimes on the mountain sides. We follow Lieut. Mullen's [John Mullan] Road — he has done considerable work in places. This road is generally easy of travel. Pass thro' splendid pine, mostly the pitch pine. 24 miles W. of N.W.

Tuesday [*sic*] 2. At first a cold raw morning, but clears off. Pass along a pleasant valley of pines. Before getting into the Hell-gate pass (Hell Gate proper) we come

[46] The following sentences, inserted after the word "noon," appear in the Strong version of Dibb's Diary: "On the way the Captain and I meet a wounded Indian, suffering from a bullet wound in the shoulder. I fix him up and he, in the fullness of his gratitude, tells us of a mountain of gold over in 'the yellow country.' We pay little attention to the fellow, who evidently has been drinking." In Bond's journal entry of the same date there is a blank in the manuscript after the sentence: "I have obtained from Mr. Burritt the following succinct account of his prospecting tour."

[47] The name Clark Fork is now generally applied to the entire river, the different sections of which were earlier known as the Deer Lodge, Hell Gate, and Missoula rivers.

on a high bench which is on a level with the prairie on the other side. The road thro' Hell gate is very good — the pass being about a mile in width, with high mountains on either side. Then opens into a prairie, or valley, the "Bitter root Valley" — in wh there is a settlement, store &c. We camp near the Store & near which the Bitter-root river joins with the Hell-gate river, & forms what is called the St Mary's, Hell-Gate, or Missoula River [Clark Fork]. 14 miles. N.W.

Friday 3. Start down the valley of the St Mary's or Missoula. Pass thro' a french s[e]ttlement of farms — good land. Saw some winter wheat growing, & looking well. Good stock. Bought some oats for feed ($2.50 per Bushel). The roads are good. Camp on a small stream run[n]ing into the river. 18 miles N.W.

Saturday 4. Start at 8:30 a. m. Go 2 miles to a creek — in crossing which we make a mistake, & take a wood track for 5 or 6 miles — when discovering our blunder we back up — get on the right track & camp on a creek. Charlton & I passed thro' splendid pine, & tamarack in crossing to the right trail. (on dire[c]t road) 7 miles. N. of W.

Sunday 5. As we made a short trip yesterday we travel today — road good up to noon (10) — then we got on a very rocky road. All afternoon we travelled on sidling grades, & hard going for the teams. It seems to us it would be much better to throw a bridge over the river, here, as the other side is a level pine bench all along. 21 miles. Course everyway.[48]

Monday 6. Today we repacked, & lightened our load as much as possible. Our horses on scant feed are giving out & that infernal howitzer will kill a dozen horses before we get across. Leave one wagon, & put 4 horses, or mules to each wagon. Burritt, Bond & I go back to see after a horse we left yesterday — he was hurt by a fall & yesterdays work tuckered him out — had something like the blind staggers. We found him in the bed of the river, into which he had rolled some 2 or 300 ft, & was considerably bruised & scratched. With some trouble we got him out, & slowly he travelled some 5 miles, when he again gave out & we had to leave him. The train had moved a short distance & we were caught in a heavy storm, & thoroughly drenched before we got to camp. 5 miles N. of W.

Tuesday 7. Leave the river, & go up a long hill — then down to the river again — some 4 miles up & down — road pretty hard up to noon (10). Good road in the afternoon. Camp on the river. Grass pretty good in places. Today a Panther stopped one of our party who had only a shot-gun — he came to us for help — but when we returned he could not be found. 20 miles W.N.W.

Wednesday 8. Morning dull. Start at 8:30 — reach the crossing of the Missoula by 1 p. m. There is a ferry here. The Flathead River comes in 12 miles below this ferry, the river then takes the name of the South, or Clark's Fork of the Columbia. After crossing we camp on some bottom ground of thick timber, on a Creek — no grass — dull, sloppy evening. 17 miles W.

Thursday 9. It rained last night up to midnight. The Packers go on ahead to cross the Co[e]ur D'Aléne ridge. Train starts at 9 a. m. Road today thro' a thick pine growth of timber — road muddy & full of grubs, & holes. Lunched on a small opening — called prairie. This afternoon roads as bad until we get to the "St Regis

---

[48] Mullan located the road on the rocky side of the river in order to avoid difficult crossings. See *Military Road from Fort Benton to Fort Walla-Walla*, 45 (36 Congress, 2 session, *House Executive Documents*, no. 44 — serial 1099).

de Borgia" [St. Regis River] where we camp — good grass. This river is a pretty, fast running mountain stream. The woods are full of Partridge, or Ruffed Grouse. 13 miles W.

Friday 10. Start at 8 a.m. Travel up the river, and cross every half mile or so. Roads are bad, rocky grubby, & holey. Lunch on a timber opening. The day is cold, & often nearly dark the road is so shaded. We continue our crossings of the river. Camp on an opening, where there was once grass. Meet here with Mr Chas. Hutchins, Indian agent, who has lost his pack mules, & is stopped here on that account. 16.25 miles N.W.

Saturday 11. Started early this morning. I walk on ahead, & reach the summit of the Cour d'Alène by 9.30. Shot a bullet into the summit post as "my mark." There had been over a foot of snow 10 or 12 days ago — but there was only a little on our crossing the summit. Over the summit, & down a long, steep, winding mountain side. The "Cour d'Aléne River" commences immediately over the summit as a small stream. The road is good until we strike this river down which we travel, crossing & recrossing as we did the St Regis in ascending. The road now is rocky & bad. It has been cold all day, and very cold tonight. Camp at "Johnson's Cut-off."[49] No grass — & our poor horses suffer. They even browse on pine branches, & it is dangerous to pass in front of a mule. 13.50 miles W.N.W.

Sunday 12. Travel for feed — passing over bad timber roads — holes, grubs, & rocks — crossing the river every half mile. I go on ahead & shoot some half dozen partridges. Camp at "Long bridge" the feed being somewhat better. 12.50 miles W.N.W.

Monday 13. Fine morning — rain last night. Keep along the river — roads as of yesterday. At a crossing I shot a salmon, weighing over 12 lbs. Got 2 grouse & 1 duck. At noon we come to a prairie with good grass, & determined to let our stock fill up for once. 8 miles W.N.W.

Tuesday 14. Our stock did well last night. We had visitors — the Express-man & two others. They gave us the news &c. This morning we passed thro' a pretty country to the "Mission." The roads much better. Pass the Mission & camp 2 miles below, where there is good marsh feed. Get fresh beef, vegetables, peas &c from the Mission. 12 miles W.N.W.[50]

Wednesday 15. Fine warm day — intend to rest here for a few days. Go to the Mission, & see the [Father] Superior & 2 or 3 other Priests. The Superior was about starting for Ft Benton, alone. Went into the church, pretty for Indians. The Mission is on a splendid site — they have a good farm of 80 or 100 acres under cultivation — grow good grain & vegetables   bought oats, & peas for horsefeed.

Thursday 16. Still at rest. Saw some good winter wheat. Quite a number of indians at the Mission. The old Chief of the Cour d'Alénes came to see us.[51] The

[49] Johnson's Cutoff crossed the mountains to Thompson's Prairie on the Clark Fork River, according to the map accompanying Mullan's *Report* (serial 1149).

[50] The expressman, Haggard, proposed to establish a pony express line from Walla Walla to Fort Benton. See Bond, "Journal," October 13, and *Press*, March 19, 1863. The Sacred Heart Mission to the Coeur d'Alene Indians was located at this time on the Coeur d'Alene River. See Edmund R. Cody, *History of the Coeur d'Alene Mission of the Sacred Heart*, 39 (Caldwell, Idaho, 1930).

[51] This was probably Chief Vincent. See Bond, "Journal," October 16; Hiram M. Chittenden and Alfred T. Richardson, eds., *Life, Letters and Travels of Father Pierre-Jean de Smet, S.J.*, 2:748–756 (New York, 1905).

Indians here dirty & poor looking — altho' they are indifferent about trading — they seem to depend mainly upon their salmon fishing for a living. Some few go to hunt buffalo towards the Missouri. I smoke my antelope skins, & dress my otter.

Friday 17. A.M. 9. Started, & passed thro' timber for 3 miles — then strike a creek up which we go for 3 or 4 miles on bad rocky road. (10) then the country is rolling — roads level & good. We make "Wolf-lodge" [Creek] where there is good feed & water. Camp. 16 miles W.

Saturday 18. Fine day. Pass over the "Cour d'Aléne Hills" — fine country, & plenty of feed. Reach "Lake Cour d'Aléne" by noon. On one of the hills 2 or 3 miles from the lake there is a splendid view — the lake — river & valley of the Spokane. The lake has clear, gravelly shores. What we can see of it is 3 or 4 miles across, & 6 or 8 in length. Indians are fishing here, & at the mouth of the river. 10 miles W.

Sunday 19. Today we move on to the farm — road good & country level.[52] We keep along the river. The Cour d'Aléne River enters Lake Cour d'Aléne & runs thro' it, but on leaving the lake, it takes the name of the Spokane river. Reach the farm early. No one living on it — there is some wheat and oats in the straw, both good. This farm belongs, & is worked by the indians, who are away now fishing. Grass is good — the country is gently rolling & quite refreshing after our mountain travel. 5 miles W.

Monday 20. Pass thro' pine openings, & small prairies along the Spokane — roads good — the soil is light & gravelly. Lunch at the ford of the Spokane the train crosses here — but Capt. Burritt, Charlton & I go with the flagwagon to the ferry to get flour &c. Reach Antoine Plant's, but he is out hunting, so we must camp here tonight.[53] We sup with Antoine, & sleep under some trees near our wagon. Some Spokane indians visit us, & bring us a salmon, which the[y] broil on sticks for us. They appear quite chatty & agreeable. Antoine makes me a present of a buckskin gun cover. 19 miles W.

Tuesday 21. Get some flour, recross the river, & meet the train which had camped below us. Cross a prairie some 6 miles wide — then have pine openings. Lunch at a spring (9) — then travel to a pond in a marsh — good feed — left the stock out all night. Shot a goose & 4 ducks on ye pond. Country is rocky & barren in places — rock crops out. 18 miles S.W.

Wednesday 22. Travel over a rolling, rocky, hard looking country — covered in places with trap rock — roads good & hard. Reach "Rock Creek" by 2 pm. Grass thin & dry — but stock appear to like it. Winged another goose but did not get her. 14.50 miles S.S.W.

Thursday 23. Fine morning, cooler. Travel over a rolling prairie. Cross the "Three Creeks" (Tcho-Tcho-o-seep). Lunch here. Country more rolling — on our left, ⅓ a mile there is water, which we suppose to be the Pelouse [Palouse] River — pass on & camp at the "Cottonwood Springs" which form a small creek running down the valley. Good feed. 17 miles S.S.W.

Friday 24. Had a very strong, cold wind last night. Our stock felt this very much.

---

[52] The farm was probably one of the plots which the Indians had been cultivating for several years under the tutelage of the Jesuits. See William N. Bischoff, *The Jesuits in Old Oregon*, 133–135 (Caldwell, Idaho, 1945).

[53] Plant, a French half-breed, and his son operated the ferry across the Spokane River at this place. See Bond, "Journal," October 20.

Pass over a rolling prairie — very rocky in places, & formed into curious looking walls, mounds, turretts &c like some old fortifications. Cross a creek (O-say-tāy-ouse). Keep along a valley & camp at the "Sulphur Springs["] — grass & water plenty — not much wood. Some of our party intend to go ahead to the Snake-river ferry tomorrow. 14 miles S.S.W.

Saturday 25. Capt. & Burritt go on ahead. We still pass along the Pelouse River — grass pretty good all along — not much wood. Cross the river at the bends. Camp early, on the river, to let our stock fill up. 10.50 miles S.S.W.

Sunday 26. Stock feels better. Continue along the river. See the indians (Pelouse) fishing along the river. Some of our people get into trade with them for ponies &c We reach the last crossing, & camp near some falls (16 or 18 ft) & very pretty 18.75 miles W.

Monday 27. Train kept on the wagon track. We, Bond, Charlton, & I took the Indian trail along the river to see the "Falls of the Pelouse." Soon after starting we passed two falls, which were small, & where the river makes a bend at right angles. About 5 or 6 miles from Snake river we come to *the* "Falls," which are really splendid — the water making a clear shoot of 120 or 150 ft into a large basin. This basin is hemmed in by perpendicular rock walls 3 to 400 ft high, except at the Exit of the stream. We stayed some time here viewing it from different points. The banks of the river today are very bold & rocky as if for some mighty river. Reached the "Snake River" & crossed, to join our party already on the other side. 13 miles S.W.

Tuesday 28. Left camp on "Snake River" early, as we have 20 miles without water. "Snake River" here is a wide, & shallow R. banks generally low, & sandy, — no timber, wh gives it a bleak barren appearance. Travelled over prairie up one ravine to a divide & down another to the spring. Killed a fine sage Cock. Camped at this spring (or rather 3 or 4 of them). 20 miles S.W.

Wednesday 29. Started from the springs for the "Touchet" [River] which we reach in 2 hours, & camp. The "Touchet" is a small river, with settlers all along the valley — on good farming land but not much farming done yet. See here an English-man, a sporting character (a runner). Says he has been on a tour thro' the mines & won some $1800 in one race at Deer Creek. 7 miles S.W.

Thursday 30. Start today for "Dry Creek" — on which we intend to stay until we see our way clear in selling out the stock, as this is only 6 or 7 miles from "Walla Walla," and here we are secure from horsethieves. Reach the creek by noon. Some go on to town for mail — none for me. Get news from Minn: by the [St. Paul] "Press" & California papers. 11 miles S.W.

Friday 31. Camped on Dry Creek. Most of our folks are off to town. I overhaul my Medicine Chest. Clean my gun — pistol &c preparatory to packing away.

November 1. Moved this morning for our last camp. Reach the town of "Walla Walla," & camp in town on a vacant lot; near our stock. "Walla Walla" seems to be a very lively place stores all busy — streets full of people — houses are small, & there appears to be enough for 1500 inhabitants, but they say they have 3000. Fix our camp, then walk around to see the sights of this great City. 6 miles S.W.[54]

[54] The town which grew up around the military post of Fort Walla Walla was incorporated in 1862. See Henry L. Talkington, "Mullan Road," in *Washington Historical Quarterly*, 7:302 (October, 1916).

Sunday 2. Today the town (Walla Walla) is alive with business. They make no difference, or if any, it is the busiest day in the week. Horses &c selling at auction in the streets, packers busy loading up for the "Boisé" mines. Saloons — gaming houses full & doing a thriving business — in fact the only place closed for the day is the Church, or meeting house. We walk over to the fort in the evening.

3, 4, 5, 6, 7. Still at Walla Walla. Have sold all the stock, camp equipage &c., and intend to leave tomorrow for Wallula.[55]

Saturday 8. Start for "Wallula" at 7:30 by stage which is crowded (13 outside, 9 inside). Good farming land along the river for about one farm in width — the rest rolling, sandy prairie — not much timber on the river (Walla Walla). The roads are heavy & dusty — reach Wallula by 6 p.m. which is a small place, simply a convenience for boat passengers. The old Fort is here, but not used. 31 miles S.W.

Sunday 9. Take boat at 5:30 for the "Dalles."[56]

[55] Wallula (old Fort Walla Walla) was originally an important post of the Hudson's Bay Company.
[56] The diary continues until January 3, 1863, and records Dibb's homeward journey by way of San Francisco and Panama to New York City.

1863

THE FISK EXPEDITION

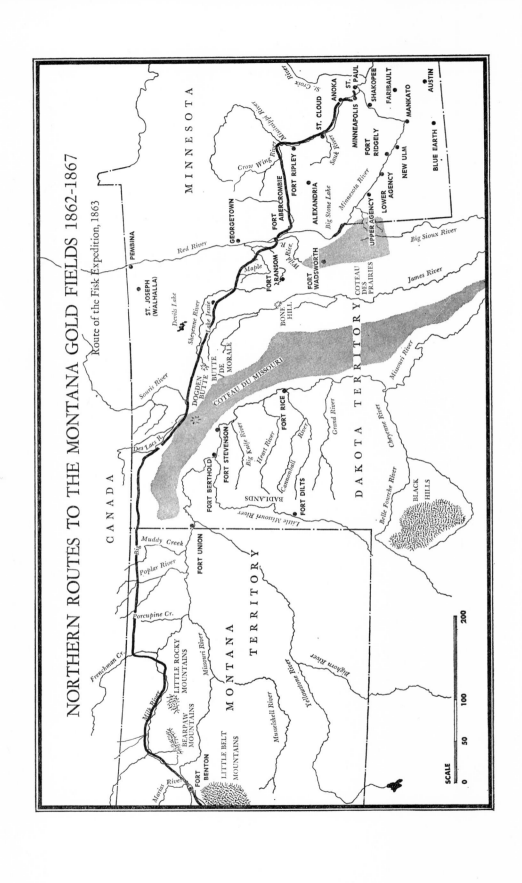

NORTHERN ROUTES TO THE MONTANA GOLD FIELDS 1862-1867

Route of the Fisk Expedition, 1863

SCALE

0   50   100   200

1863 ⊛⊛⊛⊛⊛⊛⊛⊛⊛⊛⊛⊛⊛⊛⊛⊛⊛⊛

The Fisk Expedition

ONLY ONE EXPEDITION — a group of about sixty persons led by James Fisk — crossed the northern plains in 1863. Despite fresh gold discoveries in the Rockies, prospective emigrants were reluctant to undertake the overland journey that year because they feared Indian attacks. In August, 1862, shortly after the Fisk and Holmes expeditions had left Minnesota, the Sioux raided frontier settlements in the state and killed several hundred people. The uprising was soon put down, but thousands of hostile Sioux fled to Dakota Territory where they threatened the safety of anyone who ventured onto the plains.[1]

Nevertheless, during the winter of 1862–63 backers of the northern route were busy in Washington setting the stage for another overland expedition. On February 7 Congress passed a new law for the protection of emigrant travel which recognized the northern route specifically for the first time and set aside for its protection the sum of ten thousand dollars, twice the amount allocated the previous year. Fisk arrived in the capital about the first of February, after a three-week visit in Minnesota, and submitted his official report to the adjutant general. Before the end of the month the report had been received by Congress, and on March 2 the House of Representatives ordered the printing of five thousand copies. Publication was prompt; within three weeks copies had reached Minnesota. In a third action of interest to the supporters of a northern route, Congress provided for the organization of Idaho Territory out of the eastern portion of Washington Territory. Idaho now embraced Prickly Pear, Bannack, and much of the area where the Minnesota emigrants had been prospecting. By these three acts Congress recognized and provided support for a northern overland route, made information about the route and the gold fields readily available to the public, and laid the foundation for the government of this frontier region. "Ho! for Idaho!" became the rallying cry for gold seekers of 1863.[2]

Fisk remained in the East during most of February, March, and April. Tech-

---

[1] Kenneth Carley, *The Sioux Uprising of 1862*, 70 (St. Paul, 1961).
[2] *Statutes at Large*, 12:642, 808–814; James Fisk, *Expedition from Fort Abercrombie to Fort Benton* (37 Congress, 3 session, *House Executive Documents*, no. 80 — serial 1164); *Congressional Globe*, 37 Congress, 3 session, p. 1478; *Pioneer*, March 21, 1863. Fisk later claimed that he had coined the name "Idaho" and suggested it to the congressional committee on territories. See *Weekly Press*, March 17, 1864.

nically he was on military assignment, settling the affairs of the 1862 expedition, but the work of completing his reports could hardly have taken his full time. It seems likely that he was also sending and inspiring news releases which appeared in Minnesota papers, calling on members of Congress, and arranging for the publication of his emigrant guidebook. Fisk obviously considered these activities well within the scope of his duties as superintendent of emigration for the northern route.[3]

In March Fisk submitted his financial reports and thereby created a snarl of red tape which was not fully untangled until the 1870s. The auditor's office found Fisk's vouchers improperly made out, his account overdrawn, and some of his expenditures apparently unwarranted. Either boldly or in ignorance, Fisk had claimed allowances which the auditor considered excessive, even by the liberal terms of his instructions. He had also paid for the transportation back to the States of four of his assistants. The auditor wished to disallow this expense, amounting to more than a thousand dollars, on the ground that Fisk was expected to recruit his staff among people who planned to stay in the gold fields. If the return fares were allowed, they would have to be paid out of an unexpended balance remaining from the 1862 appropriation for emigrant protection. Fisk was aware of the existence of this balance, which amounted to some seven thousand dollars in 1863, and would have liked nothing better than to have part or all of it diverted to the northern route. In fact, he eyed the fund covetously for the next three years.[4]

Fisk's financial problems were not solved in 1863, and they led to more complicated entanglements in 1864. His difficulties seem to have been caused by his carelessness in military and financial detail and a deliberate attempt to aggrandize the northern route by spending on it all the money to which its supporters thought it was entitled.

Fisk's lobbying techniques were more successful than his accounting procedures. On March 2 members of the Minnesota congressional delegation sent a letter to the secretary of war requesting Fisk's reappointment as superintendent of emigration over the northern route. Although it was signed by Senators Morton Wilkinson and Henry Rice and Representatives Cyrus Aldrich and William Windom, the letter was in the handwriting of the expedition's secretary, Samuel Bond, and it was couched in his graceful phrases. The document alluded to the satisfactory conduct of the 1862 expedition and suggested that in view of Fisk's experience, natural ability, and fitness to command, he was well qualified to lead a new expedition. It also recommended that his funds be augmented by the seven thousand dollars remaining from the 1862 appropriation, since the Indians posed a greater threat than they had during the previous year.[5]

Shortly before the end of March the secretary of war ordered Fisk's reappointment. His new instructions, dated April 1, did not differ significantly from those of 1862. Fisk was given permission to pay the return fare of one of his assistants, but

[3] *Press,* March 8, April 5, 14, 1863; *Pioneer,* March 21, 1863.

[4] Copies of letters concerning Fisk's accounts may be found in miscellaneous letters sent by the third auditor, 144:22, 145:374, and 147:86, NARG 217. Abstracts of Fisk's accounts and a record of their final settlement are in the records of the third auditor, NARG 217. For Fisk's explanation of his 1862 accounts, see Fisk to Lorenzo Thomas, February 28, 1863 (photocopy), James Fisk Papers.

[5] Wilkinson and others to Stanton, March 2, 1863, file 218W 1863, NARG 94.

his own transportation allowance was reduced. Although his request for unexpended funds was ignored and the old accounts remained unsettled, Fisk had ten thousand dollars in new funds and a new chapter to write.[6]

Before he went back to Minnesota, Fisk finished his book, *Idaho: Her Gold Fields and the Routes to Them* — the first guide to the northern overland route. The thin, pocket-sized volume was published in April and came from the press of John A. Gray in New York. It contained Fisk's official report of 1862, a sketchy map and itinerary from David Charlton's report, and fresh introductory material written by Fisk which commented on the significance of the northern route and quoted from emigrant letters up-to-date news on the Idaho gold fields. Early in May copies were on sale for thirty cents each at David D. Merrill's bookstore in St. Paul.[7]

Minnesota newspapers publicized Fisk's report, his guidebook, and his plans for a new expedition. In addition papers in various towns carried a spate of letters from the Holmes and Fisk emigrants of 1862 which kept people well informed about the latest happenings in the gold fields. Thomas Holmes wrote from the new diggings on Grasshopper Creek, where he had hunted for gold and laid out an addition to the city of Bannack. According to a St. Paul newspaper, Holmes had tuned his "Golden Harp to a Golden Strain" and was founding "New Jerusalems where streets are paved with gold."[8]

Despite all this publicity, it soon became evident that few people were interested in emigrating to Idaho in 1863. Continuing fears of the Indians were not allayed by the army's plans to send a two-pronged expedition into Dakota to punish the rebellious Sioux. An infantry column, led by General Henry H. Sibley, was to advance from Fort Ridgely northwest toward Devils Lake and a converging cavalry column under General Alfred Sully was to ascend the Missouri from Fort Randall. It was expected that the combined units would capture or destroy the entire Sioux fighting force.[9]

A great many of the state's able-bodied citizens had joined the army to defend the frontier or to serve in the South, and, as the *State Atlas* pointed out on April 22, Minnesota had been drained of men who might otherwise have traveled to the gold fields. The *Atlas* doubted that Fisk could get together a sufficient number of emigrants for a train, but it urged the editors of other newspapers to "talk up the subject."

Fisk returned to St. Paul about May 1 and, undismayed by obstacles, published official notices of the new expedition. With more time and money at his disposal than he had in 1862, he purchased an elaborate outfit and soon overspent his budget, buying more than eleven thousand dollars' worth of goods in St. Paul. Expenditures for camp equipment, animals, wagons, and supplies ran two to three times higher than the previous year. More than $2,600 was spent for weapons and

[6] Stanton to Fisk, April 1, 1863 (copy), file 218W 1863, NARG 94.

[7] *Pioneer,* May 15, 1863. The MiHS has a copy of Fisk's guidebook.

[8] For news about Fisk, see *Pioneer,* March 21, May 15, 1863; *Press,* April 9, 14, 1863; *Goodhue Volunteer* (Red Wing), May 6, 1863. For examples of letters from emigrants, see *St. Cloud Democrat,* February 5, April 9, May 21, 1863; *St. Peter Tribune,* April 4, 1863; *Press,* March 19, 1863; *Weekly Press,* April 9, 1863; *Pioneer,* March 25, May 10, 1863. Holmes's letter appeared in the *Weekly Press,* May 14, 1863.

[9] Carley, *Sioux Uprising of 1862,* 72.

ammunition alone, compared to $130 in 1862. The larger expenditures reflected not only a more complete outfit, but also the inflated prices which Fisk was forced to pay. The equipment he needed was in great demand for military outfits that year, and many items were in short supply. Further, a severe drought on the plains and in Minnesota raised the price of grain and at the same time made it prudent to carry large amounts of feed for the animals.[10]

The central Minnesota town of St. Cloud rather than Fort Abercrombie was designated as the rendezvous for 1863 so that emigrants would not have to travel unprotected across western Minnesota. Fisk also chose a somewhat more northerly route to the Dakota border than he had in 1862, because of the drought conditions and the Indian menace. The day of departure was postponed on one pretext or another while Fisk waited for ordnance supplies, "tardy emigrants," and a party of government surveyors whom he had been ordered to escort to the Pacific Coast. He had only thirty-five men with him when he finally left St. Cloud in the middle of June and started the train up the east side of the Mississippi toward Fort Ripley. Three of the government surveyors and more emigrants joined him at a camp below the fort, where the train delayed another five days. Fisk drew additional supplies and obtained a howitzer, which, like the one taken on the 1862 journey, was expected to impress both emigrants and Indians. Despite this evidence of military might, some of the emigrants were afraid; at least one man left the expedition just beyond the fort.[11]

By this time there were some sixty men in camp, of whom thirty-six were on Fisk's payroll. With such a small party Fisk would perhaps have been justified in disbanding his corps and canceling the expedition. Yet his instructions did not specify a minimum number of emigrants and he had purchased an elaborate outfit. Cancellation would have been a serious blow to the ambitions of those who were interested in the northern route as an artery of trade and a pathway of empire to the West. Fisk undoubtedly considered a crew of thirty-six men an adequate task force to scout, improve, and advertise a route to the gold fields. The thought of abandoning the project seems never to have entered his head.[12]

Fisk's staff included George W. Dart, a tinsmith from St. Paul who acted as second in command. Dr. Dibb, whose brother John was also among the emigrants, again served as physician. George Northup, the son of an early Minnesota steamboat captain, signed on as wagon master but deserted the expedition in July. Little is known about Fisk's secretary, Lieutenant Samuel H. Johnston, although he seems to have been a newspaperman. Antoine Freniere, the Sioux interpreter and guide, was a member of a renowned family of French-Indian traders and pioneers. Freniere sent news of the expedition to St. Paul newspapers and wrote further

---

[10] Abstracts of Fisk's accounts, 1862, 1863, records of the third auditor, NARG 217; *Pioneer*, June 23, 1863.

[11] The departure of the expedition is described in Fisk's official report, published as *Expedition of Captain Fisk to the Rocky Mountains* (38 Congress, 1 session, *House Executive Documents*, no. 45 — serial 1189). See also *Press*, May 20, 24, 1863; *Pioneer*, May 27, June 10, 1863; *St. Cloud Democrat*, June 18, 1863; William H. Clandening, "Across the Plains in 1863–1865," in *North Dakota Historical Quarterly*, 2:249 (July, 1928).

[12] The signatures of fifty-eight emigrants are appended to a letter of P. Hannay and others to Fisk, September 7, 1863. Another testimonial of appreciation lists thirty-six members of the escort and staff. Photocopies of both are in the James Fisk Papers. For a roster of members of the train see Appendix, below.

impressions of his experiences to his niece. A number of the protective corps were French Canadians, whom Fisk described as men accustomed to prairie life, attentive to their duties, and gay and lighthearted when the day's work was done.[13]

Leaving Fort Ripley at last on June 25, the expedition moved westward to the Red River in leisurely fashion, much to the annoyance of the emigrants. Delay, as one of them wrote in exasperation, was the whole story of the expedition from St. Cloud to Fort Abercrombie. The thirty-six men of the protective corps, who had few more than themselves to protect, were set to work repairing bridges and putting corduroys in the road. These repairs retarded the progress of the train, but in Fisk's view escorting emigrants was a minor part of a larger duty, that of opening a roadway for another season, another expedition.[14]

Road work was only one reason for the train's slow advance. Men and animals unaccustomed to trail routine suffered the usual mishaps, causing further delays. The train waited five days in camp for two missing members of the surveying party and finally moved on without them. Another day's layover took place on the Fourth of July, which was marked by a howitzer salute and the singing of patriotic songs.[15]

For men who had been ready to travel on June 1 the lost time was costly, lengthening the journey and using up supplies of food and forage. The emigrants were also disturbed by the sight of abandoned farmhouses and Indian-ravaged settlements, by the clouds of mosquitoes, the stench of grasshoppers rotting thick on lake shores, the choking dust on the prairie, and the smoke from forest and grass fires.

Both Fisk and Dr. Dibb, whose diary is printed in this text, were able to ignore the petty annoyances of the journey. Fisk viewed the expedition in larger perspective. Throughout the trip he noted the agricultural potential of the land and commented on outcroppings of coal near the trail, ever mindful of a future northern Pacific railroad, which in veritable sound and smoke was never far behind.

On July 13, almost a month after leaving St. Cloud, the expedition reached Fort Abercrombie. There more supplies were obtained, animals were shod, wagons repaired, and the organization completed. The shake-down phase of the journey was over and the train now faced the Dakota plains.[16]

Fisk led his party close to the 1862 trail until the end of July. During the first few days beyond the fort, the emigrants followed General Sibley's Indian expedition, and some of them dined one day with members of his command at an entrenched camp near Lake Jessie. Here Fisk purchased several animals from one

---

[13] For Dart, see Leeson, ed., *Montana*, 481, 985. For John Dibb, see United States Manuscript Census Schedules, 1860, Hennepin County, Minnesota, p. 93. Northup's desertion and Fisk's comments on the French Canadians are in *Expedition of Captain Fisk*, 7, 8. In 1869 Northup was killed in a street brawl in Duluth. See Walter N. Trenerry, *Murder in Minnesota*, 53–60 (St. Paul, 1962). An article signed "SHJ" appeared in the *New York Weekly Tribune*, April 23, 1864.

For Freniere's letters, see *Pioneer*, June 10, August 14, September 2, 1863; *Weekly Pioneer*, November 13, 1863; *Press*, November 6, 1863; Freniere to Ellen Brown, June 22, July 13, October 5, 1863, March 2, 1864, Joseph R. and Samuel J. Brown Papers, in MiHS. See also *Pioneer*, June 30, 1864.

[14] *Taylors Falls Reporter*, April 2, 1864; *Expedition of Captain Fisk*, 3.

[15] *Taylors Falls Reporter*, April 2, 1864; Clandening, in *North Dakota Historical Quarterly*, 2:250–253; William H. Holyoke Diary, July 4, 1864, Holyoke Papers, in MiHS.

[16] *Expedition of Captain Fisk*, 4.

E. D. Cobb, a transaction that was to cause him trouble in Washington the following spring. Sibley's men expressed the fear that Fisk's slender forces would not
be able to make the trip safely through Indian country. The Fisk party, they said,
must be "either heroes or madmen." [17]

Fortunately, the journey was a safe one, and the emigrants were free to enjoy the
beauty of the land, the excitement of the chase, and the encounters with peaceful
Indians and Red River hunters. On guard in the middle of a moonlit night, William
H. Clandening, a Canadian mining engineer who had complained for days about
the choking dust, succumbed to the charm of the plains. Never had he seen such
beautiful country as the White Wood Lakes area in north-central North Dakota —
"the high hills which smooth and blue rise one above another and the pretty little
lakes filling the valleys." He and others were also struck by the wintry appearance
of a chain of dry saline lakes in northwestern Dakota. Clandening thought their
salt-covered beds resembled "ice just before breaking up, and the white dust about
the shore when blown by the wind [looked] like snow drifts." Farther on, Fisk
wrote, the expedition passed a "full clear stream . . . bordered by grass, green
as an emerald, and thickly dotted with flowers — daisies, lilac and white, mari-
golds, &c." On their approach, a startled "herd of graceful antelopes who were
drinking at the river . . . disappeared like a cloud shadow from the landscape." [18]

From day to day the emigrants encountered antelope, wolves, blacktail deer,
grizzly bears, rattlesnakes, prairie dogs, and a great variety of wild birds. At Lake
Jessie they saw geese and ducks and a "perfect rookery" of nesting cranes, crows,
gulls, storks, and shitepokes. Birds and game as well as wild cherries, black currants, and prickly pears were a welcome addition to their diet. Of all the wild
game, the most spectacular was the buffalo. Antoine Freniere killed the first one
on July 17, and for more than a month the emigrants were never far from herds
which offered food and sport. They ate the meat in a variety of ways; Fisk wrote
of buffalo ribs roasted hunter-style on bent stakes placed on either side of the
campfire. On the vast rolling hills of the coteau the travelers saw great herds of
buffalo covering the distant landscape like swarms of flies. Clandening estimated
that in one day they had seen fifteen thousand; another emigrant put the number at five hundred thousand, while Fisk, who had scanned the hills with a field
glass, wrote "certainly over one million were in sight during the day." [19]

In the buffalo country the expedition encountered Red River half-breeds on
their summer hunt. Fisk and several members of the corps visited their camp near
the White Wood Lakes. About six hundred men were away hunting while the
women and a few old men remained in camp. Their carts were drawn into a
circular corral, hubs adjoining; inside were their conical skin tents. Outside the
cart circle a framework of stakes, like a red wall around the camp, was covered
with buffalo meat drying in the sun. The women, neatly dressed, modest, and
industrious, were cutting up the meat for pemmican, drying small cakes of wild
cherries and berries, and scraping skins. Later several of the hunters visited the

[17] *Expedition of Captain Fisk*, 6 (quote); *Pioneer*, August 15, 1863; *Weekly Pioneer*, September
4, 1863.
[18] Clandening, in *North Dakota Historical Quarterly*, 2:256, 260; *Expedition of Captain Fisk*,
15, 16.
[19] *Expedition of Captain Fisk*, 4, 5, 8, 11, 12, 18; Holyoke Diary, August 3; Clandening, in
North Dakota Historical Quarterly, 2:257, 258.

Fisk camp. One of them played his violin, and members of the Fisk party had a lively time dancing "French Fours."[20] The next day other Red River hunters came to Fisk's camp and waited while the emigrants wrote letters which the hunters promised to forward from Pembina to Minnesota. Fisk described one of the half-breeds in detail. Middle-aged and well-mannered, he "spoke good French and was most animated and even eloquent." His colorful costume included "a felt hat with a gay wreath; a dark blue coat, with a hood; drab leggins, fringed with scarlet and black cloth, with beadwork and gilt buttons on the outside; and moccasins embroidered with stained porcupine quills." Elaborate designs worked in colored beads decorated his crossbelts and other accouterments.

Traversing the Sioux lands of Dakota, the expedition saw numerous Indian signs — a medicine arrow painted on a rock, a war sacrifice in the form of a scarecrow, and a number of abandoned campsites — but met only one small party of Sioux. Farther west on top of a peak named by the Indians Haraka-o-weran (Where the Elk Feeds), some of the emigrants saw a spectacular figure of an elk cut into the earth. They estimated that the peak, a landmark which could be seen for a great distance, was about fifteen miles from the Canadian border; they renamed it "Mount Fisk."

This was Assiniboin country, where Fisk renewed his acquaintance with Chief Broken Arm and some of his followers. A party of Assiniboin came into view toward sunset on August 8 and dismounted near the camp. Fisk, surrounded by his staff, received Broken Arm and some fifteen followers in his tent. The Indians presented certificates testifying to their friendship for the white men. Broken Arm spoke at great length of his tribesmen's peaceful habits and their need for guns, blankets, flour, and other supplies.

According to Antoine Freniere's translation, Broken Arm concluded his speech: "My grandfather was born on these plains, like the wolf; he owned this land, and he told me always to be a friend to the white man. I have been so. I now claim this country. . . . If the white man comes here, he will drive away the buffalo, and my people will starve and perish. I want you, chief soldier, to tell the Great Father of all these things."

Fisk assured Broken Arm that the lands of the Assiniboin would not be taken. As long as they kept their treaties and did not harm white men, the Great Father would protect them. Fisk added that soldiers "as numerous as the buffalo or the leaves of the forest" were coming into the Indian country. He reminded Broken Arm that some of his band had insulted the expedition the previous year, and he cautioned the chief to take care that his tribesmen were not troublesome in the future.

Indians and white men smoked the peace pipe, and Dr. Dibb handed round his snuffbox. This occasioned "much laughter," and Fisk wrote that it "was amusing to watch the efforts of the Indians to maintain their gravity and imperturbability. The tears ran down their faces, and finally they were obliged to sneeze repeatedly, while looking at one another after the explosion with the most sheepish air imaginable." As a parting gift, Fisk presented the Indians with medicine, flour, sugar, coffee, and tobacco.

[20] The encounters with Red River hunters and Indians, here and below, are described in *Expedition of Captain Fisk*, 6, 7–15, 18, 25.

During much of August the expedition's route across Dakota and Montana lay north of the 1862 trail, probably close to the Canadian border. Near Frenchman Creek Fisk turned southward again to join the 1862 trail along the Milk River. On the evening of August 25 thirteen Gros Ventres Indians came to the camp and spent the night with the expedition. Fisk wrote that "their gaily embroidered robes, scarlet leggins and plumes" gave them a "picturesque and martial appearance by the light of our camp fires." After the Indians were fed, they sat in a circle with the white men, attempting to converse, and passed around their long pipe filled with kinnikinnick. Their language, according to Fisk, was "extraordinary and uncouth" and seemed to consist of a cough, a groan, a grunt, a whistle, and a 'tst tst.'" He quoted Robert Meldrum as saying that it was almost impossible for a white man to learn their language. The Indians, Fisk further noted, were clean and "tolerably well dressed," but three of the eleven men were lame. Dr. Dibb stated that the whole tribe was terribly diseased. After an unsuccessful attempt at horse trading, the Indians went on their way.

On September 7 Fisk and fifty-eight men reached Fort Benton, just one year after the arrival of the 1862 expedition. Here Fisk's official duties ended; he sold his heavier equipment at auction and with twenty of the men moved along the Mullan Road, planning to close out the expedition farther west. Although his orders instructed him to proceed to Walla Walla, he had apparently planned all along to visit the new mines south of the Mullan Road. In any case the Bannack–Virginia City area became his destination. The remainder of the emigrants chose a new captain and followed a day or so behind on the Mullan Road, not certain where they should prospect for gold.[21]

One of the men who remained with Fisk was William H. Holyoke, a young New Yorker who had been a messenger for the Office of Indian Affairs in St. Paul. Holyoke suffered from tuberculosis and undertook the western journey in the hope of improving his health. Although he looked forward eagerly to crossing the summit of the Rockies, it became more and more difficult for him to breathe in the thin mountain air. Young Holyoke insisted on proceeding, but on the morning of September 17 he died quietly as he lay in the expedition flag wagon. "With but a piece of one lung," Fisk wrote, "he undertook a great journey." Word of Holyoke's death was sent to the emigrants traveling behind. When they caught up, the members of the reunited expedition buried Holyoke on a mountain slope overlooking the Little Prickly Pear Valley.[22]

After Holyoke's funeral some of the emigrants stopped to prospect in the valley of the Prickly Pear. Fisk and others followed the Mullan Road to Deer Lodge, where they took a trail which led southward, not far from present-day Butte and Anaconda, through the valley of the Big Hole to Bannack. Nathaniel P. Langford, postmaster of Bannack, headed a delegation of Minnesotans who greeted the Fisk party on Yankee Flats, a grassy plain at the outskirts of the town. "We seemed to have met a band of brothers, so kindly and hospitably were

[21] *Expedition of Captain Fisk,* 22; P. Hannay and others to Fisk, September 7, 1863, James Fisk Papers; Clandening, in *North Dakota Historical Quarterly,* 2:263; *Pioneer,* October 23, 1863. Clandening says the new captain was "G. Diab," apparently a misprint for "G. Dart."
[22] *St. Paul City Directory,* 1863; *Press,* December 16, 1863; *Expedition of Captain Fisk,* 25.

we received," Fisk wrote. He and his men spent several days in Bannack while the captain collected information about the mines and the Minnesotans there.[23]

It was Antoine Freniere's first view of a western mining town and he found conditions shocking. "If there is such a place as hell," he wrote his niece, "this must be the back door to it." When the American flag was hoisted by the Fisk party, Freniere reported "considerable excitement" among the miners, many of whom were secessionists. A great number of the thousand or so persons in Bannack, the guide thought, were the "very worst of characters from all parts of the United States." Half of them did nothing but gamble, drink whisky, "and shoot each other." Knives and revolvers were freely used to settle disputes.[24]

At Bannack Fisk heard that early snows had blocked the passes in the Rockies between him and Walla Walla. He was thus furnished with a good reason for following his inclination to go home by a new route. Assigning Freniere to take the government surveyors on to San Francisco and leaving Johnston in charge of the animals and equipment at Bannack, Fisk went off to investigate conditions at Alder Gulch.[25]

A "sink hole of creation," one of the emigrants called the new settlements, and forthwith made plans to go back East. Fisk received a better impression. The diggings were "said to be as rich as any mines ever worked." He noted that the average miner made about twenty dollars a day, while some claims yielded as high as a hundred dollars daily.[26]

At Virginia City, as at Bannack, Fisk looked for Minnesotans and took note of their activities. A number of them entrusted him with bags of gold for their families back home. One old Minnesota miner gave him some nuggets to deliver to President Lincoln.

In addition to the nuggets, Fisk acquired two pieces of information that were to be valuable to him in the year that followed. Virginia City, he learned, was just north of the forty-fifth parallel, that mystical line of destiny which had inspired some Minnesotans for a decade. He also heard that a party of miners intended the next spring to "get a foothold" in the valley of the Yellowstone, a region supposedly rich in agricultural and mineral prospects. Traces of gold had been found at the mouth of the Bighorn River, and the miners hoped that the government would establish a military post there to protect them from the Crow Indians.

Fisk, beginning to see a role for himself in this enterprise, returned to Bannack and sold the rest of his animals and government equipment. With a valise full of gold and a mind full of equally golden prospects, he, Dibb, and Johnston took the stage for Salt Lake City. During a wretched journey on the Overland Stage Line, Fisk was delayed eighteen days by the loss of his valise, which contained the gold nuggets and his official papers. He recovered it, and he and his party finally reached Minnesota in the middle of December.[27]

---

[23] *Expedition of Captain Fisk,* 26–29.

[24] Freniere to Ellen Brown, October 5, 1863, Brown Papers.

[25] Freniere to Ellen Brown, October 5, 1863, Brown Papers; *Expedition of Captain Fisk,* 29; Fisk to Thomas, October 15, 1863, file F163 AGO 1862, NARG 94; *Pioneer,* October 23, 1863.

[26] *Weekly Press,* November 19, 1863. For Fisk's experiences here and below, see *Expedition of Captain Fisk,* 30, 31.

[27] *Expedition of Captain Fisk,* 31, 33; *Press,* December 15, 1863.

Some of the emigrants Fisk left behind him in the gold fields played noteworthy roles in the settlement of Montana. Antoine Marceau, a French Canadian, became a pioneer settler and wagonmaker at Butte, as well as part owner of a mine near that city. The Reverend Andrew M. Torbet, who conducted Holyoke's funeral, had been a Baptist minister in Minnesota. One of the first Protestant clergymen in Montana, he organized the society that built the Union Church in Virginia City, where he preached a memorable sermon at the funeral of the outlaw, Joseph A. Slade. Accompanying Torbet on the expedition was Thomas G. Merrill, a former principal of schools in St. Paul and Taylors Falls, Minnesota. In Montana he invested in mines and mining machinery before returning to Minnesota, where he married Torbet's daughter. Some years later he settled in Helena and managed the Merrill Mining Company, which reportedly owned some of the most valuable mines in the territory.[28]

It is likely that J. R. Anderson of the Fisk train was the picturesque Joseph R. or "Skookum Joe" Anderson who was one of the discoverers of the copper mines in the Stillwater, Montana, area. Simeon Estes, who drove the expedition's flag wagon, was originally from Maine and a house painter by trade, though he had also worked for a cotton-buying firm in Alabama before he moved to Minnesota. In Montana he joined the Vigilantes who fought road agents in the mining settlements. He later raised stock and operated a stage-freight station at Watson.[29]

Perhaps the most unusual of the group who went with Fisk in 1863 was Reginald Stanley, an Englishman. Born in Cornwall in 1838, he was the son and grandson of Wesleyan Methodist ministers. He had come to the United States in 1857 at the age of nineteen and spent the next five or six years in logging, farming, trapping, and fighting Indians. Stanley was known as "Bob" or "Robert" because, as he wrote many years later, "Reginald was voted altogether too sentimental a cognomen to suit the buckskin period of Montana." Early in 1864 he and three companions discovered gold at a gulch they named Last Chance — the future site of Helena. Three years later Stanley returned to England with a fortune in gold which he invested in a variety of business and philanthropic enterprises. His buffalo coat embroidered in fine Indian beadwork is now among the treasures of the British Museum.[30]

[28] For Marceau, see Fogarty, "Butte in the Sixties," and *Helena Independent*, November 10, 1906. For Torbet, see United States Manuscript Census Schedules, 1860, Chisago County, Minnesota, p. 613; Henry A. Castle, *History of St. Paul and Vicinity*, 2:545 (Chicago, 1912); "Historical Address by Hon. H. S. Blake," owned by Frank Carey, Virginia City, Montana; and the diary of Mrs. Wilbur Fisk Sanders, owned by Charles Bovey, Great Falls, Montana. For Merrill, *Weekly Pioneer*, July 27, 1866; *Taylors Falls Reporter*, April 2, 1864; Leeson, ed., *Montana*, 1236.
[29] For Anderson, see *Billings Gazette*, February 4, 1898, June 30, 1927, p. 17; for Estes, *Anaconda Standard*, May 17, 1909, p. 3; Leeson, ed., *Montana*, 968.
[30] *Helena Weekly Herald*, October 19, 1882; S. H. Barlow, Nuneaton, England, to the author, April 14, 29, June 2, 10, September 10, 1964, in MiHS; Leeson, ed., *Montana*, 1253.

1863 ✿✿✿✿✿✿✿✿✿✿✿✿✿✿✿✿✿✿✿

Dr. W. D. Dibb's Diary of
the Fisk Expedition[1]

THE RENDEZVOUS THIS YEAR was Fort Ripley[2] and the time for gathering was the 20th June, but we did not leave the fort until the 25th June owing to some delay in lost horses, getting provisions, gun &c. From [Lieut.] Col: [Henry C.] Rogers commg the post we received every kindness & attention. Here we got a 12 lb Howitzer & ammunition, & filled our stock of supplies, clothing &c.

We were joined here by Mess[s] [Frederick G.] Hesse, [Peter] Hannay, & [John] Major. These gentlemen were to form part of an Expedition for the survey of the boundary between Oregon and Washington Tery.[3] While in Camp we had daily Exercise in Cavalry drill. Here we secured "Shortie" for a cook.

June 25. We broke camp. Previous to getting off, we went across the [Mississippi] river to the fort to take leave of the Col: & Officers. [4 miles]

[June 26.] We then passed the Indian Agency at "Crow Wing" and remained in camp on June 27. Camping on Crow Wing River. Emigrants & Guard were assembled to hear the rules & regulations of travel & of camp duty. [9 miles][4]

[June 29. 4 miles.]

[1] Dibb's diary, in the possession of Mr. Gerald E. Fitzgerald of St. Paul, is reproduced with the permission of the owners; the MiHS has photostatic and typewritten copies. Dibb did not give mileages for portions of the journey which followed the 1862 trail. Figures have been supplied in brackets from the diaries of William H. Holyoke in the MiHS and Clandening, in *North Dakota Historical Quarterly*, 2:247–271. The figures are approximate, since the two diarists did not always agree.

[2] Fort Ripley, a military post established in 1848–49, was located on the west side of the Mississippi River, a few miles below the mouth of the Crow Wing. From its preliminary rendezvous at St. Cloud the expedition traveled up the military road on the east side of the Mississippi, camped on that side, and crossed to the fort by the military ferry to get supplies.

[3] Daniel G. Major — astronomer, surveyor, and former acting master of the United States Naval Observatory — contracted with the General Land Office in May, 1863, to survey a portion of the Oregon-Washington boundary. Associated with him were Hesse, former professor of mathematics at the observatory; Hannay, a Washington patent lawyer; John Major; and Alfred H. Jones. Neither Daniel Major nor Jones joined Fisk. See Contract no. 72 and Bond, file 21512, and vol. 20, p. 103–115, 425, division E, records of the surveyors general, NARG 49; *Boyd's Directory of Washington, D.C.*, 1860; *Hutchinson's Washington and Georgetown Directory*, 1863.

[4] The train apparently crossed the Mississippi River at Crow Wing, an important trading center and mission site at the juncture of the Mississippi and Crow Wing rivers in the 1860s. The

July 1. Reached the [Wadena] Crossing of Crow Wing River — after much delay in mending the Corduroy roads and bridges. [16⅔ miles] [5]

5. Remained in camp, waiting for Major [Alfred H.] Jones & Major Jun[r].

6. These men not arriving we left the crossing, & started for Ottertail lake — bridges bad — & all need repair. [17½ miles] [6]

July 8. We passed "Ottertail City" and found the City entirely deserted by White men, on account of indian Massacre of last year. Some few families of Chippewa indians occupied some of the houses. Camped this evening on "Ottertail Lake." Country around is rolling, with clumps of trees — feed good. This will be a good & pleasant country when settled. [15¾ miles] [7]

9. Today we passed a beautiful chain of lakes "Wood Lake" — "Battle Lake" &c, & camped on "Long Lake." Country like that around Ottertail — these lakes are good water. [13½ miles] [8]

10. Passed thro' thick timber Oak, Elm, Bass &c. Afternoon we found the wood afire on either side of the road, & on getting out of the timber, found the prairie or [sic] burning for miles around. Pushed on for "Bass Lake" which we reached in the evening, & camped — good water grass, & wood.[9] [15½ miles]

11. Travelled over beautiful prairie to Dayton & here nooned. Here the people had been murdered by the Sioux. houses & mill burned — broken wagons, machines, plows &c were broken & scattered around. Went on & camped at the old crossing of Ottertail river. A party of Cavalry camped on the other side. [20½ miles][10]

12. When the Cavalry started, our horses took a stampede, & ran back some 8 or 10 miles. We started & passed over level prairie to the Red river & camped some 4 miles below Breckenridge. The hotel was burned down since last year. [18½ miles]

Chippewa Indian Agency was located on the north side of the Crow Wing, some three miles above its mouth. From June 26 to 28 the train camped about six miles from the agency on a bend of the Crow Wing, near its juncture with the Gull River. Holyoke Diary, June 26–28; June Drenning Holmquist and Jean A. Brookins, *Minnesota's Major Historic Sites: A Guide*, 73 (St. Paul, 1963); William W. Folwell, *A History of Minnesota*, 2:374 (St. Paul, 1961).

[5] On June 29 the camp was moved four miles to get more feed for the cattle. The train forded the Crow Wing at the Wadena crossing, just north of the mouth of the Partridge River. This crossing, which was also the site of a frontier trading post, should not be confused with the present-day town of Wadena, some miles to the west. Holyoke Diary, June 29, July 1; Clandening, in *North Dakota Historical Quarterly*, 2:250.

[6] On July 6 the expedition nooned on the Wing River and camped on "Bungo Creek." Dibb had no entry for July 7. Since the doctor probably attended an emigrant who was injured when he fell under a moving wagon, he may have been too busy to write in his diary. On that day the expedition traveled sixteen miles and camped on the Leaf River. Holyoke Diary, July 6, 7; Clandening, in *North Dakota Historical Quarterly*, 2:251.

[7] During the 1850s Otter Tail City, at the northeast end of Otter Tail Lake, was an important trading post on the Red River Trail from Crow Wing to Pembina. See Upham, *Minnesota Geographic Names*, 390. The night camp was about seven miles west of the city. Holyoke Diary, July 8; Clandening, in *North Dakota Historical Quarterly*, 2:251.

[8] The larger lakes of this chain are now known as East and West Battle lakes in Otter Tail County. Long Lake is probably the one located in Tordenskjold Township in the same county. See also Clandening, in *North Dakota Historical Quarterly*, 2:252, and Holyoke Diary, July 9.

[9] This was probably the Bass Lake directly east of present-day Fergus Falls.

[10] The cavalry was escorting a mail carrier and a supply train returning to St. Paul from Fort Abercrombie. Holyoke Diary, July 11. The emigrants followed close to Fisk's 1862 route from this point until August 4. See above, p. 52–60.

13. Nooned about one or two miles from fort Abercrombie. Afternoon train passed the fort & went on to the "Wild-rice" river & camped. The river was dry at the crossing — only water in a pool a little down the river — grass not good, parched wood plenty. [15 miles]

July 14. Remained in Camp all day. Got stores &c from the fort — repair wagons — shoe up horses & mules &c. In the eveng — got instructions as to the order of March — keeping guard — feeding stock &c. Capt. & I dines with Major [George A.] Camp, Commg. the post.

Officers this year were Capt. Fisk — commg. 1st Assistant Geo. Dart — 2nd d[itt]o. S. H. Johnston — Physician & Surgeon W. D. Dibb — Wagon Master Geo. Northup — Sioux interpreter — Antoine Freniere — Chippeway interpreter R. D. Campbell. The guard was 50 men. Wagons were numbered.

15. Broke camp passed Mud Lake & forded the Sheyenne river without much trouble only a little grading.[11] There was only one stringer left of the bridge we built last year [July 9, 1862]. Camped on our old ground — feed good. [10 miles]

16. Travel over to Maple river — very little water in the river — feed good. [18 miles]

17. Loaded with three days wood as there is none to the second crossing of Sheyenne. Nooned at a small branch of the Maple river. About noon Antoine killed the first buffalo. I got one after nooning. We saw a few antelope today. Camped on second crossing of Maple. [20 miles]

18. Rainy morning — travelled a marshy country but good for travel this dry sun [summer?]. Camp on a pond. [18 miles]

19. Reached second crossing of Sheyenne. Crossed & camped on the bank. Here struck Sibley's trail. [8 miles][12]

20. Rolling prairie with good feed — passed one of Sibley's camps — earth-works & rifle pits — picked up 2 mules & a horse. We used water got from the well dug by Sibley. [20½ miles]

21. Reached lakes Lydia & Jessie, Lydia named after the Capt's wife. Were here visited by some officers & men from Camp Atchison, left there by Sibley who had gone towards the Missouri. [11 miles][13]

July 22. We laid over today & dined by invitation with the officers of Sibley's expedition, & had a good time. Genl Sibley had gone south after the Sissiton Sioux who were making for the Missouri. [113 miles from Fort Abercrombie]

23. Some of the officers rode with us this morng some distance & then bade us a hearty good-bye. Crossed Stevens' "bad slough," but it was dry. Halted at

[11] Clandening wrote that the river was two feet deep and about twenty feet wide; the west bank was so steep that some wagons used seven teams of oxen to get up. *North Dakota Historical Quarterly,* 2:253.

[12] Sibley, with about 3,300 men, was traveling from the Minnesota River Valley toward Devils Lake, North Dakota. For his campaign, see Carley, *Sioux Uprising of 1862,* 72, and Sibley Diary, 1863, Sibley Papers, in MiHS. For his route and camps of July 16 and 17 mentioned in the next entry, see Wright, in *North Dakota History,* 29:283–296.

[13] The train left Sibley's trail about four miles before making camp, traveled to the west of Lake Lydia (Addie), and camped between the two lakes. Clandening, in *North Dakota Historical Quarterly,* 2:254; *Expedition of Captain Fisk,* 5. Sibley's entrenched Camp Atchison was about two miles to the southwest. The general had learned of a concentration of Sioux on the coteau and set out after them on July 20, taking about two thousand men of his command. See Sibley Diary, July 18–20, 1863.

noon on a small circular lake which was named "Lake Dibb," feed good — no timber. Camped on a small pond. [17 miles]

24. Passed "Lake Townsend." Nooned at a pond of good water — & camped on the James river. [25½ miles]

25. Prairie travel. Nooned with good feed & water. Two of our scouts saw 5 men & 1 squaw — learned there were 20 or 30 Sioux lodges, south of us — but [on] our approach they moved off. Camped on three lakes which were named "Trinity Lakes" — feed & water but no wood. [20½ miles] [14]

26. Crossed the third crossing of Sheyenne river nearly dry — travel for the Butte [de] Morale near which we camped.

Today Geo. Northup — George Geire — & R. D. Campbell deserted us, taking with them three good horses, a mule, Carbines, revolver &c. [24½ miles] [15]

27. To[day] pushed for Bass-wood island. Good feed — water — & wood near. I ran an old buffalo & wounded him on the lake shore. When he swam to the middle, & stayed there showing only his head but a good shot reached him there. So he came quietly out to be killed. [11½ miles]

28. To day we visited a large camp of Red river hunters, their camp was 2 or 3 miles south of our track. They were busy drying meat. The party numbered 600 hunters. Capt. F. gave authority to the head hunter [Captain Edward Harmon] to recover the property taken by the deserters. They speak [of] seeing about 1,000 Sioux one day S[outh] of us. [20½ miles] [16]

July 29. Crossed Wintering river. Saw large herds of buffalo here & killed all we wanted. Made the crossing easily, as it was nearly dry. Visited by 3 or 4 hunters. [16 miles]

30. Travel towards Mouse [Souris] river. Today saw immense herds of buffalo. We keep at the heads of the Coulées — & camp on last years ground (wh[ich] was on July 27). Good camp — intend to stay here tomorrow — as some hunters visit us who are about to return, we write home. [18 miles] [17]

31. In Camp — tinker up — shoot at a mark.

August 1. Travel along the heads of the Coulés towards the Côteaux du Missouri — dug in a coulé for water — feed good. [23 miles]

2. Same kind of travel [as] yesterdays. Lieut. Johnston found a curious figure, made by stuffing a wolfskin & setting it upright on a stake — a cross stick supported the forelegs like arms — & wolf's head, covered with a gay scarlet cloth

[14] The lakes may have been those northeast of Hamburg in Wells County, North Dakota.

[15] The third crossing of the Sheyenne was seven and a half miles from the evening camp, which was made on a small lake north of the butte. In the Robert Strong version of Dibb's diary, the July 26 entry, after the first sentence, reads: "During the evening there was considerable talk around the camp fire of the gold country to the west of us, and in the morning we found that George Northrup [sic] George Geire [sic] and R. D. Campbell had deserted us, taking with them three good horses, a mule, carbines, revolver, etc. The captain said he believed the men had headed for the gold country, thinking to 'make a stake.'"

[16] On this day the expedition took a "pass" through the coteau which Fisk claimed to have discovered in 1862 and traveled near the chain of White Wood Lakes which extended almost to the Souris River. See Bond, "Journal," July 22, 1862; Clandening, in *North Dakota Historical Quarterly*, 2:256; *Expedition of Captain Fisk*, 7.

[17] The camp of July 30 and 31 was about five miles from the Souris River and approximately 268 miles from Fort Abercrombie. Fisk to General [Lorenzo Thomas], July 31, 1863, in file 194F 1863, NARG 94; *Pioneer*, September 2, 1863.

cap, worked with beads &c. On the arms were hung small wooden arrows, painted red, — tobacco &c. Antoine calls it a "War Sacrifice" of the Sioux. [9½ miles]

3. High level prairie. Camped near 3 lakes — one good water — other two bad. Buffalo out of all number. [18 miles]

4. This year we kept nearer the Côteau du Miss: on account of water — about 12 [2?] miles from the "Riviere des Lacs" — which is here only a chain of lakes — the bed of the stream between was dry this year. This afternoon we left the old trail of last year, as it led to Ft Union, & we intended to strike nearly direct west, & reach Milk River somewhere about the second or third crossing. Camp near 2 or 3 small lakes. [21 miles]

August 5. We passed thro' part of the Côteau taking a westerly course. About noon we passed the highest hill — a good land mark, which was named "Freniere Mount." We observed around the Mount the marks of old indian Encampments. In the afternoon we came out to level prairie, & took a N.W. course to get round a point of the Côteau which juts out to the N. Travel 16 miles N.W.

6. Our course still partly in the Côteau, but soon get out on prairie. Camped near our old Camp [August 2 and 3, 1862] — here was a medicine lodge, with recent traces of teepees.[18] 12.25 miles N.W.

7. Today we struck out into the prairie a little north of the Côteau — passing a good large lake a few miles to the right. Camped on a coulé feed scarce, & not much water. 23 miles.

8. Rolling prairie. Lieut: Johnston & myself saw an indian, & after a little race brought him in to the train. Antoine had a talk with him — he was an Assiniboine of "Broken Arm's" band — said they had 145 lodges a little to N. & they would see us at our night camp. Our course got a little S of W this afternoon. Camped on a Coulé & opened an old spring [.] Travel 16.50 S of W.

9. The indians (some Chiefs) came over last night, & we [kept] them until this morning. The Chiefs had a great talk with the Capt. They (or old "Broken Arm") remembered me at once & wanted more medicine, especially some "Smelling Medicine" (snuff). he said he had given [it] to his young men, I suppose in all cases, & it was very good, so he had to get a further supply. They admitted me into their tribe under the name of "Pejuta-wish-ash-ita." which Antoine says means "the Medicine-Man of the Whites." The Capt was admitted under a name still more terrible "Ah-Kichita-honka-na-me-ne-she-ne." *i.e.* "The Chief Soldier that never turns back." (from the remembrance of last year). Lieut: Johnston they called "Wa-to-pan" *i.e.* "dug-out" or "Canoe." In asking as to the country direct W they gave a very poor account. No water — no grass, all burnt — in fact nothing. They strongly advised us to strike & follow the Missouri & Milk rivers — but they appeared to have other reasons for this account & we paid little or no attention to it. We remained in camp all day (Sunday). They stayed with us until noon, examining horses, guns &c. I gave them medicines, as near as I could guess, for their sick.[19]

[18] See *Expedition of Captain Fisk*, 12.

[19] The Robert Strong version of the Dibb diary contains this additional sentence: "Old 'Broken Arm' called me aside just before his party went off, gave me a handsome whip ornamented with a human scalp, and told me in a mysterious way of a 'yellow land' off to the west, which he said the Indians there guarded closely and drove out everyone but members of their own tribe."

August 10. Travelled over prairie until noon, & then entered a chain of mountains (afterward known to be "Wood Mountains"[)]. Camped at night on a nearly dry pond, but with a good spring in the middle — good feed — no wood. 19.50 course W.[20]

11. Our road was thro' these mountains. Nooned on a lake with good water, & feed — in the afternoon passed a number of saline lakes quite dry. Camped at a spring, water, & grass. Mr [Joseph O.] Hamel has not come in yet — fire the gun & get out lights — but no Hamel. 16 [miles]. Course W.

12. Mr H came in early this morning — heard one of the guns, but was too far off — so concluded he would try in the morning. Today passed more dry saline lakes. Nooned on a marsh with good water & grass. Camped on a lake — water not first rate — feed good. About 2 miles north of camp — is a steep, high mountain — good land mark. Known to the indians as "Haraka-o-weran" *i.e.* "Where the Elk feeds." We voted one & all to call it "Mount Fisk." 22. miles W.[21]

13. Having found a fine spring with good feed about ½ a mile up a ravine the train moved there & stopped for the day. While scouting near Mount Fisk — Lieut: Johnston saw an indian watching him from a distance — he went to him & brought him to camp — he was Assiniboine of Whirlwind's band — had with him 3 squaws, two wives & his mother-in-law — said he had been hunting buffalo in the mountains north. When asked how far this range extended — he said there was "no end to it — he had been travelling two or three weeks in order to join his band." He was carrying dried meat on "travaires" [travois] hauled by dogs — he had a poor pony to carry his goods. Altogether he was a poor, dirty looking fellow & did not seem to know much.

14. Today we Kept in the valleys, & by noon got among some pretty rough looking mounta[i]n scenery — broken & worn by the action of rain & winds. We wound our way thro' the valleys without trouble, & camped in a large valley on a stream which we supposed to be one of the heads of the Big Muddy [Creek] — good grass good spring water — wood in Coulés near. Travel 17 miles. W.

15. Kept on a W course in the valleys — the ridges lofty. Camped on a small stream running S — which we named "Antelope Creek" [Big Muddy] from the number on it when we approached — grass good — water slightly saline — no wood. 16.50 miles W.

16. Remained in Camp (Sunday).

17. Our road thro' the valleys today was good — ridges not quite so high, or abrupt. Halted at noon at a pool; good spring nearby. Camped on Porcupine [Poplar] river — 15 or 20 feet wide, & from 3 to 5 ft deep. Water good — grass splendid & green. Must have had rain here, & heavy, as the old grass was beaten flat, & the ground marked with it. 15 miles — S. of W.

---

[20] Wood Mountain in southwestern Saskatchewan rises more than three thousand feet above the prairie. *The Encyclopedia of Canada*, 10:358 (Ottawa, 1958). The Fisk train probably traveled in the highlands south of the border on a route across the northern part of Sheridan, Daniels, and Valley counties in Montana. It is very difficult to trace the journey from this point to the Milk River crossing on August 25.

[21] Fisk estimated that the mountain was about fifteen miles south of the border (*Expedition of Captain Fisk*, 15). It may have been in northwestern Divide County, North Dakota, or in northeastern Sheridan County, Montana. The figure of an elk was cut into the top of the peak; see Clandening, in *North Dakota Historical Quarterly*, 2:260.

18. Started at 7 a.m. forded this stream easily — good gravelly bottom. We travelled over the hills this morning in W.S.W. course and halted at noon on a small river. A short distance above us this stream has 3 forks coming from N.W. — W. — & W.S.W.[22] Grass & water good. The prairie was burnt between porcupine & this — but not beyond. 22.50 S. of W.

August 19. Took a W. course halted at noon near a spring. Afternoon travelled about 8 miles in same valley — then crossed some ridges a little S. of W. & got into another valley running parallel with the last. Camped on a small river, some 15 or 20 ft wide & 2 or 3 ft deep. Crossed a large indian trail going N. Saw some buffaloes today. Yesterday in the afternoon we saw a large seam of coal on the bank of a small stream, the seam as we saw it was from 10 to 15 ft thick & the coal burned well. Camped on the above river — good grass, & water, no wood 21.50 S. of W.

August 20. Course along the same valley — halted at noon on the head waters of porcupine [Porcupine Creek] — good grass. Afternoon we had some rather rough travelling — & Camped on a nearly dry stream. Capt. made a good shot at an Antelope, running hitting him at 250 yards — he ran about 50 yards & dropped. 20 W.

21. Travel rough — at 3 miles we struck Little Porcupine [Rock Creek] — & camped on it in the Eveng with good feed & water — no wood. 15. W.

22. Mountain travel all morning — towards night passed down a long & narrow coulé to the banks of a large river (heard at Benton they call it "Frenchman's Fork" [Frenchman Creek] of Milk river). This river varies from 50 to 100 ft — no stream now — but water in pools at the bends — the banks &c & the Cottonwood timber makes it resemble Milk river. Plenty of wood & water, but grass poor & scarce. I killed 2 buffaloes coming down to the river — one old bull being worried by the dogs dashed towards the train — went between two yoke of cattle & snapped the chain like a thread. Antoine got us a splendid fat cow for supper, & tomorrow. The valley here is narrow — hemmed in by bold & lofty bluffs. 19 S. of W.[23]

23. Sunday — remain camped here.[24] Capt. & I rode out this morning to explore the country ahead of us — & try to find a good route towards the Milk River. After riding near 20 miles & getting on the highest peak we could see the Milk river winding thro' the valley below us — we could also see the Little Rocky & Bear's Paw Mountains which made us quite easy as to our whereabouts — found a good road to the Milk & got home in the Eveng having ridden some 40 or 50 miles. Professor Hesse had taken an observation to day & found we were in Latitude 48° 46' [4]7".

24. Crossed Frenchman's fork & ascended the heights to the S. working our way thro' the Coulés — rough road but with removing the large boulders, the train got along pretty well. Nooned near a bend of the river. Afternoon went over

---

[22] This stream, unnamed in the diaries, may have been the west fork of the Poplar River.

[23] Clandening said the coulee was "the worst place I ever drove a waggon through." Fisk reported that half an inch of ice formed in a pail of water during the night. *North Dakota Historical Quarterly*, 2:262; *Expedition of Captain Fisk*, 18.

[24] The camp would have been north of Valleytown, Montana, and about fifteen miles from the Canadian border.

a rough hilly country & camped at night near same stream — tolerable feed plenty water & wood. 13 S.W.

25. Crossed some rough hills this morning. Came in sight of Milk river about 11 am   the Little Rocky & Bears Paw being just visible. We saw these last year on the same day.

We descended to the [Milk] river, & crossed, a few miles W. of Frenchman's fork — & camped at noon a short distance up the river. River nearly dry — but water in pools — grass very poor plenty of cottonwood. 8.50 S.W.

We remarked towards sunset that Mr Major had not come in — he had started to walk ahead this morning & had not been seen since. We suppose he may have struck our old trail, which is not far from here, and followed that. We fired the howitzer several times but he did not come in. After sunset some 13 indians came dashing thro' the cottonwood, crossed the river, & rode into camp — they were Gros Ventres — they made us understand by signs that they heard our guns — their camp being some miles up river on the other side — they stayed the night with us. No news of Mr Major.

August 26. Left at 7 am. We left a large govern[men]t wagon, & packed the commissary stores in the others. Struck the old trail in about 3 miles & followed it. We had scouts out all around on the look out for Mr Major — & two were sent back to yesterdays camp — last night was cold, & he had no blanket. Halted at noon on a dry lake, 11 miles out, no wood or grass. This afternoon I was certain I had discovered Mr M's track in the dusty road on a head of us — two men were sent on with food & drink. We found a good spring & feed 6 miles from nooning & camped. At 12:30 [A.M.] Mr Major was brought in — the men [Johnston and Hugh Miller] who went to seek him say they rode some 16 miles to another crossing of the river — they saw the tracks in the road for only a short distance — so that on reaching the crossing, they felt sure Mr M. must be back & off the road. After riding 3 or 4 miles back, they saw some dark object lying on the ground near the trail — it was Mr. M.   his cry was for water, as he had drunk nothing since 10 am. the previous day — they got him on one of their poneys — & in coming back they met two other scouts, whom they sent on to camp — when the Capt. sent the flag wagon with provisions & water — but he only wanted drink, his mouth & throat were completely parched — he had travelled night & day to overtake us feeling confident we were on ahead when he struck the old trail. Capt. & I shot an old grizzly bear on the river bottom — he appeared to be hunting for roots. Two very large rattlesnakes were also killed today. There was a large camp of Gros Ventres near our nooning place. 17. W.[25]

August 27. Travelled over rolling prairie to the second [Milk River] crossing — good ford. Followed the old trail, & camped on the river — poor feed — plenty of wood & water. We had a regular chase after a grizzly among the trees & willows — a number of shots were fired at him, but he got away by crossing the river. 19.50 W.

28. Road along the bottom. Camp on river   grass poor. I killed a nice black tailed deer. 15. W.

29. Still along the river — & camp with more feed. Today I got a wild goose &

[25] See also *Expedition of Captain Fisk,* 19.

some [prairie] Chickens. Some of the others got 3 buffaloes & a fine doe. 22.25 N. of W.

30. Sunday. Remained in camp. Had quite a variety for dinner — venison — buff. steaks — wild-goose — chickens, &c &c.[26]

31. On the river bottom — road sandy. Met some teams going down to Fort St Charles for Quartz Mill Machinery for Col. Hunkins of Bannack. They tell us of the new discovery on the Stinking water which they describe as rich. Grass better. 22.25 N. of W.[27]

September 1. Travelled today 10 miles & halted for noon & camped in a fine clump of cottonwoods with good grass & water 10. N. of W.

2. Go over rolling prairie, noon on a bend of [Milk] river. Afternoon we leave the river & strike towards Bear paw Mountains. Camped on Beaver Creek. 20. S.W.[28]

3. Good road to Box Elder Creek — passed the Bears Paw. Camp on Box Elder. Meet a large oxtrain belonging to the Fur Company — also one from Virginia City. Lieut: Johnston & Antoine Freniere started on ahead for Fort Benton — to get shoes &c prepared. The men having charge of these trains say there is little difficulty in passing thro' the Bear Paw range with wagons to the Missouri. 16.50 S.W.

4. Crossed the Big Sandy at 5.50 miles — good grass & water — then put across the prairie for the springs & camped. We met here Mr Vanderburg who gave us a fuller account of the new "diggins." [23 miles][29]

5. The road was over high rolling prairie to the Marias river — getting down to the river bottom is by a long steep pitch — but luckily sandy — so the wagons can hold back a little. We met here with Mr [Andrew] Dawson who has charge of the Fort who was going after his train — but he gave us letters to Mr [George] Steele to get all we wanted. This is a good camping place — we here taste the first sweet mountain water. 13. S.W.[30]

6. Left at 8 a.m. followed the valley of the Marias to the Teton river — & camped. This is the nearest camping ground to the Fort, some 4 miles from us. We reached here last year on the same date. Fired a salute with the howitzer — and prepared for a 2 or 3 days rest. 7.25 S.W.

September 7. Rode over to Ft Benton & were well received by Mr Steele who forwarded what goods &c. we wanted as fast as possible. We met here many freighters from Virginia [City] & Bannack — they had to go down to Shreveport

[26] The wild game was served with " 'Worcester sauce,' good hot bread, sirup, tea, coffee, &c; pretty good living for the wilderness." *Expedition of Captain Fisk,* 20.

[27] The expedition probably crossed Battle Creek during the day and camped on Lodge Creek; see p. 63, above. For more details of the encounter with the teams, see *Expedition of Captain Fisk,* 21.

[28] As in 1862, the train crossed the Milk River at this point, near present-day Havre. See p. 63, above.

[29] In the Robert Strong version of the Dibb diary this additional sentence appears: "He had heard vague rumors of a rich gold hill in the 'yellow country,' but could not trace it to anything definite. 25.50 miles S W." "Vanderburg" may be the C. C. Vandenburg of the Holmes 1862 train.

[30] Andrew Dawson of Pierre Chouteau, Jr., and Company had been at Fort Benton since 1854. See Bond, "Journal," September 4, 1862; *Montana Historical Contributions,* 10:266. Steele was a clerk at the fort. See *Montana Historical Contributions,* 3:286.

for their goods as the boats could not get up to Benton on account of the low water. In the afternoon the Capt. sold by auction the heavy wagons, tents, & stores. Capt. bid farewell to the Emigrants & received a letter, signed by all, of thanks for his care & approval of his conduct along the route. We saw here a party going to the Saskatchewan river — they report the diggings there as being very rich. Having given the measured distances from here thro' the mountains in our first trip it will not be necessary to repeat just giving a few heads as we go along.

11. Reached Sun River. [55 miles]

12. Went up to the crossing. Mr [Malcolm] Clark is on the Govt farm — he does not farm much, but has a good quantity of stock. Saw one of the Fathers from the Mission some 15 miles from here. There are 3 missions thro' the mountains — by the Jesuit Fathers — this one — one among the Pend d'Oreilles, & Flatheads — one among the Co[e]ur d'Alenes. [7 miles][31]

13. Crossed Sun river — passed Crown Butte — & camp near the Bird tail rock. [17 miles]

14. Travelled over for the Dearborn river & camp. While riding a-head of the train towards the river in company with Capt., Lieut: Johnston, & Antoine — armed & in our usual rig — we observed a man riding up a ravine leading to the river — we spurred on to intercept him, thinking to get news from Bannack — the stranger catching sight of us rode up slowly — looking scared — but on seeing Lieut: J. he rode up & saluted him cordially, having seen him at Ft Benton. Having talked a little he asked us to help him look for his purse which he had thrown among the grass as he was coming up to us, taking us for "Road Agents" *i.e.* highwaymen. After some searching we found his bag of gold dust — about $3,000. [17 miles][32]

September 15. Struck the Little Prickly Pear river & followed the valley. Crossed the P. Pear Spur — & the Medicine rock — & camped near [John B.] Morgan's ranch on the river at last crossing [18 miles?][33]

16. Remained in camp — poor [William] Holyoke suffers heavily in this sharp mountain air. Morgan gets a good many beaver on the river here. He is building a large log house & corral.

17. Start at 8 am. Holyoke did not rest last night, had to be raised up to breathe at all — this morning he was very anxious to be starting had a great wish to reach or cross the summit ridge — made him a bed in the flagwagon so that he could

[31] On Clark, formerly of the American Fur Company, see Bond, "Journal," September 5, 1862; Charlotte O. Van Cleve, "A Sketch of the Early Life of Malcolm Clark," and Helen P. Clarke, "Sketch of Malcolm Clarke," in *Montana Historical Contributions,* 1:90–98, 2:255–268 (Helena, 1876, 1896). James Vail, who had been in charge of the farm in 1862, had gone to the Bannack gold mines. *Expedition of Captain Fisk,* 23.
St. Peter's Mission to the Blackfeet was located on the north bank of the Missouri, six miles above the mouth of the Sun River. The others mentioned were probably the mission of St. Ignatius and the Coeur d'Alene mission. See Bischoff, *Jesuits in Old Oregon,* 86–94, and Chittenden and Richardson, *Life, Letters and Travels of Father De Smet,* 60.
[32] Fisk said that his party wore buckskin suits, were fully armed, and probably looked "somewhat 'wild.'" *Expedition of Captain Fisk,* 24.
[33] The first sentence of this entry apparently belongs with the events of September 14. According to Fisk's account, the group crossed the Little Prickly Pear twenty-one times that day and camped near the spur. The next day they crossed the spur, as Dibb states. For more details of the campsite and Morgan, see *Expedition of Captain Fisk,* 25; *Montana Historical Contributions,* 10:295.

either sit or lay. We had travelled about a mile — I was at the head of the train, some 50 or 80 rods in advance — a messenger came for me to see him — rode quickly back — but he was dead — he appeared to have died without a struggle. We turned back to Morgans & camped to wait for the Emigrants to come up as they were one or one & a half day behind us. He bore his sufferings very patiently — never complaining — & generally in the best of cheer.

18. The Emigrants arrived last night. Today we buried Holyoke — Mr [Andrew M.] Torbet conduct'd the burial service. The coffin was covered with our old flag — every one followed to the grave — the guard firing three volleys over the grave. he was buried on a knoll near Morgan's Ranch — a rough headstone was got out — having the name cut on it. The Capt. arranged with Morgan to fence, plant trees around it, &c. This was felt to be a sad day by all of us — he was so generally well liked. He always expressed a strong wish to reach & cross the summit of the mountains — he failed by one days travel.

September 19. We again left the Emigrants — crossing Silver Creek — camping on the Big Prickley Pear with wood, water, & grass. Met today with a band of 300 Pend d'Oreilles, going on a hunt for buffalo south of Benton. They are mostly Catholic — civil & well behaved. The diggins in the P. P. valley are S.E. of our camp — but not much has been done yet. Our party of the first year stopped here — but not long — leaving for Bannack & Virginia. [22 miles]

20. Crossed the Summit of the Rocky Mounts about 3 or 4 miles from camp — fired a salute & passed along Summit [Otter?] creek towards the Little Bl[ac]kfoot river — camping on that stream. This creek abounds in Beaver dams every 30 or 40 rods. Prospected on this river & found from 2 to 10 cts to the pan. Plenty of speckled trout in this stream. [17 miles]

21. Along the valley of Little Blkfoot to Livingstone [Cottonwood?] Creek — then descend into Deerlodge valley, & camp near Johnny Grant's. [17 miles] [34]

22. Crossed the Deerlodge, & moved 3 or 4 miles further up river — stop to recruit stock. Got about 60 trout this afternoon.

23. Moved on — forded 3 creeks, & halted at noon on Warm Spring Creek — near us are the "Warm Springs." The largest one has formed from deposits of the water a circular conical mound about 50 ft high — appears to be Magnesium limestone — the water now bubbles up to the surface but does not run over — temperature about 100° F. Around the base of this are numerous springs on a level with the surface of the ground — & some other mounds forming — the temperature of some of these was 150° F. & over. Afternoon crossed the river, & Camped on the last crossing [Silver Bow Creek].[35] Capt. & I shooting together got 2 nice deer. Lost a mule today.

September 24. Passed over the Divide thro' the Big Hole this morning — this is

[34] DeLacy's "Map of the Territory of Montana" shows the Mullan Road branching before the confluence of the Deer Lodge and Blackfoot rivers and uniting again at American Fork. The route of 1863 appears to have followed the southern branch, or a trail close to it. For a description of the valley, see *Expedition of Captain Fisk*, 26; for Grant, p. 67, above. Fisk's party apparently turned off the Mullan Road the next day, traveling toward Bannack on a branch road which is shown on DeLacy's map.

[35] The crossing of Silver Bow Creek was west of present-day Butte. The Warm Springs mentioned above still exist near the Montana town of that name.

a very [easy] pass — ascent hardly noticed. Camped on last crossing of Divide creek — good feed, & willows. [21 miles][36]

25. Crossed "Moose Creek" & at noon came in sight of "Big Hole" (or "Wisdom") river, a tributary of the Jefferson fork of the Missouri — this is a fine stream 100 or 150 ft wide — with plenty of Cottonwood on the banks — follow'd down to a bridge but this was out of repair — so we forded — the current was rapid, & the bottom full of loose boulders in about 3 ft of water. This must be deep & rapid in the spring. We met this noon with Geo. White who had been to "the diggins" with vegetables. [18 miles][37]

26. Crossed "Rock Creek," "Willow Creek," and nooned on "Birch Creek" — stopped on this last for camp. The Big hole has a fine valley, some 50 miles long by 15 wide. [9 miles]

27. Travelled to Rattlesnake river & camped.[38] Mines both here & on the Big Hole have been opened, paying from 5 to 10 dollars to the man. [13 miles]

28. Our road today was pretty good, but hilly between here & Bannack City — had a pretty sharp snow storm while on the ridge. We gave them a salute — & camped over the creek, on "Yankee flats." We met here a good many of our last years Comrades, who gave us a hearty welcome. A great many had left for the "Stinking water diggins." This has the appearance of all the mining "Cities!" — log cabins, stores, bakeries, Saloons &c. [16 miles]

The Gulch diggings here are not so rich as at Virginia — quartz is abundant, but the machinery to crush it is wanting. There is only one mill of two horse power, a very primitive affair, but which gets out about 1500$ a week. No doubt a great deal lost in the tailings.

There are plenty of other lodes discovered, but not worked. That [Dakota Lode] being worked (by the two horse power Crusher just spoken of) is very rich. The quartz they are crushing appears to have been burnt, is of a chocolate color, & easily crushed & yields from $300 to $2,000 per cord. Very most of the miners have left here for the Stinkingwater, which as yet is all gulch digging.[39]

We stayed at Con. [Cornelius] Bray's while in Bannack. Pat [Bray] & he have a saw mill which they are having refixed.

We now proceeded to the Stinking water travelling over a hilly sandy & rocky road — the distance being 65 miles Easterly from Bannack.[40] There are 3 points or cities on the [Alder] creek [,] Nevada, Virginia, & Summit, — the whole length of the Claims are 15 miles. Some do not pay much, some very rich. The population on the Creek is about 4000. The houses, stores &c, the same in appearance as at

[36] According to a table of distances appended to the diary, the Fisk party traveled twelve miles to Divide Creek and nine miles farther to the last crossing. The road shown on DeLacy's map makes three crossings of the creek. The camp was probably in the vicinity of present-day Divide in Silver Bow County.

[37] White may have been one of the farmers, described by Fisk, who traveled from Hell Gate to Virginia City to sell potatoes and onions to the miners at very high prices. See *Expedition of Captain Fisk,* 27.

[38] On the Big Hole prairie or basin, see *Expedition of Captain Fisk,* 28. Rattlesnake Creek is shown on DeLacy's map. It is a branch of the Beaverhead River.

[39] For more details on mining operations at Bannack, see *Expedition of Captain Fisk,* 28, 29.

[40] DeLacy's map shows two roads to Virginia City from Bannack and it is not clear which route the Fisk party took. The mines were located on Alder Creek, a branch of the Stinkingwater (the present-day Ruby River).

Bannack but here we have a mining city in full blast — stores, saloons, gaming houses, & streets crammed full — dust everywhere plentiful — & the price of everything at the utmost stretch. It would be difficult to give the average yield of the claims. I was at [William] Fairweather's claim twice at the time he washed up — his claim yielded from 75 to 100 to the man per day — others we knew were taking out from 30 to 70 per day — strangers will not tell you what they are doing.[41] We were glad to find most of our fellow travellers of last year doing well. Bevans Gulch is about 12 or 15 miles North of here, which yields well, without so much stripping. There have been discoveries lately at Brown's & Harris Gulch in this vicinity. The U. S. Marshall Estimates the population in & around Virginia diggings at 12,000. A party from Bannack went last year [*sic*] to prospect on the headwaters of the Yellow Stone & found very good promise, but were driven off by the Crow Indians.[42] They went down as far as the Big Horn, on the Yellowstone. We sold most of the stock, wagons, &c &c at Virginia then returned to Bannack, on our way home.

The Express from Bannack to Salt Lake is a primitive affair. A covered wagon drawn by indian ponies. We have to take our provisions along. In crossing the Divide we had a snow storm & very cold weather — some 20° below Zero. We met numerous freight trains & Emigrant wagons. Passed thro' settlements of the Mormons, who farm along the valleys, & have scattering villages all along as you near Salt Lake.[43] Passing in view of the Lake we reached Salt Lake City — which has the appearance of a big country Village — from the lots being of 4 acres, & in many grain is brought from the farms & stacked in the city lot. It is a pleasant site for a City. On many of the streets there is one or two streams of water running by the edge of the sidewalk. Visited the old tabernacle & heard some preaching — saw the foundation for the new one, which is to be a splendid building. Went to the theatre (lately built) which is a very neat building & well fitted up internally. Had a bath in the hot springs in the vicinity of the City. Paid a visit to General [Patrick E.] Connor's Camp, near the City. Then we prepare for the "Overland Stage" trip.

We left Salt Lake City by 4 A.M. — the stage not too full — but full enough, as we travel day & night. Capt. & I stayed over one stage at Fort Bridger to wait for his bedding, robes, &c which had not been put on our stage. We got along pretty well as far as Latham (opposite Denver City) going over a miserable road — with carcasses of Cattle &c all along the road — sandy roads, bad alkali water — &

[41] William Fairweather was one of a party who prospected on Alder Gulch and made the original gold discovery there. See "Journal of Henry Edgar — 1863," in *Montana Historical Contributions*, 3:124–142.

[42] The expedition led by James Stuart in the spring of 1863 to prospect on the Yellowstone is described in "The Yellowstone Expedition of 1863," in *Montana Historical Contributions*, 1:149–233. The party returned to Bannack in June and made plans to renew the project in 1864.

In the Robert Strong version of the Dibb diary the following insertion occurs at this point: "We were shown some of the quartz from a secret lode in the Yellowstone country, and the captain and I determined to go after it, sometime, if we could do so."

[43] Dibb, Fisk, and Johnston traveled from Bannack to Salt Lake City by a road, shown on DeLacy's map, which crossed Horse Plain and Camas creeks and struck the Snake River at a point somewhat north of the mouth of the John Day River. From there they followed General Patrick E. Connor's military trail to Salt Lake by way of Soda Springs, the Bear River, and the present-day towns of Brigham, Logan, and Ogden, Utah. The itinerary is appended to Dibb's diary.

poor feed for ourselves, make this a miserable journey. (Once we had to go 36 hours without food). When we changed coach at Latham, we found the Capt's valise missing — Capt. went back to Cache-la-poudre valley — then got a sargeant & 10 Cavalry, & went up the road some 90 miles & luckily recovered it — it had been picked up by a hay teamster, & taken to their hay-camp. While recovering the valise we had a very heavy hail storm — then snow — which continued for 2 nights & one day — & we had to travel thro' snow down to Atchison. Taking it altogether it was as miserable piece of travel as anyone could go thro'. It took us 3 or 4 days to get our limbs stretched & to get us accustomed to sleeping on a bed. From here we travelled by rail to Chicago, thence to La Crosse — then by stage to St Paul & St Anthony our destination.[44]

[44] Dibb later contrasted his unpleasant experiences on the return journey with the relative ease of travel over the northern trail in a letter to the *State Atlas*, March 9, 1864.

1864

THE HOLMES AND FISK TRAINS

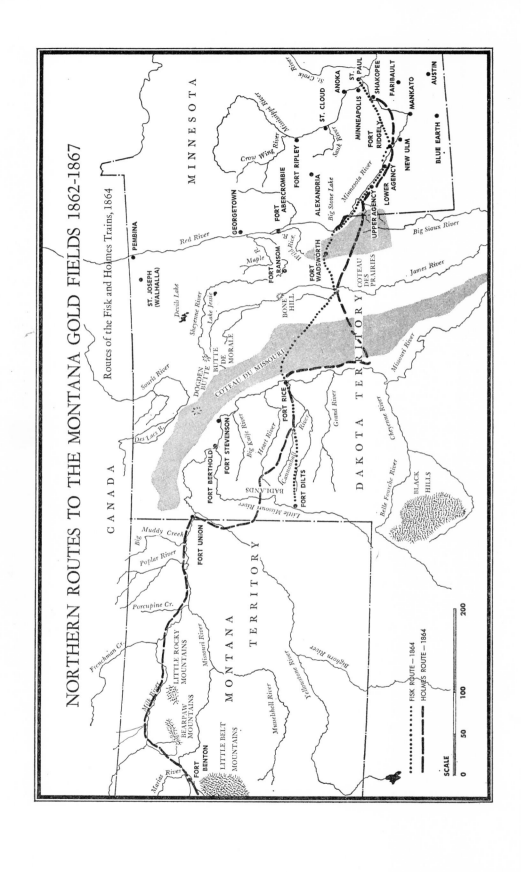

NORTHERN ROUTES TO THE MONTANA GOLD FIELDS 1862–1867

Routes of the Fisk and Holmes Trains, 1864

CANADA

MINNESOTA

M O N T A N A   T E R R I T O R Y

D A K O T A   T E R R I T O R Y

PEMBINA

ST. JOSEPH
(WALHALLA)

GEORGETOWN

FORT
ABERCROMBIE

ALEXANDRIA

ST. CLOUD

ANOKA

MINNEAPOLIS

ST.
PAUL

SHAKOPEE

FARIBAULT

MANKATO

AUSTIN

NEW ULM

BLUE EARTH

FORT
RIDGELY

LOWER
AGENCY

UPPER AGENCY

FORT RIPLEY

FORT
RANSOM

FORT
WADSWORTH

BONE
HILL

FORT BERTHOLD

FORT STEVENSON

FORT RICE

FORT DILTS

BADLANDS

DOGDEN
BUTTE

BUTTE
DE
MORALE

COTEAU DU MISSOURI

COTEAU
DES
PRAIRIES

FORT UNION

FORT
BENTON

LITTLE ROCKY
MOUNTAINS

BEARPAW
MOUNTAINS

LITTLE BELT
MOUNTAINS

BLACK
HILLS

Mississippi River

St. Croix River

Crow Wing River

Sauk River

Minnesota River

Big Stone Lake

Big Sioux River

Red River

Maple R.

Wild Rice R.

James River

Souris River

Des Lacs R.

Sheyenne River

Devils Lake

Lake Jessie

Missouri River

Cannonball River

Little Missouri River

Heart River

Big Knife River

Grand River

Cheyenne River

Belle Fourche River

Missouri River

Big Muddy Creek

Poplar River

Porcupine Cr.

Frenchman Cr.

Milk River

Missouri River

Musselshell River

Yellowstone River

BigHorn River

Marias River

SCALE

0   50   100   200

FISK ROUTE – 1864
HOLMES ROUTE – 1864

1864 ✻✺✺✺✺✺✺✺✺✺✺✺✺✺✺✺✺✺

The Holmes and Fisk Trains

ALTHOUGH SUPPORTERS of northern overland emigration were disappointed because so few emigrants went west in 1863, they soon had cause for a more hopeful outlook. By the end of the year fear of the Indians had somewhat subsided, and the headline news of Fisk's return from his successful journey caught the public's attention. Gold fever once again spread throughout Minnesota. By late spring of 1864 more than four hundred emigrants were ready to leave the state for the gold fields of Idaho Territory, which included what is now Montana. Thomas Holmes led nearly three hundred people safely to Helena; Fisk took a train of perhaps one hundred and seventy emigrants almost to the present Montana border before being turned back by Indian attack.

When St. Paul newspapers gave Fisk banner publicity in December, 1863, the captain moved quickly to take advantage of the bright prospects. On December 29 members of the Minnesota Historical Society braved a bitter north wind and drifting snow to hear Fisk blow the bugle for a splendid new expedition. It was the first lecture in a campaign that took him in the next six weeks to more than half a dozen cities, including Chicago and New York.[1]

Reports in the press suggested that his story was much the same wherever he went. Unfurling the tattered flag which had flown at the head of his two successful expeditions, Fisk demonstrated bugle calls, exhibited gold nuggets, and recounted colorful anecdotes of life on the trail. Describing the valuable mineral deposits of eastern Idaho Territory, he accepted for himself and "his" emigrants a lion's share of credit for their discovery. "Fair Idaho," he proclaimed, welcomed the emigrant "with cheer on her cheeks, and her apron full of nuggets." Gold from the placer mines, promised Fisk, would enrich the enterprising emigrant and help Uncle Sam win the war in the South.[2]

The heart of the 1864 publicity campaign was the promotion of a new, shorter route to the Yellowstone Valley, as well as to the Virginia City and Bannack gold fields which Fisk had investigated at the end of the 1863 season. In focusing on this route, Fisk embraced many ideas attractive to Minnesotans. For some years

[1] *Pioneer,* December 15, 17, 31, 1863, January 1, 1864. For other examples of enthusiasm for the gold fields, see *Mankato Union,* January 1; *Winona Republican,* January 4, 20; *Pioneer,* January 8; *Press,* January 25; *Anoka Star,* January 30 — all in 1864.

[2] *Press,* February 16, 1864.

men like William Windom and James Taylor had favored a route along the forty-fifth parallel, on which lay both St. Paul and Virginia City. Others had proposed a trail due west from the railhead at La Crosse, Wisconsin, across southern Minnesota to the Missouri River, close to the old Nobles wagon road. The practicability of such a road had supposedly been demonstrated by a winter expedition to the Missouri in 1863. Above all other considerations, Fisk emphasized that the proposed route would be as much as five hundred miles shorter than the Stevens trail previously used by himself and Holmes. Combining various proposals, Fisk linked La Crosse, St. Paul, southern Minnesota, the Yellowstone, Virginia City, and the Pacific Ocean in one grand pathway of empire.[3]

Although the idea may not have been his originally, Fisk with his flag, bugle, and glowing tales clothed the route in glamour. Since people of that day knew little of the northern plains, grandiloquence was more important than geographical information. On "a day not far off," Fisk predicted in the *Press* of January 16, 1864, "the Trade of the Eastern Hemisphere shall pass over the world's thoroughfares" on the new route.

In encouraging emigrants to follow this trail to the West in 1864, Fisk saw for himself a greater task than merely guiding travelers. He advocated a generous congressional appropriation to build a wagon road, a line of forts to protect it, and a military campaign to sweep the Indians forever from the line of march. Fisk envisioned himself in a stellar role. He would be a colonel with a cavalry force of a thousand or more men, grandly marching west, building a road and exterminating the savages. Following him, and under his banner, would come a host of emigrants bound for homes and fortunes in the West. Settlements, "populous and rich," would follow in their wake. "Let us reach out our hands and cla[s]p them by a wagon road, soon to give way to a railroad, telegraphs, &c.," Fisk proclaimed. He urged his listeners to demonstrate their support by writing to the President, to Congress, to the secretary of war, and to the generals of the army.[4]

In the little town of Anoka, just north of Minneapolis, the citizens could hardly hear enough of Idaho, perhaps because the rails of the long-awaited St. Paul and Pacific Railroad had just reached the town. Fisk lectured there to a crowded house on January 14, and a month later John F. Hoyt of the 1862 Holmes train gave two talks. Hoyt was less optimistic than Fisk, and some townspeople publicly expressed considerable skepticism about both mining and agricultural prospects in the West. Despite these warnings, Idaho fever burned hotly in Anoka. William L. Larned, a former army officer, stated that he "never attached much importance" to Fisk's picture of the wealth of Idaho, but he was sufficiently impressed to invest heavily in hardware stock for sale at the mines and make plans to go with him.[5]

[3] *Press*, May 30, 1862, January 16, 1864; *Mankato Union*, January 1, March 11, 1864; *Pioneer*, February 26, 1864; *Faribault Central Republican*, March 16, 1864; *Expedition of Captain Fisk*, 33–35. An account of the 1863 winter trek is in William E. Lass, "The 'Moscow Expedition,'" in *Minnesota History*, 39:227–240 (Summer, 1965).

[4] *Pioneer*, December 31, 1863; *Press*, January 16, 1864 (quotes); Fisk to Ignatius Donnelly, January 19, 1864, in Donnelly Papers, MiHS.

[5] *Press*, January 16, 19, 1864; *Anoka Star*, January 16, February 13, 20, 1864. For expressions of doubt about the gold fields, see *Anoka Star*, January 30, February 6, 20, 1864, as well as *St. Cloud Democrat*, January 28, 1864, and *Faribault Central Republican*, February 3, 1864. See also Larned Diary, September 10, 1864.

The captain found other receptive audiences. On January 20 Fisk delivered a lecture sponsored by St. Mark's Episcopal Church of Minneapolis. With him on the platform was Nathaniel Langford of the 1862 expedition, who announced optimistically that miners had already laid out a city at the mouth of the Bighorn River and that steamboats could ascend the Missouri and Yellowstone rivers to that point. Several weeks later John Hoyt gave his "candid and intelligent" observations on Idaho from the same platform. On January 25 Fisk addressed an overflow audience in St. Paul. Following the lecture, the *Pioneer* of January 27 reported indignantly that someone had carried away Fisk's collection of gold nuggets. Either the rascal was caught or Fisk had a reserve supply, for the nuggets continued to be the *pièce de résistance* of his lectures along the course of his journey to Washington.[6]

Fisk was expected to lead several thousand emigrants to Idaho, and Minnesotans concerned with the state's economy were quick to note the implications of such an extensive migration. Governor Henry A. Swift in his annual message to the legislature urged a number of measures to strengthen communications between Minnesota and Idaho. If the northern route were safe from Indian attack, Swift asserted, much of the "immense emigration to those mines with the business it creates, would undoubtedly flow through this State." The legislature adopted memorials to Congress which it hoped would achieve this aim. The St. Paul Chamber of Commerce conferred with Fisk as to the best means for opening a route from St. Paul to Idaho Territory. The businessmen decided to send copies of a memorial to the President and to the army authorities setting forth the reasons why such a route should be opened and fortified. The chamber also allocated money for the publication of a map and other information about the new trail.[7]

Between speaking engagements in January Fisk and his journalist, Samuel Johnston, completed a detailed report of the 1863 expedition and added a prospectus for the proposed new wagon road. In answer to numerous letters inquiring about his plans, Fisk announced in the press that he was too busy to reply to each one and that the War Department had not yet indicated who would lead overland emigration in 1864. Despite the death of his father on January 29, Fisk, accompanied by Johnston, was soon on his way to Washington. He addressed an audience in the Winona County courthouse on January 30 and, in the opinion of the local paper, spoke in "a very ready and fluent manner" to an attentive crowd.[8]

Moving across the Mississippi to La Crosse, Wisconsin, the captain called at

[6] *State Atlas*, January 20, February 3, 1864; *Press*, January 23, 24, 1864.

[7] *Chicago Tribune*, January 20, 24, 1864; "Proclamations and Messages of the Governor, Executive Journal, 1858–1864," p. 219, Governor's Collection, Minnesota State Archives, St. Paul; Minnesota, *House Journal*, 1864, p. 28, 178; *Senate Journal*, 1864, p. 57, 63; *Memorials* (38 Congress, 1 session, *Senate Miscellaneous Documents*, nos. 36, 54 — serial 1177); *Press*, January 24, February 7, 20, 1864.

Money from the chamber was probably used to publish two maps in 1864. One was D. D. Merrill's "Minnesota Route the shortest and best to the Idaho Gold Mines," issued in St. Paul with an accompanying travel guide. See Seymour Dunbar, *A History of Travel in America*, 4:1225 (Indianapolis, 1915). The other was Fisk's "Map Showing Proposed Military & Emigrant Roads to the Gold Fields of Montana or East Idaho," probably published in Washington. Copies of both are in the library of the MiHS.

[8] *Press*, January 21, 1864; A. J. Fisk Diary, February 3, 1864; *Winona Republican*, February 1, 1864.

the office of the *Daily Democrat*. Fisk "is a trump," the editor wrote, "wide between
the eyes, and knows his business to a dot." Citizens and businessmen were told
that Fisk's forthcoming lecture would promote "the establishment of a thoroughfare
of travel through the northwest via this city to the new gold fields." The *Democrat*
afterward reported that Fisk's talk "set everybody who heard him crazy" about
Idaho, and the paper soon carried notices that two steamboats loaded with passengers and freight for the gold fields would leave La Crosse in April, as soon as
"ice will permit." [9]

Quitting La Crosse and its Idaho ferment, Fisk and Johnston took the train for
Milwaukee. There the captain called on General John Pope at the headquarters
of the Department of the Northwest and later reported to the press that Pope had
agreed to make the proposed new route his line of communication on the plains
"whenever at all consistent with his instructions and plans." The Milwaukee Chamber of Commerce listened to an address by Fisk and shortly thereafter adopted a
memorial to Congress in support of the new route.[10]

In Chicago two hundred members of the Board of Trade heard Fisk give what
the *Chicago Tribune* of February 10 described as "an interesting sketch of Idaho,
and the practicality of establishing a wagon route soon to give way to a Northern
Pacific Railroad to the new gold regions." The *St. Paul Press* reported on February
16 that the Board of Trade had appointed a committee to meet with Fisk, consider his proposals, and "lay the matter before the public."

Until this time Fisk's press had been largely complimentary, but as he traveled
eastward, unfavorable accounts began to appear. Several reports, said to have
originated in Chicago and Cincinnati, Ohio, minimized the significance of his
1863 expedition and characterized him as "considerably windy, much given to
brandy and blowing."[11] The *St. Paul Pioneer* of February 25, 1864, objected to this
"punching of our Minnesota lion," but as reports of Fisk's "lionizing" continued to
come back, the editor remarked impatiently on March 4 that "we have had too
many gaseous speeches, resolutions and memorials" and "too little practical
common-sense work." Fisk should be getting on to Washington, the editor asserted.
The *Faribault Central Republican* of March 16 commented acidly that no one
would object to Fisk's traveling any route to Idaho, "with all the gudgeons he can
induce to follow him, provided they pay their own expenses." But the editor felt
that the expenditure of government money on the so-called direct route to the
West would benefit not the public, but rather "blow-hard Fisk," "wooden generals," and businessmen — particularly St. Paul merchants who hoped to receive
government contracts.

When issues of the Minnesota newspapers reached the gold fields, the miners
there sent back their two cents' worth of information and opinion. Some agreed

[9] The quotations are from the *La Crosse Democrat,* February 1, 2, 4. See also issues of February
3, March 2, 14, 17, April 16, 19, 1864. The steamers, the "Chippewa Falls" and the "Cutter,"
left La Crosse on April 18 loaded with 250 passengers and a large amount of freight. The
"Cutter" reached Fort Benton, but the "Chippewa Falls" was commandeered by General Alfred
Sully to carry military supplies and later ferried Holmes emigrants across the Yellowstone River.
See John E. Parsons, "Steamboats in the 'Idaho' Gold Rush," in *Montana, the Magazine of
Western History*, vol. 10, no. 1, p. 52–54 (January, 1960), and p. 127, below.
[10] *Pioneer,* February 12, 1864; *Milwaukee Sentinel,* February 6, 1864; for the *Memorial,* see
38 Congress, 1 session, *Senate Miscellaneous Documents,* no. 72 (serial 1177).
[11] *St. Cloud Democrat,* March 3, 1864.

with Fisk and Langford in their sanguine reports on Idaho; others felt that Hoyt had a more practical view of the mines.[12] Amos W. Hall, a member of the Holmes train of 1862, described Fisk in the *Pioneer* of May 22 as the "originator of monstrous but pleasing and ingenious fictions" about the gold fields. Opportunities to make a fortune certainly existed, Hall wrote, but prospective emigrants must be willing to hunt gold "without whining about a bed to sleep on, about coffee and sugar, and vegetables, which they don't get[,] or about dirt, and mice, and fleas, which they do get." The public, however, seemed little concerned about the reliability of the various spokesmen, and the debate served only to raise the Idaho fever.

While the country was "getting wild" over the gold stories from Idaho and men busily "swore in" for the journey, Fisk — contenting himself with a short press interview in New York — moved on to Washington. To complete his duty as expedition commander, Fisk had only to turn in his financial records, a matter which should have been accomplished quite readily. Yet he lingered on in the capital for more than three months, suffering a number of embarrassments which began the day of his arrival when he was arrested for being in the wartime city without a pass. Short of funds, he was hounded by a creditor for payment of an overdue draft for the purchase of oxen in Dakota the previous summer. Repercussions from his alleged misconduct on the central overland trail in search of his lost valise also rose to plague him. All these matters distracted Fisk from his chief interest in the capital: the passage of a bill for the construction of a wagon road from Minnesota to Idaho Territory over the new route he had so enthusiastically publicized.[13]

In support of the wagon-road project, Fisk and Congressman Ignatius Donnelly arranged a splendid publicity coup shortly after the captain reached Washington. On February 29 the two men, with Senator Ramsey, William Nobles, and probably Samuel Johnston, called on President Lincoln at the White House. Senator Ramsey read the memorial of the St. Paul Chamber of Commerce to the President and showed him a map of Fisk's proposed route. With suitable verbal flourishes Fisk then gave Lincoln the much-traveled gold nuggets. The largest was said to be worth $122. Attached to it was a smaller, head-shaped nugget with "features strongly resembling the President." A third nugget bore the message: "Give this to Old Abe for me. A Minnesota Miner, East Side, Idaho, 1863." Fisk told the President that the miner had "'heern tell that "Old Abe" was the humliest man in the U-nited States, and that nugget was the *gol durndest* humliest nugget in the whole gulch.'" Lincoln "enjoyed this complimentary reference to his personal beauty and laughed heartily," and shaking the captain's hand, requested him to "'Give my respects to that miner when you go back, and tell him that's the work of the best artist that ever took my portrait.'"[14]

The President assured his visitors that he favored the development of the

[12] *St. Peter Tribune,* March 2, 1864; *St. Cloud Democrat,* June 23, 1864.

[13] *Milwaukee Sentinel,* January 26, 1864 (quotes); *New York Tribune,* February 19, 1864; *Press,* February 20, 1864. Fisk's difficulties are discussed in detail in Helen M. White, "Captain Fisk Goes to Washington," in *Minnesota History,* 38:220–226 (March, 1963).

[14] *Press,* March 2, 1864; *New York Weekly Tribune,* April 23, 1864; *Pioneer,* April 28, 1864 (quotes); Donnelly Diary, February 29, 1864, Donnelly Papers. A sketch of the nuggets appeared in *Leslie's Illustrated Newspaper* (New York), March 19, 1864. Fisk's map discussed in note 7, above, was probably the one shown to the President.

mineral region, recognizing its potential value in paying the country's debts. He expressed sympathy with the Minnesota proposals for the road but was apprehensive about the cost of building and fortifying it. He nevertheless endorsed the memorial to the attention of the secretary of war and promised to have it sent on by special messenger to Congress. Although little but publicity came of the interview with the President, it was easily the high point of Fisk's army career.

Early in March Congress passed a bill allocating ten thousand dollars for the protection of the northern route. On March 15 both the Senate and the House approved the printing of five thousand copies of Fisk's 1863 report. One senator remarked that its publication would save him "much trouble in correspondence" because he had received so many requests for the information it contained. In view of Fisk's cordial relations with the Minnesota congressional delegation, he would probably have had little trouble in securing a speedy recommendation for reappointment as superintendent of emigration over his old route. However, the weeks passed and no letter of recommendation was written. The reason for the delay was undoubtedly Fisk's interest in the outcome of the wagon-road legislation.[15]

Before the middle of March, Donnelly and House members from Iowa and Idaho Territory introduced bills for the construction of roads to link the Midwest to Idaho. The three bills were referred to the committee on roads and canals and eventually emerged as House Resolution 323. This omnibus bill provided for the construction of a number of roads, including one along the forty-fifth parallel for which a hundred thousand dollars was to be appropriated. During the spring backers of the bill made a number of unsuccessful attempts to secure its passage while Fisk lingered in Washington. He was obviously unwilling to settle for ten thousand dollars and the job of protecting an emigrant train when any possibility remained of obtaining ten times as much money and the superintendency of a wagon road.[16]

In March the new route proposed by Fisk received recognition of another sort. General Pope announced plans for a second military expedition against the Sioux on the northern plains. The campaign had three objectives: to further subdue and punish the Indians for the outbreak of 1862; to drive them from the overland routes to the gold fields; and to establish a line of forts to keep the Indians from again harassing the frontier and the emigrant trains. Pope, perhaps unaware that Fisk's project had not received official sanction, proposed to locate three of the new posts close to the captain's intended line of march. The general also issued a circular to prospective emigrants, advising them to travel west in large parties under the command of persons skilled in Indian warfare, and not to go in advance of the military forces.[17]

All signs pointed to a heavy wave of emigration to the West in 1864. In Minne-

[15] *Statutes at Large*, 13:14; *Congressional Globe*, 38 Congress, 1 session, p. 960 (quote), 1108, 1121.

[16] *Congressional Globe*, 38 Congress, 1 session, p. 1174, 1736, 2607; *St. Cloud Democrat*, March 10, 1864; *Press*, March 4, 1864; *Weekly Press*, May 5, 1864; A. J. Fisk Diary, April 26, 1864. The three original bills, H.R. 323, 326, and 343, are contained in the files of 38 Congress, 1 session, Committee on Roads and Canals, records of the House of Representatives, NARG 233.

[17] *WRR*, vol. 34, part 2, p. 154, 608, 622–625; *St. Cloud Democrat*, March 24, 1864. Pope's circular was published in various Minnesota newspapers, including the March 25 issues of the *Pioneer* and the *Mankato Union*.

sota, as the snow melted and spring advanced, the Idaho fever spread unchecked, and for a time Governor Stephen Miller was afraid that the state would be unable to supply its quota of men for the Union army in the face of an exodus of "hundreds" of people who "propose leaving within a few weeks" for Idaho.[18]

↓ While Fisk tarried in Washington, Thomas Holmes returned to Shakopee from the gold fields. On April 30 the *Shakopee Argus* announced that Holmes would again go west with a party whose members would travel "on their own hook" and "beat Cap. Fisk 'all hollow.'" On May 7 Holmes called to order a mass meeting of emigrants at the National Hotel in Shakopee. The prospective travelers resolved to leave on May 16 and to communicate with General Sibley and Captain Fisk about a military escort. A letter was sent at once to Sibley asking whether it would be advisable for 250 well-armed emigrants to attempt the Idaho journey without an escort. "Emphatically no!" Sibley replied. The danger of Indian attack was grave, and the emigrants were advised to travel with army troops as far as the Yellowstone River. Sibley could give the Shakopee men no information about Fisk and his plans, but he told them that within a few weeks troops under the command of Colonel Minor T. Thomas would leave Fort Ridgely to join General Sully's forces on the Missouri. This military contingent, Sibley said, would protect any emigrant parties which wished to travel with it. The information in Sibley's letter, in effect, determined the rendezvous, the time of departure, and the route of the Holmes overland train of 1864.[19]

In the middle of May, Shakopee's main street was thronged with emigrants and cluttered with their wagons. Most of the group came from towns and farms in southern Minnesota. One of them, Thomas E. Cooper, had heard Fisk speak in February at La Crosse. Cooper was so stirred by Fisk's picture of the favorable prospects in the gold fields that he resolved to try his fortune, but he was unwilling to wait for the tardy captain and left with Holmes instead. More than thirty emigrants from eastern states had also been attracted by Fisk's propaganda and had come west expecting to travel with him. Fifteen men arrived from Middletown, Connecticut; smaller parties came from Saratoga and Glens Falls, New York. Among the Glens Falls group was Gilbert Benedict, a thirty-four-year-old harness maker who undertook the journey in an effort to improve his health. Benedict was ambidextrous, and his careful record of the journey, which is included in this text, was said to have been written right- and left-handed on alternate pages of his journal. Other men who joined the Holmes train came from Massachusetts, Ohio, Michigan, and Wisconsin.[20]

The emigrants left Shakopee on May 19. A week later, as they straggled up the Minnesota River Valley, President Lincoln signed a bill creating Montana Terri-

[18] Stephen Miller to James B. Fry, March 16, 1864; Gordon E. Cole to Miller, March 17, 1864 (quote); "Executive Journal B, 1863–1865," p. 198, 202; Ramsey to Miller, March 28, 1864, file 141-18, all in the Governor's Collection, Minnesota State Archives.
[19] *Press*, May 13, 1864; G. S. Benson to Sibley, May 9, 1864, Department of the Northwest, NARG 98; *WRR*, vol. 34, part 3, p. 541 (quote).
[20] *Shakopee Argus*, May 14, 1864; Cooper, "How the Tom Holmes Expedition . . . Crossed the Plains in 1864 to Last Chance Gulch in Montana," reminiscence in MoHS. For a roster of known members of the expedition, see Appendix, below. It was compiled chiefly from the Cooper Papers in MoHS; *Shakopee Argus*, May 14, 1864; Nicholas Hilger, "General Alfred Sully's Ex-

tory. Included in the new territory were the now familiar gold fields of eastern Idaho. Thus overnight Montana, rather than Idaho, became the emigrants' destination. At Fort Ridgely the train was organized into six divisions, each under the command of a wagon master. Holmes was elected captain, and an executive committee was chosen to act as a court "for the trial of any cause that might arise." Farther up the valley the emigrants remained in camp for several days, waiting for their military escort. Thomas Cooper remembered that on a typical morning some people "were eating breakfast, some washing dishes, some cutting their neighbors' hair, some out hunting, some coming in with a string of fish." Hundreds of cattle belonging to the emigrants grazed near the camp. The size of the train can only be approximated. Contemporary estimates ranged from 113 to 175 wagons and 200 to 300 people, including fourteen women. The names of fewer than half the emigrants are known.[21]

On June 7 the wagon train fell in behind some thirteen hundred men of Colonel Thomas' Minnesota Brigade marching out to meet Sully at the Missouri River. The emigrants passed through the valley of the upper Minnesota with its frightening reminders of the Sioux Uprising of 1862, traveled on to Lac qui Parle, and then followed a branch of the Lac qui Parle River into Dakota. Moving slowly across Dakota, the emigrants enjoyed pleasant associations with the troops. They washed the soldiers' clothes and sold them milk and fresh bread. When the soldiers butchered cattle, the train members were able to buy beef tongues and livers to supplement their diet. East of present-day Watertown, South Dakota, the expedition saw its first buffalo and soon added the meat of these animals to the bill of fare.[22]

It was probably on this portion of the journey that a young Indian traveled beside the train for several days and showed great interest in the infant son of Mary Anna Weydert, a German-born woman who had come with her husband from Shakopee. The Indian indicated in sign language that he wished to hold the baby. Mrs. Weydert, doubtless with misgivings, handed him the child. He gently wrapped two beautifully tanned buffalo robes about the baby and gave him back to his mother.[23]

South of present-day Aberdeen, South Dakota, the expedition crossed the James River, then traveled over the Coteau du Missouri and joined Sully's command at Swan Lake Creek on the Missouri River. The combined force moved upriver to Long Lake Creek, some twenty miles south of present-day Bismarck, North Dakota. Troops and emigrants crossed the river with the assistance of Sully's supply steam-

pedition of 1864," in *Montana Historical Contributions*, 2:321; and the Gilbert Benedict Diary in MoHS. For biographical information on Cooper, see *North Dakota Historical Collections*, 1:354 (Bismarck, 1906), and *Pioneer Press and Dispatch*, June 20, 1915, p. 8. For Benedict, see *Montana Record-Herald* (Helena), June 28, 1920, p. 2; Alva J. Noyes, "Gilbert Benedict," 9, in MoHS.

[21] Cooper, "Tom Holmes Expedition," describes the train organization and camp life. For varying estimates of the train size, see also A. J. Fisk Diary, June 3, 1864; Ebenezer Rice Diary, June 7, 1864, in MiHS; Hilger, in *Montana Historical Contributions*, 2:314; Weydert, "Biography"; Frank E. Best, comp., *John Keep of Longmeadow, Massachusetts, 1660–1676, and His Descendants*, 151 (Chicago, 1889).

[22] Morning report, May 30, 1864, and returns for June, Second (Minnesota) Brigade, Northwestern Indian Expedition, Department of the Northwest, NARG 94; *WRR*, vol. 41, part 1, p. 168–170. For the emigrant-soldier associations, see Weydert, "Biography"; A. J. Fisk Diary, July 3, 17, 22, 1864; Gilbert Benedict, "Trip to Montana," prose, 9.

[23] Weydert, "Biography."

boats, the emigrants paying one cord of wood for each wagon ferried over. Here Sully chose a site for Fort Rice, the middle post in the line of three proposed for establishment on the route to the gold fields, and soldiers began construction of the fort. The emigrants lay in camp for five days, resting their animals and putting their wagons in condition for the more difficult part of the journey which lay ahead. Hot winds blew and temperatures of 106 degrees in the shade were recorded. While in camp, the train members elected Oliver D. Keep as their new captain, replacing Holmes whose particular talents were not those of an organization leader.[24]

From Fort Rice Sully proposed to march to the Yellowstone River, where he would meet supply steamboats and build the westernmost of the new forts. On the way he expected to encounter and attack a concentration of Sioux warriors. Just before sunset on July 18, Sully, Thomas, and their staff officers rode into the emigrant camp. The captain of the train raised the flag and called a meeting of the emigrants. Sully, irritated at the prospect of having an emigrant train on his heels all the way to the Yellowstone, spoke frankly to them. "Gentlemen," he said, "I am damn sorry you are here, but so long as you are I will do the best I can to protect you." He told them that he planned to "jump an Indian Camp and give them hell," and warned the travelers to follow his instructions during the expected battle. Cheers from the emigrants and the swinging of hats followed the general's speech. Early the next morning soldiers and emigrants moved slowly away from Fort Rice.[25]

On the trail up the north fork of the Cannonball River they found many specimens of petrified wood and increasing signs of Indians. As the hot, dry weather continued, oxen and mules died of heat and exertion. On the Heart River, south of present-day Richardton, North Dakota, the emigrant train was ordered to stay in camp under the protection of a detachment of troops. The larger part of Sully's forces moved northward to the Killdeer Mountains, where they fought the Indians and destroyed their camp.[26]

Returning to its base camp, the military force gathered the emigrants under its wing again and moved along the Heart and Knife rivers close to the present-day path of the Northern Pacific Railroad. Most of Sully's Indian guides thought it impossible to get through the Badlands of the Little Missouri, but one of them, a young Blackfoot-Sioux, claimed to have been through the region and insisted that he could lead the expedition to the Yellowstone in eight days. Because Sully's commissary department had made a mistake in calculating the supplies needed, military rations were short. Since the expedition was now closer to the Yellowstone than to Fort Rice, Sully decided to follow the young guide.[27]

After a few days the Indian brought the expedition onto a narrow tableland.

[24] Maps of the route followed by the Minnesota Brigade erroneously indicate that it first met Sully at Fort Rice. See Folwell, *Minnesota*, 2:296.

[25] Cooper, "Tom Holmes Expedition."

[26] *WRR*, vol. 41, part 1, p. 141–144; Louis Pfaller, "Sully's Expedition of 1864," in *North Dakota History*, 31:38 (January, 1964).

[27] Material here and below is based on *WRR*, vol. 41, part 1, p. 144–146; Hilger, in *Montana Historical Contributions*, 2:315–317 (quote). See also Robert N. McLaren to his wife, August 15, 1864, in McLaren Papers, MiHS; *Minnesota in the Civil and Indian Wars*, 1:391 (St. Paul, 1890).

Neither soldiers nor emigrants were prepared for the spectacle before them. As far as the eye could see, were the vast, worn, and wrinkled Badlands — gray and red hills tumbled about in fantastic shapes like the ruins of a gigantic prehistoric civilization. "Hell burnt out," General Sully called it.

The guide led them on a winding path through the Badlands. The heat continued, the air was stifling, and dust hung thick over the train. Grasshoppers had consumed most of the grass, leaving only sage and cactus as food for the stock. Water in scanty pools was usually muddy or alkali. For eight days the emigrants traveled, one of them remembered, "without as much water as a chicken could eat . . . going up hills and down hills as you never saw and never will." Tongues swelled and lips parched, and the people suffered from dysentery caused by the water. Horses and oxen died of thirst or were killed to put them out of their misery. All broken wagons were abandoned so as not to delay the march.[28]

From time to time Indians harassed the train, shooting, shouting, and charging down on the expedition from the tops of the buttes. The young guide — one of six men wounded on August 8 — was shot in the shoulder. The train halted and went into corral as soon as a suitable campsite was found. Batteries quickly put into position soon drove the Indians back. When the guide had "recovered from the shock of his wound," he was "held up by the men in a carriage, and thus riding was able to point out the course." Emigrants and soldiers moved on, fighting their way through the Badlands.[29]

The expedition had to march more than thirty miles one day in order to reach water and grass, leaving a trail marked by the carcasses of animals shot by the rear guard. The emigrants did not reach camp until 10:00 P.M. After dark, one of the soldiers wrote, "we did not dare shoot [any more of] the Animals for fear of shooting the Idaho Emmigrants who were trying to coax their cattle into Camp . . . we saw Women belonging to the Idaho Train pulling grass among the Brush in Ravines forgetting [the Indians] in their anxiety to save their cattle."[30]

The guide's promised eight days became ten before the expedition finally reached the Yellowstone. Men and animals rushed to the river, plunging into the cool, sweet water, drinking all they could hold, washing off dirt and sweat. Two of the expected government steamboats were at hand, but a third had struck a snag and sunk with its supply of corn for the animals. Sully had intended to go farther up the Yellowstone to establish another post, but the steamboats were unable to move upriver because of low water. Poor forage, low water, and the loss of the corn led Sully to change his plans and begin his homeward march by way of Fort Union and the Missouri. At this point, then, some thirty-five miles south of Fort Union, Sully crossed the Yellowstone with his troops and followed the river toward its junction with the Missouri.[31]

The emigrants crossed the Yellowstone after the troops, ferrying their wagon boxes and swimming the stock across. Two men from Shakopee, Xavier Kopp

---

[28] Clark K. Reynolds, "The Civil and Indian War Diaries of Eugene Marshall, Minnesota Volunteer," 324–326 (master's thesis, Duke University, 1963, photocopy MiHS); *Shakopee Argus*, November 26, 1864 (quote).

[29] Hilger, in *Montana Historical Contributions*, 2:318.

[30] John H. Strong Diary, August 11, 1864, in MiHS.

[31] WRR, vol. 41, part 1, p. 147.

and John Brounworth, were drowned in the difficult crossing, and animals belonging to emigrants and soldiers were lost. The rest of the train moved north through the valley along a splendid level roadway. The fringes of the river were green, and the travelers found game and berries. Men feasted on steaks of elk and black-tailed deer and ate chokecherries to cure their dysentery.[32]

At Fort Union the Holmes people obtained a guide, left the Sully expedition, and moved out on the old emigrant trail to Fort Benton. No sooner had they turned their wagons west than military officers at Union reported the loss of army oxen, horses, mules, and rifles. Soldiers dispatched after the train discovered that a few emigrants and a number of army deserters were far ahead with the missing goods. The army did not recover its property, and General Sully added another grievance to his list of complaints against overland emigrants.[33]

Meanwhile, the greater number of the Holmes emigrants traveled respectably onward to Fort Benton, where they arrived in mid-September. From there they followed the Mullan Road to the Prickly Pear turnoff and went to the diggings near a new settlement which one of their number was to name Helena. Apparently few had the benefit of any previous mining experience. They worked with blunt picks, like "chickens on a grain pile," according to a correspondent of the Virginia City *Montana Post* of April 29, 1865, and they obviously knew more "about raising wheat on the prairies, digging ginseng in the 'Big Woods,' gathering cranberries in the Minnesota swamps, or logs in the pineries, than using a pick and shovel." However, many of the greenhorns found gold. A substantial number also prospered at other occupations and thus made a permanent place for themselves in the new district.

John Marvin Blake, who had lived in Wisconsin and spent a winter trapping on the Dakota plains before he joined the train, found a gold nugget worth $2,300 in the Helena area. This find enabled him to study dentistry in Philadelphia; he returned to Helena where he practiced until his death in 1927. Blake also raised sheep, purebred cattle, and horses, including a prize-winning hurdle racer named "JMB." Another emigrant, Edwin Howe, started a grocery and hotel business in Helena. Howe, an Englishman, had earlier been employed as a bank courier in New York, London, and Paris.[34]

Gilbert Benedict, the ambidextrous diarist, found his health much improved in Montana. He prospered as a miner, farmer, and real estate operator, surviving to a ripe old age. He owned several buildings in Helena, but in spite of his wealth he lived simply without electricity and other modern conveniences. Over the years he developed unusual ideas concerning temperance, medicine, and spiritualism. At his death he left much of his property to his tenants.[35]

---

[32] Reynolds, "Diaries of Eugene Marshall," 334; John Strong Diary, August 15, 1864; A. J. Fisk Diary, August 12–14, 1864; *Press,* October 8, 1864. On Kopp and Brounworth, see also *Press,* October 8, 1864; United States Manuscript Census Schedules, 1860, Scott County, Minnesota, p. 2, and Carver County, p. 73.

[33] *WRR,* vol. 41, part 1, p. 149.

[34] On Blake, see *Montana Record-Herald,* November 17, 1927, p. 5; *Helena Independent,* November 18, 1927, p. 3. On Howe, SMP *Register,* 149; Leeson, ed., *Montana,* 1223.

[35] *Montana Record-Herald,* June 28, 1920, p. 2; Gilbert Benedict Scrapbook, in Benedict Papers, MoHS.

Several of the emigrants from southern Minnesota were foreign born. Nick Grommisch, a shoemaker from Luxembourg, mined for gold and later worked as a departmental manager in Nick Mullen's Boot and Shoe Company at Helena. Two other Luxembourgers, Nicholas and Matt Hilger, became miners and ranchers in Montana. Philip Constans, a St. Paul saloonkeeper who was born in the Rhine Valley of France, turned miner and merchant at Unionville. German-born John Henry Jurgens, a blacksmith, became a merchant and also engaged in mining and lumbering. He was postmaster of Marysville and served in the Montana legislature.[36]

Other Holmes emigrants who served in the legislature were Joseph W. Hartwell, John H. Shober, and Thomas J. Lowry. Hartwell was variously a miner, lumberman, and brickmaker. Shober, a lawyer and Minnesota pioneer, had served two years in the legislature of Dakota Territory before he and a small party of men from southern Dakota joined Holmes's train on the Missouri River. Lowry, born in Pennsylvania, studied law in his father's office before moving to Minnesota, where he continued his studies and was admitted to the bar. Shober and Lowry set up a law partnership in Helena.[37]

Some of the gold seekers found their wanderlust unsatisfied even by the long trek to Montana. Oliver Keep, whom the emigrants elected as their new leader at Fort Rice, was born in Ohio and had been a steamboat captain on the Minnesota River. He discovered one of the largest nuggets ever found in the Helena area but failed to make his fortune and later became a farmer in Kansas. Thomas Cooper, whose interest in the gold fields had been kindled by one of Fisk's speeches, was another restless pioneer. Born in Ireland of English parents, Cooper had lived for a time in Quebec and later in Wisconsin, where he took up farming and served as superintendent of schools. When he decided to join the Holmes expedition, he was living at Pine Island, Minnesota. After mining in Montana for some years, he returned to Minnesota. In the 1870s he again moved on to become one of the founders of Grafton, North Dakota, where he ran a hotel.[38]

The life of John H. Somerville perhaps best typifies the varying fortunes of the men who searched for gold. Born in Vermont, Somerville had been in the lumber business in Pennsylvania, Wisconsin, and Minnesota. He was a pioneer associate of Holmes in Scott County, Minnesota, and was farming there when he and his wife joined the train. Somerville made rich claims in a gulch near Helena but lost part of his fortune in expensive litigation over the ownership of one of his holdings. Returning to Minnesota, he put the rest of his capital into an unsuccessful manufacturing venture and died penniless in St. Paul at the age of seventy-nine. Somer-

[36] On Grommisch, see *Helena Weekly Herald,* November 20, 1890; United States Manuscript Census Schedules, 1860, Carver County, Minnesota, p. 28; Hilger, in *Montana Historical Contributions,* 2:321. On the Hilgers, SMP *Register,* 147; *Montana Daily Record* (Helena), August 12, 1913, p. 2. On Constans, SMP *Register,* 137; *Helena Independent,* December 26, 1902, p. 5. On Jurgens, Census Schedules, 1860, Scott County, Minnesota, p. 20; SMP *Register,* 150.

[37] On Hartwell, see SMP *Register,* 185; *Helena Weekly Herald,* October 12, 1899. On Shober, SMP *Register,* 165; *Helena Independent,* August 22, 1925. On Lowry, Leeson, ed., *Montana,* 1233; *Helena Weekly Herald,* December 2, 1886.

[38] On Keep, see Best, comp., *John Keep of Longmeadow,* 151; Cooper, "Tom Holmes Expedition"; *Montana Post,* July 1, 1865. On Cooper, see note 20, above.

ville is best remembered for his role at a public meeting held in a log cabin in Last Chance Gulch, when he proposed that the yet-unnamed settlement be called Helena, after a little village in Scott County, Minnesota.[39]

At the end of May, when the Holmes emigrants had already left Shakopee, James Fisk was still in Washington. On May 31 the House of Representatives killed his dream of becoming a colonel and a road builder when it buried the wagon-road bill in committee. Almost immediately Senator Wilkinson wrote to the secretary of war urging Fisk's reappointment as a superintendent of emigration. Wilkinson suggested that Fisk be instructed to travel over the direct route from southern Minnesota, and he also tried to amend the protective legislation to specify this route. His efforts on its behalf were unsuccessful; on June 7 Fisk was notified that he had ten thousand dollars to spend for the protection of emigration over the old Abercrombie–Benton trail.[40]

Fisk, however, apparently never considered following this trail, but planned all along to travel the more southern direct route. He was not a career army officer, and he felt no compulsion to operate through the regular chain of command or to obey instructions when they conflicted with his own judgment. Samuel Johnston sent out word from Washington that Fisk would leave not from Fort Abercrombie but from more southerly Fort Ridgely. It seems very likely that on the return trip to Minnesota Fisk and Johnston called at General Pope's headquarters in Milwaukee, for on June 20 Pope wrote to Sibley and Sully suggesting that they co-operate with Fisk. The captain, Pope said, planned to leave about July 1 with an emigrant train. He would travel overland to the Missouri, go up the Grand River, and strike directly west for the mouth of the Bighorn River. Pope asked Sibley to give Fisk a military escort to the proposed site of Fort Wadsworth; from there, the general recommended that Fisk be given further support if it were deemed necessary and did not prejudice other military movements.[41]

The captain arrived in St. Paul on June 18. Five days later he called on Sibley and was assured of full co-operation. He was authorized to obtain army ordnance and quartermaster supplies and conditionally promised a troop escort to the Missouri. It would thus appear that neither Pope nor Sibley saw Fisk's instructions directing him to travel farther north. In any case, it was perhaps too late to consider making the journey that way. The army was deployed farther south, and emigrants were already waiting at Ridgely. From St. Paul, Fisk announced boldly that he would go overland to Montana by way of Fort Ridgely, the Grand River, and the Yellowstone, and that he would leave about July 10.[42]

Outfitting proceeded rapidly in spite of a few vexing delays, the most serious of which was the death of Antoine Freniere, Fisk's 1863 guide, who was killed by

[39] Minnesota Historical Society Scrapbooks, 49:129; *Helena Herald,* August 15, 1890. For the naming of Helena, see p. 131n, below.

[40] *Congressional Globe,* 38 Congress, 1 session, p. 2607, 3533; Wilkinson to Stanton, June 4, 1864, file 763W 1864, NARG 94; Stanton to Fisk, June 7, and Fisk to E. D. Townsend, June 7, 1864, file 218W 1863, NARG 94.

[41] *Press,* June 8, 1864; *WRR,* vol. 34, part 4, p. 478.

[42] *WRR,* vol. 34, part 4, p. 556; *Press,* June 18, 25, 1864; *Pioneer,* June 19, July 3, 1864.

Indians while on his way back from Montana to serve as trail maker for the new expedition. Fisk then vowed to be his own guide, and amid the "roar of fire-crackers and music of the band," the nucleus of the expedition rolled out of St. Paul on the trail to Fort Ridgely.[43]

When the expedition was organized at Ridgely, it included Fisk's staff, members of his protective escort, and other emigrants — a total of about a hundred wagons and some 170 people.[44] On Fisk's staff were two veterans of the 1863 expedition, Dr. Dibb and Samuel Johnston. August Chemidlin, a French-born farmer and watchman-tollkeeper of the Minneapolis Suspension Bridge, was in charge of the commissary. His nephew, Nicholas Chemidlin, drove the commissary wagon. The wagon master of the expedition was Fisk's brother Van. Born in Conneaut, Ohio, twenty-four years earlier, Van had lived on the plains for various lengths of time since he was sixteen years old. He served in the First Minnesota Regiment and was discharged for disability in 1863. Fisk's brother-in-law, George W. Burson — known as "Laughing George" — drove the flag wagon. Little is known of the other staff members. George W. Marsh, assistant wagon master, was a St. Paul printer. The expedition's surveyor, W. Ellis Smith, was said to have been a "big hearted man strongly addicted to gazing at the sun and moon through a long necked bottle" and was probably the same Smith who had gone to the Fraser River gold fields in 1858.[45]

The names of only a few of the emigrants are known, and very little information about them has been found. Some apparently came from the St. Croix Valley, Minneapolis, St. Anthony, Anoka, and St. Cloud. They were a "cheerful and whole souled lot," reported the St. Paul Press on July 7, well armed and "used to bushwhacking and skirmishing." Fisk was disappointed that the Holmes emigrants had gone west without him. Although by this time they were more than a month ahead of him, he assumed with characteristic optimism that they would wait for him somewhere along the way.[46]

It was not until July 23 that the expedition, accompanied by some fifty cavalrymen from Sibley's command, started up the Minnesota River Valley toward Big Stone Lake. They crossed the height of land which separates the rivers flowing to Hudson Bay from those draining into the Mississippi system, and moved on into southern Dakota Territory. There were signs of Indians along the route but

[43] Pioneer, June 30, July 1, 3, 6; Anoka Star, July 2; State Atlas, June 29 — all in 1864. The quotation is from Noyes, "Lost on the Plains," 1.

[44] This was Fisk's estimate of the size of the expedition; see p. 133, below. For others, varying a good deal, see Pioneer, July 20, 1864; "Expeditions of Capt. Jas. L. Fisk to the Gold Mines of Idaho and Montana," in North Dakota Historical Collections, 2 (part 1): 431 (Bismarck, 1908); Willoughby Wells, "Brackett's Battalion," in Daughters of the American Revolution, "Geneological [sic] Records," 1945, p. 122 — cited hereafter as DAR, "Geneological Records."

[45] On the Chemidlins, see United States Manuscript Census Schedules, 1860, Ramsey County, Minnesota, p. 301; Alva J. Noyes, "Nicholas Chemidlin," in MoHS. On Van Fisk, see his pension file, SC 12523, in NARG 15, and Leeson, ed., Montana, 1182. On Burson, see Noyes, "George W. Burson," in MoHS. On Marsh, St. Paul City Directory, 1864. For Marsh's letters from the expedition, see Press, August 9, September 10, October 11, 1864. On W. E. Smith, Pioneer, January 25, 1859, July 20, 1864; Noyes, "Lost on the Plains," 3 (quote).

[46] For the names of known emigrants, see Appendix, below. The roster was compiled chiefly from the William Larned Diary and Ethel Collins, "Pioneer Experiences of Horatio Larned," in North Dakota Historical Collections, 7:6–9 (Grand Forks, 1925). See also Stillwater Messenger, August 2, 1864; St. Cloud Democrat, October 13, 1864.

no Indians troubled the train. On July 23 Fisk dispatched a casual note to the adjutant general explaining why he had left from Fort Ridgely.[47]

At the head of the Coteau des Prairies — not far from the present-day town of Eden, South Dakota — the train stopped near the camp of army troops which had been sent out to construct Fort Wadsworth, the easternmost in the line of new posts authorized that year. Here Fisk gave the military some assistance in locating the fort and received advice from army scouts about a route to the Missouri. Armed with this information, he guided the train through the James River Valley and northwest over the Coteau du Missouri. Fisk had originally intended to cross the Missouri River at the mouth of the Grand, but because of the location of Fort Rice farther to the north, near the mouth of the Cannonball, he was obliged to steer his course to the latter point. Three men, sent ahead to find the fort, were lost for several days on the plains, but Fisk had no serious difficulty in reaching the Missouri. Emigrants and wagons were ferried by steamboat across the river at Fort Rice.

The detachment of troops which had accompanied the train to Fort Rice returned to Fort Wadsworth, despite Fisk's attempts to press them into service as far as the Yellowstone. Fisk was further frustrated when he discovered that the Holmes emigrants had gone westward with Sully and that the general had left no instructions for an escort for Fisk. Colonel Daniel J. Dill, the officer in charge at Fort Rice, felt that he could not spare any men, but after several interviews Fisk prevailed on him to furnish an escort of some fifty convalescent soldiers who were to accompany the expedition as far as the Yellowstone.

Leaving Fort Rice, Fisk followed Sully's trail for about eighty miles up the Cannonball River. At this point he made a crucial decision. Sully had turned northward; Fisk wanted to go southwest toward the headwaters of the Little Missouri. It was a more direct way to the mouth of the Bighorn, and the captain was convinced that he could avoid the worst of the Badlands. So it was that the train, in Fisk's words, "struck out from the tracks of the white man to try and solve the problem of route or no route . . . through that unexplored region, toward the valley of the Yellowstone." In so doing, the train rolled on toward a disastrous encounter with the Sioux.

The land was smooth and hard, "generally better after leaving Sully's trail," Fisk wrote, and the journey was pleasant, without Indian signs for a hundred miles. However, on September 2, near present-day Rhame, North Dakota, a band of Hunkpapa warriors attacked two wagons at the rear of the train. Before the sun went down that day, the Indians killed nine men and mortally wounded three more. The expedition spent a miserable night huddled in corral. The wounded were cared for and the dead buried, while wolves howled in the blackness. A sudden storm with thunder, lightning, and heavy rain lasted for several hours, and in the morning the cattle in the corral stood in two feet of water. Under continuous Indian attack, the expedition moved twelve miles in the next two days. Finally, about fifteen miles east of the Montana line, they established an entrenched camp and Lieutenant DeWitt C. Smith with fifteen men started for Fort Rice and help.

The events of the following sixteen days, while the emigrants waited for relief

[47] Fisk to Thomas, July 23, 1864, in file 328F 1864, NARG 94.

to arrive, are recounted in Fisk's official report, which is included in this volume. Fisk described in some detail his unsuccessful efforts to ransom Mrs. Fanny Kelly, a white woman whom the Indians had captured earlier and wanted to exchange for supplies of food. The captain mentioned more briefly an incident that was to have serious repercussions. Some of the emigrants left hardtack injected with strychnine at a campsite and about twenty-five Indians were poisoned.

After a few days the attacking Indians withdrew. Time dragged heavily in the camp. Jefferson Dilts, the expedition's scout, and two soldiers died of their wounds and were buried under the entrenchments of the camp, which was named Fort Dilts. Fisk's twenty-ninth birthday passed unheralded as he, impatient at the long wait, made a short reconnaissance to the west. Heavily guarded work parties prepared fords over two nearby streams so that the expedition could move on to the Yellowstone. Some emigrants wanted to go on, others preferred to stay in camp until help came. An emigrant named McCarthy, who was taking a stock of saloon supplies to the mines, concluded that he would never reach the gold fields and offered to sell his whisky at twenty-five cents a cup. Someone on the head-quarters staff, perhaps Fisk or his brother Van, composed a poetic version of the events of the Indian battle.[48]

On September 20 a relief expedition from Fort Rice reached the camp. Fisk hoped to go on, but he was told that no troops would be allowed to escort him farther west. Under these circumstances the expedition returned to Fort Rice. Johnston and Van Fisk remained there for the winter to look after the outfit and the animals. Some emigrants also waited at the fort until the following spring in the hope of resuming their journey to Montana, but most of them apparently traveled with parties of soldiers down the Missouri or back to Minnesota. Fisk and several men of his command went down the Missouri and overland to St. Paul.

Various assessments were made of the cause of the expedition's failure and of Fisk's responsibility for the disaster. Charles F. Sims, whom Fisk had delegated to represent the interests of the emigrants on the expedition, reported that despite the frustration of his high hopes of the spring, "I am well pleased that I still exist, that the Indian arrow, scalping knife and tomahawk has harmed me not." Sims thought that in four months he had learned more of human nature than ever before in his life. "In all of our train," he wrote, "I cannot think of more than twenty that to me were congenial spirits, and who were always ready to do their duty without complaint." He thought that military rule on such an expedition was the only way to make "some men take care of their own interests."[49]

Although Sims was reluctant to criticize Fisk because of their amicable relations on the trail, he censured him privately for his overconfidence in leaving Fort Rice without an adequate escort and for his rashness in turning off Sully's trail. Sims felt that Fisk had counted too heavily on the good luck which had so far attended him. On the other hand, wrote Sims, Fisk was a "noble hearted and generous man. He is intelligent, has a large experience, and is a good leader in such an expedition, where there is no danger of Indians." In spite of the heavy financial

---

[48] The poem is on the last page of vol. 1 of the James Fisk Papers. The story about McCarthy is told by Wells, in DAR, "Geneological Records," p. 124.

[49] For Sims's comments here and below, see *North Dakota Historical Collections*, 2 (part 1): 431, 434, 437, 438.

JAMES L. FISK, *who led four expeditions across the northern plains in the 1860s, struck a symbolic pose for a Washington photographer probably before he set out for the Montana gold fields in 1864.*

THOMAS A. HOLMES, *veteran frontiersman and townsite promoter, led three wagon trains from Minnesota to the Montana gold fields in the 1860s. Engraving from* The Southern Minnesotan, *March, 1931.*

PETER B. DAVY, *a bearded veteran of the Civil War, conducted the last wagon train expedition over the northern route to Montana in 1867. Courtesy Faribault County Historical Society.*

THE OFFICERS OF THE 1862 FISK EXPEDITION *probably sat for this photograph in Minnesota before their three-month journey across the plains. Standing left to right are Dr. William D. Dibb and Nathaniel P. Langford. James Fisk, in buckskins, is seated in the center, and the other two men have been tentatively identified as Elihu H. Burritt and David Charlton. Courtesy Mr. Gerald E. Fitzgerald, St. Paul.*

PIERRE BOTTINEAU, *an experienced scout who was already famous on the frontier, guided Fisk's first expedition across Dakota in 1862.*

THREE *of James Fisk's brothers accompanied him on the Montana expeditions— Andrew, Robert, and Van. Both Andrew and Robert left accounts of their journeys, which are printed in this book. Photograph of Andrew, at right, courtesy Montana Historical Society.*

THIS PHOTOGRAPH *of Robert E. Fisk was taken in 1865.*

VAN H. FISK *went with his brother on two gold-seeking expeditions. Courtesy Montana Historical Society.*

ST. PAUL, *the capital of Minnesota and the head of navigation on the Mississippi, served as the outfitting point for many members of the trains. Photograph by B. F. Upton, 1861.*

Ho! for Montana!

All persons going to Montana by way of Fort Abercrombie can obtain a complete outfit of Fire Arms, Ammunition, &c.,

At St. Cloud, Minn.,

(The rendezvous for Capt. Fisk's train,) from

H. W. HANFORD,

DEALER IN

Breech-Loading Rifles, Shot Guns,

Revolvers, Fishing Tackle,

And a general assortment of Sportsmen's and Hunter's Goods, which *I will guarantee to sell as low as any House in the West.*

H. W. HANFORD.

my1-1m-1st¶

THIS ADVERTISEMENT *of H. W. Hanford, an outfitter who offered to sell the emigrants firearms and ammunition, appeared in the* St. Paul Press *of May 1, 1866. A great deal of advertising and promotion preceded the departure of the wagon trains.*

MINNESOTANS *living in the vicinity of Shakopee formed the nucleus of the three Holmes trains. This photograph of Shakopee's main street, with the Minnesota River in the background, was taken in the 1870s.*

THE MINNESOTA RIVER VALLEY TOWN *of Mankato was Davy's headquarters in 1867. The valley formed a natural highway to Dakota. This sketch, showing the town as it looked in 1866, is from Thomas Hughes,* History of Blue Earth County *(Chicago, [1909?]).*

ST. CLOUD, *a thriving town in central Minnesota, was the rendezvous for several expeditions. Photograph taken in 1868.*

AT LEFT IS PART *of the roll of the Fisk expedition of 1866, listing the names of those who traveled in the train and the fees they paid. Courtesy Mrs. Catherine Fountain, Pewaukee, Wisconsin.*

ONE of the more than 1,400 emigrants who crossed the northern plains with the wagon trains in the 1860s was "Whack" Ryan, an adventurer who was later shot by the Spaniards in Cuba. Courtesy Montana Historical Society.

AN AMERICAN FLAG flew over the camp of the Fisk expedition at St. Cloud in June, 1866. Two photographers — William H. Illingworth and a Mr. Bill — accompanied the train that year. This is one of twenty-four known stereopticon views taken on their journey. Courtesy Montana Historical Society.

THE ROLLING, WOODED VALLEY *of the Sauk River was followed by several wagon trains on their way across Minnesota. They found the trail rough and difficult. Lithograph by John Mix Stanley from Isaac I. Stevens,* Narrative and Final Report of Explorations for a Route for a Pacific Railroad *(Washington, 1860).*

THIS PHOTOGRAPH *taken by Illingworth and Bill shows the Fisk train of 1866 probably encamped in the Sauk Valley. Andrew Fisk stands in the foreground. Courtesy Montana Historical Society.*

AFTER MOVING OUT *from Minnesota towns, the emigrant parties stopped at frontier military posts before starting across the plains. Fort Ridgely on the Minnesota River was visited by expeditions in 1864 and 1866. Water color by Alfred Sully, 1855; courtesy Thomas Gilcrease Institute of American History and Art.*

FORT ABERCROMBIE *on the Red River played host to trains in 1862, 1863, 1866, and 1867. Sketch by Robert O. Sweeny, 1862.*

AFTER LEAVING *Fort Abercrombie on the present Minnesota–North Dakota border, the trains headed west across the plains. The emigrants crossed the Sheyenne River and traveled northwestward toward the Missouri River. Lithograph of the Sheyenne River by Stanley, from Stevens,* Narrative and Final Report.

BEYOND LAKE JESSIE *in northwestern North Dakota, emigrants of the Fisk train of 1863 met Red River half-breeds on their summer buffalo hunt. Lithograph of the hunters' encampment by Stanley, from Stevens,* Narrative and Final Report.

FOR BETTER DEFENSE *against Indian attack, the wagons formed a corral each night. This photography by Illingworth and Bill shows a corral of the Fisk expedition of 1866 probably near Bears Den Hillock on the Sheyenne River, where Fort Ransom was later built. Courtesy Montana Historical Society.*

MEMBERS *of several trains encoun-tered large herds of buffalo near Lake Jessie. Lithograph by Stanley, from Stevens,* Narrative and Final Report.

THE EMIGRANTS *hunted buffalo for food and sport, and the killing of the first buffalo was an exciting event for members of every expedi-tion. From* Harper's New Monthly Magazine, *October, 1860.*

BUTTE DE MORALE, *named for a half-breed hunter killed near there, was a landmark on the trail near present-day Wellsburg, North Dakota. Lithograph by Stanley, from Stevens,* Narrative and Final Report.

THE VALLEY *of the Souris or Mouse River in the vicinity of present-day Minot, North Dakota, was on the route taken by three expeditions to the gold fields. Lithograph by Stanley, from Stevens,* Narrative and Final Report.

THE INTERIOR of Fort Rice looked like this in 1864. The post was one of three authorized by the army in 1864 for the protection of emigration on the northern routes.

FORT BERTHOLD, an old fur post on the Missouri River, was described by one emigrant as a "poor, dirty little stockade." Sketch by Granville Stuart, 1866; courtesy Montana Historical Society.

A WAGON TRAIN of gold seekers is depicted under attack by Indians. Only the expeditions of 1864 had any major encounters with hostile Indians. When the Davy train met unfriendly Indians in 1867, trouble was averted with the help of the expedition's brass band. Illustration from an old calendar entitled "Montana Gold Seekers Crossing the Plains," courtesy Montana Historical Society.

GENERAL ALFRED SULLY's *punitive expedition against the Sioux in 1864, on its way down the Missouri Valley, encamped on the plains near Fort Berthold. Members of the Holmes train traveled with Sully's soldiers to the Yellowstone River.*

MEMBERS *of the Fisk train saw Badlands formations between Forts Berthold and Union in 1866. This photograph was taken that year by Illingworth and Bill. Courtesy Montana Historical Society.*

GENERAL SULLY, *pictured in uniform at right, said the Badlands look like "Hell burnt out." His troops traveled through the Little Missouri Badlands in 1864.*

FISK WAGONS *crossed the White Earth River in the rough country of the Coteau du Missouri. Andrew Fisk said this view by Illingworth and Bill was taken on July 27, 1866, before the train reached Fort Union. Courtesy Montana Historical Society.*

PICTURED HERE *is a camp of the Assiniboin Indians near Fort Union. The log structure in the center was probably a trader's store. During the summer of 1866, when Illingworth and Bill took this photograph, many tribes were gathered at the fort to make a treaty with the United States government. Courtesy Montana Historical Society.*

FORT UNION, *the largest of the fur posts on the route, stood guard on the upper Missouri River. When the overland emigrants visited it in the 1860s, the fort was operated by Pierre Chouteau, Jr., and Company of St. Louis. These two views, taken by Illingworth and Bill, are perhaps the only known photographs of Fort Union, which was bought by the United States Army in 1867 and later wrecked. Courtesy Montana Historical Society.*

ALL BUT ONE *of the expeditions traversed the Milk River Valley. The Bearpaw Mountains, which can be seen in the distance, marked the emigrants' entrance into the mountain region. Lithograph by Stanley, from Stevens,* Narrative and Final Report.

FORT BENTON, *a fur post at the eastern end of the Mullan Road, was an important terminus for Missouri River shipping and a gateway to the gold fields in the 1860s. This lithograph is the work of Gustav Sohon, an artist who accompanied Captain John Mullan's expedition to build the road. From Mullan,* Report of the Construction of a Military Road from Fort Walla-Walla to Fort Benton *(Washington, 1863).*

NEAR FORT BENTON, *the emigrants encountered such tribes as the Blackfeet. This painting by Charles M. Russell depicts Indian warriors watching a wagon train invade their territory. Courtesy Montana Historical Society.*

BIRDTAIL BUTTE *on the Mullan Road was a striking landmark seen by the emigrants as they approached the end of their journey. Lithograph by A. E. Mathews, from* Pencil Sketches of Montana *(New York, 1868); courtesy Montana Historical Society.*

THE MULLAN ROAD *ran between steep cliffs in Prickly Pear Canyon. One of the Holmes emigrants of 1864 called this "the finest scenery on the route." Water color by Danish artist Peter Tofft; courtesy Montana Historical Society.*

OFF THE MULLAN ROAD *in present-day Montana the emigrants stopped to prospect for gold and founded mining settlements. Some of these grew into permanent towns; others died quickly. This water color of what was probably the mining town of Unionville was painted by Tofft in the 1860s. Courtesy Montana Historical Society.*

OTHER MINING SETTLEMENTS *boasted log cabins like these erected at Last Chance Gulch on the site of Helena. Courtesy Montana Historical Society.*

THE FIRST HOME *for many a miner's family was a wickiup — a rough hut made of brush and poles. This one was erected at Prickly Pear diggings on the site of Montana City, where Fisk emigrants found gold in 1862. Courtesy Montana Historical Society.*

WAGONS AND BUGGIES *of the Last Chance Gulch miners crowded Helena's main street in the mid-1860s. Andrew Fisk, who worked with his brothers on the Helena Herald, dated this photograph 1866. Courtesy Montana Historical Society.*

THE DEER LODGE VALLEY *became a permanent home for gold seekers who found agri-culture more profitable than mining. Lithograph by Mathews, from* Pencil Sketches of Montana; *courtesy Montana Historical Society.*

JOHNNY GRANT'S RANCH *in the Deer Lodge Valley was a stopover place for several emigrant trains. Sketch by Stuart, 1865; courtesy Montana Historical Society.*

OTHER MINNESOTA EMIGRANTS *became pioneer residents of Bannack on Grasshopper Creek. This sketch of the settlement was made in the winter of 1862–63 by Robert Halliday, an Englishman who crossed the plains with Fisk in 1862. The cabin in the foreground at the far right belonged to James Fergus, for whom Fergus Falls, Minnesota and Fergus County, Montana, were named. Courtesy Montana Historical Society.*

VIRGINIA CITY *is shown as it looked about 1865, a few years after the discovery of gold in Alder Gulch, one of the richest placers in the world. The town has been restored as an example of a gold-mining city of the 1860s. Courtesy Montana Historical Society.*

By the end of the 1860s the day of the pick-and-pan gold miner was over. From Montana Historical Contributions, *vol. 4 (Helena, 1903).*

These gold nuggets *from Alder Gulch were given by Fisk to President Lincoln. Sketch from* Leslie's Illustrated Newspaper, *March 19, 1864.*

Promoters *of the northern wagon trains of the 1860s saw them as forerunners of a great commercial empire, which would come into being as soon as a railroad linked Minnesota with the Pacific. This photograph of an early Northern Pacific train was taken in 1873 along a route pioneered by the gold seekers.*

loss Sims had suffered, he insisted that if he were ever to travel west again he would go with Fisk.

A somewhat harsher evaluation was made by William Larned. When the history of the expedition was finally written, asserted Larned, it would "shed no luster around the name of him who has undertaken its direction." Fisk's conduct had been sadly lacking in energy, system, and thoroughness in the "commonest duties." In order "to gain a little personal fame," Fisk had turned off Sully's trail, although he was "utterly ignorant" of the region to be traversed and although his surveyor was "often unable to sit on his horse from intoxication." Indeed, Larned added, "If Whiskey often & much is an element of success, we lack nothing — for all from the head of the Command down . . . drink deep & long." Fisk himself, according to Larned, "urges Moderation Yet passes the bottle often." However, Larned added, "I like him, for his great good nature covers a great many defects."[50]

As the story of the expedition became known, Fisk was bitterly assailed in eastern newspapers for the poisoning of the Indians. The army, too, shared the blame for this seemingly inhuman conduct. The opinion of westerners was probably summed up by the Stillwater, Minnesota, editor who wrote that "the man who can by no matter what agency — *bad bread* or bullets, — put the greatest number of Indians out of the way, is a benefactor of the human race."[51]

Fisk and the army exchanged recriminations. Fisk was criticized for insubordination, for not following Sully's trail, for irresponsible behavior, and for speaking disrespectfully of his superior officers. He defended his conduct vigorously in the public press and in his official report, criticizing Sully for escorting the Holmes emigrants and for not providing enough assistance for his own train. In a sense, the army had the last word, for the captain's intemperate remarks about Sully and Fisk's account of the Indian poisoning were censored from his report for a hundred years.[52]

A curious epilogue to the Fisk expedition of 1864 is the so-called "Mountain of Gold" story which appeared in print more than fifty years later. In 1919 William Dibb's son-in-law, Robert D. Strong, published in the *Minneapolis Journal* a colorful article about the deceased doctor's experiences with the Fisk expeditions. The account, which later appeared in more dramatic form in a travel and adventure publication, *Wide World Magazine,* purported to be based on the doctor's diaries and included alleged quotations from them. Among other events the article described the discovery by Dibb and Fisk of rich gold deposits not far from their 1864 line of march. The description of a fabulous Mountain of Gold, supposedly discovered just before the train was attacked by Indians, aroused considerable public interest and led the Minnesota Historical Society to make an extensive search for records of the Fisk expeditions.[53]

[50] Larned Diary, September 10, 1864.

[51] *Faribault Central Republican,* October 19, 1864; *Pioneer,* November 13, 30, 1864, January 26, 1865; *Stillwater Messenger,* January 31, 1865.

[52] *Pioneer,* November 22, 30, 1864; *WRR,* vol. 41, part 1, p. 132, 152.

[53] *Journal,* March 2, 1919, Magazine Section, p. 1, 7; *Wide World Magazine,* 43:415–419 (September, 1919). Both articles included a map, purportedly drawn by Dibb and showing the location of the "Mountain of Gold." The map confuses the headwaters of the Missouri and Little Missouri rivers, locating the supposed mine in the vicinity of both Fort Rice and Butte, Montana. Dibb died in St. Anthony in 1871.

Strong gave a typed copy of the diaries of Dr. Dibb to the society in April, 1919. Four years later the institution obtained a photographic copy of the original diaries. When the two copies were compared, it became apparent that more than half a dozen references to gold discoveries in the "Strong version" were not present in the original diaries. Careful readers also noted that the highly romantic description of the Mountain of Gold was quite unlike Dr. Dibb's usual spare prose. The Strong version, moreover, contained factual errors about gold mines and mining not likely to have been made by Dr. Dibb after his firsthand acquaintance with the mining region of the West.[54]

Since no other records of the Fisk expeditions support the Mountain of Gold story, historians have supposed that it was invented by Strong out of whole cloth. However, evidence turned up during the course of research for this book sheds new light on the golden mountain. Correspondence preserved in the National Archives reveals that in the 1890s Fisk himself returned to Dakota to search for "certain supposed valuable mineral deposites" along the route of the 1864 expedition. Probably during the same period, Fisk was said to have visited the Dibb home to inquire about a map which had been among the doctor's papers. Fisk undoubtedly knew of the rumors of gold in the Black Hills, which circulated among Indians and frontiersmen for years before the Black Hills gold rush of the 1870s. Whether he and Dr. Dibb had picked up any more specific information about where to look for gold is not known. Perhaps they had once possessed a map of some modest, long-forgotten claim which Fisk's fertile imagination had turned into a golden mountain by the 1890s.[55]

In any event, it now appears that an oral tradition in the Dibb family, perhaps a memory of an old map, and perhaps the inquiries of Fisk himself may have inspired Strong to rework the Dibb diaries and create a Mountain of Gold. Whatever its origin, the belief in such a mountain has persisted to this day. Men are still searching for it, and some of them have offered, in return for information now incorporated in this book, to share the gold with the author if it is found.

[54] The interpolations appeared in entries of September 19, 25, 1862; July 26, August 9, September 4, 28, 1863; September 1, 21, 1864.
[55] Fisk to H. C. Corbin, May 3, 22, 1893, Corbin to Fisk, June 7, 1893 — all in file 7350 PDR 1893, NARG 94; interview of the author with Mrs. Katherine Dibb Fitzgerald, 1945.

1864 ⚙⚙⚙⚙⚙⚙⚙⚙⚙⚙⚙⚙⚙⚙⚙

Gilbert Benedict's Diary of the Holmes Train[1]

WEDNESDAY, APRIL 27, 1864. Started from Glenn's [Glens] Falls N. Y. for Idaho in good spirits. Weather dark and rainy. Baggage car took fire by friction produced by my extra trunk, of course. — 358 miles through New York State.[2]

April 28. Arrived at the Suspension Bridge [Niagara River] at noon, and at Detroit at ten o'clock P.M. — 259 [229] miles.

April 29. Arrived at Chicago at ten o'clock A.M. — 284 miles. From Chicago to Milwaukee 85 miles, & from Milwaukee to La Cross[e] 200 miles.

April 30. Arrived at La Cross at six o'clock A.M. At 8 o'clock A.M., took the packet Keokuk for St. Paul — 208 miles. River low. Boat goes as crooked as a rail fence to find a channel.[3]

Sunday, May 1. Arrived at St. Paul at 8½ o'clock A.M. Cold wind. The inhabitants number 15,000. Commenced boarding at Payne's Temperance House [Moffet's Hotel] at noon.[4]

[1] Benedict's diary is reproduced with the permission of the MoHS. This version is a copy of the original diary, now lost, which was made with Benedict's permission by William F. Wheeler sometime before 1884. (See *Montana Historical Contributions,* 2:34.) In preparing Wheeler's copy for publication, the form of entry has been regularized and the punctuation standardized. Comments made on diary entries by Wheeler have been omitted.

Three manuscripts in the MoHS supplement the Wheeler copy and have been used in editing it. Two are undated reminiscent accounts of the journey in Benedict's handwriting, one in prose and one in verse form. The third is an undated biographical account of Benedict prepared by Alva J. Noyes, apparently based on an interview and including quotations from the original diary. These manuscripts are cited respectively as Benedict, "Trip to Montana," prose; Benedict, "Trip to Montana," verse; and Noyes, "Gilbert Benedict."

[2] Benedict was accompanied by Hiram Krum, a carpenter and neighbor, D. G. Norris, and Henry Fenton. See obituary of Krum in Benedict's Scrapbook, in MoHS; Benedict, "Trip to Montana," prose, 1, and verse, 7–9; United States Manuscript Census Schedules, 1860, Warren County, New York, p. 96, in the National Archives.

[3] Benedict's route was probably by way of Schenectady and Rochester to Niagara Falls, chiefly over the New York Central Railroad, and then over the Great Western Railway of Canada, the Michigan Central, the Milwaukee and Chicago, and the Milwaukee and St. Paul Railway to La Crosse. The mileages given are approximately the same as those in *Ashcroft's Railway Directory for 1865,* 52, 115, 117, 124, 135 (New York, 1865).

[4] The population of St. Paul in 1865 was nearly 13,000, according to *St. Paul City Directory,*

May 2. Weather cool and dry. Many soldiers in town, at the forts and military stations, not to fight the white, but the red rebels.

May 3. Went to Ft. Snelling, six miles above St. Paul. In the Fort 25 Sioux Indians were in the barracks as prisoners and more squaws and their children. A soldier shot an Indian boy by accident. Boy was 12 years old.[5]

May 4. Dry and dusty. At 11 P.M. a man jumped from my hotel, and was almost killed. Was drunk.

May 5. First Minnesota Regiment was discharged. — has been in 21 battles. Noble large men. One of them six feet and seven inches high, — had been shot twice in the head.[6]

May 6. Nothing of importance transpiring now, except getting our outfit.[7]

May 12. Heard from a man just returned from Idaho by the southern [central] route that there are a thousand wagons on the plains with no teams. They started too early in the Spring, got caught in a snow storm, cattle starved, leaving the men without means of transportation.[8]

May 17. Took passage on boat up the Minnesota river to Shakopee. It is a beautiful river — no islands — and looks as though its banks had been cut by hand. Met [D. G.] Norris with oxen and put the wagons together.

May 18. Still at Shakopee. The sun looks red and angry and it is very dry.

Thursday, May 19. *Started* from Shakopee with three yokes of cattle and one cow. Made 12 miles. Roads quite good. Run into a stump and nearly broke an axle.[9] Tom Holmes lost one pair cattle in the woods and had to leave them. We passed through Jordan.

May 20. Went four miles. Found good feed and stopped for the night. Good road but very dry. Indian shot six miles from New Ulm. His hand is preserved in alcohol.

May 21. Saw a deer before sun rise. Passed through Belle Plaine. Traveled 18 miles to Leseur [Le Sueur], where we found good feed and water and a beautiful spot or grove.

Sunday, May 22. rested all day. Had a fine rain which did much good.

May 23. Went 14 miles. Crossed a ferry near Ottowa [Ottawa].

May 24. Went 14 miles. Are now in the section where the Indians in 1862 committed such depredations.

1866. Moffet's Hotel, also known as Moffet's Castle, was a temperance hotel. A clerk named Payne is listed in the *St. Paul City Directory, 1864*.

[5] On May 4 there were nearly ninety Sioux men, women, and children in the custody of the military at Fort Snelling, awaiting removal to a new reservation. See Sibley to Pope, May 4, 1864, in Department of the Northwest, 10:289, NARG 98.

[6] This was probably Jacob George, a corporal in Company C, who had been wounded in the battle of Bull Run. See Descriptive Book, First Minnesota Volunteer Infantry, and George's compiled service record, both in NARG 94.

[7] Benedict, Krum, and Fenton assembled their wagon and supplies in St. Paul, while Norris "went out among the farmers" to buy oxen. See Noyes, "Gilbert Benedict," 7. At this point in the diary Wheeler noted that there were no further entries until May 12. Other lapses between May 12 and 17 and on May 29 are not accounted for.

[8] Benedict later recalled that he had asked this man's advice about supplies for the trip. The man replied: "'By all means take some whiskey.' Two of us did not believe in liquor so did not lay in a supply and we got along better than some who did. (I never tasted any liquor in my life)." Noyes, "Gilbert Benedict," 7.

[9] Benedict later said that the cattle had been purchased from a German farmer and did not understand commands given in English. Noyes, "Gilbert Benedict," 1.

May 25. Traveled six miles. Camped two and a half miles from New Ulm, where 125 houses were burned, on the 19th and 23d of August, 1862. Twenty people were killed and sixty wounded by 800 Indians.[10]

May 26. Passed through New Ulm at Six A.M., where are breast works and cannon. Find many bullet holes in some houses. Made two and one half miles.

May 27. Camping near New Ulm.

May 28. Received good news in relation to the expedition. We are to have 1900 military from Ft. Ridgley to the Missouri river, where we will meet Genl. Sully, with 8,000 men to guard the emigrants through.[11]

May 30. Traveled over the ground that was the scene of many sanguinary conflicts with the Indians. Fifteen hundred whites were murdered and a large amount of property burned.[12]

May 31. Started from New Ulm, crossed the [Minnesota] river again and traveled ten miles.

Wednesday, June 1. Traveled seven miles near Ft. Ridgley. Visited the Fort. It is surrounded by extensive high land, which is covered with cavalry and artillery.

June 2. Went five miles to the gathering of wagons opposite Ft. Ridgley on the south side of the river, where the train and companies were formed and officers elected for the expedition.

June 3. Went ten miles. Camped on an Indian [Lower Sioux] reservation, where are the ruins of an Indian village [Little Crow's], but it was deserted in August 1862, at the time of the great massacre. The boys dug open ten Indian graves, found two gold dollars and plenty of other trinkets, silver, brass, spoons, basins, cups, &c.[13]

June 4. Traveled six miles. This reservation had about 3,000 red-skins and their houses cover miles of ground, some of which are quite good; — Also a church built by Uncle Sam. All are now in ruins since 1862. The boys go among and in the houses and find what articles are left. Were stopped by a shower.[14]

June 5. To-day made six miles to Camp Pope. We now wait for the military escort.[15]

June 6. Remain in Camp Pope. Find good hunting and fishing, and plenty of grass, water and wood.

[10] According to Carley, 190 structures were destroyed, 34 people killed, and 60 wounded during attacks by perhaps 100 Sioux on August 19 and by about 650 on August 23. *Sioux Uprising of 1862,* 38–46.

[11] Like many of the emigrants, Benedict and his friends had expected to travel with Fisk, but when no word came from him, they decided to accompany the military expedition. There were 1,308 men in the Second or Minnesota Brigade at Fort Ridgley. Sully's command totaled 4,203 men. See returns of May 30, 1864, for Department of the Northwest, and returns of the Northwestern Indian Expedition for June, 1864, both in Department of the Northwest, NARG 94.

[12] A recent estimate is that between 450 and 800 settlers and soldiers were killed. Carley, *Sioux Uprising of 1862,* 11.

[13] The Lower Sioux reservation and that of the Upper Sioux, which was contiguous to the west, extended in a narrow strip along the south side of the Minnesota River. Little Crow's village was near present-day Redwood Falls. Carley, *Sioux Uprising of 1862,* 12, 40.

[14] There were some 7,000 Indians on the Upper and Lower Sioux reservations. Carley, *Sioux Uprising of 1862,* 12. The church, St. John's Episcopal, is mentioned in George C. Tanner, *Fifty Years of Church Work in the Diocese of Minnesota,* 391, 393, 396, 404 (St. Paul, 1909).

[15] For Camp Pope, used by Sibley in 1863 and located near present-day Redwood Falls, see Carley, *Sioux Uprising of 1862,* 71.

June 7. Cavalry came to Camp Pope for the expedition and camped a mile above us. Man shot at Indian but did not hit him.

June 8. Made 20 miles. Camped at a beautiful lake near the Minnesota river.[16]

June 9. Remained in camp. Day very warm and dry. The Indian reservation is 150 miles long and ten miles wide. Our Camp is near Wood Lake, where are rifle pits. It is the place where a battle was fought with the Indians in August, in 1862.

June 10. Passed through the Upper Agency. Found large numbers of brick houses built by the government in ruins. Crossed the Yellow Medicine river. It abounds in fish. Made eight miles and camped at a brook.[17]

June 11. Traveled sixteen miles. Roads good. Scouts found an Indian trail. Camped on the Minnesota river. The ground is so dry for want of rain, that there are cracks wide enough to put my hand in. River very low.

Sunday, June 12. Halted at Camp Release for this day.[18] Military horses made a stampede for camp, for some cause. No damage.

June 13. Made 12 miles. Camped on In-the-Pah creek [Intpah, or Lac qui Parle River]. Found large tracts of prairie on fire.

June 14. Made 14 miles. Followed In-the-Pah creek — good fishing.

June 15. Went 16 miles to a lake [Lone Tree Lake? South Dakota], — good fishing — no wood.

June 16. Traveled 16 miles over hills. Party saw the first herd of buffaloes, that has been seen since the train started. Camped on the Sioux river [Willow Creek]. Found a lake [Two Woods Lake] with many dead fish on the banks, also buffalo bones.[19]

June 17. Saw more buffalo. Scouts killed two yesterday. Camped at a pleasant lake [Lake Nicholson]. Made 22 miles.[20]

June 18. Made 20 miles. Some of the party saw buffalo, wolves and antelope. Camped at a fine lake [Horseshoe Lake], a number of which we passed on the route. At ten P.M. had a very hard shower and wind.

Sunday, June 19. No travel this day, but we strewed the ground with quilts, blankets and whole loads of stuff to dry, in the sun. Two tents blew down, and much property was wet by the shower last night. The [Second Cavalry?] band in our camp made good music at 3 P.M. which was quite delightful. There was preaching.

[16] The train camped on Lone Tree or Battle Lake (since dried up), five miles north of present-day Echo. For the misnamed battle of Wood Lake, mentioned below, see Carley, *Sioux Uprising of 1862,* 55–59.

[17] The Upper Sioux Agency, located near present-day Granite Falls, included about half a dozen buildings. See Carley, *Sioux Uprising of 1862,* 12, 26.

[18] Camp Release, near present-day Montevideo, was the spot where white captives were released by the Sioux after the battle of Wood Lake. See Carley, *Sioux Uprising of 1862,* 60–62.

[19] The train apparently passed between two lakes of the group in northwestern Deuel County, South Dakota, which includes Two Woods, Round, and School lakes, a few miles north of present-day Highway 212. See the diaries of Ebenezer Rice and Robert McLaren, June 16, 1864, both in the MiHS.

[20] The route taken by the train from Lake Nicholson to the crossing of the James River on June 22 has been traced with the diaries of Rice, John Strong, and McLaren; *WRR,* vol. 41, part 2, p. 514; and with the assistance in the field of Mr. Herman P. Chilson, Webster, South Dakota. See Chilson to the author, April 20, 1965.

June 20. Went 16 miles. Saw two buffaloes and two wolves. Road good. The air is so clear we can see far off.[21]

June 21. One vast level prairie; — No lakes until we get to camp 22 miles, near James river [Crow Creek] — a very muddy stream at this point.[22]

June 22. Camp Salts. Crossed [James] river. Two upset in canoe. Two Dutchmen fought about a rope, when one being worsted went to his wagon got his pistol, cocked it, but before he got to his man was taken, and his pistol discharged. He was tried and sentenced to take the rear and to leave the train on getting to the Missouri river. Made one mile.[23]

June 23. Made 12 miles. Camped on James [Elm] River. Weather hot and dry. Have on our journey, found water tinctured with alkali, salts, sulphur, iron &c., much of which is not fit to drink.

June 24. Camped on Elm river. Made 17½ miles. Saw the boys kill an antelope. Good wood, water, and grass. Plenty of buffalo. This is the ground on which the treaty was made with the Dakota Indians.[24]

June 25. Made fifteen and a half miles. Arrived at 12½ o'clock P.M. Good grass and water. The boys killed a large buffalo bull, and might have killed more, but they showed fight. The men being on foot ran for a more safe place. At 7 P.M. took team and went for the animal killed. Remained out all night.[25]

Sunday, June 26. Brought in the buffalo this morning. He was very large. No travel this day.

June 27. Made 19½ miles this day. Camped by the side of a fine lake [Long Lake].

June 28. Made 20 miles. Good water and grass. Saw two antelope. Boys shot at and missed them. Wind blew the tents down.

June 29. Made 25 miles. Antelope plenty. Train struck Sully's last year's trail and followed the same. Tuesday Sully lost his Chief Engineer [Captain John Feilner], by shot from three Indians, who were caught and killed.[26]

June 30. Continued on the old trail and found Gen. Sully's camp, with two com-

---

[21] A rifle pit is still visible on the campsite in Scotland Township, Day County, South Dakota. See Chilson to the author, April 20, 1965.

[22] Benedict probably means that there had been no water during the day's march of twenty-two miles. Crow Creek is an eastern branch of the James River.

[23] The train apparently crossed the James south of present-day Columbia, South Dakota, and then followed the Elm River and its branches south and west into the Coteau du Missouri. The two men involved in the shooting affair were probably Edwin Howe and Paul Kratke. According to Benedict, "Trip to Montana," verse, 6, Howe was sentenced to travel at the rear of the train for the rest of the journey.

[24] Benedict probably refers to a treaty made with the Yankton Sioux in 1858, although the boundary of the land ceded by the Indians lay somewhat south of the route of the Holmes train. See Charles J. Kappler, ed., *Indian Affairs, Laws and Treaties*, 2:776–780 (Washington, 1904); B. M. Smith and A. J. Hill, "Map of the Ceded Part of Dakota Territory Showing also portions of Minnesota, Iowa & Nebraska" (2 ed., 1863), in the National Archives.

[25] The camp was at the eastern foot of the coteau, probably at the head of the Willow Creek branch of the Elm River, east of present-day Leola, South Dakota. The route over the coteau from this point to the camp of June 29 is difficult to reconstruct, but appears to have gone to Long Lake and the vicinity of present-day Eureka, South Dakota.

[26] The train struck Sully's 1863 trail south of Bordache or Spring Creek, probably in the vicinity of present-day Mound City, South Dakota. The camp was probably about seven miles south of Mound City. Sully's 1863 route is shown on John H. Wagner, comp., "Map Exhibiting the Route . . . of Brig. Gen. H. H. Sibley, 1863," in *WRR Atlas*, plate 33. On Feilner, see A. M. English, "Dakota's First Soldiers," in *South Dakota Historical Collections*, 9:275 (Aberdeen, 1918.)

panies of cavalry, one battery of guns and one Regiment of soldiers, on six boats on the Missouri river. Made 20 miles, camped in a shower.[27]

Friday, July 1. Heavy rains last night. Also one man killed by an Indian, and his horse taken. No travel this day. 2100 Indians seen the other side of the river, who pretended to be fri[e]ndly.

July 2. No travel this day. Boys saw six Indians on horses. Cattle get mired and have to be pulled out by the dozen.

Sunday, July 3. Made four miles on a back track. Col. [Minor T.] Thomas having got supplies from the steam boats, we go north to the Long Lake to fight Indians.[28] Eleven having been seen by two of our men and then driven into camp, but who in turn were pursued by the scouts.

July 4. Traveled 15 miles. Camped where we did last Thursday [Wednesday] night. Some of the boys celebrated the day by getting drunk.

July 5. Made 20 miles due north up the Missouri river towards Long Lake.

July 6. Made 32 miles and stopped on Beaver [Sand] Creek. After getting fifteen miles we came to a lake, and after preparing to make camp, we found the water to be alkali, which induced us to go farther. Plenty of beaver on this creek.

July 7. Having one creek [Horsehead?] and a slough to cross and a hilly road to travel, we made but nine miles and camped at 1.30 P.M.

July 8. Traveled 12 miles and camped on the bank of the Missouri. It is a fast stream and quite muddy, but the soldiers say the water is quite healthful. Opposite to us Gen. Sully is going to build a post, to be called Ft. Rice.[29]

July 9. Went one mile to-day to better our location and wait for our turn to cross the river. Seven steamers are taking the military over.[30] The steamer Yellowstone arrived last night with passengers and furs from Ft. Benton. They report buffaloes so plenty swimming the river, that they had to stop the boat to let them cross. They also report 7000 Indians who intend to fight us.

Sunday, July 10. Genl. Sully crosses more of his troops to-day. They caught a large wolf swimming the river and took him to camp alive.

July 11. Col. Thomas' force (the Minnesota Brigade) cross the river to-day. The river is now up enough for business, showing that there has been rain above — up the river.

July 12. The emigrants cross on the Steamboats. We find business driving, building Ft. Rice, and store houses, landing goods &c. One steamboat ["Chippewa Falls"?] has arrived with mail &c. Our train was crossed on condition that we cut one cord of wood to each wagon for the steamboats.

July 13. Cut our cord to-day. One hundred and seventeen wagons make quite

[27] The camp was on Swan Lake Creek, near present-day Alaska, South Dakota. For the route of this part of the journey, see Henning Von Minden, "Map of the Route of Brig. Gen. A. Sully," 1864, in Cartographic Records, No. Q107½, Office of the Chief of Engineers, NARG 77. Troops of the Thirtieth Wisconsin Infantry were on steamboats bound upriver for Fort Rice. See returns of the Northwestern Indian Expedition for June, 1864, NARG 94.

[28] Benedict here refers to the Long Lake in Kidder and Burleigh counties, North Dakota.

[29] The camp was at the mouth of present-day Badger Creek. For the fort, see Ray H. Mattison, "Fort Rice — North Dakota's First Missouri River Military Post," in *North Dakota History,* 20:87–108 (April, 1953).

[30] The names of the steamboats are given in "Diary Kept by Lewis C. Paxson, Stockton, N.J. (1862–1864)," in *North Dakota Historical Collections,* 2 (part 2):140.

a pile of wood. We elected a Mr. O[liver] D. Keep our Captain to-day. The soldiers killed 13 buffalo out of a herd of 200.

July 14. The air or wind is so hot that we cannot keep cool in the shade — 106° degrees. We have a fine young wolf in camp kept by a Dutchman.

July 15. Last night a wolf came into camp and frightened the dogs much. Business is driving in this place. Many men are at work building the Fort, store houses, making brick &c. One man occupies the burying ground, who started for his health.[31]

July 16. Wrote home. No travel around camp. All quiet.

Sunday, July 17. No travel. General parade in Sully's Camp. Weather hot and dry.

July 18. An improved condition in our camp since the election of our New Captain Keep. Got a visit and a speech in our camp from Gen. Sully, who proposed to carry us through to Powder River safe.

July 19. Made 16 miles over a rough road, in 13 hours. Killed a rattle-snake. Camped on Cannon Ball river. Good water, grass and wood. Two births in camp since we started. One child died and one [Dakota Hanchild] lived.[32]

July 20. Made 20 miles. Scouts report 400[0] Indians 12 miles from here. Gen. Sully says that we are two days march from the Indians, and they are the same he fought in 1862, and with whom he found fifty white women's scalps, which he buried.[33]

July 21. Our hunters say they saw 300 antelopes. We find many petrifactions of wood on the hills. Made 22 miles to-day.

July 22. Made 15 miles. Got news from Scouts that Fisk's train was taken by Indians, Sixty miles above Ft. Rice — men all killed women taken prisoners. Camped on Cannon Ball river.[34]

July 23. Made 20 miles. Crossed [North Fork of the] Cannon Ball river. Found an Indian dead, laid on a scaffold above the ground, wrapped in two buffalo robes, with a supply of 4 bags of tobacco, paint, rings, beads &c. Pony [had been] tied to the post and starved.

Sunday, July 24. Made 22 miles. Very hot. Four oxen and one mule, belonging to Gen. Sully died on the road. Camped on Heart river. Water good and wood plenty. Seventeen herd of stock, belonging to the military died on the road from the heat and work.[35]

July 25. Laid over to wait for Gen. Sully to go to hunt Indians a few days, and to recruit the cattle. Organized two companies out of the train. The boys find many specimens of petrified wood, stumps & leaves. Get them under our feet, any where on the ground.

[31] C. P. Clark, an emigrant from St. Anthony, died on July 8. See Paxson, in *North Dakota Historical Collections*, 2 (part 2):140, and records of the military cemetery at Fort Rice in file R362, August 9, 1867, and file 2608, 1873, both in Fort Rice Consolidated File, NARG 92.

[32] Dakota or Hannah Hanchild was the daughter of Henry Hanchild.

[33] Sully fought the Sioux in 1863 in the battle of White Stone Hill. His published account did not mention the scalps. See *WRR*, vol. 22, part 1, p. 555–568. The camp for this date was on present-day Louse Creek.

[34] The scouts could not have brought accurate news of Fisk's train, for on this date it was still in western Minnesota.

[35] The campsite, on the Heart River about twenty miles southeast of Richardton, North Dakota, is now identified by a marker, according to Pfaller, in *North Dakota History*, 31:38.

July 26. Gen. Sully started his force up Heart river to fight the Indians, while we guard his train with the help of a few [sick] soldiers, who were left at our camp. June berries plenty.

July 27. No travel. The men of the Idaho train stand on picket all the time now, watching for Indians. Weather very dry and hot. No danger of taking cold by sleeping on the ground. Night or day, without cover or shelter of any kind.

July 28. No travel. Not heard from Gen. Sully yet. Great excitement last night from a stampede of mules. We dug rifle pits around the corral to protect ourselves against Indians during the absence of Gen. Sully's force.[36]

July 29. No travel. All hands roused up to man the rifle pits to defend against Indians last night. I have been all day on picket with others watching for Indians. No pay. No rations from Uncle Sam. Most of the troops are gone.

July 30. No travel. Wolves had a fine time fighting and howling around camp.

July 31. No travel. Went hunting at 4 A.M. Saw four wolves before breakfast. Genl. Sully returned.

Monday, August 1. Fine rain last night. No travel. The soldiers and horses are much exhausted from the march and fight, but are recruiting fast. Most have some interesting story to tell about the fight.[37]

August 2. No travel. Moved our camp one mile yesterday, near to Col. Thomas' camp. Every man in our train is now ordered to take a gun out on cattle guard, as the Indians followed Gen. Sully to do mischief.[38]

August 3. Made 20 miles. Camped again on Heart river. A government wagon broke down.

August 4. Made 19 miles. Camped again on Heart river. Crossed over some sand hills, but found plenty of grass.

August 5. Made 22 miles, and after a hard day's work crossing sloughs & mud holes, we got into camp near sun down. Little water and grass. The water we got was made by the last shower. This is the roughest country we have found on the journey.[39]

August 6. Made 12 miles, going over this rough country, through ravines, over high hills. Overturned two wagons, and another broke down. All the scouts say we cannot go through but one. He thinks we can.[40] The boys kill many rattlesnakes.

[36] The emigrants dug rifle pits near each wagon, as well as a large pit near the center of the corral for the women. When the mules stampeded, the men thought Indians were attacking and ran to the outside pits. See Benedict, "Trip to Montana," prose, 7. Some of the soldiers said that the emigrants also made a Quaker cannon — a hollowed log reinforced with iron bands. See Pfaller, in *North Dakota History*, 31:55.

[37] Benedict later wrote two accounts of the battle of Killdeer Mountain — one in "Trip to Montana," prose, 7, and the other in a memorandum added to the Wheeler version.

[38] Because of a cattle stampede, the emigrants believed that Indians were in the vicinity. See John Strong Diary, August 2, 1864.

[39] The train had entered the Little Missouri Badlands. For the route from August 5 to September 8, see "Journal of the March of . . . Brig. Gen'l. A. Sully," 1863, in miscellaneous file 219, NARG 94; Journal of the Northwestern Indian Expedition," Department of the Northwest, vol. 67, NARG 98; Ray W. Lingk, "The Northwestern Indian Expedition . . . The Sully Trail (1864)," in *North Dakota History*, 24:182–197 (October, 1957); Pfaller, in *North Dakota History*, 31:61–65.

[40] The route followed Sully's Creek to the Little Missouri Valley; the camp was just south of present-day Medora, North Dakota. The scout who served as guide through the Badlands may have been William Jackson, about seventeen years old and of Blackfoot-Sioux descent. See Robert

Sunday, August 7. Traveled three miles. Great Indian excitement. Many seen. Gen. Sully throws shell at their pickets all the afternoon. One of our men shot through the jaw [by another picket].[41]

August 8. Fight commences again. Indians all on ponies, but dare not come very near. Our Chief guide shot but not killed. He was an Indian. A hundred red skins were killed by our shot and shell. One horse and rider got an arrow each. Made eight miles can see indians on all sides.[42]

August 9. Made 18 miles. The soldiers drove an encampment of several thousand [*sic*] Indians. Fighting in front and rear. Red skins on all sides but dare not come very near. This morning, before light, great excitement. Guns fired but no red skins seen. Got to camp at ten o'clock P.M.[43]

August 10. Made 18 miles. Roads much better. Picket shot through three fingers before daylight, causing half the camp to mount horses. Few, if any Indians seen this day.[44]

August 11. Made 33 miles. Water and grass very scar[c]e. Gen. Sully's horses, oxen and mules laying dead on the road. They have too much work, and to[o] little grass and water. Found water at ten P.M. where we camped. Damage to government to-day, from loss of stock $30,000.[45]

August 12. Made 10 miles. Little grass, — very dry. No Indian trouble. Camped on the Yellowstone 35 miles from its mouth by water.

August 13. No travel. The boys are having a great time killing deer, elk, &c. which are very plenty. The military are crossing the Yellowstone river. Two men were drowned and some horses mules and wagons were lost. It is a swift stream.[46]

Sunday, August 14. Idaho train crossed the river. Had very good success. Two more men [John Brounworth and Saffer (Xavier) Kopp] were drowned and some wagons tipped over. Some crossed on two steamboats, & some on tight wagon boxes. Cattle swim over.[47]

McLaren to Mrs. McLaren, August 15, 1864, McLaren Papers; Lingk, in *North Dakota History*, 24:183; Jackson's compiled service record, Christian Stuffts Independent Company, Indian Scouts, U.S. Volunteers, NARG 94.

[41] The expedition traveled up the Little Missouri, crossed the river twice, built a road out of the valley up present-day Custer's Wash, and camped near the site of the present-day Custer Trail Ranch. The bracketed information comes from Benedict, "Trip to Montana," prose, 9.

[42] The expedition crossed the Little Missouri again, traveled out of the valley, and camped on a pond on the northeast side of Flat Top Butte, about seven miles southwest of Medora.

[43] Sully estimated that about a thousand Indians appeared; see *WRR*, vol. 41, part 1, p. 146. The morning excitement occurred when a disgruntled soldier walked away from the camp "to let the Indians kill him." When the Indians charged, he started back and was rescued by the troops. See A. J. Fisk Diary, August 9, 1864. The night camp was on Little Beaver Creek, about seven and a half miles north of present-day Beach, North Dakota.

[44] The camp was on Beaver Creek, in Wibaux County, Montana.

[45] The camp was on a branch of Smith Creek, south of the Lindbergh Hills, in Richland County, Montana.

[46] The camp of August 12 and 13 was north of the mouth of Shadwell Creek and about half a mile north of the Pyramid, a landmark in Richland County, Montana. The crossing was made south of the Seven Sisters Islands. The names of the soldiers who drowned are not known.

[47] One of the steamboats was the "Chippewa Falls." See p. 104n, above, and Joseph M. Hanson, *The Conquest of the Missouri*, 59 (Chicago, 1909); Sully, "Journal," August 13, 1864 (Miscellaneous file 219, NARG 94). At this point some of the emigrants proposed to travel to Montana via the Yellowstone, but Sully advised that the route was too dangerous and suggested they accompany the troops as far as Fort Union. See Benedict, "Trip to Montana," prose, 10.

August 15. Made eight miles down the Yellowstone for Fort Union. Plenty of grass and water.

August 16. Made 24 miles to the Missouri opposite the Fort. Saw great numbers of deer, elk &c. Nine before breakfast.

August 17. Crossed to the Fort, which is mostly made of wood. Used a barge and small boat and tight wagon boxes in crossing. Some of Uncle Sam's cattle were lost. The nights are quite cool now.

August 18. No travel. The military went twelve miles last night after Indians, but found none. We are camped one and a half miles from Ft. Union. Prospects are poor and we are afraid of the Indians. No more military protection.[48]

August 19. Left Ft. Union. Made nine miles, but starting without a guide took the wrong road. Guide came up this afternoon.[49]

August 20. Made 12 miles. Boys had a fine time shooting. Grass plenty.

Sunday, August 21. Made 15 miles. Killed more buffaloes than the whole company can eat. See plenty more. Camped on the Big Muddy river. Cattle are sick drinking alkali water from the river.

August 22. Made 20 miles. Saw large herd of buffalo. Road and grass good, but water scarce. Crossed the Big Muddy by laying a large quantity of willow brush over it, in water 18 inches deep. Hundred of Wild geese seen and some shot.

August 23. Made 20 miles. Saw many large herds of buffalo, and more killed than we can use, also deer. Crossed the Quaking asp [Poplar] river.

August 24. Made 14 miles. Any quantity of buffalo. Shot some. Rolling land but not much grass, except in low ground.

August 25. More buffalo. We are drying the meat for winter use. Camp on Ft. Charles river [Wolf Creek]. Made 10 miles.

August 26. Made 15 miles. More buffalo than we want. Hunters get in too late. Get lost or too far from camp to get back before dark. Camped on [Little] Porcupine river.

August 27. Traveled 16 miles. Camped on the Little Porcupine river [Porcupine]. More buffalo and other game. Roads continue good over rolling land.

Sunday, August 28. No travel. Good feed and water where we camped.

August 29. Made 20 miles. Four deserters from Gen. Sully's force arrived this day. They left him where they crossed the Yellowstone river. Went 75 miles and were attacked by Indians. They lost one man and two horses, and then proceeded back. They say so far as they traveled the grass and water are good.[50]

August 30. Made 14 miles. Crossed Willow [Rock] Creek.

August 31. Made 20 miles. Crossed a creek and Milk river. Cow mired and left. Good roads, — poor grass. Camped after sundown.

[48] For the troops' unsuccessful pursuit of the party of Sioux Indians, see WRR, vol. 41, part 1, p. 148. At least two men left the train at this point: Hiram Krum, "who got homesick and . . . worked his way back to St. Louis on a boat," and John H. Tibbetts, a Shakopee jeweler, who returned with some of the soldiers. See Noyes, "Gilbert Benedict," 7, and Winona Republican, October 12, 1864.

[49] The emigrants wanted to hire Basil Clement, one of Sully's guides, but the general would not release him; instead they hired a half-breed named Pete. See "Basil Clement," in North Dakota Historical Collections, 1:342. Benedict mentions "Pete" in an undated memorandum added to Wheeler's copy of the diary.

[50] Benedict wrote later that only two deserters caught up with the train. "Trip to Montana," prose, 10.

Thursday, September 1. Made 14 miles. Very rough, hilly road, and no water till night. Camped on a creek.

September 2. Made 20 miles. Camped on Milk river.

September 3. Made 28 miles up the Milk river. The guide and two others drove a large buffalo up to the road and shot him, and each man took a piece. Camped in a wood. No water for cattle.[51]

Sunday, September 4. Laid over after making eight miles to get water near Milk river.

September 5. Made 20 miles. Camped on creek with a little water. See no buffalo now.

September 6. Messrs Haws [Edwin Howe?] & Goodman went back to get a lame ox and two cows. Remained all night with eleven indians, who cared well for them, and next day robbed them of all they had except one pistol.

September 7. Made 14 miles. Camped on a creek. Good water and grass. Our largest ox got mired, but we got him out safely after a long pull. Also another ox same.

September 8. Made 28 miles. Good road. Camped on Box Elder Creek. Passed Beaver Creek, and found a good spring. Less game now. Passed Bear Paw Mountains, also struck Fisk's old trail.[52]

September 9. Made 25½ miles Camped at 11½ P.M. No water. Cool in the night. Wolves ate Mr. Haws cow alive.

September 10. Made 20 miles. — Crossed the Marias river near its mouth, and camped on the Teton river. Were visited by a party of the Blackfeet Indians, who were quite friendly, and begged for food which they got.[53]

Sunday, September 11. No travel. More Indians. We are six miles from Ft. Benton.

September 12. Made 18 miles. Meet more Indians who are going to the Fort to trade. Our boys are buying robes of them, but are afraid of lice. Camped on the Teton river. A M[r. Benjamin] Bear was run over by his wagon, and injured much in the chest.

September 13. Made 18 miles over good roads. Camped on a lake about 10 feet wide and half a mile long. Twenty miles to Sun river. We see a mirage often, but we don't run for water where there is none.

September 14. Made 24 miles. Quite a frost last night. We have had two or three frosts. The air is very dry — little or no dew and little rain the whole distance. Camped on the Sun river, — a beautiful stream.

September 15. Made 17 miles. Hilly road. Little wood or grass, but fine view of the mountains. Camped near Bird Tail rock. Good water. Warm days, — cool nights. An old man in our train died. Don't know what ailed him.

September 16. Started at 4:30 A.M. Made 17 miles. The change from prairie to

[51] On this date Benedict also reported a quarrel between Philip Constans and the guide, who threatened to lead the train into a hostile Indian camp because he was denied as much liquor as he wanted. See Benedict, "Trip to Montana," verse, 3.

[52] It is not clear what Benedict means by Fisk's "old trail," since a comparison of mileages indicates that the Holmes train had traveled close to Fisk's 1862 trail since leaving Fort Union.

[53] Benedict added a memorandum for September 10, commenting that the group arrived at Fort Benton, which he described as "nothing but a trading post, owned by the American Fur Company."

mountain scenery, from slough or alkali water to the pure mountain stream is quite agreeable as well as conducive to health. Camped on the Dearborn, which is a fast running, pure stream.

September 17. Made 14 miles over a hilly road. Crossed the Little Prickly Pear river eight times. The cliffs each side are three to five hundred feet high. I find no fish in this stream, no game in the woods, but the finest scenery on the route.

Sunday, September 18. Made eight miles over mountains very steep. Crossed the Prickly Pear river thirteen times. Camped in a valley between two mountains.

September 19. Made three and a half miles over another part of the rocky mountains. Camped at Morgan's Ranch. Grass good. Crossed the Prickly Pear for the last time.

September 20. Made 15 miles. Arrived at a branch of the Little Prickly Pear river, where we found a number of men prospecting for gold. Found some. Some took claims and more looking. See plenty of friendly Indians. Bought a robe of a squaw for a red coat and two dollars in greenbacks.

September 21. Laid over to feed and recruit our cattle, and to prospect for gold, other parties having found some. The day is show[e]ry and quite cool.

September 22. Some rain last night and this morning. Find plenty of snow upon the mountains in the west. More rain and a little snow. Men out gold hunting who find some. They call this the Piegan river.[54]

September 23. Make 22 miles. Camped on Ten Mile Creek, a stream three miles from what they call the "Last Chance" creek. Passed Silver creek where they are getting gold. But little water.

Sept. 24. Made 13 miles to the Prickly Pear river where they are getting some gold. Plenty of water and grass.

Sept. 25. The wagon remained at the toll-gate on this river, but I went back ten miles to Last Chance Creek [Helena] to see about some claims that were bought for us, while the others prospected the Prickly Pear river.

Sept. 26. Returned to wagon on foot after looking at the claims &c. Heavy frosts now every night.

Sept. 27. Went up the Prickly Pear river eight miles to see the country. Plenty of chances to buy claims at four to six hundred dollars each. Visited the [Alhambra] Hot Springs and took a bath. The water has a good taste, there seems to be no mineral in it. It froze quite hard last night.

Sept. 28. Made ten miles on a back track to Last Chance, where we have bought or staked six claims, and are going to build a cabin to winter in.[55] The chance seems poor for us on the Prickly Pear. They say that Virginia City is more than full — claims all taken.

Sept. 29. Drew logs for a cabin. We learned that Bannack City has its claims all taken, so we stay at this place, for we know that there is gold here. We have but little water, yet if we club together, we can get or bring it five or six miles to wash the gold.

Sept. 30. Preparing to build. We have on one side a vast plain and much grass,

[54] Piegan River may be a branch of Canyon Creek.
[55] "There were only two cabins [at Helena] and they were occupied by six men. We built our cabin about where the Eddy Hotel is now. We could have our choice of building lots in those days." Noyes, "Gilbert Benedict," 8.

the Ten Mile Creek running through it. On the other side are high mountains covered with timber, full of game. Fine scenery. Snow on the distant mountains.

Saturday, Oct. 1. Drawing logs & stone. The weather is quite cool. Some nights water in the pails freezes, a quarter to a half inch thick. Rather cold to sleep in tents and eat out in the wind, but it is good weather to chop logs, it makes us so tough and hardy.

Oct. 4. An indian stole a man's coat and pipe, and made a threat to kill him. They will steal.

Oct. 5. Continued our building. Saw this day Mr. W. E. *Bass,* that lived at Glenn's Falls, and who left there in 1854. He is living at the Bitter Root river farming, 185 miles west from here.

Oct. 6. The Indians stole six horses, but one was found, and after the man had knocked two of them, he got on the horse and ran off with him.

Oct. 8. The wolves howl around our little village. We call it *Crab Town.* No post office here yet. No farming done in this section. I think it too cold for corn, but cattle feed on the bottoms all winter.[56]

Oct. 12. It is more of a job to build a good log cabin than I thought, but we are gaining every day.

Oct. 13. This country or this section has fed many buffaloes, judging by the number of bones we find, but they have all left.

Oct. 14. They have given this place a better name — *Helena City.*[57]

Oct. 15. We have got the cabin done and moved in. We find it much more comfortable than eating out doors and sleeping in a tent at night, and everything frozen in the morning.[58]

[56] One of the discovery party at Last Chance Gulch was John Crab, after whom, presumably, "Crab Town" took its name. *Helena Weekly Herald,* October 19, 1882.

[57] Other accounts suggest that Helena was not named until October 30 and purport to quote minutes of a meeting held that day in the cabin of George J. Wood. Chairman and secretary of the meeting were respectively John Somerville and Thomas Cooper of the Holmes train. Most accounts agree that it was Somerville who suggested the name for the new settlement. Cooper quotes him as saying: "I propose to call it Helena, in honor of Helena in Scot[t] County Minnesota, the best county in the State, and the best State in the Union by God." See *Helena Weekly Herald,* August 24, October 19, 1882; Cooper to Mrs. Cooper (copy), November 12, 1864, Cooper Papers.

[58] Benedict later said that because the best claims in Helena had been taken up his party located claims in Nelson Gulch nearby. After mining for two years, he "took up a ranch which was adjoining the ground which is now the Fair Ground," and farmed there for eighteen years. Noyes, "Gilbert Benedict," 8.

The Wheeler copy continues to the end of 1864; the original diary (now lost) contained entries up to August, 1865, according to Wheeler. Other Benedict diaries covering the period from August, 1865, until 1895 are in the possession of John Schroeder, Helena. Mrs. Harriet Meloy to the author, April 20, 1964.

1864 ✺✺✺✺✺✺✺✺✺✺✺✺✺✺✺✺✺✺✺✺✺✺✺✺

The Report of James L. Fisk[1]

Washington D.C. January 13th 1865

L[ORENZO] THOMAS
ADJT. GENL. U. S. A.
WASHINGTON D.C.

GENERAL, Immediately upon receipt of instructions from the Secy. of war, I proceeded at that very late day, (the seventh of last June) to organize a protective Corps of about 50 able bodied men for the protection and guidance of emigrants from the border of Minnesota westward to the mineral fields of Montana and Idaho in the Rocky Mountain region embraceing the heads of the Missouri and Columbia Rivers.

Makeing the best possible use of the small amount set apart for my expenses, I managed by about the first of July to have at least the nucleus of an expedition and gave my order for a march on the 4th of that month from St Paul for the Rendezvous.

The emigrants, without exception having taken it for granted that I would be ordered to pursue the new and direct route I had urgently recommended to the Department and which had been favorably considered in Congress during the winter, had assembled at Fort Ridgely as the most secure outpost along the new route, and there awaited my arrival.

My instructions with reference to the route I should pursue were not changed from those of the two years previous, but feeling assured that the real design of these expeditions from the beginning, was to explore the country of which so little is definitely known, and establish, if possible, the feasibility of a shorter and more direct route for the use of the Military, mails and emigration between the northwestern border and the Rocky Mounta[i]ns: and as a second consideration, to protect such emigrants as chose to avail themselves of the oppertunity thus afforded by the government, I did not hesitate, as I wrote you on leaveing Fort Ridgely,

---

[1] Fisk's report may be found in file 63F 1865, NARG 94. The file also includes three documents supplied by Dr. Dibb: his "Report" as physician and surgeon of the expedition; "Notes," a day-to-day summary of the events of the journey; and "Itinerary from Fort Ridgely," which gives a running total of mileage to September 4.

to deviate from the letter of my instructions so far as by takeing the route I did, to make it of some account to the people and the Government.[2]

Had the emigrants gone out as far as Big Stone Lake to rendezvous, I would have gone direct across the State to that point, but as it was, I took the usually traveled road up the St Peter [Minnesota River] to Fort Ridgely, where I found a Camp of covered wagons, about one hundred in number, and about one hundred and Seventy men women and children ready and anxious for the journey. A train of more than two hundred wagons [the Holmes train] had already started some four weeks previous under cover of the military expedition from Minnesota, going across to participate in General Sully's campaign against the Indians.

Here I fully organized the train and my escort for the long march before us.

OFFICERS OF THE EXPEDITION

First Assistant	Lieut. S[amuel] H. Johns[t]on
Second ″	E[ugene] F. Mitchell
Surgeon	W. D. Dibb
Commissary	A[ugust] Chemidlin
Engineer	W. E[llis] Smith
Train Master	V[an] H[aden] Fisk
Asst Train Master	G[eorge] W. Marsh.[3]

Not being able to find, much less to pay a guide, I decided to be my own pilot and trust to the compass as I did in my journey of 1863. In the list above it may be noticed that this was the third trip by Dr Dibb and the second by Lt. Johnson in my overland expeditions.

I had procured a 12 pound Mountain Howitzer at Fort Snelling, and for this a squad was organized and drilled in Artillery Tactics. I consider such a piece in Indian fighting, equal to one hundred men in line.

General Sibley kindly detailed fifty mounted men of the 2nd Minn Vol. Cavalry who were to accompany us, if possible, as far as the Missouri. The whole of this Company (Capt [Isaac Bonham] Bonhams) [went] as far as Fort Wadsworth where Lt H. S. Philips [Henry F. Phillips] took command of the 50 men.[4]

I had of my own about fifty men all told, who were variously disposed as Scouts, Herders, Teamsters, Cooks &c. all of whom were well armed, and none were excused from guard duty at night.

RULES AND REGULATIONS

The following are some of the rules and regulations by which my party was governed, and which were read to them before starting.

1. For my Aids or assistants who have been announced to you I shall want your respect and cheerful obedience to all reasonable requests or orders emenateing from them. I shall expect these Officers to be prompt and faithful in the

---

[2] See Fisk to Thomas, July 23, 1864, file 328F 1864, NARG 94.

[3] Fisk's orders provided for three assistants, physician, clerk, wagon master, and guide or interpreter. See Stanton to Fisk, June 7, 1864, file 218W 1863, NARG 94.

[4] See Sibley's Special Order 146, June 27, 1864, District of Minnesota, in Department of the Northwest, vol. 44, NARG 98; Special Order 82, July 14, 1864, Headquarters second subdistrict of Minnesota, and Special Order 19, July 31, 1864, Fort Wadsworth, both in Order Book, Second Minnesota Cavalry, NARG 94.

discharge of their several duties as they now understand them, and as they may from time to time be instructed.

2. The men, whose duties are less responsible but more laborious, are to be treated on all occaisons, with respect and justice.

3. Drunkenness occurring with officers or men is not only disgusting to me, but works evil to the expedition, and I now warn you all that I will not suffer the int[e]rests that are intrusted to me to be imperilled by those whose appetite for liquor cannot be checked short of inebriation.

4. I shall hold each horseman responsible for his horse, saddle, bridle and gun and other equipments: each teamster liable for such freight as may be intrusted to him and for the good treatment of his animals.

5. Ev[e]ry article of Property in my train is as sacred to me as my purse, and for the slightest disturbance of any thing not belonging to them, men will be promptly disgraced and punished.

6. I enjoin upon you all to be careful of evry article committed to your care, be friendly and social to one another, avoid all quarreling and boisterous herangues; be like *men* in your deportment, faithful in your work whatever it may be, and you will find your task not only easy, but pleasant on your long journey.

7. The order of march will be a single file of Wagons regulated according to numbered sections, to be arranged this evening; and the Train Master will see that all take their places in order; that none, from breakage or other misfortune, are left behind without help, and that for any ordinary mishap to a team those in the rear will not pass by, but help the Wagon to proceed.

8. Generally a march of from seven to twelve miles will be made in the forenoon, then a halt of from one to two hours, and afterwards a similar march until evening, when the train will be formed into a corral, into which the Oxen will be driven at dusk the Cows remaining outside.

9. The Tents should be pitched at least twenty feet from the Wagons, and the Mules, Horses, and other animals should be picketed just outside of the Tents.

10. A Camp Guard will be detailed each night to patroll around the tents and amongst the picketed Stock. This guard will have a Countersign, will be armed, and will allow no one to pass in or out of the lines without giving the countersign or obtaining permission from the officer of the guard.

11. The Cavalry accompanying us will furnish a picket guard at night and will constitute the flank and advance guard by day. There will be certain bugle calls which must be observed.

12. At daybreak Revielle will be sounded, which will signify that it is time that all were astir attending to their stock, Cooks at work, prepareing for the march &c.

The second call in the morning will be to bring in stock and hitch up.

In the evening there will be the first call after Camp is made for driveing in Stock.

The second call will be for guard mounting at 8½ oclock when the detail for guard will report promptly, armed and equiped, in front of my tent for instructions.

The third evening call will be tapps at 9 Oclock, when all lights must be put out and perfect quiet in the camp.

14. [*sic*] The Picket for the present will consist of five men and a Sergeant or corporal, the number of reliefs to be determined by the Officer commanding the Escort.

15. The lines of these pickets cannot be approached from within or without with safety, and can only be passed with the Countersign. These precautions are necessary to prevent surprises and Stampedes by the Indians through whose country we have to pass.

16. Both the guard and the emigrants will be expected to keep their fire arms in good order, to place them where they sleep, so that they can lay their hands on them at a moments notice, and to have everything ready for defence or offence as occaison may demand.

17. The train will always lay by on the Sabbath whenever the camping place is suitable.

18. I ask of the emigrants a strict observeance of the regulations herein prescribed, and with their good will and proper behavior toward each other and to me, I shall expect to meet with the same success that has attended me on other expeditions. Relying upon the good will of the military forces that are ahead of us, I have the best hopes of a good trip. But the march is a long one, and there will be times when the experience will seem hard, — Sometimes hot weather, other times a lack of water, a rough piece of road or poor grazeing. But all of these things which none of us can change, if encountered with a good will, are quickly and easily overcome.

19. Mr Charles F. Sims is delegated to represent the intrests of the emigrants, and to coöperate with me in such capacity.

Be ready to move from here by Six Oclock tomorrow morning.

Leave Fort Ridgely

We made our start from Fort Ridgely, where I had received the kindest attentions and important favors from the officers in charge, on the afternoon of the 15th of July makeing a march of 9½ miles and encamping in the River bottom, through which flows the St. Peter or Minnasota River.

The Old Sioux Agencies

Next morning we crossed the stream and ascended the bluffs on to that magnificent pra[i]rie plateau which extends from Mankato to Big Stone Lake, passing, as we fairly reached the summit of this rise, through the ruins of what was once the Lower or Redwood Indian Agency,[5] where that terrible massacre, which laid wast[e] Minnasota's fair frontier, and brought death and desolation to so many homes, first broke out. While I stood on the spot, I could not refrain from indulging in the contemplation of how, for years our government had lavished its millions of money and all the benificence of its generosity upon these savages, and then how the thirst which flattery and overkindness had bred, must have the life blood of 800 defenceless and innocent settlers to seal the compact.

Recollecting well the great gathering of the Sioux at Yellow Medicine in 1857

[5] Portions of the agency, now owned by the state of Minnesota, still stand on the south bank of the Minnesota River near Redwood Falls. See Holmquist and Brookins, *Minnesota's Major Historic Sites,* 96.

when for the same benevolence they threatened the same thing and were only prevented by the timely arrival of [Major Thomas W.] Shermans Battery and a company of Infantry from Fort Ridgely, I could see just how it all happened five years afterwards.[6] I recollect too, of hearing the interpreter repeat the threats and words of defiance uttered by the haughty Chiefs of the Yanktonias and how the "Young men" of that great tribe of the plains declared that before a hundred moons, they would have war with the whites, and how as they then fell back to their prarie homes, they laid waste the outer settlements along the Big Sioux.

Col. Wm H. Nobles with a command of sixty five men, sent out on a wagon road expedition to the south Pass, and which I now believe was an entirely feasible public enterprise, was detained here at the same time by those Indians, endeavoring to treat with them for a right of way, until he finally pushed forward, in spite of their protest, as far west as the Missouri River, but the season being too far spent, the party returned and the expedition was abandoned. I enjoyed the pleasure of this trip with Col Nobles as my first experience on the plains.[7]

I did not, however, apprehend for my little party any serious difficulty east of the Missouri, as the Buffalo were then rangeing north of my line of march, and while such of the hostile tribes as were hunting would be obliged to follow the game, it was well known that the greater number of Indians were west of that River, gathering their hosts in the fastnesses of the bad lands, or the "*Mauvaises Terres.*"

After spending the sabbath at a Camp about 5 miles above the Redwood Agency, we moved along the River, keeping it in sight, and encamped on the hills of the west bank of the Yellow Medicine River, on the night of the 19th near the ruins of that well known and excellently conducted [Upper Sioux] Agency and Mission, which had also been destroyed by the Indians. All the wooden buildings had been burnt to the ground, and but a few walls of the neat brick and stone buildings still stood. Here also had been fine farms opened, fenced and highly cultivated, splendid gardens laid out, good Schools established, Churches, Mills, &c &c, all the gift of a good and paternal government to the "*poor Indian*" as a means of coaxing him into civilized habits; But ingratitude and fiendish barbarity were the fruits of all of our pains. There were many green graves here of those who fell victims of savage fury. Their teachers and best friends were the first to fall beneath the tomahawk and scalping knife. Then came helpless babes, women and children. But I leave this subject, for the story has been many times told, and because I have no heart to dwell upon butcheries which so tax the english language and human nature to describe.

HEAD OF THE ST PETER, BIG STONE LAKE

Leaving the Yellow Medicine on the morning of the 20th over open, smooth and rolling praries with plenty of grass and wood for a distance of 137¼ miles from Fort Ridgely to the head of the Minnasota River which we reached on the

[6] The Sioux gathered for annuity payments at the Upper Agency in July, 1857, at a time when a renegade band remained unpunished for the Spirit Lake massacre which had occurred some months earlier. Contemporary observers believed the unsatisfactory conclusion of the affair led to the outbreak of 1862. See Folwell, *Minnesota*, 2:400–415.

[7] For Nobles' account of this incident, see Albert H. Campbell, *Report Upon the Pacific Wagon Roads*, 14 (35 Congress, 2 session, *House Executive Documents*, no. 108 — serial 1008).

26th of July. We nooned on the bluff overlooking the waters of Big Stone Lake, the source of the Minnasota River flowing south, and those of Lake traverse, source of the Red River of the north. We found this place to be what I had always supposed very suitable for a border post and small garrison. This place must naturally be the junction of highways and a rendezvous for emigration.[8]

THE COTEAU DE PRARIE

Bearing westward from this point we reached, after a drive of ten miles, a good camping ground on a small stream just under the base of the Coteau De Prarie.

As you near this distinguishing feature of the great prarie, which forms the conspicuous land mark between Hudson's Bay and the Gulf of Mexico, looking out upon the blue cloud as of water looming up against the horison; you may easily imagine yourself approaching the sea Shore. This Coteau, enveloped as it almost always is in summer, by smoke and mirage, can well be mistaken for the ocean. The front is smooth, grassy prarie cut evry half mile by wooded ravines, generally moistened by springs of excellent water. A good natural road is easily found up the slopes between these ravines, and after reaching the summit you encounter a somewhat more broken prarie, stretching away in the distance, and covered with good grass, and dotted with numerous beautiful lakes, many of them skirted with timber. These lakes abound with fine fish of various kinds, and both lakes and ponds are always well covered with Ducks, Geese, Swan, Pellicans &c. The roadway is fair, and by care in selecting, and a little grading would be good enough for a carriage way.

LAKE BOWL[E]S

On the 27th we reached a very desireable and most romantic camping ground, on one of the highest plateaux on the Coteau, at the head of quite a large [Enemy Swim or Parker] lake, on the left of our route, and which was belted by groves of timber, had its promontories and peninsulas, and afforded sport for the angler and hunter, and luxuries for our table. This lake not having a name, was christened by common consent, "Lake Bowles," in honor of the patriarch of our party, an intelligent, active old gentleman [William Bowles] of that name and 74 years of age.

BUFFALO

July 27. Saw our first Buffalo today — a small herd — of which our cavalry, by a *grand* charge, succeeded in killing one.

REINFORCEMENTS

July 28. Distance from Fort Ridgely 162 miles. During a night attack last night a patriotic Irish lady of the emigrants reinforced the *infantry*, by presenting a

[8] Fisk's "Map Showing Proposed Military & Emigrant Roads" shows two roads across Minnesota meeting, not at Big Stone Lake, but at the James River. In 1866, however, he advocated a Big Stone Lake rendezvous. The route from July 15 to 26 is described in detail in Dibb's "Notes." From Fort Ridgely Fisk crossed the Redwood, Chippewa, Yellow Medicine, Lac qui Parle, and Yellow Bank rivers and traveled between the Whetstone River and Big Stone Lake to a camp on Bullhead Lake. The route appears to have been close to that of Major John Clowney, who led troops from Fort Ridgely to build Fort Wadsworth a few days ahead of Fisk. See *WRR*, vol. 41, part 2, p. 512.

healthy young soldier weighing 12½ pounds. Dr Dibb had command, and deserves special credit. Of course we ran up the colors and made this a day of congratulation and rest. By the following morning, mother and child were so hearty that we were able to again resume our march.[9]

FORT WADSWORTH

July 30. Reached that magnificent cluster of Lakes known as Kettle [Fort] Lakes, so graphically described by [Joseph N.] Nicollet.[10] Here we found the Camp of the expedition that had been sent out from Fort Snelling to locate and build a Post somewhere near or on the James River, on the proposed line of travel, to be called Fort Wadsworth, in honor I suppose of the brave and lamented General [James S. Wadsworth] of that name. I soon had a visit from Officers and men of the camp, many of whom I was acquainted with. I was told that they had halted there and sent forward a reconnoitering party to the James River, who were hourly expected back, with a report whether the site they were on, or some other on the James River, which is about 40 miles west, would be selected for the post. The party returned next morning just as we were moveing on, and reported unfavorable for the James, so Fort Wadsworth is being built amidst those blue, oak skirted lakes, well upon the Coteau De Prarie, surrounded on three sides by water, glorious praries stretching away in evry direction, stocked with game of evry description, and on the route which must, of all others, be established from the western border to Montana and the Pacific side. I received several favors from the party and for courtesies extended by all officers of the command, I am their debtor.[11]

FROM FORT WADSWORTH TO FORT RICE

I had intended, in case of makeing a trip on this parallel to strike from this point to the Grand or Moreau River, as I had supposed that would be the better point for the general supply post and base of operations on the lower upper Missouri.[12] But as Fort Rice became the point, I was obliged to steer for that Post in order to find the means of crossing the Big River; So again launching out on the sea of praries which stretch away on all sides to the horison, we took our leaveing, West-North-West, bearing a trifle more north and without any other guide than my horse's nose which I kept pointed by the Compass, and takeing markers to run by, after a march of about 180 miles in eleven days, over a track-

[9] Dibb stated that a Mrs. Murphy had a "fine girl." Diary, July 28, 1864. For other comments on the Murphy family, see Larned Diary for the same date.

[10] Nicollet's description appears in *Report Intended to Illustrate a Map of the Hydrographical Basin of the Upper Mississippi River*, 10 (26 Congress, 2 session, *Senate Documents*, no. 237 — serial 380).

[11] Fisk actually received advice from two army scouting parties: the James River party, which was guided by Pierre Bottineau, and another, led by Joseph R. Brown, which had gone to the Missouri. See Dibb Diary, July 31, August 1, 1864; *WRR*, vol. 41, part 2, p. 513, 514, 546.

[12] Fisk's "Map Showing Proposed Military & Emigrant Roads" put the route somewhat farther south along the Grand River, close to the forty-fifth parallel. His actual route between Fort Wadsworth and the Missouri is not clear. From Wadsworth to the James River the expedition probably followed the trail of Bottineau's party, by way of present-day Mud Creek to a crossing of the James south of the mouth of Moccasin Creek. West of the James, according to Lieutenant Phillips, the escort commander, the train made "a new trail north of any of those previously established." Dibb said they traveled north of Long Lake in McPherson County, South Dakota. See *WRR*, vol. 41, part 2, p. 514, 546–548, 947; Dibb and Larned diaries, July 30–August 20, 1864.

less country we came to Camp on the left bank and opposite the anxiously looked for *Fort Rice*.

THREE MEN LOST. FOUR DAYS WITHOUT FOOD

On our arrival here, I learned with the deepest concern that three men, (my brother, Eugene Smith and Asst Mitchell) whom I had dispatched four days previous, on good horses to make a forced march and reconnoitre for the Fort, and then report to me, that I might not go wide of the mark, had not been seen or heard of. The presence of a large hunting party, Some nine hundred of what are called "friendly Indians" hunting in the region they were to pass through, made me doubly anxious, as I feared their natural treachery.

On the fifth day towards evening, my scouts met them, half starved and much fatigued by their long tramp, comeing along the trail we had made. There was great rejoiceing throughout the Camp. A light vehicle was run out by hand, the wanderers taken from their horses and placed in it and hauled into camp, amidst cheers and a salute from our Howitser, and the general rejoiceing was kept up far into the night after they had told their story.[13]

On their first morning out Smith's horse fell with him and broke the Compass. Not willing to return, and thinking they could keep their direction without one, they proceeded on the voyage. On the second morning they came to the high bluffs overlooking the Missouri River, but could not see anything like a camp or a fort. No sign of life could be seen either up or down the river, yet at that same moment they were standing within four miles of Fort Rice, which was concealed from them by a thick curtain of timber just below them, and on the opposite side of the river. Decideing that they had struck below the Fort they rode on and on up the river, over bluffs and ravines, through thickets and over praries, sometimes on the river bank and sometimes several miles back over the heights. For two days they kept on up the river. As they had seen fresh Indian signs, they dared not to use their firearms on the game, an article they were much in want of, as their one day's ration had not lasted long. Returning from a point which proves to have been near Fort Berthold, they struck back and on the fifth day found our trail where they met my scouts who were searching for them, 12 miles back from the river.

They were obliged, as they said, to camp in secluded places in order to rest in safety. Their food for four days consisted of three ducks and a few rosebuds which they ate spareingly. When they struck the trail they were steering for a small clump of timber, where they intended to kill one of their horses that had nearly given out, and make beef of him; stop long enough to dry or jirk it, and then continue their search for the train or the Fort.

My trail from Fort Wadsworth to Fort Rice was pronounced by the Indians and "voyageurs" at and about Fort Rice, to be the very best one that could be made between these two Posts. I certainly hit the mark exactly, and the pass opening out from the great Coteau Du Missouri down to the river, is the best I have ever seen. It is known as the Long Lake Outlet.[14]

[13] For more details, see Noyes, "Lost on the Plains."
[14] The Outlet is the pass through which Badger Creek (then known as Long Lake Creek) flows to the Missouri.

We saw but few Antelopes and very few Buffalo along this route although grass was plenty. The season was intensely dry, but on nearing the Missouri Valley, it was evident more rain had fallen there.

T[h]e water found in crossing a greater part of the Coteau Du Missouri, a distance of 75 or 80 miles, is strongly impregnated with alkali or Salt, in ponds and lakes some of rods, others of miles in diameter. But after a road is once established, the fresh springs and watering places noted in a carefully prepared itinerary of measured distances, the very best of camping places may be had evry night, water and feed being evry-where in abundance, so the route will become certainly a desireable one.

AT FORT RICE

☞Agreeable to his orders Lieut Phillips and his brave and jolly boys, returned from this Post two days after our arrival. I here take occaison to acknowledge their good behaveior, their ability and their readiness at all times to do their duty. The detachment returned safely in nine days over the same ground.[15]

On visiting the Fort I found the command composed of five Companies of the 30th Wisconsin Infantry, and a hundred or more convalescents, still in their tents, in a very neat camp indeed, near the bank of the River and on one of its small tributarys comeing in at the same place. The garrison was in a state of rapid progress, and I never saw men work harder nor more cheerfully than did the Wisconsin Troops at this Post. As the Fort is a large one, and the season unfavorable, it required evry effort to put it in condition for winter. The steam mill was kept running from morning till night, a Ferryboat in course of construction, a fleet of Flatboats were building to transport troops down the river on their return from the Indian Expedition. Hay makeing was hurrying up, and a train of Ox teams were busily plying to and from the woods near by, hauling logs and timbers, & Considering all, Fort Rice certainly presented a lively scene. Col [Daniel J.] Dill the Commandant is a staid and pleasant gentleman who extended to me the usual civilities. Lt. Col. [Edward M.] Bartlett, Q. M. [Henry A.] Wilson, Captains [Edgar A.] Meacham and [Arthur L.] Cox were earnest, hospitable, soldierly gentlemen to whom I owe a great many obligations for their many kindnesses.

BRIG. GENL. SULLY

Brig Genl Sully with a command of about 4,000 consisting of Cavalry, Infantry and Artillery, had been absent about three weeks on his march for the Yellow Stone, where it seemed he was headed more for the purpose of finding a rout and protecting emigrants, than for the building of forts and fighting the Indians. I was not aware until I reached Fort Rice that this distinguished military leader was authorized or disposed to supercede me in the special duties of pioneering routes and protecting emigrants. However, I suppose I can square accounts with the General by offsetting my battles with his Indians against his pains with my emigrants. Genl Pope had early addressed a letter to General Sully, requesting him to co-

---

[15] Fisk ordered Phillips to continue with the expedition, but Phillips protested that his orders required him to report to Fort Wadsworth without delay. See *WRR*, vol. 41, part 2, p. 947, 948; Henry F. Phillips, pension file WC 675409, NARG 15.

öperate with me if it might not conflict with his general plans, or interfere with his Expeditions against the Indians.[16]

I, at least, expected to find the Emigrants who had come across with Col [Minor D.] Thomas, and reasonably hoped that he had left for us a small detachment of mounted men. I did not consider that in the discharge of my duty, and with the verbal assurance of the Hon. Sec. of war himself and of many others of high standing, but that the military would certainly encour[a]ge and assist the little expedition much less that I was intrudeing myself into the Kings parlor or pinching the cubs of Bruin.

Col Dill informed me that there was not a man to spare from the garrison. But I would not think of abandoning the expedition at this juncture when it was just fairly under way. The reports of terrible massacres by the Sioux along the Platte added to the condition of things here, made matters look blue enough with a good number of the party.[17]

I called the emigrants together and stated to them exactly as it was, and gave it as my candid opinion that with Genl. Sully and his heavy force in our advance (as I supposed he had gone direct to the Big Horn) it was about the same as though we had a complement of troops with us, and that I thought we could get through, and would try it, if only a few were ready to accompany me. All decided to go forward.[18]

CROSS THE MISSOURI

About the same time the Steamer U. S. Grant came down, halted at this post and finally set us across the river.

ESCORT — LEAVE FORT RICE

After several interviews with Col. Dill, I persuaded him to muster about 50 men from the convalescents Camp, mount them, give them 20 days rations, and let them accompany me, that I might at least have a respectable number of scouts, if I had to do without main force or reserve.[19]

Lt. D[ewitt] C. Smith, of the second Dakota Cavalry was detailed to this command which represented evry company in the Generals whole Command. But the men were of good material, were tolerable well equiped and with their indefatigable Lieutenant who possessed no fear, did nobly their parts.[20]

[16] See *WRR*, vol. 34, part 4, p. 478.

[17] For reports of the Indian raids see, for example, the *Milwaukee Sentinel*, August 8–11, 15, 18–22, 26, September 1, 1864. On August 15 the paper quoted news from St. Louis indicating that the outbreak was "the most extensive Indian war yet waged."

[18] Fisk was advised, probably by Colonel Dill, not to go west from Fort Rice because grass and water were scarce. He replied that this advice "was a damned trick of the traders; they wanted him [Fisk] to go ninety miles out of his way, by Berthold, to get money out of his men." See *WRR*, vol. 41, part 1, p. 151.

[19] Sully had left 155 men in the convalescent camp; by this time 134 were judged fit for duty again. Colonel Dill assigned some 50 of them to guard the Fisk train under Special Order 80. See Fort Rice, Post Returns, July, August, 1864, NARG 94; *WRR*, vol. 41, part 1, p. 153. Willoughby Wells, a member of the escort, recalled that only 45 men were detailed to guard the expedition, and 5 of them deserted the first night out from Fort Rice. See DAR, "Geneological Records," 121.

[20] Smith had submitted his resignation from the service in July but Sully refused to approve it, and Smith was awaiting action on an appeal to Washington. He was subsequently given a dis-

After obtaining here what was needed to make my meagre outfit something of
what it should be, I bade a hasty goodbye to Fort Rice and again moved on to
the plains:

Camping on the night of the 23d of August, on a small Stream 8½ miles west
of the Fort, our road lay along the general course of the Cannon Ball River, Sometimes in its immediate valley, and several crossings of the stream were made. The
details of our march up this river (topography &c) as well as for the first part
of the journey are supplied in the notes of the itinerary attached to this report.

LEAVE SULLEYS TRAIL

At the fourth crossing of the Cannon Ball, distant 80 miles from Fort Rice, we
left Gen. Sully's trail, as from this place he bore due north in search of large bands
of Indians said to be on the Big Knife River, some 40 or 50 miles away.

The course still along the Cannon Ball River, being directly in our favor for
the mouth of the Big Horn River, and opening such a favorable natural road, that
I could not hesitate to resort again to the Compass: & After arrangeing for moveing the train in two or ten colum[n]s; if necessary, we struck out from the tracks
of the white man to try and solve the problem of route or no route for emigration
along that parallel and through that unexplored region, toward the valley of the
Yellow Stone.

I followed the Cannon Ball to its source and then bore more southerly, as far
as necessary — by the indications of signs, to avoid the dreaded "Mauvaises
Terres" of the Little Missouri.[21]

Nothing of any particular moment occurred along this portion of the route.
Plenty of game, very favorable weather, abundance of good water and grass, no
fresh signs of Indians, and our way extending over smooth hard plains, like pas-
tures and meadows of the old States, cut by small streams and dotted with isolated
mounds, "Buttes" and towering reefs of earth. Stock in good condition, health of
the party excellent: We were making good time and at no part of the journey
had there been such general cheer and interchange of congratulations; But it seems
that this fair sailing and these glorious days were only the forerunners of a storm
we were to experience.

We had traveled nearly one hundred miles after leaving General Sully's trail,
had camped one night without water, though there occurred a fine shower during
the night, and after going ten miles before baiting the animals, we halted for
breakfast on a small stream of good water. Grazeing and Buffalo chips being in
abundance we stopped till about one Oclock, when the train was again straight-
ened out in two columns, crossed the stream, ascended a splendid plataux open-

honorable discharge for "debauchery, gambling with cards, and fighting with the enlisted men
of his command." See his compiled service record, Company A, First Battalion Dakota Cavalry,
and file N611VS64, both in NARG 94.

[21] Fisk's course, like that of Sully, lay up the north fork of the Cannonball and its branches.
On August 29, Fisk reached the point near present-day New Leipzig, North Dakota, where Sully
had turned north on July 23; from here Fisk traveled south and west to the south fork of the
Cannonball and followed it upriver to a point near Chalky Buttes, where he turned southwest
again. See Dibb's "Itinerary"; Collins, in *North Dakota Historical Collections,* 7:8. Fisk claimed
that his choice of route was based on information about the region which he had gained in
previous years. See *Expedition of Captain Fisk,* 34, and p. 151, below. Sully, disregarding the
advice of his guides to follow this route, struggled through the Badlands farther north. See *WRR,*
vol. 41, part 2, p. 767.

ing away through the picturesque Red Butte [White Butte?], high and conical in Shape — a broad smo[o]th pass out to broader praries beyond.[22]

INDIANS. THREE DAYS OF FIGHTING

The flankers were well out, advance and rear guards strictly at their posts, the signal scout telling us, from the highest mound near, that all was well, when, as we had not traveled more than four miles a cavalry-man from the right flank dashed in toward the train and reported to me that the rear was attacked by a larg[e] party of Indians, and there was eminent peril of the loss of two wagons which had become somewhat detached from the main train by an upset, but were guarded by a rear guard of nine men and three Teamsters.[23]

Being ahead of the train I rode quickly back, ordered a halt and the forming [of] a close corral, which was done in the very best order although considerable excitement prevailed.

Lieut Smith, who was as usual with the main body of his little command, in the advance, but just then on an eminence, hearing the alarm did not wait for special orders, but put his horses under their best speed toward the scene of conflict: for he well knew that Indian attacks were sudden and quickly ended. A signal gun was fired, calling in scouts, flankers or others who might be beyond the reach of the bugle sound, and a good part of my own men were sent to the assistance of Lt Smith. At this juncture a scout rode up with the word to look out for a camp! hurry up the Corral! &c as the Indians were swarming in the bluffs on all sid[e]s. A few minutes after Corporal [Thomas C.] Williamson of the Cavalry rode in terribly wounded but without support. He sat straight up in his saddle as he rode up to me, while he had nine different cuts from Tomahawks, knives and war clubs, besides arrows sticking deep in his back and sides. Blood streamed from his head and body and was dripping down his horse's sides. Surely that was a shocking sight to most of the party who had never before witnessed scenes of blood. Soon another and another came up; but to their high credit be it said, that in the midst of all this, the emigrants and teamsters under the direction of my Brother and G. W. Marsh, formed a Corral with the wagons, perfect in shape and impregnable by Indians, in which we enclosed the entire herd of stock, besides a partition for the women, children and wounded.

From the firing some of which could be seen, and all distinctly heard, it was

---

[22] The Robert Strong version of Dibb's diary for September 1, 1864, contains a long entry describing in colorful, if improbable, detail a fabulous gold discovery made by Fisk and Dibb at this time, about 550 miles from Fort Ridgely and supposedly near the headwaters of the Knife River. The two men set out alone on a prospecting trip and shortly came across a rich quartz deposit — "a veritable mountain of gold." The outcropping was "so rich that the gold stuck out all over it and . . . was so loosely fixed that we could pull out many of the threads with our fingers. . . . Here was riches beyond belief — and it was all ours. . . . we planned to return there without delay . . . and establish the biggest gold camp in the world." According to this version, the men were attacked by Indians and forced to fight their way back to the train, losing en route all the gold specimens with which they had stuffed their pockets. On their return they found that the train was also under attack.

[23] The attack occurred about twenty-two miles east of the Little Missouri River, at the crossing of Deep Creek. For more details, see Collins, in *North Dakota Historical Collections*, 7:9, 10, 39; Wells, in DAR, "Geneological Records," 123; Larned and Dibb diaries, September 2, 1864; and Dibb, "Report" and "Notes." Sully estimated, probably correctly, that about 60 warriors took part in the initial attack and up to 300 harassed the train later. *WRR*, vol. 41, part 1, p. 152.

evident that Lieut Smith was engageing the Indians in earnest near the captured wagons. Upon sending him word that he must if possible occupy the ground and recover the wounded and dead, he replied that he must have the howitzer and a few more men to do it, as the Indians far outnumber[e]d him and flushed by the capture of the wagons were defending themselves obstinately while the plunder could be taken away. I immediately dispatched more men, the Howitzer and an ambulance for the bodies. The fight lasted about two hours, when the sun went down, and Lieut Smith and his brave boys returned to camp, tired, but with some glow of satisfaction upon their sunburnt faces. They had in a regular fight driven many times their number of Indians from the field, with considerable punishment, and recovered all the wounded and the dead bodies except two which they could not find. We remained here for the night. We could not water our stock nor could we let them out to graze at dark. Made no fires, nor pitched our tents.

That night

It was a sad and gloomy night. Our camp was on a smooth level plain between two ranges of bluffs or conical hills peculiarly red from their tops one third the way down. But we were three hundred yards from the base of the nearest one, and consequently out of range of the enemy's guns, except the sharp's carbines they had taken from our dead men, and of which they had hardly yet acquired the use.

As soon as the wounded were cared for, we buried our dead with such military honors as circumstances permitted.

A strong Camp and picket guard were posted for the night,— a cold lunch was passed around at nine Oclock, and then some tried to sleep. But soon the night darkened into blackness. Hundreds of Wolves, attracted by the scent of blood and of corpses set up a most unearthly howling and yelping, while there gathered and broke over us a thunder storm more grand and terrific than anything I had ever experienced. There was incessant and intensely vivid lightening for nearly an hour, and then came peal on peal and treble peal of heavy continued and incessant thunder which lasted for two hours. A shower, not in drops but in sheets poured for an hour upon our parched camp, till within the corral, in the natural basin around which it was formed, cattle were standing in the morning in two feet of water. The fatigue of the day, the groaning of the wounded, the howling of wolves, the unprecedented Storm under such circumstances, made this a night in my experience never to be forgotten.

Our losses in this surprise were,

Killed

1 T. Rasch [Theodore Rosch, Co. K] 8th Minn.
2 J. Delaney [Joseph Deloney, Co. I]   Do
3 J. Quin [John Quinn, Co. I] 6th Iowa [Cavalry]
4 [William] H. Chase, Bracketts Batt[alion]
5 H. Hoffman [Ernst Hoffmaster]   Do
6 H. Higgins, Cavalry
7 Walter Fewer, Teamster
8 W. Greaves   Do
9 L. Nudick   Emigrant.

WOUNDED

1 Corp. [Marmaduke] Betts, [Co. F, 6th Iowa] Cavalry, Mortally.
2 [Thomas C.] Williamson, [Co. A, 6th Iowa]   Do   Do
3 Jeff. Dilts   Signal Scout   Do
4 L. Dostaler, Teamster, Slightly.[24]

The two days following we made in all a march of about twelve miles[,] nine in the first day, and three in the second. With evry available man in the lines and no reliefs, the train moveing in five columns and being the continual object of attack by a most persevereing and desperate foe. The Indians had gathered strength and added largely to their numbers, and seemed to have the most sanguin[e] hopes of createing a panic or getting us into a trap by flank movements, and take, if not all, at least a portion of the train. But the good behavior of evry man on duty as teamster, aids and guards prevented any further disaster, while a destructive fire was poured upon them whenever they appeared.

These red devils charged repeatedly within pistol shot, upon the advance, rear and flanks, with yells and volleys of arrows and bullets. But while they were always repulsed with severe loss from our superior rifles aided by the Howitzer which filled the place of at least a hundred men for defence, our only suffering during the two days marching, although there were many very narrow escapes, was in the loss of animals, of which quite a number of valuable ones fell. The Indians contested inch by inch, evry foot of the ground we advanced upon, occupying all the ridges and mounds in the advance, and on the flank and from which they had to be driven by skirmishers and the use of the Howitzer, before the train could pass; while they continually sough[t] to break in upon the rear with their main force.

LT D. C. SMITH

Lieut. Smith was given command of the rear guard with orders to muster evry available man from among the emigrants, when needed, to strengthen his forces and I cannot neglect to express, not only my own admiration and gratitude, but that of all the party without a single exception, for the indefatigable exertions and success of that brave and soldierly officer. He was evrywhere with his men, his coat off, a trusty rifle in his hand, and his hand, and his deeds always following his commands. When, after a second council, it was decided to corral and entrench, and send to Fort Rice for help, Lieut Smith volunteered his services for this perilous ride.[25]

WE ENTRENCH AND SEND FOR HELP

Reaching a desireable point, we entrenched on the high grounds on the east side of the Little Missouri or Thick Timbered River, on the 4th of September. We were then in Latitude 45°:40ᵐ: and ten or fifteen miles east of the Montana Line.

[24] Bracketed information was drawn from compiled service records, NARG 94. For Dilts, see *Minnesota in the Civil and Indian Wars*, 1:529. "Nudick" may be the Louis Neudick who was a member of Fisk's 1863 expedition.

[25] For Fisk's message to Colonel Dill, see *WRR*, vol. 41, part 3, p. 466. The site of the fortified camp, now Fort Dilts State Park, is near present-day Rhame, North Dakota. The fortification was built of sod plowed up east of the camp and laid on the ridge of dirt left when the trenches were dug. Collins, in *North Dakota Historical Collections*, 7:14.

In getting possession of the ground, we had a sharp skirmish in which one man named [Charles L.] Libby, received a ball in the shoulder, and several animals were mortally wounded. Bullets and arrows poured upon the train. But that did not last more than an hour before we occupied all important points commanding our camp. We then threw up rifle pits and the Indians dispersed, leaveing their dead on the field.

The son of the old chief of the band, which proved to be the Unk-pa-pa- [Hunk-papa] Sioux, on[e] of the strongest and most desperate bands of the nation, tried repeatedly, after their defeat, to rally his men for a charge upon our lines. He rushed upon the lines several times with fifteen or twenty men, but a single volley from our boys on the hill to the right and left would hurl them back in confusion. Finally he dashed deliberately alone, up to within 75 yards of our pits, when he received a ball through the heart, and as he fell, several of his "braves" rushed out to recover his body, so strong is their habit or pledge of burying of their dead. But they too bit the dust. There was more or less skirmishing on all sides of the camp during the whole day, but at sundown the Indians with-drew, leaveing only a line of pickets on the prominent bluffs, north and east, covering the trail we had made on the mornings march.

It became evident that we could not, without hazarding the whole train, any longer march and fight the continually increasing force that had gathered to harrass us, we knew not how long, so it was decided to strongly intrench where we were, as we held a commanding position, with plenty of grazeing, and good promise of water near by, and dispatch to Fort Rice for assistance.

At ten Oclock that night, Lt Smith reported himself with fifteen comrades, ready for the task, and after getting his instructions he was soon in the saddle and disapeared in the darkness, followed by the heartfelt adieus of all. It was a threate[n]ing misty night. He was to take the back tra[c]k and that to run a most desperate gauntlet during the first hours ride, although there was no security until within the walls of the Fort. This journey of 175 miles through the enemy's country, without the means of recruiting or shelter, with somewhat jaded horses, was made between 10 Oclock on sunday night and three P.M. on Wednesday, when my dispatch was delivered to Col Dill.

Genl. Sully, with his command, having just been heard from, as being but one days march up the river on his return from a campaign, was at once apprised of our situation, and under considerable and publicly expressed bitterness curses, and a protest as I am reliably informed, dispatched Col. Dill with a command of three Companies of Infantry, one battallion of Cavalry, and a section of Artillery.[26]

THE SIEGE. THE RESULT

In the mean time we were engaged with the Unkpapas, reconnoitering for a route &c.

At 12 Oclock on the night of the fourth, a volley of arrows and bullets were fired over the pickets and into the Camp from a range of about 300 yards. It was supposed to be the parting salute of braves who had come to recover their slain, but the wolves had got the start of them.

---

[26] For names of the military units sent to Fisk's relief, see *WRR*, vol. 41, part 3, p. 466, 467.

Next morning early, we explored for water and found an abundance of it immediately at the foot of the hill in front of our camp, not more than 400 yards distant. Besides that we found a fine spring not half a mile away, boiling out from under a fine bed of lignite Coal. The Stock was grazed from daylight till about nine A.M. when the Indians again appeared in force gathering and closing around us. One of them clothed with a long robe, was seen on one side to harangue us, to divert our attention from a desperate band working around to the other side and preparing to make a desperate dash. All this was soon attended to and evry preparation made for an assault. It Should be noted that we had lost two thousand rounds of fixed am[m]unition, in the wagons that were captured, and in consequence we were not well provided with the means of resistance in a long seige, so far as the use of our best fire-arms was concerned.[27]

THE TRUCE. A CAPTIVE WHITE WOMAN

Soon there was a gathering of what appeared to be all the Indians about, on an eminence of prarie one mile away, and in full sight of the Camp. There came from the crowd three unarmed warriors towards the train, holding up a white flag which they planted in the ground about seven hundred yards off, and then retired.

This was an unexpected phase to the affair. While we were makeing extra preparations for war, there came a truce. I sent Mitchell, my brave and efficient officer of the guard, with two Sioux halfbreed interpreters to ascertain the meaning of this overture. They found, on reaching the ground, a letter stuck in a stick, and directed to me. Without pausing to converse with the Indians who were a few rods distant, my assistant returned to camp with the letter. That letter appeared to have been written by a white woman, a captive in the hands of the Indians and read as follows[28]

> Makatunke says he will not fight wagons, for they have been fighting two days. They had many killed by the goods they brought into camp. They tell me what to write. I do not understand them. I was taken by them July 12th. They say for the soldiers to give 40 head of Cattle.
>
> Hehutatunca says he fight not. But they have been fighting. Be kind to them and try to free me, for mercy's sake. I was taken by them July 12.
>
> (Signed) [FANNY] KELLEY [KELLY]
>
> Buy me if you can and you will be satisfied. They have killed many whites. Help me if you can.
>
> Unkpapas, (they put words in and I have to obey) they say for the wagons, they are fighting for them to go on. But I fear the result of this battle. The Lord have marcy.

I replied to this letter as follows:

[27] Contemporary accounts vary on the contents of the captured wagons, but agree that they carried liquor as well as ammunition. See Wells, in DAR, "Geneological Records," p. 123; *North Dakota Historical Collections*, 2 (part 1): 430, 439; 7:10; Fanny Kelly, *Narrative of My Captivity Among the Sioux Indians*, 148 (Hartford, Connecticut, 1873).

[28] The white woman, Mrs. Fanny Kelly, had been captured west of Fort Laramie while traveling in a wagon train to Idaho. The Indians instructed Mrs. Kelly to tell Fisk to move on so that they could more easily ambush the expedition in the Badlands ahead, but she contrived to send a warning in her letters. Her second sentence below probably refers to the poisoned hardtack.

Mrs Kelley. If you are really a white woman Captive in the hands of these Indians, I shall be glad to buy you and restore you to your friends, and if a few unarmed Indians will deliver you at the place where your letter was received, I will send there for them, three good American Horses, and take you to our camp.

I cannot allow any party of Indians, few or many, to come to my train or Camp while in this Country.

Tell them I shall move when I get ready and halt as long as I think proper. I want no advice or favor from the Indians who attacked us, but am prepared to fight them as long as they choose to make war. I do not in the least fear the result of this battle.

Hopeing that you may be handed to us at once for the offer I have made[.] I am truly

(Signed) Jas L Fisk, Capt. Comdg.

The above letter was sent back by the Indian messenger and we awaited the result. In the afternoon we received the following reply.

I am truly a white woman, and now in sight of your camp, but they will not let me go. They say they will not fight, but don't trust them. They say "How d'ye do." They say they want you to give them Sugar, Coffee, flour, Gunpowder, but give them nothing till you can see me for yourself, but induce them, takeing me first. They want four wagons and they will stop fighting. They want 40 cattle to eat. I have to write what they tell me. They want you to come here; you know better than that. His name Chatoanco and the other's name Porcupine.[29] Read to yourself, some of them can talk english. They say this is their ground. They say go home and come back no more. The Fort Laramie Soldiers have been after me, but they (the Indians) run so; and they say they want knives and axes and arrow Iron to shoot Buffalo. Tell them to wait till you go to town and they can get them, I would give them anything for liberty. Induce them to show me before you give anything.

They are very anxious for you to move now.

Fannie Kelley

My residence formerly Geneva Allen Co. Kansas. Read to yourself. He says he wants shirt.

I returned by the Indian the following reply:

Dear Madam, Your second communication convinces me that you are, what you profess to be, a captive white woman, and you may be assured that myself, and my party are eager for your release; but for the present I cannot accede to the demands, or gratify the wants of your captors. We are sent on an important trust and mission by order of the great War Chief at Washington, westward to the mountain region: with a small party of well armed and determin[e]d men, feeling entirely capable of defending ourselves, — but we are not a war party, and our

[29] On Porcupine, see Kelly, *Narrative of My Captivity*, 129, and Collins, in *North Dakota Historical Collections*, 7:17, 24–29.

train is not intended for war purposes. Powder and shot we have, but no presents for the *Hostile* Indians.

I am an officer of the government but am not authorized by my instructions to give any thing but *destruction* to Indians who try to stop me on my march. However I will, for your release, give three of my own horses, some flour, sugar, and coffee, or a load of supplies. Tell the Indians to go back for the night, and tomorrow at noon, if they will send you with five men to deliver you to my soldiers on the mound we occupied today — their main body not to advance beyond their present positions, I will hand over to them, the horses and provisions which they will be permitted to take away to their Head Quarters.

Should there be occaison, the same opportunity for communicating will be granted tomorrow.

The Great Spirit tells me that you will yet be safely returned to your friends, and that all wrongs that have been committed on the defence-less and innocent shall be avenged.

In warmest sympathy I am — Madam Jas L. Fisk
Capt & A. Q. M.[,] U. S. A.

After the delivery of my first note to the Indians, a conversation, lasting for half an hour, was held with them by 2d Asst. Mitchell through our two interpreters.

They said they had fought enough and desired to make a treaty with me. They wanted to be permitted to come to my camp and have a feast and council, which of course was denied.

Said they were hungry and thought they could capture our train and thereby get food for the winter, had fought as desperately as they could, but after trying three days, they could not fight any longer. They had lost many braves killed and many hurt that were dying. Wanted to see the Chief Soldier, (meaning myself) and have a talk with him. To which reply was made, (as instructed) that they could at once show their good faith, by giving up the captive white woman, and then, and not till then, would I treat with them, see them, or make friendship with them.

They were told that the truce ground would be held for another day, for the purpose of negotiateing for the woman: that what I would give would be promptly delivered to them upon their giving up the woman, but that they need not expect the slightest favor or negotiation on our part before they did it.

It being now near night, the Indians with-drew in a body to their camp with the promise that they would bring the woman the next day at noon and deliver her up for the ransom I had offered. I could not even be liberal in dealing with them, so villianous and barbarous had they been by my experience.

Their hands were yet red with the blood of our brave comrad[e]s they murdered and scalped, on their return from their recent raids upon the old emigrant trail along the Platte River, where they had captured trains and butchered men, women and children without remorse.

Feeling now that we had whipped the devils thoroughly, yet there was but one course to pursue, that of defiance, and although we were bound to do all that lay in our power to ransom Mrs Kelly, we could not, with safety to ourselves, show our weakness, and lay it at the mercy of that fiendish treachery, against which Mrs Kelley had herself warned me.

During these negotiations, the work of completeing the entrenchments went on, and the Howitzer was placed in position to command the nearest rise on the left, but could be shifted so as to be used from any part of the breastworks. The remaining cavalry, with my own men and the emigrants were formed into one guard, numbering in all 168 guns. Among the emigrants, good men were appointed Sergeants over evry twelve, and all were instructed in their duties, and took their regular turn in camp, outpost and all other guards.

Encamped as we now were, we could hold our position against a large number of Indians, but on the march nearly one hundred men being necessary to drive the teams, only 60 or 70 were left to do the fighting and guard the entire train.

DEATH OF BETTS AND WILLIAMSON

On Sept. the 8th M. D. Betts of Co "F" 6th Iowa Cavalry died at sunrise. He had suffered terribly from his wounds and had been delerious almost the whole time since he had been brought into Camp. We buried him at noon with military honors.

On the evening of the same day T. Williamson of Co "A" 6th Iowa Cavalry died. Poor Williamson had also been a great sufferer, and was delerious most of the time. We buried him at sunrise by the side of Betts, at the *Northwest Corner* of *the entrenchments*.

On the same day the reconnoitering party sent out in the morning, reported that the Indians had left.

THE STRYCHNINE AFFAIR[30]

On the afternoon of Sept 5th Mr Larnard [Larned] who had been out grazeing the animals, reported to me that they had found quite a number of human carcasses, the flesh having been mostly eaten off by the wolves.

These were supposed to be some of the many Indians who had perished from the effects of Strychnine, which it seems, had been thrown into a box of soaked Hard Bread, left upon the camp ground and which was pounced upon by the Indians the moment we left the ground, and eaten with avidity, as they did with all the offals of our camp. The night before this had been done [*i.e.*, September 3], several of the Cavalry escort and of the emigrants suggested to me, that on account of the loss of amunition, the furious and merciless character of the enemy, it might be well for our salvation to resort to poison; which they thought might be successfully administered. I did not for a moment entertain the proposition, but dismissed it with emphatic reasons why it should not be done. When those carcasses were discover[e]d around our entrenched camp, and the Indians themselves, having confessed on the truce ground, that they had lost half their tribe by bad bread and bullets, I understood how that deep hate and thirst for revenge that justly has possession of the hearts of Minnesotans had done its work.

[30] The following three paragraphs of Fisk's report were censored by the War Department for nearly a hundred years, probably because it did not wish to be associated with the Indian poisoning incident. In order to defend himself, Fisk furnished a copy of this section to the *Pioneer*, which printed it in slightly different form on January 26, 1865. According to one emigrant, strychnine was injected into the hardtack with a hypodermic needle and about twenty-five Indians died of poisoning. See Collins, in *North Dakota Historical Collections*, 7:12.

This incident, becomeing generally known, has been a choice bit for a number of monomaniac humanitarians throughout the country; and they have showered upon my head shameful and infamous epithets, at the same time holding up the general Government as a party to the crime. As for myself I have no apologies nor furt[h]er explanations to make in the premises; simply rejoining that I cannot say but that the use of that unwarlike means of destruction may have been the salvation of my weak and beleaugered party, and finding after it was done, that it *was* done, *I was glad 'twas well done!*[31]

The 6th being rainy, the Indians did not appear, but on the 7th they appeared again before our Camp, and another talk was had with them through Messrs. Mitchell[,] Johnsen [Johnston,] and the interpreters. They had concluded that we could not give enough for the captive, and they must take her to Fort Rice or Fort Sully on the Missouri; where they could get winter's food in exchange for her they said. They stated that they were makeing for their hunting grounds when they discovered us. They turned and followed us, thinking they could easily capture our whole train, and thereby have enough food for the winter. But now they were ruined in strength, had wasted their arrows, and they must go to the Forts to make a treaty. During the progress of this interview I had a span of good horses harnessed and hitched to a wagon, loaded with Flour, Sugar, Coffee &cc. tied a fine saddle horse behind the wagon, and had the whole driven to the truce ground, where it was offered in exchange for Mrs Kelley. But it was evident that their minds were made up to try the forts for a much larger amount, and that they had come to this truce (about one half of them) only to scheme for provisions, and upon their receipt, retain their captive. The team was ordered back to camp, the truce closed and the Indians, withdrew in haste and were not again seen until our return to the Missouri, where we found their delegates at Forts Rice and Sully, apparently rouseing competition between these two posts for bids on the Captive woman, and expecting to make a peace with the government.[32]

On Sept 12th, takeing with me eight men, I rode down to the Thick timbered River, a fork of the Little Missouri, distant about five miles. We found the country very broken near the river, and in the Coulees, groves of Cedar, Cottonwood and Box Elder. The bed of the River was wide, but the crossing would be on a hard gravel bed, and easily made. The water was good and the grass excellent. The country beyond looked very favorable for a road. Towards the north, some five miles distant like a vast city on the plains, loomed up the bad lands of the Little Missouri, and that jumbled up and wrinkled face of dame nature which reached northwestward beyond the vision. But ahead of us there was none of that broken land and I could scan my route for twenty miles in the distance.

Here also we discovered the plain marks of Indian trails, many of them years, and some a few days old, all showing that this ford is one very much used by the Indians and in compareing it to the description given me by a voyaguer of the American Fur Company, two years previous, felt positive I had again been favored in finding the very route that would admit of the passage of my train.

On the 18th, after a monotonous awaiting of 12 or 15 days for the escort I had

[31] "If it were done when 'tis done, then 'twere well it were done quickly." William Shakespeare, *Macbeth*, Act I, scene 7, lines 1-2.

[32] Mrs. Kelly was released at Fort Sully in December, 1864.

sent for, I was pursuaded in my own mind that if it did come at so late an hour, it would be to take us back. So I ordered a fo[r]ward movement for the next morning, having already made a good road down to, and across the Thick Timbered River.

DEATH OF DILTS

Before daylight on the following morning Jefferson Dilts, my brave Signal Scout, who had killed his three Indians and wounded a fourth, in a hand to hand fight, during the first day's engagement, and at last received his mortal wounds, died, and was buried in the entrenchments.

Mress Sims and Larnard beseeched me to wait till Wednesday. I told them I could not refuse to grant such a request, as some of them for whom they spoke were women and children; but gave it as my opinion that we could and ought to go fo[r]ward, and that if we waited for relief, we would probably be helped back instead of fo[r]ward.

On Sept. 19th at noon, we buried poor Dilts. He bore his terrible sufferings with great Courage, and was perfectly resigned to die. He was a brave, honest and good man.

Only two wounded men now remained Charles Libby and Louis Dostaler, both rapidly recovering.

Soon after breakfast on the 20th, twenty or thirty horsemen were seen on the ridge to the north. Many of the boys ran to the hill on our rear and fired three volleys as they approached. They proved to be the advance guard of the troops sent to our assistance from Fort Rice. We learned from them that Col Dill was a few miles behind with four hundred Cavalry, four hundred Infantry and a section of Artillery.[33]

I rode out with my assistants to meet Col. Dill and was not disapointed in ascertaining that Genl. Sully's orders were virtually for the train to return to Fort Rice. The 25 cavalry men we had were ordered to join Col Dill's command. After trying in vain to persuade the Colonel to let his lame and weary Infantry rest, while his cavalry might set us beyond danger, I then called all of the party together, includeing the emigrants and plead with them not to turn back. But I could not prevail against Gen. Sully's schemes, and was obliged to turn back.[34]

RETURN TO FORT RICE
DISBANDING OF ESCORT. SCATTERING OF EMIGRANTS.

We reached the fort in safety on the 30th of Septr and without experienceing any particular incidents on the return trip.

The usual order of march was preserved and the Train, entire when it reached the Missouri was in the very best condition, minus the slight loss of Government property during the battles.

Here after the first nights camp, the Expedition for this year was declared at an end and there was a general "good-bye" and scattering. The different detachments

---

[33] Dill had 550 infantrymen, 300 cavalrymen, and one section of artillery; see his report in *WRR*, vol. 41, part 1, p. 795. In the following sentence, Fisk means that he was not *surprised* at Sully's orders; he was certainly disappointed.

[34] According to Dill's report, twenty emigrants at first agreed to go on with Fisk without military support. Overnight some of them changed their minds and Fisk then decided to turn back.

of the military Expedition afforded cover, under which the scattering emigrants could reach the states in security, and of which they dilligently availed themselves.[35] Instead of sacrificeing the expedition property at an auction sale, I negotiated with friends for part funds, at the Fort, and at St. Paul for the ballance to pay off my men, and close the indebtedness of the expedition by leaveing the animals &c in camp on the Missouri, as I did, in charge of my Brother and Lieut Johnson with 8 or 10 good men.

HOMEWARD BOUND. ARRIVE AT ST PAUL

After provideing a suitable camp for this fragment of the expedition, I took passage on board of the Quartermaster's boat of the fleet of flatboats or transports conveying the 30th Wisconsin down the Missouri to Sioux City, [Iowa] accompanied by Dr Dibb, who was this time closeing his three years companionship and service with me — Also Commissary Chemedlin and ten others.

We experienced a pleasant journey home, reaching St Paul via the River to Sioux City thence across the country to Mankato on the St Peters River, by the close of November.[36]

SOME SUGGESTIONS. THE PROPOSED ROAD. THE MILITARY.
MY FAILURES. COL DILLS REPORT. THE INDIAN CAMPAIGN &C.

In closeing this report, I cannot refrain from expressing some convictions which have forced themselves upon me, through the sad experience of my late Expedition; and from the embarassments I have labored under on previous journeys through this Indian country.

My last Expedition from St Paul to the Red Buttes of Western Dakota, was neither attended with casualties or impeded by obstruction in any shape (except as stated) and the route over which the train was moved is emphatically a good one, evry rod up to the entrenched Camp, from which we returned. Beyond that — leaveing the Bad Lands to the north there opens the only "pass" Known through that wild region — along the plateaus between the "Mauvaises Terres" of the Black Hills, or Big Sheyenne [Cheyenne], and those of Little Missouri through to the mouth of the Big Horn on the Yellowstone.

But the Expedition instead of having the good will, encouragement, and cooperation of the Military Commanders in the field has experienced their illwill, discouragement, and opposition. It was not a failure at my hand, but it was in the power of General Sully to have set me across to the Yellowstone from where I fought and whipped away the Indians, it seems to me, without derangeing or delaying any other plans at that time — for he was simply "on his return to Quarters" &c. Even had he let me alone I believe I should have gotten through — but the extent of his cooperation, solicited by Genl. Pope was in compelling the expedition to return, and become the mess for an auctioneer at an isolated frontier Post.

The Official Report of Col Dill Comdg. the expedition for my relief, is I pre-

---

[35] Twenty emigrants returned to Minnesota, and ten to twenty wintered at Fort Rice. Fifty wagons went down the Missouri River Valley. Some of the emigrants settled in the Big Sioux Valley in present-day South Dakota; others went on to Montana in the spring. Collins, in *North Dakota Historical Collections*, 7:19; Wells, in DAR, "Geneological Records," p. 127.

[36] The following section of Fisk's report, to the beginning of the letter on page 154, below, was also censored by the War Department.

sume before you. — The Col; suggests that I should be "censured at least, for trying to urge the emigrants forward" — and in reply to which, I respectfully submit: that if an earnest endeavor to urge forward your forces, or your expedition in charge, after having fought your way so clear, that 12 days of reconnoitering failed to discover our enemies, or any signs of them — but a good route, the way open; in short if trying to accomplish within the spirit of your instructions, what you undertake, is ground for *censure* — then I am guilty — and probably always shall be.

As to the "folly and madness" of my proposition to the Col: to allow his footsore Infantry to rest a very few days, while his cavalry could set us on our way for two or three days march which would bring us within the friendly crow Country — beyond which an escort would not be absolutely needed — I also submit, as a question to whether it was even courteous in the Col: who was then further west than he had ever been before — then makeing his maiden expeditionary travel — to call me a fool and a madman.

It seems to have been the pride of the Indian Expeditions to make a late, but pompous "go out" and an early and victorious "git back," staying in the enemy's country just long enough to find him — then with a long stick (as the schoolboy would a hornets nest) stir him up and run, leaveing those who may confidingly follow that way to the mercy of the devils sting. Buncomb reports are packed into the Department, and one would suppose the country freed from all traces of the savage Redman. It is not unworthy of consideration, however, that while the most flattering progress was reported from Gen. Sully — year to year, as the result of the Indian War, that outrages, outbrakes, attacks, and massacres increased on the old trails and byways of the Emigrant and pioneer.

At the close of '64, we have to cite — with sorrow, the long list of depredations and butcheries indulged in by different bands of the Sioux, during the last summer & fall along the great trails of the West. They assembled their hosts & defied Genl Sully. the Genl tried them a few days and came back the Indians getting in the last shot on the field & following him to Fort Rice, where they killed under the very nose of the Garrison some of his best men & stampeded his stock at their leisure.

But upon the head of all this even Maj. Genl Pope reports to Washington as follows: "The Government may safely dismiss all apprehensions of Indian Wars in the North West &c &c" — I need hardly state that at the time of writing this, the telegraph informs us that the Great Overland Mail between Omaha and San Francisco is suspended on account of the depredations of these *subdued Indians*[.]

The following private letter just received from my first assistant at Fort Rice is pertinent to this subject, and I feel at liberty to use it in this connection.

Fort Rice D. T. Dec 2/64.

CAPT J. L. FISK
DR SIR

I was glad to hear from Mr Chemidlin that you arrived at Sioux City and well & safe.

Van will tell you all about the stock and doubtless of the attack on Lieut [Samuel B.] Noyes and Sergt. [C. D.] Thompson last Sunday.

Both had arrows through them. Thompson through the arm & Noyes through the thigh, they are getting on well. A private [G. W. Townsend] was captured the same night by this party of Cut Head Indians, near the Cannon Ball River, nothing heard of him since.[37] [*blank in ms.*] A large number of Cut Heads and Yanktonas are above here at "Painted Wood" near Fort Berthold, they are yet hostile.

Some half breeds from Red River, are among them, have supplied them with ammunition and whiskey telling them to keep at war with us. This they do of course out of a mean pityful selfishness, hoping to keep the trade with the Sioux.

Their conduct aught to be thoroughly represented to the Department.

They are keeping up this war by supplying the Sioux with powder, lead &c, encourageing them as to their final success.

The Government should at once stop the trade of these British subjects and their treasonable acts. I shall be glad to hear any news from St Paul, and how you progress with your matters. Remember me &c. Yours sincerely

(signed) S. H. JOHNSTON

I do not know if it is consistant with my rank to criticise high officers, as I have, although they them selves may have condescended to provoke it; or to offer conflicting opinions as to the future management of this vast Indian business. I am constrained to believe however that if I have, or do violate a rule in the endeavor to furnish your Department with the vital information it is seeking, as well as in justification of myself you will suspend that rule & admit my testimony.

I am still of the opinion that the present & past policy of the Government towards the Indians is fruitful only of evils, & cannot refrain from repeating what I have asserted in my previous reports that the War Department with its military arm & dictation, instead of the Interior Department with its civilian coaxing and solicitation, is the proper means of controling and correcting the awful calamities that have befallen and are yet brewing in the cauldron of the powerful tribes of the Sioux.

It seems to me that if this whole business were left to the Secty of War and the President, who would detail or commission some suitable person to take hold of the matter, it would not be a twelve month before there would be submission and permanent peace on the border.

A single Brigade of mounted men with Prairie Batteries, distributed from Fort Kearney on the Platte, and a part on the upper Yellow Stone, with the forces along the Missouri from Fort Randal[1] to Fort Union and commanded by a leader whose functions would include and control all sorts of intercourse with the Indians, would bring that serious trouble to a close in a very short time.

This Indian Dept. should be circumscribed by the limits of the troubled country and the Head Quarters of said command, should certainly be further west than Milwaukee.

I would even if neccessary keep out a Battallion of Cavalry during the hunting

[37] The bracketed names were supplied from Fort Rice, Post Returns, November, 1864, NARG 94.

season herding the Buffalo to prevent the Indians during the hostilities from obtain[in]g their great staple of food.

By the time snow fell I would know by diligent reconnoitering, the rendezvous of their main bands for winter quarters, and would organise & dispatch a winter expedition against them, as was done so successfully in ridding Oregon, California and Washington of the Red Mans sway.[38]

Another rehearsal of the Sully's campaign can scarcely result otherwise than in the aggravation of non-committed tribes who are related to the Sioux, and it is not improbable may force into alliance with them the powerful mountain tribes whom the miners have thus far kept in subjection.

Surely one cannot neglect nor overlook the fact that between the western bound[a]ry of Minnesota and the Eastern base of the Rocky Mountains there are at least twenty thousand warriors, portions or all of whom are at Knives end with the Government and all the whites.

What is to be done should be done quickly without mercy and with such fearful effect as will preclude the possibility of their again rising against us.

If they cannot or will not, as we have experienced at great sacrifice of life & treasure, receive the endowments and adopt the customs of our race, how can we continue that charity which makes a bad matter worse.

We have tried leniency, it has not succeeded. Let us now try Severity.

A MINING BUREAU

The following suggestions with regard to the importance of establishing a Mining Bureau by the Government were submitted in my last report & are still held as not unworthy the attention of Congress.[39]

"It has frequently occurred to me that our Government was deficient in one important branch, actually demanding a head at Washington; and that is a Mineral Bureau with a Commissioner General or registrar general, who should have an accurate registry of all mineral discoveries, & for each community to have power to appoint under sanction of the President a local registrar. In visiting the various mining camps in the mountain country & beyond, this question suggested itself every day or every hour in the day and many men have asked me if there could not be some means provided by which a more reliable & indisputable record could be made of their claims. These men, in fact every miner in our land would cheerfully pay ten or twenty dollars for the satisfaction of having his claim registered under a United States officer, which would insure him against

[38] Fisk refers to the winter expedition of California volunteer troops under Colonel Patrick E. Connor, which defeated Bannack and Shoshone Indians in January, 1863, on the Bear River in present-day Idaho. This action effectively ended harassment of travelers and settlers in the region. See *Dictionary of American Biography*, 4:352 (New York, 1930).

[39] See *Expedition of Captain Fisk*, 35. Fisk made this suggestion because of chaotic conditions in the new mining districts. Federal mineral lands in the west were not officially opened for occupation until the passage of legislation in 1866 and 1870; earlier there was no federal agency to register claims. In most areas miners took matters into their own hands and elected recorders, but they were not able to effectively prevent claim jumping even when backed by territorial legislation. A federal Bureau of Mines, as suggested by Fisk, was established in 1910, but the registration of claims is not one of its functions. See J. Ross Browne and James W. Taylor, *Reports upon the Mineral Resources of the United States*, 218–257 (Washington, 1867); Clarence King, comp., *The United States Mining Laws*, 1–3, 7–9, 497–508 (47 Congress, 2 session, *House Miscellaneous Documents*, no. 42, part 14 — serial 2144).

abuse & litigation. The revenue (in gold) and the vast benefits resulting in many ways from such a measure it seems to me must be plain to evry one who will give the subject a moments attention.

["]Through these agencies a very much greater amount of gold might be secured to our Mints & National Treasury.["]

I would be glad to see established some system of exchange for the benefit of the miners by which our Government might reap the advantages from the many tons of gold & silver which is annually taken out & shipped abroad, before it goes thus abroad or passes into circulation.

The Road

The route urged before the department and Congress last winter is with perhaps a trifling deviation to suit the new posts already established, a very direct & feasible one for the purposes of emigration mails & military, and if permanently located & improved under the auspices of the Government will become a very important highway.

With Forts Ridgely, Wadsworth & Rice substantial posts along this line & with the location of a small Garrison at Big Stone Lake, at the Thick timbered or Box Elder River of the Little Missouri and another supply depot or Garrison at or near the mouth of the Big Horn on the Yellowstone the road could be well guarded.

Leading directly to the riches of Montana or Idaho; with a saving of not less than 500 miles over any other, it is an established fact, and the public interest of the communities as well as that of the Government would certainly be greatly enhanced by its opening. The bill endorsed by the committee on Roads & Canals last winter & which lies in the committee of the whole asking for an approbriation of $100,000 for its establishment may meet this winter with approval & be passed by Congress, & the North West be connected by the route desired with the rich gold fields of the eastern slopes of the Rocky Mountains.[40] I may be excused from speaking of the special deed of daring & valor that any particular one of my party may have performed during the Expedition for all did well & discrimination is out of place.

If I may express a choice I do not wish any more Emigrant duty to perform under similar auspices, yet after three years & a half of service I am still proud of serving my country in what ever way it may be pleased to order.[41]

Dr Dibb has kindly furnished the following notes for the itinerary by my request, on account of loss of notes by Mr. Smith.

With high regards I have the honor to be Yours very truly.

JAS. L. FISK
Capt & A. Q. M Comdg Expdtn

[40] Fisk refers here to House Resolution 323 of the 1864 session of Congress. The legislation passed in 1865 authorized the Niobrara–Virginia City wagon road. See p. 106, above, and p. 160, below.

[41] Fisk means, of course, that he would prefer to be a wagon road superintendent. For the itinerary mentioned below, see note 1, above.

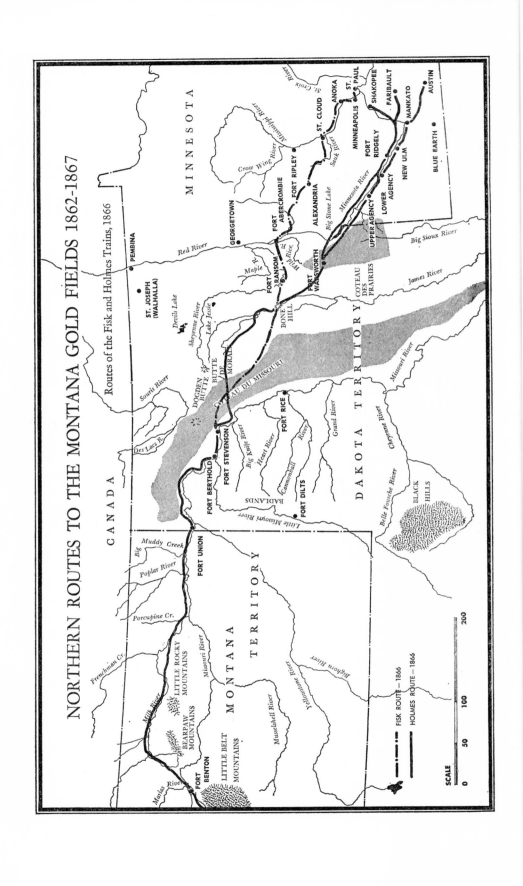

NORTHERN ROUTES TO THE MONTANA GOLD FIELDS 1862-1867

Routes of the Fisk and Holmes Trains, 1866

1866

THE HOLMES AND FISK TRAINS

1866 ❀❀❀❀❀❀❀❀❀❀❀❀❀❀❀❀❀❀

The Holmes and Fisk Trains

DURING 1866, THE BANNER YEAR for emigration over the northern plains, Minnesota sent two large wagon trains to Montana. The Civil War was over and scores of discharged soldiers — uprooted and unemployed — were ready for adventure in the gold fields. Merchants, in need of new outlets for goods to replace wartime government contracts, prepared to ship wagonloads of merchandise to Montana for sale at the mines. Thomas Holmes came back from Helena ready to organize a third train, and southern Minnesota merchants talked of sponsoring it. During the winter and spring, James Fisk lobbied, planned, propagandized, and recruited for his fourth expedition, which was to be the largest and last he took over the northern plains.

For Fisk, success followed a year of disappointment and failure. After the 1864 expedition he had fallen on hard times. Returning to Washington early in 1865, he ran up hotel bills which he was unable to pay. In the spring raiding Indians stole the government stock that he had left at Fort Rice. Far worse, all his efforts to secure a new government appointment came to nothing.[1]

Fisk first worked to obtain the superintendency of a wagon road under legislation then pending in Congress, but when the bill was passed in March, 1865, it brought joy neither to Fisk nor to Minnesota. Its key provision authorized the construction of the so-called Niobrara road through northern Nebraska Territory to Virginia City. Not only was this route located too far south to be of use to Minnesotans, but Iowans persuaded the secretary of the interior to appoint their candidate to superintend its construction. The same bill also authorized twenty thousand dollars for a branch known as the Big Cheyenne wagon road, which was to run from Minnesota's western border to an intersection with the Niobrara route beyond the Black Hills. Wilmot W. Brookings, a Dakotan, was appointed superintendent of this road. He expended six thousand dollars in 1865 on a survey as far as the Missouri, but the road was not completed. No emigrant trains passed over it, and Minnesota reaped no tangible benefits from the enterprise.[2]

An attempt by Fisk and Senator Alexander Ramsey to obtain an emigration

---

[1] A. J. Fisk Diary, February 13, 1865; Francis Keyser to Donnelly, July 13, August 4, 1865, Donnelly Papers; *WRR*, vol. 48, part 2, p. 434; R. E. Fisk to Elizabeth Chester, March 27, June 12, 1865, R. E. Fisk Papers; White, in *Minnesota History*, 38:229.

[2] *Statutes at Large*, 13:516. Brookings' report is in *Wagon Road from Niobrara to Virginia City*, 1–10 (39 Congress, 1 session, *House Executive Documents*, no. 58–serial 1256).

superintendency and part of the unexpended funds previously allocated for emigrant protection proved equally fruitless.³ Fisk may have alienated both the War and Interior departments by his intemperate remarks and his conduct of the 1864 expedition. The unfavorable publicity which followed the Indian poisoning incident, a decline of Minnesota political influence in Washington after the death of Lincoln, and the reorganization of the War Department at the end of the Civil War were all possible factors in Fisk's lack of success.

Since no government appointment seemed likely to come his way, Fisk resigned from the army in the spring of 1865 and turned his efforts in another direction. In association with his brother Daniel and Senator Ramsey's brother-in-law, John Nininger, Fisk drew up a grandiose plan to lead an expedition to the Yellowstone Valley and plant a colony there. The project, clearly designed to appeal to demobilized soldiers, called for a joint-stock company to finance a sawmill, mining and farming equipment, and a printing press for the settlers. Unfortunately, few veterans were ready to join Fisk in the summer of 1865, and he quarreled with Nininger. Even the support of Thomas Francis Meagher, the Irish war hero who had just been appointed secretary of Montana Territory, did not bring him the money, men, and military support necessary to carry out his plans. Early in September, 1865, Fisk met a bedraggled company of adventurers at the St. Cloud rendezvous and announced the postponement of the expedition until the following spring.⁴

By this time Fisk was overextended, and creditors were suing him, it was reported, for more than seven thousand dollars. He said that he had sustained losses totaling over twenty thousand dollars — his own money and that invested by friends and relatives — during the years he had been promoting the northern route.⁵

In spite of these difficulties, the thirty-year-old captain remained undaunted. "My spirit never droops," he said, and by December he was planning another journey to the gold fields. In view of the heightened interest of Minnesota merchants in trade outlets at the mines, the old dream of commercial empire in the West seemed closer to realization, and Fisk attempted to capitalize on this ambition by promoting a permanent wagon road from Minnesota to Montana. In a compromise between his trails of 1862 and 1864, he advocated a route which avoided both a far northern swing and a journey through the Badlands. He said that he favored a rendezvous at Big Stone Lake, and he projected a line of march which would strike the Missouri some two hundred miles south of Fort Union and then follow the river north to the fort. From there, Fisk suggested two routes: one through the Yellowstone Valley and the other over the familiar Missouri–Milk River trail to Fort Benton.⁶

³ Ramsey to Andrew Johnson, May 24, 1865; William P. Dole to Johnson, May 27, 1865 — both in file F231CB 1864, NARG 94.

⁴ Fisk to Thomas, May 22, 1865, file F231CB 1864, and compiled service record of Daniel W. Fisk, 132 New York Volunteer Infantry — both in NARG 94; *Pioneer*, June 10, August 10, 16, 17, 1865; *Press*, September 6, 1865; *St. Cloud Democrat*, September 7, 1865; James C. Devine to Thomas Howard, August 29, 1865, in William P. Murray Papers, MiHS. A promotional circular, dated May, 1865, is in the Alexander Ramsey Papers, MiHS.

⁵ Devine to Howard, August 29, 1865, Murray Papers; *Press*, March 10, 1866.

⁶ *Press*, March 10, 1866 (quote); Fisk to Donnelly, December 23, 1865 (quote below), and enclosed map, Donnelly Papers.

The enthusiastic captain set forth in glowing terms to Congressman Donnelly the advantages of this route for Minnesota and the whole Northwest. Thousands of gold seekers would outfit in Minnesota, and thousands of wealthy prospectors would return to settle in the state. Minnesota, it was asserted, could supply Montana's estimated annual consumption of twenty million pounds of flour and offer a product of better quality at lower prices. Fisk envisioned a daily stagecoach service and hundreds of profitably laden freight wagons rolling across the northern plains.

Reverting to the dream of Minnesota's manifest destiny, he found some symbolic meaning in the fact that the heads of three great rivers — the Mississippi, the Missouri, and the Columbia — lay along the same parallels of latitude, and he predicted that emigration would naturally flow along this course. Yet, he pointed out, "here is Minnesota occupying the Head of the Mississippi, — right along the natural geographical highway . . . the very gateway, yet she has no *gate* . . . through which the clamoring tide can be ushered out and shown along on their journey."

Many of the same arguments appeared in a letter published by the *St. Paul Press* on January 16 which was very likely written by Fisk, although it was signed "Board of Trade." The communication again underlined Minnesota's economic destiny by reviewing the benefits of a permanent road, especially in terms of sales of the state's pork, beef, and flour. In frequent letters to Donnelly during the early months of 1866, Fisk enlarged on these points and emphasized his own qualifications for the position of surveyor, guide, road builder, superintendent, expedition leader, or whatever post might become available. He wanted a government appointment for the "bread-and-butter" which he hoped would accompany it, and also because official status would attract emigrants and private capital to his enterprise. Even more he wanted the "honor of determining the location of the great overland highway which we seek to open." This was, he said, "the whole aim of [his] unceasing endeavors, risks and sacrifices since 1862."[7]

In February Donnelly announced that the army had authorized an expedition to investigate the routes between Minnesota and Montana to determine which one should be fortified. Fisk seized avidly on this project as a means of furthering his own purposes. He urged the congressman to secure for him some official position with the army expedition, under cover of which he could take a "little party of friends and emigrants" to the gold fields. In a postscript to his advertising circular, he implied that the army's route and the path of his own forthcoming expedition would be identical and that the presence of the military would ensure the safety of emigrants who accompanied him. Later he went so far as to announce, apparently without authorization, that his expedition had permission to travel with the military force. Fisk's stratagem of linking his own name with the

[7] Fisk to Donnelly, January 15, February 4, 14 (quotes), 22, 27, March 7, 15, 1866, Donnelly Papers. For Fisk's emphasis on western trade outlets, see also *Weekly Press*, February 15, 1866. The importance attached to economic benefits of a northern road is shown, too, by the vigorous opposition of northern Minnesotans to an apparent attempt to revive the Big Cheyenne road, on the grounds that it would adversely affect their business interests. See *Press*, January 31, February 9, 11, 1866; *St. Cloud Democrat*, February 15, 1866; and the Donnelly correspondence for February, 1866, especially Fisk to Donnelly, February 22.

army's plans was to backfire some weeks later when the proposed military expedition failed to materialize.[8]

While Fisk corresponded with Donnelly in the hope of obtaining some official position, he was also busily occupied at home in publicizing his fourth expedition. He had originally proposed a rendezvous at Big Stone Lake in the hope of harmonizing the interests of the several rival outfitting towns. However, the vigorous efforts of St. Cloud citizens and businessmen finally made him change his mind. As early as January 11 the *St. Cloud Democrat* had scoffed at the idea of a Big Stone Lake rendezvous. Since inevitable delays occurred while the trains were organizing, the newspaper said, it was "folly to collect a large body of men at a point where they were consuming what they could not there replace." The *Democrat* thus viewed the rendezvous and the outfitting center as one. The logical rendezvous, the newspaper suggested, was St. Cloud, well out on the frontier, yet supplied with the necessary outfitting stocks to meet all emigrant needs.

After three public meetings sponsored by the town's businessmen, Fisk more or less capitulated. St. Cloud offered substantial public support at a time when his attempts to gain assistance elsewhere were unsuccessful. By March 1 newspaper announcements and posters distributed about the state proclaimed St. Cloud as "the starting point and place of rendezvous" for the 1866 expedition. Not quite willing to abandon Big Stone Lake entirely, however, Fisk cordially invited those who did not join him in St. Paul or St. Cloud to "unite with the main party at Big Stone Lake, preparatory to crossing the Plains."[9]

The *Democrat* expressed pleasure at Fisk's decision, and he was invited to address a fourth public meeting on March 7. His large audience included residents of St. Cloud and citizens of "other towns and communities in the surrounding country for a considerable distance." The speech evinced Fisk's enthusiasm for the new empire unfolding in the mountains and his undiminished faith, imbued with the exuberant ideas of manifest destiny, that the northern route would soon become the permanent line of a railroad to the Pacific. He dramatized himself and the cause in simple, colorful language and clothed his mission in patriotism.[10]

Fisk's speech was a splendid performance, frequently interrupted by "enthusiastic applause," and the *St. Paul Press* considered the address of sufficient importance in its effect on emigration to warrant publication on March 10 in a large extra edition. The St. Paul Common Council urged all prospective emigrants to travel under Fisk's auspices and requested Minnesota's governor and congressional delegation to co-operate in the effort to establish a permanent road to Montana.

There was still no word from Washington on either military aid for the northern route or a specific appointment for Fisk. At the end of February Fisk was asking Donnelly both for a position as superintendent of emigration and for

[8] *Press,* February 11, 1866; Fisk to Donnelly, February 14 (quote), 22, March 7, 1866, and Thomas J. Galbraith to Donnelly, March 9, 12, 1866, Donnelly Papers; *Weekly Pioneer,* March 31, 1866. A copy of the circular, dated February 12, 1866, is in the Donnelly Papers.

[9] *St. Cloud Democrat,* January 18, 25, February 1, 8, March 1; *Weekly Press,* March 1 (quote); *Weekly Pioneer,* March 2 — all in 1866.

[10] *St. Cloud Democrat,* March 1, 1866. Three versions of Fisk's speech survive: his manuscript notes in vol. 1, James Fisk Papers; a printed account in the *Press,* March 10, 1866; and a somewhat abridged version in *Weekly Pioneer,* March 31, 1866 (quote). The *Pioneer* contains the council resolution mentioned below.

some assignment with the army investigation of routes to Montana. He assured the congressman that there was no conflict between the two proposals. On February 27 he suggested that Donnelly co-operate in a new scheme. Fisk asked the congressman to call at the War Department, where he would find on the books an unexpended balance of nine thousand dollars in the fund for the protection of overland emigration. The captain urged Donnelly to *"go for"* that money and have it placed to the credit of the northern route. The next step would be to obtain from the army Fisk's appointment as superintendent of emigration under terms similar to those of his three previous assignments.[11]

In Fisk's view, his services to the government should be worth the nine thousand dollars in the emigrant fund, the fourteen thousand dollars still in the Big Cheyenne road fund, or the total of the two if that amount could be obtained. The captain offered to share with Donnelly any money that became available. He had begun to see that he would have a large number of emigrants, and it occurred to him that their labor and fees could provide all the services and supplies necessary for a government expedition. Since his private organization would thus take care of all the emigrants' needs, the federal funds could be used to reward Donnelly and Fisk for their enterprise and effort. Fisk in "plain English" justified his offer to split the money with Donnelly: "while you and me have made ourselves poor by a spirit and practice of *false* honesty and been laughed at for it, [others] all around us, high and moral, have taken and quietly pocketed all legitimate 'margins' of the kind."[12]

Fisk's proposal seems not to have impressed Donnelly, and there was no word from Washington. As public interest in his expedition grew and Fisk could count on solid support from St. Cloud, he began to feel less strongly about the need for government funds or official appointment. But he still wanted some sort of government recognition which, widely publicized, would inspire confidence in his expedition and bring tangible support from the Minnesota business community. In March a Fisk promoter was pleading on his behalf for an appointment in any capacity, even if unpaid. Nothing came of these schemes for official appointment, support, or notice. In spite of considerable pressure from prominent Minnesotans, army buck-passing finally brought a military decision not to send the Donnelly-heralded expedition to investigate overland routes.[13]

Thus Fisk was left on the same footing as any other prospective emigrant leader — dependent upon the protection promised by the army for groups traveling between military posts. The army had been blamed for not preventing Indian attacks on emigrants, and it now claimed the right to lay down firm rules governing journeys through Indian country. General Pope issued a detailed order which required military commanders of frontier posts to inspect all wagon trains and see that they were properly outfitted, armed, and organized. Emigrants must travel under responsible captains in trains of at least twenty wagons with thirty armed men. Pope's order assumed that all trains would follow routes between

[11] Fisk to Donnelly, February 22, 27 (quote), 1866, Donnelly Papers.

[12] Fisk to Donnelly, February 27, 1866, Donnelly Papers.

[13] Galbraith to Donnelly, March 3, 9, 12, 1866, Donnelly Papers. On the army expedition, see *St. Cloud Democrat*, February 22; *Press*, March 10, April 3, 15, 19; *Weekly Press*, March 22 — all in 1866.

military posts, and it recognized Forts Ridgely and Abercrombie as rendezvous points for those going west by either the northern route or the Big Cheyenne road.[14]

Fisk was annoyed by the military regulations. He felt that they did not recognize the superiority of his proposed route. He also feared that the regulations regarding the organization of trains might deprive him of emigrants, since Pope seemed to suggest that they would be safe in small parties and need not travel in one large expedition under one captain. The designation of both Ridgely and Abercrombie as suitable rendezvous could also deprive Fisk of parties of emigrants because he intended to go only to the latter fort. Later events proved that Fisk's apprehensions were not entirely groundless.[15]

The captain made one last try at getting more specific military endorsement of his expedition by writing to General John M. Corse, commander of the District of Minnesota, who had shown an interest in the northern route. Corse's prompt reply, which was published in the *St. Paul Press* on April 18, confirmed Pope's order, but added that since Fisk's expedition appeared to comply with all the regulations, the emigrants who traveled with him could be assured of adequate protection and a safe journey to Montana. The general concluded by offering his best wishes for Fisk's success. With this crumb of official approval, Fisk had to be content.

By the spring of 1866 Fisk the wagon-road builder had disappeared with the wagon road into the clouds; Fisk the army officer on special assignment to open a military road or superintend emigrants had gone in the same direction. The captain now assumed the role of private expedition leader, and emigrants clamored for advice and information.

"Ho! For Montana!," the four-page promotional circular which Fisk had issued in January, answered many of the questions people were asking about his expedition. By the end of March he had sent out more than three thousand copies from his St. Paul headquarters. The circular described the attractive opportunities which Montana presented and announced the terms for joining the expedition. Individuals were to pay a fee of a hundred dollars each for passage, subsistence, and the transportation of fifty pounds of baggage. Families who provided their own outfit and wagons were charged ten dollars per adult. Fisk noted that he needed mounted men for scouts and hunters; he also promised that some men could earn their passage by driving the expedition wagons.[16]

He encouraged people to travel in groups, suggesting that they send him their fees jointly and assuring them that they would be able to travel next to each other in the line of march. Families were welcome for, as Fisk pointed out, "the mother and children, the young wife and the lass, are all fully as capable of enduring the hardships and inconveniences . . . and much more cheerful generally than the men while on the long march." The circular also urged businessmen sending goods

---

[14] *Press*, March 8, 1866.

[15] Fisk's dissatisfaction is expressed in his letter to Donnelly, March 7, 1866, and in Galbraith to Donnelly, March 3, 9, 1866, Donnelly Papers. Pope expressed a preference for the Big Cheyenne road; see Albert M. Holman, *Pioneering in the Northwest: Niobrara-Virginia City Wagon Road*, 7 (Sioux City, Iowa, 1924).

[16] Circular, February 12, 1866, Donnelly Papers. On its distribution, see *Press*, March 10, and *Weekly Pioneer*, March 31, 1866.

to the mines to communicate with Fisk as soon as possible, so that he could make adequate arrangements.

By the middle of March the circular had been put in the hands of Fisk's agents in a number of states. Ellsworth H. Denslow, a New York stockbroker who had accompanied the 1863 expedition, was the representative in New York City. One agent traveled through the oil regions of Pennsylvania, interviewing prospective emigrants, and others operated in Buffalo, Cleveland, Chicago, and the Minnesota towns of Red Wing, St. Peter, and St. Cloud. Fisk in the meantime met the crowds that had begun to "roll in for talk" at his St. Paul headquarters and worked until twelve or one o'clock every night answering letters.[17]

Three other men joined Fisk to help in organizing the expedition. His brother Robert Emmet Fisk arrived in St. Paul on March 24 to become second in command of the office staff. Robert had been born in Pierpont, Ohio, in 1837 and had lived with the family in New York and Indiana. He, too, had worked for the *Lafayette Daily Courier*, where brother James had served his newspaper apprenticeship. By 1861 Robert had been a compositor, reporter, printer, writer of fiction, and, as he wrote later, the "conductor of a live newspaper." His Lafayette employer described him as a "young man of inestimable character and reputation — of superior business qualifications — and withall a sound, reliable Republican." Robert was working on a newspaper in New York City in 1861. He then joined the army and became a captain in the 132nd New York Volunteer Regiment.[18]

During the war, Robert corresponded with a young New England schoolteacher named Elizabeth Chester, who belonged to a sewing circle which had sent him a quilt. After his discharge from the army in the summer of 1865, he made a trip to Vernon, Connecticut, to meet Miss Chester in person, and the couple became engaged. Robert then went to Minnesota, having promised to join his brother's expedition to the Yellowstone. When that project was postponed, he waited out the winter working for the Burlington, Iowa, *Hawk Eye*. Robert's frequent letters to his fiancée provide a wealth of information about the organization of the train and his trip to Montana.

The headquarters staff also included Nicholas Chemidlin, who had accompanied Fisk in 1864, and an adventurer named William Albert Chester ("Whack") Ryan, a resident of Buffalo, New York, who had served in Robert Fisk's regiment. At the conclusion of his army service Ryan went to Minnesota with the intention of joining the Yellowstone expedition. Twenty-three years old at the time, Ryan was a tall, handsome, apparently well educated soldier of fortune. In St. Cloud he won a saloon bet by swallowing six dozen raw eggs in an hour, and he managed to keep his wallet full of money without seeming to do any work.[19]

[17] *Pioneer*, March 11, 1866; A. J. Fisk Scrapbook, 1:5, in A. J. Fisk Papers; Fisk to Chester, March 4, 1866 (quote), R. E. Fisk Papers.

[18] For biographical information about Robert here and below, see his compiled service record, NARG 94, and pension record, file 327618, NARG 15; A. J. Fisk Diary, March 24, 1866; *Helena Record*, December 28, 1908; and the following letters in the R. E. Fisk Papers — James Fisk to R. E. Fisk, November 20, 1860; W. R. Ellis to Horace Greeley, March 26, 1861 (quote); Fisk to Chester, March 27, June 12, July 24, September 27 (quote), 1865, January 7, March 4, 1866.

[19] On Chemidlin, see Alva J. Noyes, "Nicholas Chemidlin," a reminiscence in MoHS. On Ryan, see his compiled service record, Company I, 53 New York Infantry, and Companies G, H, 132 New York Infantry; Fisk to Chester, March 4, 1866, R. E. Fisk Papers; Loren W. Collins, *The Story of a Minnesotan*, 70 (n.p., [1919?]); *Helena Weekly Herald*, November 13, 1873.

A warm sun had begun to melt the huge snowdrifts as men tramped the slushy walks to Fisk's St. Paul office over the Marine Bank on Third and Robert streets. They crowded their way upstairs, "eager for information, asking questions, giving in their names, telling where they are from, what their trades or calling." Meeting people and answering the enormous correspondence kept the staff constantly busy, and Robert Fisk wrote on March 29 that he had hardly been out of the office except at "ration time." [20]

Many of the letters asked routine questions; others were interesting or amusing. A man from Michigan inquired how "to git on to St Pall," what wages would be paid to "hands as goes to drive teams," and "how mutch grub" the teamsters would receive. Robert's sense of the newsworthy brought the expedition much favorable publicity when he released to the press a letter from a Yankee schoolma'am bound for Montana. Writing from Springfield, Massachusetts, the young lady expressed her interest in joining a brother in Montana because "minds" as well as "mines" were to be developed there. She wrote that she could pay her own way, ride with the best of them, did not fear savages, and could shoot if necessary. The editor of the *St. Paul Press* commented on April 13 that her letter was one of a number which illustrated the "enterprise of Yankee women, the fearlessness with which they undertake great missions, and the sober earnestness with which they discuss even a journey across the continent." [21]

James Fisk began to show signs of the strain of answering the multitude of questions with which he was besieged. Gilbert B. O. Bassett of Forestville, Minnesota, wrote that he had received Fisk's circular and wanted to know "what the particular services were . . . that would entitle him to $10 per head for grown persons going on his train." Bassett was perhaps understandably confused about whether the expedition was to be a private or a government-sponsored one, but when Fisk replied he did not hide his annoyance or correct his spelling. He told Bassett that he was the first of "several thousand" correspondents who had complained about paying the "pitiance I have charged for my cervices and expence in getting up and conducting this expedition." If Bassett and others objected to paying the fee, Fisk urged them to take some other route and "not impose themselves into good society." [22]

The indignant Bassett asked his son Henry, a student at the University of Wisconsin, to take up the matter with the governor of Minnesota. Young Bassett wrote the governor that thousands of people in Wisconsin would take the northern overland trail "if things were not so badly *mixed* up on that route." Some people, he said, thought Fisk was chiefly interested in making money, and others considered him a humbug because of his failures in 1864 and 1865. It is not clear how the

Ryan worked in Montana for the *Helena Herald* and with Fisk on a quartz mining project until he returned to New York in 1869 and became involved in filibustering activities in aid of Cuban independence. In 1873 he was one of the party on the steamer "Virginius," which was captured by a Spanish gunboat. Ryan and many others were court-martialed and shot. See Allan Nevins, *Hamilton Fish*, 198, 628, 667 (New York, 1936).

[20] *Weekly Pioneer*, March 2, 1866; Fisk to Chester, March 26, 29 (quotes), 1866, R. E. Fisk Papers.

[21] Fisk to Chester, March 29, April 10 (quote), 15, 1866, R. E. Fisk Papers.

[22] The correspondence is quoted in Henry Bassett to Governor William R. Marshall, April 30, 1866, file 169, Governor's Collection, Minnesota State Archives. The names of the Bassett family appear on the expedition roll (cited hereafter as Fisk Roll, 1866), photocopy in James Fisk Papers.

senior Bassett was mollified, but when the emigrants gathered at St. Cloud, he, his wife, and five children were among them, and he had paid his fees.

The office staff had other duties besides answering inquiries. "Whack" Ryan traveled to Stillwater, St. Cloud, and Marine on expedition business. James Fisk went back and forth between St. Paul and St. Cloud and took a trip to the towns in the Minnesota River Valley, where people were said to be clamoring for his appearance. Robert was sent on a short journey to the pineries of the St. Croix and Rum rivers to buy oxen. He appears also to have had a hand in preparing a new and almost completely rewritten edition of the circular, which appeared in the middle of April. The new version contained excerpts from General Corse's letter to James Fisk, assuring prospective emigrants of military protection on the journey. The circular also addressed a special appeal to two types of travelers — invalids and pleasure seekers. Emphasizing the extraordinary health which had prevailed on his earlier expeditions, Fisk predicted that "puny invalids" would become "robust and healthful" on the journey. He also stressed the pleasures of travel by horseback and urged young men to equip themselves with saddle horses and enjoy "the privileges and recognition of 'companions in the saddle.'"[23]

Two more Fisk brothers reached St. Paul in April to join the expedition. Andrew Jackson, the youngest, was seventeen and had just been discharged from the Second Minnesota Cavalry after almost three years of service on the Minnesota and Dakota frontier. Jack, as he was called, served with the Sully expedition of 1864 and had been one of the volunteers who went to the rescue of the Fisk train at Fort Dilts. James enrolled him in a St. Paul business college to study bookkeeping — training that was put to practical use in May when he began to keep the financial records of the expedition. Van Fisk, the wagon master of the 1864 expedition, came to St. Paul to take over this duty again after spending the winter trapping in Dakota.[24]

With the opening of the Mississippi to steamboat travel in the middle of April, the pace at headquarters quickened. Two staff members distributed the new circulars in St. Paul's crowded hotels and saloons. In spite of the press of business, members of the staff led an active social life. They went to dancing parties, a circus, a concert by the Hutchinson family, and saw most of the plays offered by St. Paul theaters, including "Lucretia Borgia," "The Mischievous Negro," and "Our Country Cousin." Day after day the office was thronged with "Montana folks," as Andrew called them. The gold delirium was said to be equal to, if not greater than, that of California days. On May 14 two steamboats brought twenty-seven gold seekers from eastern states; forty emigrants arrived on the sixteenth; the next day fifteen or twenty reported in and another fifteen were expected. Minnesota and Wisconsin emigrants were beginning to pour in by "squads, sections and single teams."[25]

[23] A. J. Fisk Diary, April 12, 19, May 10, 15, 17, 22, 1866; Fisk to Chester, April 17, May 15, 1866, R. E. Fisk Papers; a copy of the new edition of the circular, *Capt. Fisk's Fourth Expedition from St. Cloud, Minnesota to the Great Gold Fields of Montana,* is in the MiHS library.

[24] On Andrew, see his compiled service record, Company A, Second Minnesota Cavalry, NARG 94; and his diary, April 2, 7, 12, 1866. Information about Van is contained in *Pioneer,* March 14, 1866; Fisk to Chester, May 3, 1866, R. E. Fisk Papers; A. J. Fisk Diary, May 31, June 2, 1866.

[25] The A. J. Fisk diary for April, May, 1866, records the activities of the staff. See also *Weekly Press,* May 17, 1866; *Press,* May 20, 1866 (quote); Fisk to Chester, May 15, 1866, R. E. Fisk Papers.

Wagonmakers had more business than they could handle in manufacturing new vehicles and repairing old ones. Merchants in St. Paul and St. Cloud fitted out wagonloads of merchandise to send with the expedition — boxes of shoes and boots, barrels of pork, bags of coffee, and chests of tea, as well as stoves, tin, mining utensils, and other hardware. S. B. Loye & Company of St. Cloud advised emigrants that it had everything "from a knitting needle to an outfit for a Montana train." In the *St. Paul Pioneer* of May 19 Cunningham Brothers advertised "all the latest publications as well as standard novels in paper binding" to while away "many an otherwise tedious hour" on the march.[26]

Toward the end of May members of the staff began to leave for St. Cloud. On May 20 the *St. Paul Press* reported optimistically that three hundred people were already at the rendezvous, "waiting for the grass." It was not too late to sign up, and two young photographers decided to join the expedition. William H. Illingworth, the son of a St. Paul jeweler who had been studying photography in Chicago, and a Mr. Bill of Hartford, Connecticut, announced in the *Press* of May 31 that they would take pictures "along the whole length of the northern route." The lure of Montana became almost irresistible and one morning a young Irish housemaid succumbed. Donning a suit of her employer's "masculine habiliments," Kate Williams left the breakfast dishes on the table and the baby in its cradle and set out after a young St. Paul gentleman, determined to share his joys, his sorrows, and his profits.[27]

By May 30 only Robert remained at the St. Paul headquarters. To him had been entrusted the task of securing an army field howitzer for the protection of the expedition. James had already approached General William T. Sherman, who was in Minnesota on an inspection tour. Sherman replied coolly that if necessary a howitzer would be available at Fort Wadsworth. Since the expedition was not going to Wadsworth, Sherman's offer was of little help to Fisk. In a last attempt, Robert secured an interview with the general in St. Paul. The two reminisced for a few moments about campaigning in North Carolina where Robert had been an officer in Sherman's command. Robert then presented his request and the general without a word of dissent penned the desired order to the commander at Abercrombie. His mission accomplished, Robert closed the headquarters office and left for the rendezvous.[28]

While James Fisk and his men attended to a multitude of duties, a competing project quietly took shape in the Minnesota River Valley. As spring came on in Shakopee, two law partners, Luther M. Brown and Harrison J. Peck, contracted gold fever. Putting "Blackstone & Chitty upon the high shelf," they closed their law office and organized the third train to be led by Thomas Holmes. Brown,

[26] *Press,* May 17, 19, 1866; A. J. Fisk Diary, May 17, 31, June 2, 1866; *St. Cloud Democrat,* May 24, 1866 (quote).
[27] A. J. Fisk Diary, May 22, 24, 26, 1866; *Press,* June 5, 1866 (quote). Helen M. White, "Photographs of the James L. Fisk Expedition to Montana, 1866," in the MiHS, lists twenty-four photographs which were probably taken by Illingworth and Bill between St. Cloud and Fort Union.
[28] *Weekly Press,* May 17, 1866; *Press,* June 2, 1866; Fisk to Chester, June 1, 1866, R. E. Fisk Papers.

who was related to Holmes by marriage, had been a member of the Minnesota territorial legislature and had served as the first attorney of Scott County. His account of the Holmes train is published in the pages that follow. Peck had settled in Shakopee in 1864 after serving in the First Vermont Regiment of Berdan's Sharpshooters. His younger brother Simon, a schoolteacher, came out from Vermont to join the train, hopeful of adventure in the West.[29]

Early in May Holmes predicted that his train would be the largest that had ever left the state. His partisans made disdainful comparisons with Fisk and his enterprise. The Holmes train, they said, would go forward without the "tall puffing" that had accompanied the organization of certain other expeditions. Holmes was characterized as being neither rash nor a braggart but "a modest backwoodsman" with considerable experience on the plains. It was further pointed out that he would guide the train without charging fees and "without the least desire for making a speculation in the matter."[30]

During the latter part of May, half a dozen or so emigrant parties who planned to go with Holmes moved independently westward through the Minnesota River Valley to a final rendezvous at Fort Wadsworth. At St. Peter, where a party stopped to complete its outfit, the streets were "dotted with ox-teams, and the long canvas-roofed prairie schooners were drawn up in front of nearly every store." Silas M. McCall, a young farmer who had caught gold fever when "the spring work was nearly done," stopped at the same town two weeks later. He recalled that men from his group bought tobacco, hardtack, medicines, herbs, coffee, and other staples, including a supply of liquor which they smuggled into camp. Fourteen emigrants outfitted at Mankato, purchasing, it was said, fifteen hundred dollars' worth of provisions and clothing in the space of two hours. Most of the parties seem to have stopped at Fort Ridgely. There William Johnstone, a Canadian on his way to recoup his fortunes in the gold fields, reported a cordial meeting with General Sherman, who wished the emigrants every success.[31]

As the Holmes contingents straggled toward Fort Wadsworth, they endured nearly a week of strong winds, hail, and drenching rain. Finally all the groups combined on June 14 in a camp outside the fort. The Holmes train then comprised six companies of thirty to forty men, each under a captain of its own choosing. Johnstone reported that the full train included two hundred men, ten women, ten children, and four hundred head of cattle.[32]

About half the members were Civil War veterans, most of whose names are unknown. They came, according to Luther Brown, from almost every Minnesota regiment, as well as from Vermont, New York, Pennsylvania, Ohio, and Wiscon-

[29] Simon L. Peck, *History of Ira, Vermont,* 61 (quote), 62 (Rutland, 1910); Upham and Dunlap, *Minnesota Biographies,* 84; *Scott County Argus,* October 13, 1916, p. 1. For an earlier attempt to organize a Holmes train, see *St. Peter Tribune,* December 20, 1865, January 12, 1866.

[30] *Pioneer,* May 6, 1866; *St. Peter Tribune,* May 16, June 6, 1866 (quotes).

[31] *St. Peter Tribune,* May 23, 1866 (quote); Silas M. McCall, "Account of the Holmes Train, 1866" (quote), typescript in MiHS (original in the South Dakota Historical Society). On the Mankato outfitting, see *Weekly Pioneer,* June 1, 1866. The William Johnstone Diary gives an account of a group which started from Faribault. Johnstone's entry for May 23 describes the meeting with Sherman.

[32] Johnstone Diary, June 5–10, 14. Other estimates of the train size are given by Peck, *History of Ira, Vermont,* 62; McCall, "Account of the Holmes Train"; and *Forsyth Times-Journal* (Montana), February 14, 1924, p. 1.

sin regiments. Few of them had any acquaintance with the West, and the tender-foot view of plains life revealed in Brown's account of the journey was probably shared by most of his companions.[33]

The train passed military inspection at Fort Wadsworth and moved north and west to the Bone Hill crossing of the James River, south of present-day Dickey, North Dakota. The emigrants had planned to ford the river there, but two half-breed hunters whom they met and hired as guides advised a different course. The train therefore traveled farther north along the James, postponing the ascent of the rough Coteau du Missouri on the other side of the river, and made its crossing somewhat south of present-day Jamestown, North Dakota.

Before the Fourth of July, the Holmes train reached the Missouri, probably south of the present-day town of Garrison, North Dakota. After traveling forty miles north and west, in the area now covered by a reservoir, the emigrants came in sight of Fort Berthold, a fur trading station which also served as a temporary military post. A traveler described it as "a poor, dirty little stockade about one hundred and fifty feet square, with log bastions on two diagonal corners, and miserable little cabins on the inside for the accommodation of the traders."[34]

During a weekend stay near the fort one of the emigrant women, a Mrs. James Windslow, braved the Indians and her husband's wrath in order to bring up a lame ox which had been left thirty-five miles back on the trail. Secretly taking a loaded revolver, dried beef, and some crackers, Mrs. Windslow started out from camp with the explanation that she wanted to accompany some other women on a shopping trip to the fort. Then she rode off alone across the plains. Eventually Windslow learned what his wife had done and set out after her. When he caught up with her late in the day, she had reached the ox, fed her horse, and was enjoying her supper. The pair did not return to camp until the next day, by which time, an observer said, there was little evidence of amicability between husband and wife.[35]

Other emigrants improved their time by selling whisky to the Gros Ventres Indians encamped near the fort. Silas McCall said they got as much as eight dollars a bottle for it, and sales were brisk "until they had all the Indians' money and a horse." The sequel to this enterprise was a night attack on the train by a party of drunken Gros Ventres. Yelling and shouting, the Indians fired "two or three hundred shots" toward the camp. Fortunately, their aim was poor, and the emigrants put an end to the trouble by shooting the leader of the marauders. Luther Brown gives a somewhat different version of the encounter in his account which is printed in this text. A garbled report of the affair reached Minnesota and caused some anxiety there for the safety of the train.[36]

The diarists of the Holmes train recorded numerous other encounters with Indians, but perhaps the most dramatic was the impressive pageant at Fort Union, where several thousand Indians from seven tribes had gathered for treaty making

[33] McCall, "Account of the Holmes Train," lists eleven names; others are mentioned in the Johnstone Diary and Brown's account. For the names of known members, see Appendix, below.
[34] *St. Peter Tribune*, December 12, 1866.
[35] Johnstone Diary, July 8.
[36] McCall, "Account of the Holmes Train," 4. For an example of a garbled press account, see *Faribault Central Republican*, August 15, 1866.

with government peace commissioners. Brown met a Sioux from Shakopee whom he suspected of having participated in the Minnesota uprising, and drew his own conclusions about the efficacy of such treaties.

On July 19 the train left Fort Union on the long, last stage of the journey to the gold fields. Young Simon Peck, looking westward from the top of a small bluff, saw what appeared to be many clumps of trees far off in the distance. Next day he discovered that he had seen innumerable small groups of buffalo feeding on the prairie grass. The train was soon in the midst of the herd, and for six days it was surrounded by the animals. Peck recalled that the noise made by the buffalo "filled the air, like the roar of Niagara," and that fresh buffalo meat was served at every meal that week.[37]

The Holmes emigrants, like those who had gone before them, had memorable adventures hunting elk, antelope, deer, and bear. In camp one evening in the Bear-paw Mountains, an emigrant recalled seeing across a ravine "seven bears sitting upon their haunches and looking at us. They would play around and then sit up and look over to see what we were doing."[38]

Distances were deceiving in the mountain air. A small party set out to hunt in some seemingly nearby hills, only to discover that what had looked like ten miles was probably fifty. Some time later the train came to a small river and, according to McCall, "one of the boys commenced to take off his clothes. We asked him what he was doing this for and he said that everything was so deceiving, the water might be deeper and farther across than we expected."

It was a long journey, but a peaceful one, and in good health and spirits the emigrants reached Helena on August 24. There the travelers went their separate ways, and the names of most of them have long been forgotten.

At the end of May, while the Holmes parties were traveling up the Minnesota River Valley toward Fort Wadsworth, Fisk's emigrants were gathering at St. Cloud and moving out toward Fort Abercrombie. Plagued by bad weather and other petty annoyances, the train did not reach the fort until June 22. There Fisk discovered that his party would not be as large as he expected. Among the men waiting for Fisk was Henry B. Steele, who was taking fourteen wagons of merchandise to sell at the mines. Steele had crossed the plains with the Holmes expedition of 1862; he felt that he knew the way, and he was impatient to be off. Volunteering to act as guide and expedition leader, he promised free passage to emigrants who had already paid Fisk's fee. Others could go by paying a charge of only $2.50. Steele managed to rally some eighty persons and forty teams to his banner, more than enough to meet army regulations for emigrant travel, and his train left Fort Abercrombie on June 23, two days ahead of Fisk. Some of the emigrants thought Steele incompetent and predicted disaster for his party, but the group reached the gold fields safely a few days before Fisk's party.[39]

[37] Peck, *History of Ira, Vermont*, 69.

[38] See McCall, "Account of the Holmes Train," 8, 9, for the anecdotes here and below.

[39] A. J. Fisk Diary, June 13–17, 1866. For the Steele controversy, see *St. Cloud Democrat*, July 5; *Weekly Press*, July 5; *Weekly Pioneer*, July 13; A. J. Fisk Diary, June 23 — all in 1866. Accounts of the journey of Steele's train are in *Montana Post*, September 1, 1866, and *Weekly Pioneer*, August 10, 1866.

Despite the defection of the Steele group, Fisk had between three and four hundred emigrants and one hundred to two hundred wagons in his train. It included parties of men from Canada and from the states of New York, Maine, Massachusetts, Illinois, Connecticut, Pennsylvania, and Wisconsin, as well as Minnesota. Some of them had connections with earlier Fisk expeditions. Charles and Erwin Sims traveled with Fisk again, despite their unhappy experience in 1864. The train also included the wife and children of George Noyes, who had accompanied Fisk in 1862. Many of the men had served in the army, and most were well armed with revolvers, bowie knives, and multishot breech-loading Spencer, Smith, Wesson, or Burnside rifles. Those not already armed were furnished with weapons from the government stores at the fort.[40]

Although Fisk's train was considerably larger than it had been in 1864, his staff was about the same size. Serving as first assistant was Philip Beaupre, a veteran frontiersman who had settled at Sauk Rapids, Minnesota, and who had represented the American Fur Company in the Yellowstone country during the 1840s. "Whack" Ryan managed the commissary, with the aid of Wilson B. Harlan of Red Wing. Though he was only eighteen years old and a member of a pacifist Quaker family, Harlan had served in the army before joining the expedition.[41]

Wagon master Van Fisk had for his assistant a young French-Canadian named Etienne E. Laliberte or Stephen Liberty. Liberty's ancestors, members of an old Norman family, had settled in Quebec in the seventeenth century. Although he had been trained for the priesthood, Liberty moved to Minnesota and worked as a fur buyer at New Ulm for trader Louis Robert.[42]

Little is known of the expedition's physician, Dr. Henry Gates Weeden of Viroqua, Wisconsin. Like the other staff members, he received no salary, but charged a fee for treating those who were ill. On August 12 he reported to his wife that he had already received two hundred dollars in fees. Most of this money was probably earned in treating patients who suffered from diarrhea; it was the most prevalent illness on the early part of the journey and one for which Dr. Weeden found his cholera medicine particularly effective.[43]

As secretary-journalist, Robert Fisk was responsible for keeping a journal and for writing letters about the expedition to St. Paul newspapers. His record of the trip, published in this text, contains the type of information that would have been valuable to later emigrants on the plains trails. Written in an easy, graceful style, Robert's account was probably composed with the hope that it would be used as

[40] Information on the composition of the train can be found in Fisk Roll, 1866; Noyes, *Story of Ajax*, 3; *St. Cloud Democrat*, July 5, September 6, 1866; *Weekly Press*, June 7, 1866; *Montana Post*, September 15, 1866; Henry G. Weeden to Mrs. Weeden, June 25, 1866. The MiHS has a typescript of extracts from the Weeden letters, last known to be in the possession of Mrs. Ethel Weeden Chapman, Stevensville, Montana. Military and pension records for many of the emigrants have been found in the National Archives. For names of the emigrants, see the Appendix, below.

[41] On Beaupre, see MiHS Scrapbook, 43:33. On Harlan, see A. J. Fisk Diary, June 26, 1866, and Harlan's diary of the journey, edited by Gilbert Drake Harlan, "A Walk with a Wagon Train," in *Journal of the West*, 3:141–162 (April, 1964).

[42] On Liberty, see *Spokane Chronicle*, January 18, 1911, p. 1, and J. Porter Graham to the author, August 25, 1955, February 14, 1956.

[43] Weeden to Mrs. Weeden, June 3, 20 (quote); August 12, 1866, MiHS; United States Manuscript Census Schedules, 1860, Bad Ax County, Wisconsin, p. 9, in the National Archives.

a guide. It ignores both personal details and many of the minor hardships of the journey.[44]

Fisk's route varied somewhat from that of his 1862 and 1863 expeditions. He avoided the crossings of the Sheyenne and Maple rivers and traveled, as the Stevens report had recommended, in a northwesterly curve toward the Missouri. From the bend of the Sheyenne at Bears Den Hillock, the expedition went to Bone Hill on the James River. Unlike Holmes, Fisk crossed the river at this point and a day later entered the coteau. Not long after, the emigrants traveled through an immense herd of buffalo. They celebrated the Fourth of July by slaughtering twenty-five of the animals, and their trail westward through the coteau was marked by rotting buffalo carcasses.

Mosquitoes were troublesome; at times the weather was extremely hot; there were delays caused by lost animals and wagon accidents on the rough coteau terrain. But on this part of the journey men and animals suffered most from the effects of alkali water. One emigrant remembered its taste as being so strong "that the addition of the proper amount of grease would have been all that was necessary to produce soft soap."[45]

In the middle of July the train traveled almost a day and a half without fresh water. The cattle, put out to graze at midday, milled about and lowed, and after a dry evening camp they bellowed far into the night. At three in the morning the expedition took up the march again, journeying until noon the next day before reaching a supply of good water. That evening, in celebration of their well-watered camp, the musicians began to play and the emigrants gathered for a concert and dance.[46]

The expedition struck the Missouri, as the Holmes train had, well below Fort Berthold. To one of the emigrants the great river looked like an "immense stream of ready prepared mortar,"[47] but the two-hundred-mile trip along its banks was a welcome change from the hot monotonous trip through the coteau. Diarists recorded the wild and beautiful river scenery, the availability of driftwood for campfires after days of burning buffalo chips, the encounters with Indians encamped at Fort Berthold, the contacts with white men, and the receiving of mail from home.

The journey was only half completed, however, and the brief glimpses of civilization at Berthold seem to have emphasized the distance and the problems that lay between the pilgrims and their destination. As tempers frayed, men drank heavily, quarreled, and exchanged blows over trifling irritations. Three men — including the assistant wagon master, Stephen Liberty — struck out on their own for Montana, but a few days alone on the plains brought them back into the corral. Young Wilson Harlan wrote to his mother from Fort Union: "Some of the party are discouraged, homesick and consequently in the worst of humors." Gilbert Bassett and a companion were threatened with expulsion from the train for selling liquor to the Indians and refusing to perform guard duty. Farther along on the trail Fisk uncovered a plot by a few of the men to steal all the best horses and leave the

[44] Robert's letters, signed "Loveland," appeared in *Weekly Press*, July 5, 1866; *Press*, July 8, August 3, 25, 1866. See also his letters to Elizabeth Chester, April 17, July 21, 1866.
[45] *Minneapolis Tribune*, April 21, 1901, part 2, p. 3.
[46] A. J. Fisk Diary, July 14, 1866; Harlan, in *Journal of the West*, 3:152.
[47] *St. Peter Tribune*, December 19, 1866.

train. After a dispute with Fisk, the Sims brothers took some forty wagons and traveled in advance of the main body of the expedition for the rest of the way to Fort Benton.[48]

Lacking anything more constructive to do, "Whack" Ryan became the ring-leader in a serious escapade. When an emigrant halted along the trail and turned his oxen out to graze, Ryan and several other young men thought it would be a good joke to dress up like Indians, give the man a scare, and "learn him better [than] to stragle." The pranksters fired several shots and gave a few Indian war whoops before they discovered that a woman was in the wagon. According to Andrew Fisk, "They immediately threw of[f] thier Blankets & came up, but the woman was scart to fits." Dr. Weeden was called to attend the unconscious lady, and for some time "her life was despaired of." Although she recovered, the emi-grants were so angry that they threatened to hang Ryan.[49]

The quarrels and annoyances were real, but in spite of them a feeling of cama-raderie persisted among the wagon train emigrants — those who seceded and those who stayed with the main train — that continued throughout the journey and afterward in Montana. On the trail the Steele and Sims dissidents left notes for Fisk's train; Steele's men bridged a river and told Fisk's men where to cross; an emissary from the Sims train came back to warn Fisk that the next campsite ahead lacked water.[50]

The Fisk expedition made camp on the Teton River, six miles from Fort Benton, on August 27. A part of the train went on to Helena, while some eighty emigrants chose to accompany Fisk on a prospecting trip up the valley of the Sun River. In several weeks of searching at the headwaters of the river, they found no gold, and before winter all had moved on to Helena, making their last camp on Tenmile Creek near the ranch of the Widow Durgan, who had traveled with Fisk on his first expedition.

The diary of Andrew Jackson Fisk, printed below, tells the story of the emi-grants who settled at Helena. Within a few weeks Robert had been hired to edit a new newspaper, the *Helena Herald*. His first issue — printed on brown paper for lack of better stock — placed him on the side of virtue, patriotism, and the Republican party, and against rowdies, immoral women, and Southern sym-pathizers. Before the week was out, he had used his fists to defend himself and freedom of the press against the angry supporters of a woman who thought she had been libeled by editorial remarks in the first issue. As a result of this inci-dent, Robert was fined for disturbing the peace by a court whose prosecuting attorney was John Shober of the 1864 Holmes train. By the end of the year Repub-licans in the territory had collected enough money to enable Robert to buy out the owners and become proprietor as well as editor of the paper. His brothers were associated with him, and other Fisk emigrants filled out his staff. Down the street Martin Maginnis of the Steele party provided lively competition as editor of the opposition *Rocky Mountain Gazette*.[51]

Not all the Holmes and Fisk emigrants settled at Helena. Some of them went

[43] A. J. Fisk Diary, July 24, 26–28, August 1, 14, 18, 19, 1866; Harlan, in *Journal of the West*, 3:153, 155 (quote), 158; *Weekly Pioneer*, August 31, 1866.

[49] A. J. Fisk Diary, July 29, 1866 (quotes); Harlan, in *Journal of the West*, 3:154.

[50] A. J. Fisk Diary, August 1, 24, 25, 1866.

[51] On Robert, see p. 227, below. On Maginnis, see Leeson, ed., *Montana*, 327, 1234.

to the Highland district in the Deer Lodge Valley. Perhaps as many as a hundred "Minnesota boys" stampeded to the headwaters of the Little Prickly Pear where they named Lost Horse Gulch and established a small settlement which James Fisk christened Atlantic City.[52]

Many of the emigrants were not ardent prospectors, and they found more profit or adventure in other fields. Wilson Harlan became a pioneer fruitgrower in Montana; he was an early member of the Montana Horticultural Society and the Patrons of Husbandry. Stephen Liberty at first managed a stage station at Cabinet Landing, and later homesteaded near Liberty Lake, which was named for him. He did much to promote the welfare of the Coeur d'Alene Indians and became a familiar figure in Washington, D.C., lobbying for their interests. Martin Maginnis served several terms in Congress as representative and senator from Montana. Alva J. Noyes, who was ten years old when he crossed the plains with Fisk to join his father at Bannack, became a rancher in the Big Hole Basin and wrote books about Montana history.[53]

The most notorious emigrant of 1866 was J. D. Judd, alias Wesson, alias Judson D. Lusk, who was said to have joined the expedition after jumping bail in St. Paul. In the winter of 1867 Judd was jailed in Virginia City for horse stealing; escaping, he was tracked through the snow and shot to death. "A scoundrel of the first water," the *Montana Post* called him, "a cool desperate man, dangerous to the peace, and a useless encumbrance upon the community."[54]

Some of the emigrants failed to find El Dorado in Montana and returned home. Luther Brown became a district judge and a member of the Minnesota state legislature. Harrison Peck took up his law practice in Shakopee again, married Brown's daughter, and served as county attorney and later as state senator. Peck's younger brother Simon returned thankfully to Vermont, where he was to hold public offices for more than forty years. Thomas Holmes, too, had had his fill of overland travel and adventure in the gold fields. Now sixty-three years old, he settled down at Shakopee for a time. Then apparently still pursued by his "demon of unrest," he moved to Cullman, Alabama, where he farmed until his death in 1888.[55]

At the end of 1866, Robert Fisk made plans to go east to buy a new press, to do some politicking in Washington in the inimitable Fisk style, and to marry Elizabeth Chester. He returned with his bride to Helena in 1867, and for more than thirty years the Fisk brothers were associated in the publication of the *Helena Herald*. Van later became the publisher of the *Townsend Tranchant*.[56]

Like Holmes, James Fisk had finished his career as a pathfinder and emigrant leader. For some months in 1867, while Robert was in the East, he filled the edi-

[52] For settlement in the Highland district, see sketches of E. S. Stackpole and W. H. Fletcher in Fogarty, "Butte in the Sixties." On the Prickly Pear rush, see *Montana Post*, November 24, 1866; p. 232, below.

[53] On Harlan, see *Journal of the West*, 3:502, 512, 515 (October, 1964); on Liberty, see note 42, above. Many of Noyes's works have already been cited; see especially *Story of Ajax*, 1–7.

[54] *Montana Post*, December 21, 1867, February 29, 1868 (quote); Harlan, in *Journal of the West*, 3:309 (July, 1964).

[55] Peck, *History of Ira, Vermont*, [6], 35, 74–83; Upham and Dunlap, *Minnesota Biographies*, 84, 585.

[56] Fisk to Chester, December 6, 1866, February 29 [*sic*], 1867, R. E. Fisk Papers; Leeson, ed., *Montana*, 328; *Helena Daily Herald*, April 21, 1890.

tor's chair on the *Herald* and occupied himself with the activities of the Montana militia, to which he was appointed a colonel. Withdrawing from the newspaper, he later promoted a quartz mining project for a time and then moved restlessly between Montana, Dakota, Minnesota, and Washington, engaging in one ephemeral project after another. In the late 1890s he went to live at the Minnesota Soldiers Home in Minneapolis, where he died in 1902.[57]

[57] See files of the *Helena Herald*, January–August, 1867; *Montana Post*, June 1, 1867; *Montana Record*, November 3, 1902. For material relating to Fisk's lobbying activities in Washington in the 1870s, see special file 265, records of the Department of the Interior, NARG 75.

1866 ⊛⊛⊛⊛⊛⊛⊛⊛⊛⊛⊛⊛⊛⊛⊛⊛⊛⊛⊛⊛⊛

L. M. Brown's Account of the Holmes Train

"A TRIP TO MONTANA" BY LUTHER M. BROWN[1]

ABOUT THE 20TH OF MAY, A.D., 1866, the time previously advertised therefor, "Holmes Overland Train for Montana," was converging to its place of rendezvous, via. Fort Ridgely on the Minnesota River. By the 29th of May the greater part of the teams had arrived at that place, but there still remained behind some whom we were confident were on the way, we concluded to move up to Beaver Creek, about twenty miles above the Fort and on the easterly side of the River, which we did on the 30th of May. There the train was organized and officers elected to command the expedition as a military body. Mr. Holmes was elected as chief guide and general superintendent of the train with the title of Colonel. H[arrison] J. Peck Esq., of Shakopee, was elected as the military head with the rank and title of Major, both of whom have since, in Montana, retained their respective titles unchallenged.

At this place (Beaver Creek) all our friends overtook us, and the train was complete with the exception of the Faribault Company under Capt. [Randall] Fuller, and the Mankato Company, both of which kept on the westerly side of the River while the main train traveled all the way to the head of Big Stone Lake on the easterly side, thence passing between Big Stone Lake and Lake Traverse, we proceeded directly to Fort Wadsworth which is about thirty-five miles from the passage between the lakes last mentioned. Before reaching the Fort the entire train had united and now comprised six companies, each commanded by a Captain of its own choice, and comprising an average of between thirty and forty men each that were capable of bearing arms. At the Fort we were inspected by the Col. [Samuel B. Hayman] commanding, and by him permitted to go into the Indian country. From Fort Ridgely to Fort Wadsworth was about one hundred and eighty miles, and the train consisted of seventy-four heavily loaded wagons which moved at about the rate of from fifteen to eighteen miles per day,

---

[1] Brown's account of his journey with the Holmes train appeared in weekly issues of the *Shakopee Spectator* between August 31 and September 28, 1867.

exclusive of delays. The distance was made in fifteen days, and the road had previously been considerably traveled by Government trains and troops going to and from Fort Wadsworth and upon the expeditions against the Indians.

There were few incidents worthy of note occurring upon this part of our route. A few of us, myself among others, walked two or three miles off the road to take a look at the celebrated battle ground of "Birch Coolie," and there we found the graves of some fourteen men who had fallen there, besides a large number of mules and horses. It appeared to me that if the vast prairies had been scoured for a month by a thousand men for the purpose of finding an encampment where, if assailed, the Indians would have all the advantage, that no better place could have been chosen. On a piece of ground as level as a house floor, and about forty rods from the brow of the bluff overhanging the coolie on one side and on the other side the encampment was commanded by gentle elevations (within easy range) just sufficient for a good breast-work for the Indians. But then that event happened early in the war, and our military men had not then learned the science of strategy, so no blame is attached to the fireman or engineer.[2]

Our boys, who, by the way, were nearly one half veteran soldiers, were many of them, continually ranging about the country from one to three miles from the train, with their guns upon their shoulders, frequently coming into camp laden with ducks, curlews, wild ganders, prairie chickens and other wild game, in utter contempt of the "Statute in such case made and provided," but to the infinite pleasure of the "honest emigrant."

At one of our camps, near a large lake and several days' journey below Big Stone Lake, we came across a settler, a single man, living many miles from any neighbor, and entirely alone, with the exception of his dog and several hens, in a secluded valley out of view from the road. He had in his possession one yoke of oxen and a wagon. Upon learning our destination, he immediately conceived the idea of going with us, if he could only dispose of his plunder, which consisted of a cooking stove, six chairs, a half dozen hens and a "crower," a large lot of old harness, cavalry bridles, extra bits, Springfield rifles, Sharps' and Spencer's carbines, steel traps &c. Most of those things were purchased by some of those who could make use of such articles and the balance was packed into his wagon and he was ready to start on time the next morning.

Very much speculation was indulged in by the company with regard to what kind of a customer we had fallen in with. Some questions would be put as to why he was thus living so secluded? (a man of about thirty-five years of age) and how he became possessed of so many traps that so closely resembled Uncle Sam's trappings; but of course no one could answer the questions except by surmises. Our new companion either gave or had conferred upon him the title of "Jack." We soon became thoroughly acquainted with Jack, as he was an inordinate talker, and possessed of more egotism and vanity than I ever saw enclosed in so small a compass. He was constantly bragging of having been in all or nearly all of the battles of the recent war. He gave information to our veteran soldiers of army

---

[2] The Indian attack at Birch Coulee, about fifteen miles northwest of Fort Ridgely, was made on September 2, 1862, against a camp of some 170 men. The campsite was poorly chosen and it was possible, as Brown suggests, for the Indians to approach within gunshot range from all sides. See Carley, *Sioux Uprising of 1862*, 48–51; Holmquist and Brookins, *Minnesota's Major Historic Sites*, 105.

movements and battles and of his hairbreadth escapes from flood and field of which they had never heard before although they had served through the whole war in those very same armies.[3]

Jack was very enthusiastic and eloquent while enlarging upon the qualities of his dog "Frank." He had never been owned by a living man but himself. He had caught him the winter previous in a steel trap set for an otter. He knew nothing of his antecedents or of his ancestry but never tired of bragging of his great exploits. Some of the boys getting somewhat wearied with Jack's constant boastings of his dog's good qualities, softly insinuated that the dog was not so excellent in all respects after all, as they had caught him stealing a ham from a wagon near by, whereupon the owner of the wagon confirmed the suspicion by asserting that he had seen the dog stealing "grub" from several wagons and that he had watched him and seen him carry the stolen property to his master's (Jack's) wagon, and had seen Jack receive the stolen property and conceal it in his wagon. Another suggested that Jack and his dog had been stealing in partnership during the last winter, and that Jack had confined his stealing to hardware and that the dog, Frank, had stolen the provisions to support the twain, and that consequently the best way to provide for our own security, would be to hang Jack and shoot his dog which accusations and suggestions Jack took to be partly in earnest, at least so far as the dog was concerned, and from this time on through the entire trip, poor Jack was worried, bored and tormented. Every mishap of the train was charged to the presence of Jack and his dog. If anything was lost by any one, Jack or the other dog had stolen it, to which Jack would make the air thick with profanity and threats of punishment to his accusers. His personal appearance was criticized, his hair, which he never seemed to have combed, was represented to him as resembling the "quills upon the back of a fretted porcupine." His mouth was represented as a huge sausage machine run with belts of raw-hide, and to have been used as a huge vat or receptacle for an inferior quality of whiskey and for manufacturing fine cut tobacco.

Finally Jack was honored with a prefix to his name, viz: "Cantankerous Jack" by which he ever afterwards, as far as I have any knowledge, continued to be distinguished.

But aside from the amusement of tormenting poor Cantankerous Jack, there were other ways of whiling away our time in camp. As I have already remarked, a large portion of our company were veteran soldiers. I think every regiment raised in Minnesota during the war was represented in Holmes Train, and beside, there were soldiers from New York, Pennsylvania, Ohio, Illinois, Indiana, Iowa, and Wisconsin, soldiers that had not seen each other since they parted on some great battle-field, and in some cases in the midst of the conflict.

I recollect of witnessing a meeting between two men from different States, who had parted as one, at least supposed for the last time upon the hard-fought battle-field of Chic[k]amauga and one of them always supposed the other dead, until they met on that occasion. I heard related around the camp-fires many thrilling adventures of the war. Many a tale of suffering in prison, of hardships suffered upon the march, and many a vivid description of the "wavering fight, the covering smoke, and tumult of the contending armies."

[3] No further information on the identity of "Jack" has been found.

After remaining two days at Fort Wadsworth, on the 17th of June we started in a northwesterly direction with the intention of crossing the James River at a place known as the Bone Hills,[4] and from there to cross the Missouri Coteau and strike the Missouri river at Fort Berthold, but for reasons which will be here-after stated we did not cross the James River at the place mentioned. From Fort Wadsworth our road lay over a waste prairie which seemed almost boundless in extent, and with scarcely a tree or other object to relieve the sameness of the scenery. Our *foragers* were of course on the *qui vive* for game, and many were the longing expressions for a sight at the much talked of buffalo. Nearly every one was anxious to give him a chase *provided* the buffalo would *run*. Some declared they would shoot at any rate whether he would or not; others appeared a little shy and appeared to manifest some interest in the question as to *which way* the buffalo would be most likely to run.

After traveling three days from Fort Wadsworth, the leaders of the train an-nounced, a buffalo ahead!! and immediately thirty or forty rifles were started in pursuit, and in the course of half an hour it was announced that the buffalo was killed and that his steak would be served for dinner. There were only a few per-sons in the train who had ever seen a buffalo, and all were anxious to see and get a piece of his luscious flesh; but such were the extravagant stores taken from the carcass, that before the rear of the train came up, it was all, or nearly all gone, at which some were inclined to complain of "*hoggishness*." Soon after we went into camp for dinner and most of those who had been so fortunate (?) as to get some buffalo, "fell in" and ate with apparently the greatest of relish, while those who had none looked on with considerable envy, and threw out many insinua-tions about "meanness," "hoggishness," and the like. Among those who seemed most particularly delighted with the flavor of buffalo meat, was "Cantankerous Jack"; he ate and bragged, and ate again, until his voracious maw was completely gorged, and he left grinning thereat a ghostly smile. We soon broke camp, how-ever, and started on our way, forgetting all about the old buffalo, and thinking only of the next one — but we saw no more that day.

On the next day, the fourth out from Wadsworth, we fell in with two families of Indian Half-breeds. They had wintered at Fort Abercrombie and were out on their spring hunt. They each had their wife and children along with them, their "tepees," and nine "half-breed carts," drawn, some by horses, some by oxen, and one or two by cows. At first they were supposed to be Indians, and things were put in order for battle, but it was soon ascertained that they were not "fighting Indians" at least. On coming up to them we found that they spoke the French language, and one of them spoke passably good English. Their names were Wil-liam Davis and Jean Parisian. Mr. Davis is a half-brother of Mr. J. Wilkie, one of the members of the last Territorial House of Representatives in Minnesota. Mr. Parisian is a family connection of the famous Jo. Rolette of Pembina.[5] These men

[4] Bone Hill is near present-day Dickey, North Dakota, about a mile from the James River. "On top of it is quite a collection of bones, both human and animal, gathered there by Indians for some purpose or other." See Harlan, in *Journal of the West*, 3:150.

[5] The Jean Parisian here mentioned may have been Baptiste Parisan, a hunter listed as twenty-two years old in United States Manuscript Census Schedules, Pembina County, Minnesota, 1850, p. 15. His name is spelled as "Garest Perrise" and "Yaeset Perres" in McCall, "Account of the Holmes Train," 2, 6. For Joseph Rolette's colorful role in territorial politics, see Folwell, *Minne-sota*, 1:384–386 (St. Paul, 1956). On Wilkie, see note 7, below.

had traversed and hunted the prairies from the mouth of the James River to the British Possessions more or less for the last thirty years, and of course knew nearly every acre of ground over which we were intending to journey.

The whole company now became quite familiar with the half-breeds, and in the course of the conversation something was said about the scarcity of game. The half-breeds said the game must be farther north, as they had yet seen none except small game. "Why," says one of the boys, "we killed a nice buffalo yesterday." "Where did you find him?" asked the half-breed. Upon being informed where the buffalo had been killed the half-breed, with a sort of half smile on his face said: — "*Ah, we saw him, too; but half-breed never eat such buffalo; nor Indian, unless he very hungry; that buffalo too much old, too much poor and too much sick.*" Of course those who had partaken so freely and heartily of the poor old sick buffalo, were somewhat taken aback at this bit of information, and "Cantankerous Jack" immediately suggested that he knew it all the time, and *that was the reason why he had not eaten any of it!*

The buffalo referred to had arrived, as it appeared by the wrinkles on his horns, at the venerable age of twenty-one, and as usual, had been driven from the herd by the "young bucks," never again to be permitted to join it.

We arrived at the Bone Hills Crossing on the morning of June 21st, and should have crossed there and continued our northwesterly course but for the reasons that the Indians (a large camp of whom we found at the Crossing) together with our half-breed friends advised us not to do so, for the reason that our road to Fort Berthold would, by crossing here, lay across and through the highlands lying between the James and Missouri, known as the "Missouri Coteau," which I understand to be in English about synonymous with the words, "Prairie Highlands." These highlands average from fifty to one hundred and twenty-five miles in breadth, and extend from the mouth of the James River on the south to near the British Possessions on the north, and consist of a *violently* rolling prairie, high hills and deep valleys, with scarcity of water, and grass, and a large quantity of alkali both in the soil and water. This would certainly have been "a rough and rugged road to travel," and to avoid the "Prairie du Coteau du Missouri," was a result greatly to be desired.

The Indians encamped at the Bone Hills were a part of a Band of Sissetons who were not implicated in the massacres of A.D. 1862, and were very friendly, and many of the males were then actually engaged in the service of the United States. They, as well as our half-breed friends, advised us not to cross the James River at that place, and further, not cross but one fork of it at all. Upon consideration by the officers of the train it was concluded to employ our half-breed friends to lead us to Fort Berthold by what, in their judgment, was the best route under all the circumstances, which they agreed to do, and did do, in a manner entirely satisfactory.

The train proceeded up the James River from the Bone Hills, on the east side, a distance of about twenty-five miles, then crossing the North Fork [Pipestem River] proceeded up the same on the west bank for nearly one hundred and fifty miles, then bearing west crossed the extreme south-west branch of the Sheyenne, and thence directly to the Missouri river, which we struck below Fort Berthold and opposite the mouth of the Big Knife River.

We left the Bone Hill Crossing June 22d, and reached the Missouri, about forty miles below Fort Berthold, July 3d, lying over only one day. At this point we camped and remained over the "Glorious Fourth." The only means of knowledge that we had of our whereabouts, whether above or below the Fort, was by listening for the sound of the salute of the day by the military at the Fort, and although there was not a white man in the train, (except "Cantankerous Jack," who declared that *he* could hear the sound of cannon in the *other* direction, and that we were about forty or fifty miles *above* the Fort) that heard any sound at all, yet our half-breed guides heard the war of the cannon and told us that we were about thirty-five miles *below* the Fort, an estimate that was probably not a mile out of the way by an air line. Our guides had never been to the Fort and were slightly misled as to its precise location, and consequently led us to the Missouri too far to the south, which error probably cost us thirty-five miles travel. But with this single exception I do not believe that a better or more desirable or feasible route can be found by which to travel from Fort Wadsworth to Fort Berthold. Every noon and every night, except two, our guides led us into camp where we had a plenty of water and feed for our cattle and horses, and although *wood* is scarce on the James River, in dry weather the "buffalo chip" is a very passable substitute. We had the pleasure several times of witnessing "the chase of the buffalo," by our half-breed guides, who were experts in the business; and saw and learned how simple and easy a thing it was to kill the huge buffalo. The experienced and practiced eye of the half-breed will clearly descry a "patch of buffalo" fully five miles before the ordinary white man can see any object whatever. If a bullet strikes a buffalo from four to six inches behind the forward leg, and from nine to twelve inches high, up his side, it will almost certainly pierce his ponderous heart, and if so, of course he is mortally wounded. Sometimes I have seen them fall dead in their very tracks, and sometimes they will contend against death with the most gigantic energy.

We broke camp on the morning of July 5th, and reached Fort Berthold on the evening of the 6th, and no one was hurt. "Cantankerous Jack" assured the entire crowd that he knew all the time just where we were, and had informed the guides from whence the sound of the cannon had proceeded on the morning of the 4th, and thereupon he bragged of his great experience as a guide, and declared that had it not been for him the train would have gone the *other* way, and would then have been down to Fort Rice.

I should have mentioned in my last that when about two hundred miles northwest of Fort Wadsworth and about one hundred miles before reaching Fort Berthold, we crossed the trail of General Sibley's expedition on its return after the battle of Big Mound, some soldiers who were with Sibley's expedition, pointed out the locality of the grave of the late lamented *Dr. J[osiah] S. Weiser*, who was treacherously killed by the Indians in a parley held before the commencement of the battle.[6] We were said, by the soldiers, to be about five miles easterly from the grave. I had no time to go to the grave, nor was it considered safe to stray that distance from the train.

At about the time of crossing General Sibley's trail, we saw for the first time

---

[6] The Holmes train probably crossed Sibley's trail in present-day Stutsman County, North Dakota. On Weiser, see Folwell, *Minnesota*, 2:270; Coller, *Shakopee Story*, 37.

what could properly be called a "herd of buffalo," and we came up to seeing distance of them before they saw us; we were to the leeward side and approached to within a little over a hundred rods of them before they had any notice of our proximity. Our half-breed guides requested of the officers of the train to keep all others out of the way, and gave full assurance that they would kill all the beef that the train could dispose of at that particular time of year. They then rode ahead toward the herd and after getting as near to them as they conveniently could without being seen, they gave a shrill "whoop," reminding one slightly of a similar trait in the character of the "noble red feller of the timber," whereupon the herd raised their heads and looked in the direction of the sound of alarm, and immediately the whole herd turned in a directly opposite direction and started into a brisk run. The half-breeds, mounted upon fleet horses, now put in their spurs and overtaking the herd, rode directly into and finally entirely through the herd, firing into and killing the choicest of the young cows and calves, and in ten minutes enough had been killed to ration the whole train for several days.

The half-breeds' horses are fully trained for the chase; the rider lets go his bridle rein, indicates to his horse by a nudge of his heel, when to stop, when to hold a steady speed, and the crack of the rifle is notice to the horse to jump ahead and "lay himself along by the side of another." The Spencer Carbine, or Henry Rifle, is now quite commonly used for killing buffalo. Mr. Davis informed me that he had on one or two occasions killed sixteen buffalo, with his Henry rifle "once full." The meat which we took on this occasion was certainly of a very delicious character; some thought it superior to any meat in the western markets; all agreed that it was at least good enough for "Half-breeds or Indians," which was understood to refer to a certain other buffalo, that "Half-breeds nor Indians don't eat." "Cantankerous Jack" did full justice to the subject; and while looking on in silent wonder at his gigantic powers of mastication, [Allen M.] Easterly, of Goodhue county, was forced to exclaim: "What a d——d fool the man was who invented the sausage grinder!" For my own part, I think that buffalo flesh of the same character and age is not inferior to our domestic beef, nor do I think it superior to the latter; in fact, I cannot, as a general rule, distinguish the one from the other.

About this time, which was June 27th, as we approached the camping ground for night, our guides informed us that they could see some objects at a considerable distance ahead, which they thought might be an encampment of Indians. Very few of those composing the train could see any object whatever, but although they could see nothing, they claimed the privelage of being as much *scared* as those who could see. Many were excited and restless, expressing many forebodings of what might take place ere "another sun should rise." Supper was, however, shortly over, and about twilight our cattle and horses were gathered up and picketed inside our corral (a circle formed by our wagons) and a strong picket guard was detailed to occupy the surrounding heights with strict orders that if attacked to hold their positions at all hazards, until reinforced. Our two guides, without the least seeming uneasiness, at about twilight, mounted their horses and quietly rode away in the direction of the supposed Indian encampment. Considerable restlessness prevailed about our camp until about 11 o'clock in the evening when they were discovered on their return to camp in company with several others, and in a few moments we had the pleasure of being introduced to the Hon. John [B.] Wilkie, late member of the Minnesota Legislature, his brother and several others of his friends and relatives — the anxiety and restlessness was at once at an end. Mr. W., with about two thousand Half-breeds, (men, women and children) from the vicinity of St. Jo, and Pembina, were out on their June hunt and had that day killed about two thousand buffalo. I had not before met Mr. Wilkie since the famous "extra session" of 1857.[7] He still retains his robust health and dignity of manner. He is one of the leading men among his people, and much respect is paid him by the younger men of his tribe. He informed me that while his half-brother, Mr. Davis, before spoken of as one of our guides, was with us, we need fear no harm from the Indians this side of Fort Berthold, 1st, because there were no Indians on or near that route except "Standing Buffalo's Band," that Standing Buffalo[8] himself was an acquaintance of Mr. D. and himself, and besides was really a good Indian, although he had many bad Indians about him over whom he had no control, and 2d, that the Indians did not DARE to molest a Pembina Half-breed or one of their friends. That if they did so, they (the Indians) knew that they would be swept from the plains within a month.

The next morning when we reached the Half-breed encampment, and there saw nearly five hundred young, athletic, and sturdy Half-breed hunters, dashing about upon horseback as fierce as a "Russian Hussar" and with the recklessness of an "Arabian Knight," I saw and felt that Mr. Wilkie had made no idle or boastful remark. With this assurance we were relieved of any unnecessary anxiety this side of Fort Berthold.

On approaching the Fort from the east, we came in sight of it some five or six miles away, and approached it down a gentle slope toward the Missouri. Soon after arriving in sight our Half-breed friends noticed considerable commotion among the Indians encamped around and in the vicinity of the Fort. They had seen our train approaching and did not know whether we were friends or enemies. They had never before seen such a sight. We had traveled for three hundred miles over the plains of Dakota Territory, where no white man's oxen, wagons and cows had even been seen before. A small tribe of Indians known by the French name of *Gros Ventres* (pronounced generally, Grovons,) live in the immediate vicinity of the Fort. They are not on exactly friendly terms with the Sioux, and therefore take the liberty of carrying away each other's scalps whenever it can be done *safely* and *secretly*.

On seeing our approach they dispatched about twenty-five mounted scouts to ascertain what designs we might entertain toward them. The scouts, before starting on their mission, had used up what little vermillion red and lampblack was to be had in the vicinity, and divested themselves almost entirely of clothing; in this condition they came hurrying towards us on a "spanking gallop" and with many threatening and defiant "airs." Coming within about a mile of us our two Half-breed guides put spurs to *their* horses and immediately dashed forward toward the advancing *red* men with a fiercer gallop and with equally as defiant

---

[7] On Wilkie, see Stevens, *Narrative and Final Report*, 65; *North Dakota Historical Collections*, 1:380. For the extra session of the Minnesota territorial legislature, see Folwell, *Minnesota*, 1:394.

[8] Standing Buffalo was a chief of the Sisseton Sioux who lived in the James River Valley after the uprising of 1862. Although the chief did not support the uprising, individual members of his band participated. Folwell, *Minnesota*, 2:230, 265, 429.

an air as that manifested by the Indians. The Indians, seeing this, slacked their pace, and our guides halting their horses upon a slight elevation in full view, turned the side of their horses toward the Indians, dismounted and stood at their heads, bridle in hand. The Indians then halted, and our guides instantly sprang into their saddles and rode in a tearing gallop directly down among the Indians. All was ascertained in a moment, to be friendly, and we were that night escorted into camp about three miles below the Fort and a few rods from the shore of the Missouri, that majestic though erratic river, "whose troubled waters are continually casting up mire and dirt."

All were pleased to again see a steamboat or even to hear its horrid whistle. At the Fort we found one company of U.S. Infantry under command of a Captain, also a few Indian traders who were mostly St. Louis men, all of whom seemed pleased to see us and were very sure that Holmes had judged wisely in making *their place* a point in his "great overland route."[9] They seemed to think that he could never have gone through the country in any other *pass*, except that by Fort Berthold, but they did not give Holmes any town lots. For the purpose of rest for ourselves and our animals we concluded to lay over for one whole day (July 7th) in the vicinity, which we did by encamping about one and a half miles above the Fort, and here during the day we were visited by the whole body of the nobility of the Great Gros-Ventres Nation. Of course a contribution box was passed, and a feast followed, after which the "noble red fellers" stole what few portable articles they could find about the train and departed with many good wishes and with great dignity of deportment. Shortly after they had left our camp complaint began to be made of the disappearance of many small articles such as powder-horns and flasks, shot-pouches and sacks, and several complained that they had lost certain black bottles, which contained small quantities of the "extract of rye," "patent medicines," "rectified high wines," &c., &c. Among those who complained of the greatest losses was "Cantankerous Jack;" to listen to whose dolorous complaints and extravagant assertions of his losses one would have supposed that a hundred pounds in "dust" would hardly make him whole.

At about nine or ten o'clock and after the picket guard had been detailed and posted, vague noises and sounds were heard occasionally in the direction of the Indian encampment near the Fort. Experienced *ears* well knew what it meant — the Indians had got some whiskey from the train and were on a "bender." These noises increased gradually both in number and volume of sound, and finally they began to come nearer our camp, and we were soon forced to the conclusion that the "noble red feller" was athirst again, and was on the rampage for a drink. The whole train was at once called to arms, except the ladies, (ten in number) who come without calling, and each man stood with rifle in hand, apparently ready for whatever events might occur. The Indians, a few of them, and as we supposed, some Half-breeds, living at the Fort and in the employ of the traders, came to within a short distance of our picket posts and called for some whiskey, and also demanded leave to pass within the lines; this was, of course, positively

[9] The traders were undoubtedly pleased with the chance to sell supplies to the emigrants. (See James B. Hubbell to Clark W. Thompson, February 26, 1864, in Thompson Papers, MiHS.) Actually, the Holmes train could have struck the Missouri at any of the fortified posts, in conformance with army regulations, but its choice of route was probably influenced by Fisk's earlier announcement that he would travel via Berthold.

refused, and they were ordered to leave at once and to make no delay in getting out of rifle range. During all this parley "Cantankerous Jack" was energetically engaged in picking up ox-yokes about the neighboring wagons and carrying and piling them up under his own wagon, and finally in getting himself concealed behind his breastwork of ox-yokes.

The Indians and Half-breeds or whichever they were, retired from sight, or nearly so, and then set up a series of noises, hootings and howlings that would have been creditable to a thousand disappointed and hungry wolves, and finally they fired something like a half-dozen shots into the air which did us no harm, except to startle us a little, by their whistle over our heads — whether they intended to simply scare us or whether they were mistaken in their range is not known; at all events, Maj. PECK was in command in a moment and directed the picket lines to open *in earnest*, and kill if they could. In another moment six of Sharps' Carbines had sent their compliments towards where our visitors could be dimly seen. In another moment they had disappeared from sight and their music now ceased for the night. The Captain in command at the Fort, supposing that we had sold whiskey to the Indians voluntarily, thought he would let us take the consequences and fight it out if necessary, and therefore paid no attention to us that night, but he informed Maj. PECK the next day that our pickets had probably sent one Indian upon an extensive journey. This is the whole of the occurrence with reference to the tremendous fighting done by the Indians on one side and Holmes' train on the other, as received by the newspapers, through Indian sources, and published broadcast with no other result than to worry our friends at home.[10]

But morning came, the sun arose, and with it came Cantankerous Jack from behind his pile of ox-yokes, and assured us that he had lain down early in the evening and had quietly fallen asleep and had not been disturbed or awakened during the night, and then complimented himself for his "nerve" and want of any sensations of fear in thus being able to sleep through such noise and confusion. But upon having his attention called to the pile of ox-yokes under his wagon and directly between the place where his head lay and the place from whence the Indians had fired their shots, Jack hemmed and hawed for a moment and then declared that some of the boys had done that to injure his character as a brave man.

On the 8th day of July, 1866, we packed up and started for Fort Union, a distance by land of one hundred and thirty miles. The greater part of this distance the road lies along the Missouri bottom, though occasionally it becomes necessary to ascend and descend an abrupt bluff or embankment. The Missouri as it appeared had recently been on a big bender, and had angrily thrown its flood wood two or three miles distant from the main stream. Of course along the Missouri bottoms we found aplenty of the three necessaries for the traveler, viz: wood, water and grass.

Nothing of importance occurred on this portion of the route, nor was there anything particularly amusing or exciting, except perhaps with the foragers or hunters, who enjoyed some rare sport in hunting the antelope, the deer and Elk. These animals are quite plenty on the plains and river bottoms. The elk is gen-

[10] See p. 171n, above.

erally found near where there is timber and water in abundance. The blacktail and whitetail deer also abound in a similar locality, while the antelope may spring up at almost any moment or at almost any place on the plains. The flesh of either of these animals when in a proper condition, is, to my mind superior to any of our domestic meats. The elk resembles in texture and flavor a two year old beef. The deer and antelope are similar to each other and somewhat resemble mutton. The animals are generally hunted and shot "on the sly," but our half-breed guides sometimes showed the fleetness of their horses, by running the antelope down upon a short "heat" on the prairie. I saw them do this several times during the trip. The antelope is a splendid animal for the "turf" but soon tires out; but while his struggle holds out, to see him run, makes one think of:

> "When swift camilla scours the plain,
> Flies o'er the unbending corn and skims along the main." [11]

The distance between Fort Berthold and Union was passed over by us in ten days though there was no road between the two places except a portion of the way we were able to follow Gen. Sully's old trail of 1864, which was never much of a trail on account of the scattering manner in which his march was made and besides the growth of vegetation and overflow of the rivers had quite obliterated the trail for much the greater part of the distance, and we were undoubtedly more puzzled in attempting to follow the trail than we would have been had we taken no notice of it, and hunted our own road — we reached Fort Union, July 18th and remained over there, as we had done at Berthold for one day only.

At this Fort we met the United States Peace Commissioners as they were called. That *intolerable nuisance* that has caused the massacre of more men, women and children by the Indians, than all other causes put together. These Peace Commissioners go around just in season almost every year, to furnish the Indians with all the comforts, necessaries and paraphernalia of a glorious raid upon the emigrant trains which every year are winding westward over the plains. This Peace Commissioner business establishes in effect a Quartermaster's and commissary Department with an Arsenal attached. The Commissioners present, were the late Maj. Gen. [S. R.] Curtis the hero of Pea Ridge, Judge [Orrin] Gurnsey of Janesville, Wis.[12] The name of the other gentleman I do not now remember as I did not note it at that time. I do not wish or intend to be understood as casting any reflections upon the actions of these men. They undoubtedly were acting in good faith and no doubt when they left Fort Union supposed that they had effected a lasting and permanent peace with the treacherous devils, to whom they had distributed their clothing, provisions, fire-arms and ammunition.

But let me mention one little incident. Upon our arrival at the Fort in the morning I met a Sioux Indian who recognized me, saying that he had often seen me in Shakopee &c. was quite communicative, and inquired for many of the white people about Shakopee, among whom were Mr. [Moses S.] Titus, Rev. Mr. [Samuel W.] Pond and Major [Richard G.] Murphy. He informed me that he had left the

[11] The quotation is from Alexander Pope's "Essay on Criticism."

[12] On the commission, see *Report of the Commissioner of Indian Affairs*, 1866–67, p. 168–176 (39 Congress, 2 session, *House Executive Documents*, no. 1 — serial 1284). Treaties were made at both Fort Berthold and Fort Union. For certain considerations the Indians ceded lands to the government and yielded right of way for overland routes.

Sioux before the outbreak of 1862, had married into a Crow family and now lived with the Crows, and formed a part of that tribe. In the afternoon I was in company with him at the Fort, where the Commissioners were distributing to the Crow Indians the presents which they were told their Great Father had sent to them. A large body of hostile Sioux were a few miles below the Fort and on the opposite side of the Missouri. The Indian of whom I have spoken, pointed out to me something like a half-dozen Sioux Indians who had smuggled themselves into the Crow camp and were receiving their presents of ammunition, provisions, and clothing. The Indian of whom I have spoken informed me that he had often heard these same Sioux boasting of the number of scalps they had taken in Minnesota in 1862. He insisted that I should not mention the matter to the Commissioners or to any one else there, as he said he would be killed if it were known that he exposed them. I suspected that my informant was another of the same stripe of Sioux. Many of his answers to the questions that I put to him were quite inconsistent and unsatisfactory and he shortly disappeared. Two traders were shot on that same day by the hostile Sioux within a mile and a half of Fort Buford the new Fort two miles below the old Fort Union; but as they were across the Missouri and were selling arms and ammunition to the "Red Fellers," and as we had some fear that they intended to go up on the west side of the river cross over and head us off, we cared a very little how many such traders they might think proper to shoot.[13]

July 19th we again packed our wagons and started upon the last long pull of four hundred miles to Fort Benton, although we had had a pleasant trip and seen many things interesting and amusing, yet our journey was beginning to grow tedious and tasteless. All wished that we were at Fort Benton and wearily counted the days that would pass before we should arrive at that point. There we should be out of fear or danger of the "noble red Feller," and nearer the gold fields where all were earnestly hoping to be lucky.

We reached Milk River in eight days, a distance considerably over one hundred miles with only two incidents worthy of note, one of which was the passage of a stream called the "Big Muddy" [Creek], which was the only stream between the Minnesota River and Helena which was deep enough to wet our wagon beds. We raised them up by means of blocks about eight inches in height and passed through the stream without injury to our goods and chattels.

The other incident was the striking of an innumerable herd of buffalo. We struck this herd on the 20th of July, and remained in it for six days the buffalo surrounding us on all sides as far as the eye could reach. Much speculation was indulged in, with regard to the number of Buffalo thus seen by us. Some estimated them by the millions, some by the hundreds of thousands. "Cantankerous Jack" was entirely sure that there could not be less than six hundred millions. I estimated the herd to contain six hundred thousand, *i.e.* one hundred thousand per day for six days. I believe that there was no one that agreed with me in my estimation. Of course we regaled ourselves upon buffalo beef and veal during these six days.

The Milk River is the largest and most important northerly branch of the Mis-

[13] On this incident, see Moses K. Armstrong Scrapbook, 1:103, in MiHS; McCall, "Account of the Holmes Train," 5.

souri, and for a long distance lies almost parallel with the Missouri about one
hundred miles north of the latter. Between the Missouri and Milk Rivers, lies
a large spur or arm of the great Rocky Mountains called "The Bear's Paw," also
still farther east is another called "The Little Rocky." On striking the Milk River,
we crossed it, and continued up its valley for near two hundred miles, crossing
it in all three times, and passing entirely around upon the north side of the Little
Rocky and Bear's Paw mountains, carrying us to the distance of nearly one hundred miles northerly of Fort Benton, causing us at least to travel two hundred
miles further than would be necessary, could we have kept [to] the Missouri Bottoms. This we could not do on account of the abrupt and broken features of the
country, nor could we cross the Missouri and cut off the great northern bend on
account of the supposed hostile feelings and intentions of the "noble red fellers"
that are supposed to reside in that secluded and romantic clime.

Somewhere about the 5th day of August as we were quietly wending our way
along the bank of the Milk River, our Half-breed friends announced that we were
in the vicinity of Indians, although none had been or could be seen. The train that
was at that time moving in 2 columns, immediately "doubled up," and formed
very nearly a square and cautiously moved along, when the half breeds again
announced "Indians near by and very hungry." I could well understand how they
could detect the traces of Indians but how they could tell that such Indians were
very hungry, passed my comprehension, for none had yet been seen. Again in
a short time it was announced "Indians ahead on the left." I then went forward
and saw the half breeds going through about the same maneuvres as at Fort
Berthold, and finally closing up by running their horses down a steep side hill
and dashing recklessly into a crowd of Indian braves.

When it was ascertained that all were friendly on both sides, the Indians, men,
women and children came pouring out of the grass, from among the bushes, and
from under the river bank as thick as "eagles from the carcass." They were hungry
and thirsty. They wanted "grub," whiskey, and especially the latter, and assured
us most solemnly that if we would let them have a small quantity they "wouldn't
tell the agent." These were what are called the "Mountain Crows," from over the
Missouri. Were out of food and were on a hunt for buffalo. We told them of the
great herd we had passed, and we went ahead, and they followed our road back
in search of the Buffalo. Cantankerous Jack, as usual, lost a large amount of personal property stolen by the Indians, and looked forward with gloomy forebodings
to the day when his whiskey rations would be suspended. I had the curiosity to
ask the half breeds how it was that they knew that these Indians were "very hungry" before they had seen them. "Why," said Davis, "we found where they had
killed an old buffalo, *like that old sick one, and had eaten it all clean up.* That
is how we knew."

While passing around the precipitous heights of the "Bear's Paw" it occurred
to some in the train who had visited mining countries before, that there was no
reason why gold should not exist and be found among the ridges and ravines of
the "Bears Paw." At a place, therefore called "Big Sandy" [Creek], and about
fifty or sixty miles from Fort Benton a part of the train, consisting of twenty-eight
wagons, stopped for the purpose of prospecting in the Bear's Paw and for the
purpose of recruiting their teams, a good many of which had already begun to

exhibit signs of weakness. The number who thus remained behind composed about one-third of the train. Among this prospecting party was a man who went by the name of "Jo" and was a half-breed Sioux from Mendota or its vicinity. He was an excellent hunter and a good shot. Also among the company was "Cantankerous Jack" who, although as he claimed, was a greater hunter than had ever lived since the days of Nimrod, had not yet been able to show his great skill in that direction, for the reason that there was no one in the train that was capable of managing his *team* in his absence. But upon this prospecting tour in the Bear's Paw mountains Jack got a chance to sail and so he sailed in.

After traveling over and among the mountains for several days, the party becoming scattered considerably, a few of the boys including the half-breed Jo., Pat McGuire, Cantankerous Jack and a few others fell in company with a huge grizzly. This was not exactly the game they were looking for, but still they concluded, as their commissary was getting a little short to take it. Accordingly, the bear having concealed himself in the underbrush, Jack fired his Sharps' rifle into the patch of bushes and handsomely retired to witness the effect on Mr. Bruin; but Bruin was unhurt and consequently paid no attention to the shot that Jack had sent toward him. Upon seeing this Jack assured his companions that he had killed him sure, and began to congratulate himself upon his great talent as a hunter, a marksman &c.

Jo., or "half-breed Jo.," as he was always called who seemed to have a sort of instinct, and also some sense about such matters, of course knew that the bear had not been seriously hurt, and in all probability was entirely unharmed. Jack, although avowing himself ready to bet his life that the bear was dead, did not feel at all inclined to go into the bushes to haul out his game. Finally Half-breed Jo., who was armed with a sixteen shooting Henry rifle, cautiously approached the jungle in which the grizzly was concealed, and not being able to see or hear anything of his secluded majesty, Jo. attempted to crowd his way into the thicket until he could see the bear, then shoot him as fast as he would be able to work his rifle, retreating at the same time if necessary. Jo had not succeeded in introducing himself far into the thicket before (to use Jo's own language) the bear "rose up immediately before him as big as an elephant," and at the same time made a noise very like a "frightened hog." Jo not having the fear of wild beasts before his eyes, instantly fired at the huge animal and commenced backing out of the bushes. The bear felt Jo's first shot just enough to provoke him at the impertinence of the hunter, and immediately went for Jo.

The others who were standing back ready to help Jo, now found a difficulty which they had not before thought of. They could not shoot at the bear without standing an equal chance of killing Jo. The bear was advancing toward Jo, and Jo was constantly shooting his Henry. Crack, crack, crack went Jo's rifle, while he was coolly stepping back, the bear getting every shot. His companions began to feel relieved, thinking that Jo would certainly shoot the grizzly "all to pieces" before he would get to him. But just then, as ill luck, chance, accident or fortune would have it, one of the cartridges clogged in the breech of the Henry rifle and in an instant that formidable weapon was utterly worthless for present use, except as a club. The bear advanced and closed in upon the poor half-breed who, attempting to defend himself with his "club," became entangled in the brush and fell down, and then the bear was upon him and apparently to all lookers on, had Jo in a most perilous condition.

On seeing this, Cantankerous Jack broke for camp, and ran like a Quarterhorse. He arrived in camp near night, having run several miles in an exceedingly short space of time. Jack reported in camp that the whole crowd except himself had been killed and eaten entirely up by a numerous drove of grizzly bears. That he had hardly escaped with his life, and only by his good marksmanship, his splendid Sharps' rifle, his own gigantic strength in wrenching himself from the very jaws of death. He advised that our camp be broke at once, and that they march all night to get out of the way of the bears. But Cantankerous Jack was too well known. His account of affairs had no influence except to draw forth ridicule upon his own head for his unmitigated cowardice in running away from his companions.

But to return to the half-breed whom we left in the power of the grizzly. Jo, at about the instant of feeling the first bite of the bear, gave a most unequivocal manifestation of it, by screaming "bloody murder." At this precise point Cantankerous Jack left for camp. But Pat. McGuire a small sized wiry built Irishman —who had on his discharge papers twenty-two pitched battles and five severe skirmishes, in the 11th United States Infantry, and "nary a scratch yet," was there. Jo gave his hand to the grizzly and taking the advantage thus gained thrust his arm directly down his throat, and seized hold of the roots or lower end of the tongue, and held on with the "grip of death." Pat McGuire rushed to his rescue, came up to Mr. grizzly and coolly blew off the top of his majesty's head with a Springfield musket while Jo. was yet holding on to his tongue. Jo was somewhat injured but soon recovered, and was able to walk to camp, where they arrived shortly after dark with a good supply of stock and his majesty's hide on a rail.

Cantankerous Jack retired to bed in his wagon at an early hour, and appeared not to hear anything said or done in camp after the arrival of the party whose tragic death he had, a few hours before, reported with so many assertions that his own eyes had borne witness to the sad affair. But on coming out the next morning after all others were up and about their business, Jack came creeping out, and was of course met by a perfect torrent of ridicule for his cowardice and false and exaggerated reports. Jack answered that they might blackguard and blow just as much as they pleased, but that he knew *one thing* and that was, that his shot had so badly wounded and weakened the bear that he was unable to kill even a rabbit, to say nothing of a half-breed Sioux Indian. This event closed the prospecting in the "Bear's Paw" Mountains, some slight traces of gold were found in several places but not in paying quantities. There was, however, no thorough prospecting done in these mountains and I see no reason to suppose that there is no gold in these, as well as others of the Rocky Mountains.

August 15th the main train arrived at Fort Benton, at least eleven hundred miles from St. Paul. We had been on the road between Fort Ridgely and Fort Benton, seventy-six days, and that, too, on a road that we had made ourselves, with small exceptions. At Fort Benton we again came in contact with the world. Here we found quite a thriving little town which is known as Benton City. There are quite a number of white people, and more have since come in. At the time we arrived at the Fort they had not fully "adopted the habits and customs of civilization," but they could lie, swear, steal and drink whiskey with a remarkable degree of accuracy, and were what might be called quite "heavy on the steal." They stole my jack knife for which I doubt if I ever forgive them. But seriously Fort Benton should it remain as it now is, "the head of navigation on the Missouri," will be quite a large town in a few years, as the Montana trade increases. There was last season before our arrival there, about 7500 tons of freight landed there by steamboats from St. Louis. This trade now in its infancy will be held by St. Louis and Chicago via. Council Bluff and Omaha until the great Northern Pacific Railroad shall be opened through Minnesota and Dacotah.[14]

Aug. 16th we started for Helena in good health and spirits, seemingly almost at home a good road to travel on, was a new thing to us. A road over which 7500 tons of freight had been carried, of course must be a good road, at least in a dry season as was the case last year in that region. For sixty miles after leaving the Missouri river at Fort Benton we travelled before finding any good water and with a great scarcity of water of any kind, and very little feed for our cattle. This sixty miles between Fort Benton and the Sun River was the most severe trial to our teams that we had experienced on our trip, but we struggled through it, crossed the Sun River and entered the "gate of the Rocky Mountains."[15] This entrance of the Mountains is guarded on each side of the road by a Gate Post of such enormous size that they very much resemble elevated fortifications, but as you approach them their abruptness and great height and wondrous proportions dispel all such ideas, and you find yourself standing in the shadows of awe-inspiring mountains and amid the wreck of ancient upheavals and the ponderous convulsions of nature.

After entering the gate of the mountain there is only an occasional spot of level road the whole distance to Helena and for hundreds of miles beyond. Through the wide valleys there are some times many miles of level travelling — or nearly so — but the greater part of the way is either a decided *up* or *down* hill. We travelled the whole distance from Fort Benton to Helena, 141 miles by actual measurement, in eight days including all rests, and arrived in Helena Aug. 24th, 1866, after a journey of nearly four [twelve] hundred miles, in near one hundred days of time. Our long journey was at an end, and we who had been so long together, and with so many anxious feelings had looked to each other for assistance and defence in case of necessity, were now to separate, each going in the direction which, in his judgment, would best promote his interests. We were never to see each other again together. The "corral" would never again be formed. We should no more hear the voice of the Major [Peck] calling out: "get up the cattle boys." All these thoughts and many more rushed through the mind, and although all were glad to be there, there was, I have no doubt, many sad feelings on the part of the entire company at this last time of breaking camp.[16]

[14] The village of Fort Benton was an important steamboat terminus and trade center during the following quarter century. See Paul F. Sharp, *Whoop-Up Country: The Canadian-American West, 1865–1885,* 5, 41, 157–182 (Minneapolis, 1955).

[15] Brown is speaking here in general terms of the entrance to the mountain region. He had not seen the true "Gate of the Mountains," north of Helena, where the Missouri cuts its way through the Rockies.

[16] The concluding installments of Brown's account, which appeared in the *Shakopee Spectator* on October 5, 12, 1867, comment chiefly on the climate and resources of Montana.

1866 ✸✸✸✸✸✸✸✸✸✸✸✸✸✸✸✸✸✸✸✸✸✸

Two Diaries of the Fisk Expedition

DIARY OF ROBERT E. FISK, 1866[1]

FT. ABERCOMBIE, JUNE 22. The last section of Capt Fisk's Montana expedition, which left St Cloud June 7th, arrived here today, and went into correll on the Capt's old camping ground of '62–3, ¾ of a mile west of the Fort.

June 23. The sections of the expedition which had preceded Capt Fisk from the rendezvous at St Cloud to Ft. Abercrombie, with the exception of Mr. [Henry B.] Steele's wagons, numbering 14, together with some 20 other wagons, representing in all about 60 men, moved up to Capt Fisk's camp from their several camping grounds about the Fort, and went into correll with the organization. Mr. Steele's party of seceders moved out to-day, pursuing Capt Fisk's northern overland trail of '63.

Sunday, June 24. Brevet Maj. [Robert H.] Hall, Capt 10 U. S. Infty., Cmdg at Ft Abercrombie, escorted by fifty of Capt Fisk's mounted men, rode out to camp and inspected the arms of the Montana party, counted the whole number of persons on parade, observed the appointments of the organization, concluding with a little speech to the men assembled, in which he expressed surprise at the extent of the expedition, the number and excellent quality of the arms and equipments in the hands of a great part of them, and concluded by saying he was satisfied that, under their experienced pioneer leader, the party would be entirely safe in passing through the Indian country, and without doubt would make a speedy and pleasant march to the mountains.

Monday, June 25. The organization having been completed, and all ready for the forward movement, the bugle sounded the "assembly," and at 10 o'clock, A.M. the Montana Caravan, numbering between three and four hundred persons, and nearly two hundred wagons, took its course, three columns abreast, westward. Marched five (5) miles, forded the Wild Rice river, which occupied three hours' time, and went into camp at 4 o'clock P.M. on the west bank of the river. Wood, water, and grass plenty and of good quality.

At 10. o'clock, P.M., in latitude 49° [46° 49'?] north, while seated with several companions in front of my quarters, a luminous meteor, resembling a ball of fire several feet in diameter with a resplendent tail, apparently forty feet in length,

---

[1] Robert E. Fisk's original diary is in the James Fisk Papers, MiHS, and is published here with the permission of the donor, Mrs. Agnes Train Janssen, Salem, Oregon.

194

rose from the northern horizon and moved slowly and majestically toward the zenith at an angle of 45 degrees, passed beneath a cloud, reappeared above, assuming a curve downwards, and presently broke into miriad stars of various hues and striking brilliancy, gradually disappearing as they approached the earth. This meteoric phenomenon was one of the largest and most beautiful I ever beheld, and was gazed at with admiration, wonder and astonishment by a dozen different parties in camp during the single minute that it described its firey course through the heavens.

Tuesday, June 26. Broke camp at 8 o'clock, A.M., marched eleven miles, and went into correll near a small pond of fresh water on the open prairie. There being no wood, fuel had been previously secured on the Wild Rice river.

Capt Fisk promulgated rules and regulations which are to obtain in the preservation of order, secure the safety, and contribute to the convenience and comfort of the expeditionary force during the journey across the plains. Hearty approval was given by the entire party, and three rousing cheers rung out on the prairie air in testimony of their approval of the Captain's orders.

Wednesday, June 27. Broke camp at 6 ½ o'clock, travelled six miles, halted, took lunch, baited the cattle, mules, and horses, and then continued the march. Pursued our course over a level prairie in a southwesterly direction, avoiding the Cheyenne [Sheyenne] river — the rout[e] being to flank Devel's Lake, (the source of the above stream), on the South.[2] Marched six miles, and pitched the evening's camp on rolling ground, covered with prairie rose-bushes, and sheltered from the prevailing winds of the season by bold, broken sand hills, dotted with stunted oak trees. The air is redolent with the perfume of flowers; wood, water, and grass of excellent quality and in abundance. Whole distance traveled, 12 miles.

Mr. Charles [Erwin W.] Sims, of St. Cloud, who has a loaded train of 20 wagons accompanying Capt Fisk, went back to Ft Abercrombie this morning, driving the Capt's horse and buggy, and will rejoin the expedition on Friday, with his wife, to whom he has sent word to join him at the Fort on Thursday. The riflemen have to-day killed a good number of prairie chickens, plover, snipe, &c., together with several badgers. One of these animals, instead of running away from danger, attacked Mr. [Peter] Eckford, of St. Paul, with great ferocity, and was kept at bay with considerable difficulty. A timely blow with the butt end of a rifle in the hands of young Eckford dispatched the beast, and the game was brought in triumph to camp.

Thursday, June 28. Struck tents at 7 o'clock. Owing to the carelessness of herders, some thirty-head of cattle got strayed among the Sand Hills, and the train was delayed until 8 o'clock in consequence. On these sand hills, and especially in the little vales between them, grass shoots up luxuriantly, and though thin in spots, an abundance of good feed will always be found here for thousands of head of stock. Timber, of the black oak, white oak, elm, and basswood species, dots these hills at irregular intervals in considerable quantities. From one peak among these Sand Hills a wide sweep of wood and prairie country is visible. Even Ft. Abercrombie, 30 miles east being diserned quite distinctly with the naked eye.

The train, in the forenoon, wound through the Sand Hills, in a course little South of West, finding the roads, in consequence of the depth of the sand, heavy

---

[2] The Sheyenne actually rises south and west of Devils Lake.

and torturous. Stopped for lunch at one o'clk, after having accomplished 9 ¼ miles, about one-eight of which distance was through deep sand. Moved at 2 ½ o'clock, marched 9 miles, over a level prairie, with here and there a gentle swell or roll, and made our camp on the banks of the Cheyenne.[3] Found the three great essentials to the pilgrim caravan crossing the plains, — wood, water, and grass. This has been the warmest day of the season. Thermometer, 95° in the shade. Whole distance traveled to-day, 18 ½ miles.

Friday, June 29. Broke camp at 7 o'clock, marched to the Big Bend of the Sh[e]yenne (course s. e.), took "nooning," baited the stock, and took on Wood. A spring of delicious, cold water was found here, bubbling from the hillside on the south bank of the river. Wood and grass in abundance. Distance from yesterday's camp to "Big Bend" 4 ½ miles.

Continued the march at one o'clock, and at 5 o'clock P.M. went into camp near a coule[e] on the prairie. No wood. Water and grass plenty. Distance made this afternoon 11 ½ miles. Course due west. Total distance traveled to-day 16 miles.

Saturday, June 30. Broke camp at 6 ½ o'clock. Marched 6 miles, lunched, and baited the cattle. Moved at one o'clock, and reached "Bear's Den," (a range of high hills so designated on the map), at 5 o'clock, having made an afternoon's march 9 ⅝ miles. Total distance traveled today 15 ⅝ miles. The country over which we have passed to-day has been rolling prairie. Grass and water good and in abundance. At "Bear's Den" an excellent spring of limestone water was found in a deep ravine beneath the brow of the neighboring hillside.[4]

Sunday, July 1. Remained in camp, in conformity with the established custom of Capt Fisk in journeying across the plains. Ellingsworth [William H. Illingworth] & Bill [George W. De Bill?], photographers of the expedition, took an excellent picture of camp from the heights of "Bear's Den." The day has been exceedingly pleasant, the ardent fiery rays of "old Sol" being neutralized by a cool breeze sweeping from the S. W across the prairie.

Monday, July 2. Struck tents at 7 o'clock, and took up the line of march 7:15. Took on wood for cooking supper to-day and breakfast to-morrow, there being no fuel at the camp we shall make to-night. Marched 7 miles over a rolling prairie, with a bed hard and firm, and here and there boulders and small stones peering up white in the midst of the green grass. "La But[t]e de Sol," signifying bluff of the Lakes, — a round peak raising its head considerably above the surrounding rolls of the country — is located in the midst of a wide reaching prairie and between what at one time were undoubtedly two lakes of fresh water, but which, at the present time, are worth little more than the title of sloughs, with just tolerable water for man and beast.[5]

[3] In a letter published in the *Press*, July 8, 1866, Robert described beaver dams which extended the entire width of the river at this point.
[4] On Bears Den Hillock, see also Harlan, in *Journal of the West*, 3:149, and A. J. Fisk Diary, June 30, 1866. Fort Ransom was located there in 1867. Several emigrants joined the train at this point.
[5] No "Butte de Sol" has been found on maps of the region. Robert may have meant to write either Butte de Sal or Butte de Sable, both of which are shown on Joseph N. Nicollet's 1843 map, "Hydrographical Basin of the Upper Mississippi River" (28 Congress, 2 session, *House Executive Documents*, no. 52 — serial 464). The butte mentioned by Robert was undoubtedly located in present-day La Moure County, North Dakota, probably south of Marion. Nicollet's map was reprinted by the MiHS in 1965.

This afternoon's march comprehended 11 ⅝ miles, and camp was pitched on a small lake, the neighborhood destitute of trees or shrubbery, but the water was good and in great plenty. Grass abundant.

Weather today cool and comfortable, a constant breeze blowing from the northeast. No heat to discommode either man or beast throughout the day. Total distance marched to-day 18 ⅝ miles.

Tuesday, July 3. Moved from camp at 7 o'clck a m and reached James river at 9 o'clk a. m. — distance, 3 ⅞ miles. Repaired the ford at the "Bone Hill Crossing" by cutting down the east bank and grading with dirt and brush. Completed the crossing of the river in one and half hours, halted on the west bank, lunched, and baited the cattle. Course traveled to the river, due west.

Capt Fisk and Antoine, (half breed guide from Ft. Abercrombie to the James River) left camp at 4 o'clock a.m. on a buffalo hunt, overtook the train two miles east of the crossing of the James river at 8 o'clock, and flourished above their heads the tongues and tails of two buffaloes. Capt Fisk slew the first one; Antoine the other. While the train was fording the river Capt Fisk, accompanied by several of his assistants and men, started out with an empty wagon and returned in an hour bringing the carcasses of the slain bison. These buffalo, being the first killed, was regarded by the Capt as common property, and the meat was divided up among the members of the entire train.

The James river at Bone Hill is about forty yards wide, and the depth of water at the ford not more than two feet. An excellent spring of water, cool and with a slight taint of sulphur, was found on the west bank at the left of the crossing.

The afternoon's march was 5 miles in a course a little north of west. Went into camp on one of the several streams [Bone Hill Creek] putting into the James river in this section of the territory. Plenty of wood, water, and grass. Total distance traveled to-day, 8 ⅞ miles.

This afternoon, Mr. Hermon [James F. Harmon], a young man from Maine, while char[g]ing a buffalo, some ten miles north of the train, and within twelve miles of James river, lost both his horse and hat in the excitement of the chase. The horse escaped after the game was killed and the horseman dismounted inspecting the carcass of the buffalo. Seeing a herd of buffalo in the distance, the horse started off at full speed, eager for the chase, and all efforts to capture the beast were without avail. The hat was lost, the man didn't know just at what time or at what point, so great was the exhileration of spirit of the infatuated huntsman. Mr. Hermon got into camp about 5 o'clock P.M. weary and footsore, and minus a cream colored horse and a white felt hat. Country passed over today — rolling prairie.

Wednesday, July 4. Broke camp at 7 o'clock. Course till 1 o'clock P.M. — when we lunched, watered, and baited the cattle — due west. The nooning was taken on a small lake, shallow, and miry bottom, but affording good water and in plenty for man and beast. Country passed over — rolling prairie, covered in many places with [*blank in ms.*] denoting it to be a great and much frequented range for buffalo. Distance traveled this forenoon — 10 miles.

Several hunting parties went out early this morning, and brought in a number of buffalo tongues, livers, and other delicate parts of this royal game.

The nation's birth day was celebrated by a great portion of the party, mounted and dismounted, in the exciting sports of the hunt. The afternoon was excessively hot, the thermometer ranging at 2 o'clock at 98° in the shade, but the temptation offered by large herds of buffalo, with here and [there] a herd of antelope — the former game mustering in large force on either flank and in front at a distance of one mile — was too great to be resisted, and the horsemen, getting in rear of a thousand shaggy bison, drove the monster game in a run over the rolling prairie toward the footmen, most of whom were ranged, rifle in hand, in the vicinity of the train. The buffalo, uncon[s]cious of the dangerous path they were pursuing, came bounding over the elevations that hid the train from distant view, found themselves suddenly beset by two hundred hunters, whose unerring aim brought down a score of the lusty bovines of the plains in as many seconds. Among the number killed were several fat, young bulls, two cows, and a calf weighing 100 lbs. The hunt was of the most exciting character; and the Indian ponies, bestrode by many of the men, evinced with their riders an equal degree of enthusiasm and wild excitement with the footmen. From the carcasses of the slain animals the choicest parts were cut, and the huge bodies were left to rot on the prairie, or be food for wolves.

Direction of march this afternoon northwest. Distance marched 6 ¼ miles. Encamped for the night on the open prairie, adjacent to a slew furnishing good water and in abundant quantity for man and beast. Grass in abundance; no wood, but plenty of "chips." Total distance traveled to-day 16 ¼ miles.[6]

Thursday, July 5. Moved from camp at 7:30. Course, a little north of west. Marched 6 ¼ miles, and took nooning near a small lake; the water was scarce and of poor quality. Topography of country: rolling prairie, with hard bed. Grass good. Marched at 1 o'clock, after 1 ½ hours halt. Course W.N.W., over rolling prairie.

Vast herds of buffalo were seen at short distances from the train. A "raise" of many thousand by several mounted riflemen, started the mass toward the train, which had to be stopped and a line of skermishers thrown out with their guns. A heavy fire along the right flank, (from which direction the bison came thickest); alone saved the train from being stampeded. Brothers Van and Jackey [Andrew] each brought into camp a fine buffalo calf, the meat of which is as delicate and tender as a chicken, and far more juicey.

Entered at 4 ½ o'clock upon the first range of the Coteaus of the Missouri, (which I claim, is between 90 and 100 miles from the [Missouri] river) marched forward in a due west direction one mile, found water sufficient for the wants of the expedition, and went into camp at 6 o'clock P.M. No wood, "chips" in abundance. Grass good. Distance marched this P.M. 8 miles.[7]

Terrific storm of wind and rain continued during the night. The day has been the warmest of the season, thermometer ranging at 12 o'clock M in the shade, at 100 in the shade. Total distance traveled today 14 ¼ miles.

Friday, July 6. Broke camp at 7 ½ o'clock. Marched over "bob-tail" prairie cov-

[6] In a letter in the *Press* (August 3, 1866), Robert stated that between the James River and the Coteau du Missouri the party killed eighty-seven buffalo, more than twenty antelope, and a number of elk and blacktail deer.

[7] The expedition may have struck the coteau in the vicinity of present-day Gackle, North Dakota. By Robert's own mileage record, the distance from the coteau to the Missouri was closer to two hundred miles.

ered, at intervals, with boulders, with here and there a hill quite precipitate, and took nooning beneath a tall *butte,* a dry alkali lake at a short distance southerly from the trail. Spring water, breaking out from the base of the *butte,* and flowing sluggishly over a flat, low piece of ground, winding around N.W., and which at one time constituted a "half circle" lake several miles in length. Course traveled w; n w. Distance made, 12 ¼ miles.

While taking lunch Mr. [Charles] Grant, from Pembina, who heads 300 riders and has with him 1500 carts to slaughter and carry away the coming winter's supply of buffalo meat, visited the train, bringing with him a number of half breeds, his fellow hunters. Mr. Grant, several years ago, was the representative in the Minnesota Legislature from the Pembina district.[8] Was visited also by a Yankton Sioux, painted and in full Indian dress, who submitted an old letter, badly written and horribly spelled, signed by one John Bailey, stating in effect that the bearer was a good Indian and one to be trusted, &c.

Continued the march after two hours rest. Course west, northwest. Topography of country: "bob tail" prairie. Marched 5 miles, and encamped for the night on a lake situated in a basin a half mile in circumference, and surrounded entirely by hills. Water, tolerably good. Grass good, "chips," plenty. Total distance traveled to-day: 17 ¼ miles.

Saturday, July 7. Took up line of march at 7 o'clk. Marched diagonally across a succession of *coteaus,* many of them rockey and several quite precipitous, 12 ½ miles, when a halt was called, the cattle baited, and the men lunched. A thorough scout of the country for several miles on each flank and in front failed to develop water. Course: northwest. Weather: cool. Wind: west.

Afternoon's march was over broken ground, our course being west, northwest. After 6 ½ miles travel, went into camp near a dry alkali lake, good water being found in a ravine close by. Grass plenty. No wood. Total distance traveled to-day: 19 miles. Numbers of buffalo were killed this PM. and about 600 lbs was taken on to the wagons.

Sunday, July 8. The members of the expedition being anxious to reach the Missouri as early as possible, Capt Fisk, instead of resting on the Sabbath, as has always been his custom in his several journeys across the plains, continued the movement to-day. Course of trail, west, northwest. Face of country, more level than the ground passed over the three days preceding; like the whole country thus far passed over west of the James river, not a tree or shrub has greeted the eye; the coteaus, over which we are still passing, are here and there dotted with round boulders.

Good water found in a pond adjacent to an alkali lake, 10 ½ miles from last night's camping ground. Weather this a.m. cool, with strong wind from S.E. Grass good.

The afternoon's march was 5 ½ miles. Course: northwest. Encamped for the night near a small lake and slew, both good, fresh water. Feed good. Face of country passed over, a series of coteau prairie. Buffalo, antelope, geese, brant, and ducks have been killed to-day; and one and all continue to be fully supplied with choice game meats.

[8] Charles Grant was a member of the Minnesota territorial legislature in 1855–57. See Minnesota, *House Journal,* 1855, p. 10; 1856, p. 7; 1857, p. 10.

At sunset Capt Fisk missed a span of mules belonging to the Flag wagon. Immediate search was made for them for several miles about, but without finding the lost beasts. The Capt is of opinion that some of the half breeds or Indians that visited our camp on Friday, have been following us, and that the mules have been stolen.

Weather this P.M. extremely warm, with strong wind from the South. Total distance traveled to-day 16 miles.

Monday, July 9. Broke camp at 7 oclk a. m. Marched 9 ½ miles over broken prairie or coteau lands, and lunched, at 1 o'clk between two lakes, both slightly tinctured with alkali. Water drank by man and beast without any hurtful results. Course, west, northwest.

The afternoon's march was 7 ¼ miles, and encamped for the night among a high range of hills. One mile away was a lake which furnished water for the stock, and spring of cool, delicious water, on the left of the lake, in a small ravine beneath a lofty *butte*, furnished plenty of refreshing drink for the entire camp. Course of afternoon's march, n. n w.

Capt. Fisk's mules, lost yesterday, were not found, though diligent search was made for them. The animals were doubtless stolen by Indians. Total distance traveled to-day 17 ¾ miles.

Tuesday, July 10. Marched at 8 o'clk. Distance made this a. m. 8 miles. Water and grass, good. Course n. n. w. Afternoon's march 6 ¼ miles. Encamped for the night on the banks of a fine lake of fresh water. Feed good. Plenty of fuel ("chips").

Game continues plenty. Buffalo, antelope, rabbit, geese and ducks have been killed to-day and furnished our tables with abundance of choice meats. Brother Van killed a fine doe antelope and brother Jackey a fat buffalo calf.

No appearance of Indians; still every precaution is taken to guard against danger from savage foes on the march and in camp. This has been the hottest day of the season. Thermometer ranged at 1 P.M. at 101 in the shade. Wind blew hot from the south all day. The intense heat severely worried the cattle, and several were nearly melted. Total distance traveled to-day 14 ¼ miles.

Wednesday, July 11. The column moved at 7 o'clock. Marched 5 miles to a small lake of excellent water, give drink to the stock, and moved forward one mile to a chain of sloughs, furnishing fresh rain water, with plenty of excellent grass, where we took nooning. Course, n.w.

The afternoon's march ended at a cold spring of water found after six miles' march on a direct northwest course from place of nooning. In digging out the spring, which was located in a swail leading down from a sloping range of hills, the ground was found to be frozen solid at a depth of two feet from the surface, and chunks of ice three inches thick were taken out and used in preparing lemonade and mint julips. A pork barrel was sunk in the spring and an inexhaustable supply of ice water, with a slight flavor of sulphur, flowed over the well and down the swail for a long distance. We pitched our tents here for the night, and named the camp ground *Cold Spring*.

Buffalo have been in sight all day, and a number of carcasses were brought piecemeal to the train, and supplied one and all with the best of fresh meat. Grass, good. Fuel (chips) abundant. Total distance traveled to-day, 12 miles.

Thursday, July 12. Broke camp at 8 o'clock. Marched 5 miles, lunched, and baited the stock. Country, broken, but good roadway. Course, west, northwest.

Capt Fisk and Antoine (half breed scout) left camp at 6 a.m. on a scouting expedition, traveling west, south-west. Sighted the Missouri river after a ride of 12 miles, and rejoined the train at 3 o'clk P.M. Changed the course of march from north-west to south-west, the Capt having satisfied himself that he had already cleared the Big Bend of the Missouri, and the direction for Ft Berthold was taken in accordance with the correctly formed opinion of Capt Fisk as to the points of compass to be followed.[9] Encamped at 5 o'clock, near a small lake of fresh water. Feed good. Distance traveled — 12 miles. Course, south-west. Weather, warm and sultry.

Friday, July 13. Marched at 7 o'clock. Traveled 8 ½ miles, lunched and baited the stock. No water. Afternoon's march, 10 ½ miles, and encamped on high ground some 4 miles south of a chain of lakes, the water of which was strongly tinctured with alkali. Passed on the march at 3 o'clk two fine springs of cold, fresh water some 4 miles from nooning place on the west shore of a dry alkali lake; but gave the stock no drink, owing to the difficulty of watering no more than three or four yoke of cattle at one time, and the belief entertained of getting an abundance of water at the end of the day's journey. The men improved a short halt at the springs in filling their canteens and all empty casks with the delicious water, which precaution saved one and all from suffering from thirst during the remainder of the day. The stock, a considerable portion of which had taken no drink in the morning, suffered for want of water, and, during the hour they were turned out to feed, did nothing but roam about and low.

Afternoon's march 10 ½ miles. Course, southwest. Weather warm, thermometer ranging at 87 in the shade. Country passed over (Plateau du coteau du Missouri) rolling prairie, with here and there a mile or more of level ground. Total distance traveled to-day, 19 miles.

Saturday, July 14. Broke camp at 3 o'clock a.m., yoking the cattle from the corell, without stopping to give them feed. Marched 10 miles, and found water, (a little brackish) flowing from springs situated in a valley two miles long, between two coteaus of considerable height running east and west. Wells were immediately sunk, and water obtain[ed] in sufficient quantity for man and beast of the expedition. The cattle, having had no water for a day and a half, suffered greatly during the march, which was completed at 12 o'clk m. and drank on an average six buckets of water each.

Coteaus passed over — coteaus. Course, S.W. Weather warm and sultry.

The loss of a tire from one of the wagons delayed the train, on the morning's march, two hours. This misfortune contributed to the injury of the stock, and some 30 head of oxen were "blowing" badly when camp was reached. One ox only was lost to the expedition.

In sinking wells to obtain an ample supply of water for the stock, two distinct strata of coal were found at the respective depths from the surface of two feet

[9] On this day the expedition struck the Holmes trail and followed it until midmorning of July 16. Apparently neither Holmes nor Fisk had a "correctly formed opinion" of their location, since neither struck the Missouri where he hoped to. See A. J. Fisk Diary, July 12–16, 1866; *St. Peter Tribune*, December 12, 1866.

and 3 ½ feet — the first strata being 18 inches in thickness, and the second was cut through to the depth of two feet, without developing the extent or thickness of the bed. The coal was of cannel species, full of gas, and was successfully used in buil[d]ing fires for the use of the camp.

At 11 ½ o'clock P.M. a most fearful storm of rain and hail, accompanied by wind, loud thunder and vivid flashes of lightning, swept over our camp, carrying away tents, flooding the ground with several inches of water, and driving the stock in a crowd to the south side of the correll. With the utmost difficulty the correl was kept intact and a stampede prevented. Among the tents blown down was Capt Fisk's, subjecting the Capt, Mrs. Fisk, and little daughter [Dell] to a thorough "soaking." Distance traveled to-day 10 ½ miles.

Sunday, July 15. Moved camp at 4 o'clock P.M. to table land three miles south west. This change was made to obtain a better quality of water for the stock and to obtain higher ground for the evening's corell. Total distance marched to-day, 3 miles.

Monday, July 16. Capt. Fisk, after a thorough scout of the country for a number of miles west, made yesterday, estimated the distance to the Missouri at 20 miles, and convinced that no water could be obtained until the column reached the river, ordered all the casks to be filled and everything in readiness to move at 6 o'clock a. m. Camp was broke at the hour designated. Marched 11 ¼ miles in a course west, south west, when lunched and baited the cattle. No water. Feed, poor. Country passed over, table land, and slightly rolling prairie with solid road bed.

Afternoon's march, 9 miles. Course, west, north west. Struck the Missouri, it is supposed, 25 miles below (south) of Ft Berthold. Camped for the night within two miles of the river, near a spring of cool, clear water, tinctured slightly with sulphur. At the fountain head a solid stream of water four inches in diameter flowed constantly, and formed in the ravine below numerous ponds or lakelets of sufficient size to water a thousand head of stock at once. This has been the longest day's march since leaving Ft Abercrombie, but notwithstanding this, only one ox was sufficiently fatigued as to require the substitution in his stead of a a fresh animal.

Grass, on the prairie short and dry but nevertheless sweet and nutricious; and with the feed in the ravines and coules, the stock had no difficulty in "filling up." Total distance traveled to-day 20 ¼ miles.[10]

Tuesday, July 17. Broke camp at 6 ½ o'clock. Course northwest. Forenoon's march 10 miles. The bluffs of the Missouri and at times the river itself, were in sight, and presented to the eye, wearied with three weeks monotonous scenery on the plains, a pleasing, attractive appearance. Several of the men, following up the river course, spoke [to] several steamers downward bound from Ft Benton. In the coule where we nooned, good water and grass were had in abundance.

Afternoon's march, 5 miles, following the river bank at a distance of less than

[10] The train left the Holmes trail in the middle of the morning to strike directly across country toward the Missouri. Several men and the guide had gone scouting down the river, still presuming that Fort Berthold was to the south. At the Missouri, men on one of the steamboats mentioned below told Fisk emigrants that they were thirty miles below the fort. A. J. Fisk Diary, July 16, 1866; *St. Peter Tribune*, December 12, 1866.

a mile. Encamped for the night on a stream of excellent water which made into the Missouri a mile distant. Grass good. Wood plenty.

Mr. Bopreau [Philip Beaupre], Van H. Fisk, and Antoine (half breed) sent by Capt Fisk to ascertain the true location of Ft Berthold, did not return to camp up to 9 o'clock this P.M., and it is inferred the party tarried at the fort over night, and will meet us on the march to-morrow. Total distance traveled to-day, 15 miles.

Wednesday, July 18. Broke camp at 7 o'clk; marched 8 miles, and nooned, near a *coule*, with no water but good grass. Course, west, northwest.

Afternoon's march 4 ¾ miles. Midway between nooning place and the evening camp, in a magnificent *coule* extending north and south a distance of many miles and ending only at the Missouri, immense springs of cool, soft water, the most delicious I ever remember to have tasted, were discov[er]ed, from each of which flowed a volume of water sufficient to turn a dozen race of stone. In the stream formed from these wells of living water the stock received drink, while the fountain heads were visited by every man, woman and child in the expedition, each of whom busied himself or herself in filling canteens and casks of the refreshing beverage God had brewed and placed in the desert.

Course pursued west, north west. Typography [*sic*] of country, rolling prairie, *coules*, with bluffs of the Missouri on the south and west.[11]

At 2 o'clock, the party sent by Capt Fisk on Tuesday morning to the Fort, returned, meeting the train within two miles of the evening's camp. They reported having met on the way, going and coming, small parties of Sioux Indians, fully armed, but who declared they were good Indians and were out hunting buffalo. Total distance traveled today, 12 ¾ miles.

Thursday, July 19. Broke camp at 6 ½ o'clk. M[ar]ched 10 ¼ miles, lunched, and baited the cattle. Water, wood and grass, plenty. Course, west north west. Country, highlands, rolling, no bluffs or coules. From Ft. Berthold, distant five miles, came out squads of Indians, (Rees, Crows, Sioux, Grovans, Mandans, &c) visited camp on foot and horseback. Many of these Indians, of either sex, had little or no clothing, aside from a "breech-cloth." All the grown males and many of the small boys were armed with bows and arrows — some few with rifles and shotguns.

Afternoon's march, 3 ½ miles. Encamped northwest of Ft Berthold, with wood and water plenty. Grass, poor.

Friendly Indians of the tribes above mentioned, camped about Ft. Berthold to the number of 2,500, came to camp during the afternoon and evening in large numbers, and were a source of great annoyance while they were permitted to remain. One and all of them are great beggars, and will not hesitate to steal anything they can lay their hands on the least opportunity being offered them. At 8 o'clk guard mount took place, and the dusky intruders were ordered from camp: the force it was thought necessary to use in ridding us of their presence not being required. Total distance traveled today, 14 ¾ miles. Total distance from Ft Abercrombie to Ft Berthold, 326 ⅝ miles.

Friday, July 20. Remained in camp for the day, repairing wagons, renovating clothing and goods, and giving rest to the stock.

Indians, with their squaws and "pappooses" visited camp in larger numbers

---

[11] The expedition was now following Sully's 1864 trail. See A. J. Fisk Diary, July 18, 1866.

than yesterday, and renewed their begging and thieving. An Indian caught in the act of theft, or with stolen goods in his possession, was summarily ejected from camp, and forbidden again to come within certain prescribed limits of the tents and corell.

Some of the boys have traded ponies. Other have purchased animals, the average price paid for good young, serviceable beasts being from $12 to $25 in trade — such as hard bread, flour, or meat.[12]

Saturday, July 21. Broke camp at 8 o'clock a. m., marched 7 miles, and nooned in a *coule*. Water and grass good, no wood. Afternoon's march 9 ½ miles, and camped near a ravine furnishing good water and in abundance at the lower end, a mile distant. Course of march w.n.w., following the Gov't [Sully's] trail between Ft. Berthold and Union. Country, rolling prairie intersected by two *coules,* passed without delay. Scenery along the river s.w. abounding in succession of coteaus, bluffs, *coules,* and but[t]es, viewed from a distance of from one to five miles, presents a pleasing variety, and often strikes the beholder with wonder and admiration.

Nothing seen of Sioux reported at Ft Berthold, as being in large numbers not far distant, awaiting Capt. Fisk's train to give him fight and destroy him and all with him. Total distance traveled to-day 16 ½ miles.

Sunday, July 22. Marched 7 ½ miles to [Little] Knife river — a small stream of pure, fresh water, abounding in fish, quite deep in places, with abrupt banks, and an average width of 15 yards at a distance of 6 miles from the Missouri, into which river it flows. Encamped for the day on a bend of the stream, with water close at hand for nearly the entire corral. Grass, good.

An alarm from one of the pickets, at 1 o'clock at night, turned the camp out under arms, and for a short time produced considerable excitement. The picket who gave the alarm, reported having seen three Indians skulking in the vicinity of his post; that having challenged, without receiving answer, he fired, and cried "turn out the camp," fully convinced that appearances indicated danger, and warranted the turning out of the men. Investigation by the officer of the guard, (Mr. Van H. Fisk) developed nothing further than the report of the sentry, and the camp was allowed to retire, sleeping on their arms. Total distance traveled to-day 7 ½ miles.

Monday, July 23. Broke camp at 6 ½ o'clock. Marched 10 ¾ miles to a lake two miles from and formed by the waters of the Missouri. Numerous springs of cold water found along the north banks of the lake. Feed for the stock passably good. Wood, plenty in coules near at hand, and along the river, three miles away. Went into camp for the purpose of repairs — many of the wagons belonging to emigrants and freighters having loose tires and needing the attention of the blacksmith [W. H. Dedrick]. During the day and night wood was cut and a pit of coal was burned. Repairs will commence to-morrow. Total distance traveled to-day, 10 ¾ miles.[13]

Tuesday, July 24. Remained in camp and completed repairs to wagons.

[12] Other events of the stopover at Berthold are described in A. J. Fisk Diary, July 19, 1866; *Minneapolis Tribune,* April 21, 1901, part 2, p. 3.

[13] On this day Stephen Liberty and two other men deserted the train and started out on horseback for Fort Union. One of them returned July 27, "sound in body if not in mind," accusing his companions of having tried to kill him. The others came into camp the next day. Three men

Wednesday, July 25. Marched at 1 o'clock., P.M. Encamped for the evening on small stream of running water, flowing South, and finding its end in the Missouri. Grass, good. Wood, none; chips instead. Distance made to-day 6 ⅝ miles.

Thursday, July 26. Broke camp at 7 o'clock. Marched 14 ¼ miles, and nooned in a *coule* furnishing good water and grass.

Afternoon's march 6 ¼ miles. Encamped for the evening on the Missouri river. Wood, water, and grass plenty. Total distance traveled to-day 20 ½ miles.

Friday, July 27. The day's march, commenced at 7 o'clock, a.m., closed at 3 o'clock P.M., after traveling the short distance of 7 ½ miles. Sideling roadways, several steep hills, and the crossing of the Little White Earth River were the causes which served to delay the train. Water wood and grass plenty and of good quality. Total distance made to-day — 7 ½ miles.

Saturday, July 28. Broke camp at 7 o'clk. Marched seven (7) miles, and nooned on the Missouri Bottom, one mile from the river. Good water in a small stream flowing from a *coule* to the north. Wood, plenty; grass, excellent.

Marched in the afternoon 8 ½ miles. Road running along the Missouri Bottom, west northwest. Bed of road good, with the exception of here and there a soft place, rendered so by recent heavy rains. Abundance of timber lining either side of the river bank. Grass along the bottom, thousands of acres in extent, growing thick and rank, offering temptation to persons having frontier notions to tarry here and establish a ranchero's home. These bottoms would supply grass in summer and hay for the winter for untold herds of cattle.

Along the sides of the bluffs, on part of the day's march, huge specimens of petrified wood were seen in abundance. Whole trunks of trees, in diameter from two to six feet, have been turned to solid stone. A large number of excellent specimens were secured by different members of the train.

Encamped for the night on a level plateau of ground, miles in extent, with the river shut out from view by a belt of timber. Pond and spring water good and in plenty. Grass good. Wood plenty. Total distance traveled to-day, 15 ½ miles.

Sunday, July 29. Broke camp at 8 o'clock, and moved to bluff bordering a small stream of soft water, 6 ¼ miles distant. Encamped for the day for rest and repairs. Grass, excellent: wood and water, plenty. Distance traveled to-day, 6 ¼ miles.

Monday, July 30. Rain during the early part of the day kept the train in camp until 12 m. The afternoon's march was accomplished in four hours, and the train went into corell on the prairie near a long slough, with plenty of water in it. Grass excellent. Wood, none. Road traveled over, in part heavy rolling hills, with rocks dotting the tops; in part level prairie with good road-bed.

Buffalo seen for the first time since leaving Ft Berthold; none killed. Total distance traveled to day, 12 ½ miles.

Tuesday, July 31. Broke camp at 6 ½ o'clk. Forenoon's march 10 ¾ miles. Nooned on Muddy creek. Good water and grass, and plenty of wood in coule one mile to the south. Afternoon's march 9 miles. Water and grass; no wood. Total distance traveled to-day 19 ¾ miles.

Wednesday, August 1. Heavy rain during the night prevented a start earlier than 8 o'clk. Forenoon's march 9 miles; water, wood and grass. Afternoon's march

were also lost on July 26–27. See A. J. Fisk Diary, July 24, 26, 27, 28, 1866; Harlan, in *Journal of the West*, 3:153.

5 miles. Evening's camp pitched on a small stream flowing through a coule, distant from Ft Union 6 miles. Wood and water. Grass, good. Total distance traveled to-day, 14 miles.[14]

Thursday, Augt. 2. Marched at 7 o'clk, reached Ft. Union at 11:30. Distance traveled 8 miles. Good water; plenty of wood; grass, on the bluffs, excellent. Total distance made to-day, 8 miles. Total distance from Ft Berthold to Ft Union 145 ⅛ m.[15]

Friday, Augt. 3. Broke camp at 2 o'clk P.M., after taking in supp[l]ies and loading 6 tons of freight.[16] Road following the course of the Missouri; on the bottom lands, level; several steep hills to climb and descend in crossing spurs of bluffs. Encamped for the night on Little Muddy river, (east bank). Good water, plenty of wood: excellent grazing. Distance traveled to day 9 ½ miles.

Saturday, Aug. 4. Rain during the forenoon. Broke camp at 12 o'clk m. Moved to creek, with water in pools, in other places entirely dry, stream running s.w. With exception of three moderate hills, road level and hard bed. Numerous herds of buffalo seen on the flanks of the train at a distance of ½ to two miles. Four buffalo bulls, three cows, and two calves were killed, supplying the whole party with an abundance of fresh beef. Encamped for the night in a beautiful valley from two to four miles wide, running east and west, and extending to the Missouri river. River distant from camp 3 miles.

Water tolerably good. Grass excellent: no wood. Total distance traveled to-day, 16 ⅛ miles.

Sunday, Aug. 5. Broke camp at 7 o'clk. Marched over rolling highlands, to the east bank of the Big Muddy river, and lunched. Commenced the crossing of the river at one o'clock, and the whole train was got over by 6 o'clock. Capt Fisk built a bridge of wagons, using seven to complete the structure. The freight and baggage was conveyed across on the bridge by the men. River from 70 to 80 feet wide, and from 3 to five feet deep; bottom and banks soft and muddy.

The sections other than Capt Fisk's crossed the river by a floating bridge built of float-wood, chained together and fastened secure across the stream — the sides being built in with weeds and dirt. Wagons drawn across by hand: oxen swam the stream.

The entire crossing was perfected without accident of any kind. Distance traveled to-day, 8 miles.[17]

Monday, Aug. 6. Broke camp at 7 ½ o'clk. Traveled up the valley of the "Big Muddy" five miles, and then debouched to the west, following the west branch of the river, and finally leaving that stream altogether to the n. w. After 10 ¼ miles, nooned, finding water in a slough near at hand and plenty of grass. No wood.

Afternoon's march, 10 ¼ miles, over fine rolling prairie. Passed close to the

[14] The Steele party had passed this creek on July 27, built a bridge, and left a note for Fisk. See A. J. Fisk Diary, August 1, 1866.

[15] An anonymous letter, written from Fort Union and published in the *Weekly Pioneer*, August 31, 1866, reported dissension of various kinds in the train.

[16] Fisk had probably arranged in advance to carry this freight on to Montana. Steamboat navigation above Fort Union was often difficult because of low water.

[17] The emigrants crossed the river in several other ways. Some made rafts; one built a log bridge; others raised their wagon beds and forded. The rest used the wagon bridge, which was made by unloading the wagons, removing their head and tail boards, and then placing them end to end. See A. J. Fisk Diary, August 5, 1866; Harlan, in *Journal of the West*, 3:155.

trail, 8 miles out, two alkaline lakes and several ponds of fresh water. Buffalo seen in great plenty toward the Missouri river. Portions of several of bison, slain by the men, were brought to camp.

Encamped for the night on a slough close to a range of hills. Water, brackish; grass, good; wood, none, but plenty of chips. Total distance traveled today, 20 ½ miles.

Tuesday, Aug. 7. Road to Poplar or Aspen river, (5 miles from last night's camp) hilly but good road bed. Forded Poplar river without much delay, although the water was three feet deep and current of stream very swift. Wood, in small groves, seen at a short distance up and down the river. Grass tolerably good.

Afternoon's march 12 miles. Road over heavy rolling prairie plentifully sown with stones. Water in ponds equidistant between Poplar river and the evening's camp, pitched on a small stream of clear running water. No wood, but plenty of chips. Grass poor. Buffalo seen in great numbers, on either side of the trail: a dozen or more of the beasts were killed by members of the train and the choice parts brought to camp. Total distance traveled to-day, 17 miles.

Wednesday, Aug. 8. Forenoon's march 9 ½ miles. Road over rolling prairie; occasional knobs thickly studded with rocks and alternate short distances of soft alkaline ground; heavy pulling. Nooned on a fine gravelly creek of running water. A few trees a mile down the stream. Grass poor.

Afternoon's march 8 miles. Encamped for the night on a stream of good water; a grove of trees (poplar predominating) close by. Missouri river two miles distant. Road upland prairie and bottom land; road on river bottom soft, and much cut up by trains preceding us. Weather fair, with cool breeze. No suffering of the cattle from heat. Total distance traveled today, 17 ½ miles.

Thursday, Aug. 9. Forenoon's march 4 miles. Nooned on "Wolf Creek," a stream of running water, 30 feet wide, sloping banks, and easily forded. Feed, good; wood, near at hand, in plenty. Road on the bottom land, which we followed, soft loam, and exceedingly heavy pulling.

Afternoon's march 8 miles. Encamped for the night on a "dry creek," with good water standing in pools. Grass, tolerable; wood, plenty. Road continues to traverse the river bottom, and experience proved it "dead pulling" on the cattle. Total distance traveled today, 12 miles.

Friday, Aug. 10. Broke camp at 6 o'clk. Forenoon's march 11 miles. Nooned on Porcupine river [Little Porcupine Creek], a fine stream of water, 30 feet wide, gravelly bottom, and easily crossed. Wood, in abundance; grass, good. Road, over fine "bench land," and very generally good.

Afternoon's march, 7 miles. Road over fine rolling prairie. Encamped for the night, on a "dry creek," furnishing good water plentifully in pools. Grass, good; wood, none, "chips," plenty. Total distance traveled tod[a]y, 18 miles.[18]

Saturday, Aug. 11. Broke camp at 7 o'clk. Marched 10 miles and nooned on the "Little Porcupine" river [Porcupine Creek], a considerable tributary of the Milk river. Road over rolling prairie and in the valley of the Milk river. Wood plenty; grass, poor.

Afternoon's march over rolling prairie and bottom-land of Milk river. Distance

[18] Robert's journal here neglects a number of problems and annoyances: a stampeding pony, a man ill with fever, a severe storm, and three lost emigrants. See A. J. Fisk Diary, August 10, 1866.

made 8 ¾ miles. Road, generally good, with exception of an occasional gravelly mound on the uplands and like patches on the bottom land. Milk river, within 4 miles of the Missouri, has a depth of 12 feet and a wi[d]th of 120 feet. The banks are abrupt, and the water of the stream is on a par with the Missouri as to its proportion of mud. Encamped for the night on Milk river. Wood and water, plenty; grass, poor. Total distance traveled today; 18 ¾ miles.

Sunday, Aug. 12. Remained in camp.

Monday, Aug. 13. Broke camp at 7 o'clk. Marched 9 miles, and nooned on a "dry creek" with pools of good water along the bed of the stream. Grass, poor; wood plenty. Road over bottom land and prairie, (both of which we followed) generally good.

Afternoon's march 5 ¼ miles, following the river bottom. Encamped for the night on Milk river, with plenty of wood and water, and tolerable good grass. Total distance made to day, 14 ¼ miles.

Tuesday, Aug. 14. The day's march was made part on the upland prairie and part on the river bottom; road on the upland hard and in spots gravelly; in the bottom generally good, the exceptions being in the crossing of small tributaries of the Milk river and short spaces of soft ground. Nooned on a small stream in the valley with plenty of wood and water and tolerable grass.

The night's camp was made on the river, near a Lake formed in the spring by back water of the stream, which furnished excellent water. Wood plenty; grass, good. Total distance traveled to-day, 16 miles.[19]

Wednesday, Aug. 15. Made Milk river crossing at 10 o'clk — distance 6 ¾ miles. Nooned on east bank, and commenced the crossing at 1 o'clk. Ford, gravelly: water, 2 feet deep; west bank steep and somewhat soft. The fording was effected with east [ease?] and without material delay.

Afternoon's march 5 ¼ miles, and encamped for the night on Rockey Creek [Larb Creek or Beaver Creek], a considerable stream of clear water, tributary of the Milk river. Grass, poor: wood, plenty. Total distance traveled to-day, 12 miles.

Thursday, Aug. 16. After fording Rockey creek and crossing the bottom land on the west side, (three miles), took the highland and trundled over a rolling prairie, with good road, to a point 13 ¼ miles from yesterday's camp, finding water in a slough ¾ mile to the south of the trail, and tolerable good feed close at hand on the low land and on the upper prairie. Passed three small lakes at intervals of 4 miles each.

Afternoon's march 8 ¼ miles, and encamped on a fine lake, with good grass but no wood: chips plenty. Game in abundance. Elk, antelope, deer, and buffalo have been slain to-day, and abundance of the several kinds of delicious meats brought to camp. Total distance made today, 21 ½ miles.

Friday, Aug. 17. Forenoon's march 8 miles, over rolling prairie, to sloughs on right and left of trail. Water and grass tolerable good; no wood. Road over rolling prairie. "Little Rocky" and "Bear Paw" Mountains, seen for the first time yesterday, show up prominently to-day.

Road over rolling prairie. Long Lake to the north of trail midway between

[19] At several bad crossings on the fourteenth, the emigrants had to cut willow brush for fill. A. J. Fisk Diary, August 14, 1866.

last night's camp and nooning place. Afternoon's march 8 ½ miles, over rolling prairie and bottom land, and encamped for the night on the Milk river, at the second crossing. Grass, poor; wood, plenty.

Parties out on the hunt since morning, were late on the prairie, and succeeded in finding their way in at a late hour only through the aid of rockets and the discharge of fire arms, telling them the location of the camp. Total distance made to-day, 16 ½ miles.

Saturday, Aug. 18. Broke camp at 3 o'clk a.m., and moved forward 4 miles to obtain feed for the stock. The crossing of the river was made without delay, the ford being good and the opposite bank sloping. Water in the stream one foot: width of river, 80 feet. Four miles from crossing grass good; water found in pools in ravine to right of trail.

Afternoon's march 11 miles. Encamped for the night on a lake near Milk river, with good grass and plenty of wood. Met with a party of 4 Grovons Indians who exchanged salutations and expressed a desire to trade with us. The train was not stopped for that purpose, and the Indians departed. Total distance traveled to-day 15 ¼ miles.

Sunday, Aug. 19. Remained in camp, and gave rest to man and beast.

Monday, Aug. 20. Broke camp at 6 ½ o'clk. Marched 10 miles, and nooned on Milk river, with good water and plenty of wood near at hand, and excellent grazing on the bottom land. Road following the Milk river Valley.

Afternoon's march 12 miles, and encamped for the night on Milk river, with plenty of wood, good water, and tolerable grass. Road following the valley. Game plenty, antelope and deer, to the number of half dozen have been killed and the carcasses brought to camp. Total distance traveled to-day, 22 miles.

Tuesday, Aug. 21. Continue to follow the valley of the Milk river. Marched 10 miles to point on the river, with good grazing and plenty of wood and water close at hand, where the train was halted, and lunch taken. Good grass and abundance of wood and water at near points along the road.

Killed a Black Tail Deer, (buck), weighing 200 pounds in a wooded coulee 1 ½ miles from the trail. Brought the game in in Capt Fisk's light buggy. Afternoon's march, along the river. Distance made, 6 ¼ miles. Encamped on Milk river, with good grass and water and plenty of wood. Total distance made today, 16 ¼ miles.

Wednesday, Aug. 22. Forenoon's march 9 ¼ miles. At nooning had good grass and water, and plenty of wood.

Afternoon's march 8 miles. Forded Meldrum river at 3 p. m. Bed of stream nearly dry. Encamped for the night on Two Lands [Lances] river, with excellent water and grass, and plenty of wood. Total distance traveled to-day, 17 ¼ miles.

Thursday, Aug. 23. Forenoon's march 11 miles. Encamped (nooned) on Milk river, with plenty of wood and water, and excellent grass.

Afternoon's march 9 miles. Made the 3rd crossing of the Milk river at 5 o'clk P.M. and went into camp for the day on the west bank of the stream. Water, wood and grass in plenty. Total distance traveled to-day, 20 miles.

Friday, Aug. 24. Broke camp at 6 o'clk. Marched 11 miles and encamped (nooned) on Beaver creek, a small mountain stream with springs of delicious water at various places along its bed. It is tributary of the Milk river.

Capt Fisk prospected a pan of sand and gravel in the bed of this stream, and found one small particle of gold — sufficient to say in the language of the miner, "Here's the color." Plenty of wood, and some grass on this stream.

Afternoon's march, which extended to 10 ½ o'clk at night, counted up 17 miles. In the dusk of evening the train passed the first camping ground on the "Box Alder" [Box Elder] creek unawares, and the "tramp" was then continued to the Cottonwood creek 5 ½ miles further on, where we encamped for the day. Stream dry, but water in pools sufficient for all the wants of the stock. Considerable wood, and some grass.

Passed this P.M. a short distance to the right of trail, the several ranges of Bear Paw Mountains. Total distance made to-day, 28 miles.

Saturday, Aug. 25. Marched at 9 o'clk. Nooned on the "Big Sandy" river [Sandy Creek]. Water in pools. Grass poor. No wood. Distance 4 ¼ miles.

Resumed the march at 4 o'clk. Marched 9 ¾ miles, and encamped for the night on a long slough, one mile to the left of the trail, with plenty of water and good grass, but no wood. Road over rolling prairie, and excellent the whole distance. Total distance made to-day, 15 miles.[20]

Sunday, Aug. 26. Remained in camp until 12 o'clk m. to allow the stock to rest and feed. Marched 11 miles, to springs (found dry) in bed of stream, and baited the stock for one hour. Continued the march at 6 o'clk, it being determined to reach the Marias river to night. Marched 12 miles, descending at 11 o'clk P.M. the Marias bluffs, (very steep), and made our camp for the day on the south side of the river.

Road exceedingly good to-day, and the stock made the drive with[out] delay. Total distance made to-day, 23 miles.

Monday, Aug. 27. Marched at 9 o'clk, 8 miles to second crossing of Teton river, and encamped on the south bank of the stream, finding good water and grass, and plenty of wood. Camp among the willow and cottonwood trees, and made everything very cozy. This is the last camp before reaching Benton (4 ½ miles distant) and it is proposed to tarry where we are for two days. Distance made to day, 8 miles. Total distance from Ft Union to Ft Benton 373 ⅜ miles.[21]

Tuesday, Aug't. 28. Remained in camp, resting stock and taking in supplies.[22]

Wednesday, Aug. 29. Marched at 8 o'clk. Made 15 miles to Coulée on the Missouri river, where we nooned. Watered the stock in the river, which is here reached by a steep, winding road down the bluffs, 1 ¼ miles long. No wood here, and feed poor.

Afternoon's drive 7 miles, and went into camp on the prairie, with no water for man or beast. Feed, tolerable good; no wood. Meals were prepared, wood having been brought from the Teton valley and water from the Missouri.

The road runs over high, rolling "table lands," with the "Belt [Little Belt]

[20] The expedition planned to go on to some springs, but a member of the Sims party came back to report that there was no water there. See A. J. Fisk Diary, August 25, 1866. The Sims party traveled a day in advance of the main train after a quarrel with Fisk on August 18.

[21] Another traveler said that by odometer measurement it was 368 miles from Fort Union to Fort Benton. Several accounts mention visits to the town of Fort Benton, a little village of some twenty to forty houses, and describe a party of men who shipped more than two thousand pounds of gold taken from a claim on Confederate Gulch. See *St. Peter Tribune*, December 19, 1866; Harlan, in *Journal of the West*, 3:158; A. J. Fisk Diary, August 27, 1866.

[22] The Sims party and some of the Fisk emigrants left for Helena on this day. A. J. Fisk Diary, August 28, 1866.

Mountains" almost constantly in view. The scarcity of water and poor grass obtains along the whole of to-day's drive, the exception as to water being at the coulée above mentioned only. Total distance traveled to-day, 22 miles.

Thursday, Aug. 30. Broke camp at 4 o'clock, and marched 10 miles to some springs, where water was obtained for cooking. The stock also got part of a bucket of water each. Grazing poor; no wood.

Afternoon's march 8 ½ miles. Encamped on "The Lake" [Benton], with good water and plenty of grass. Saw this P.M. the northern range of the Rocky Mountains for the first time. No wood. We anticipated this, and brought with us a good supply. Total distance made today, 18 ½ miles.

Friday, Aug. 31. Marched 15 ¼ miles, and nooned on the Sun river. Good grass, plenty of wood, and splendid water. Afternoon's march 3 ¼ miles, and encamped on Sun river, 2 miles east of the crossing,[23] with plenty of wood, grass, and water. Total distance made today, 18 ½ miles.

Saturday, Sept 1. Remained in camp to recruit stock, and prepare for separating the party — a portion of Capt Fisk's passengers and most of the emigrants declaring in favor of going on to Helena City, while others have decided to accompany Capt Fisk up the Sun river to locate a camp and prospect for gold on the headwaters of the river. The party going up the river will number some 80 persons, including the families of Capt Fisk and Mr. [Gilbert B. O.] Bassett.[24]

Sunday, Sept 2. Preparations having been completed for sending forward to Helena the passengers destined for that point, Mr Bopreau was sent forward with them. Mr. [W. H.] Watson's teams, freighting for Capt Fisk, took aboard the supplies and baggage of the men, and the party departed at 4 o'clk P.M. in good cheer, saluting Capt Fisk with three rounds of applause as they took leave of the camp.

Monday, Sept 3. Capt Fisk, having made up his gold prospecting party, consisting of 42 of the boys who came through to the Territory with him, and the remainder made up of emigrants (all men save two [Mrs. Fisk and Mrs. Barber]), took his departure up the valley of the Sun river, passing up the north bank of the stream. Forded the river five miles above the "Crossing," and continued during the day on the south side. Encamped for the night on the river with abundance of wood and excellent grass, and the water of the Sun river, — the finest in the Territory. Total distance made to-day, 12 ¼ miles.

Tuesday, Sept 4. Forenoon's march 8 miles following the valley near the stream on the south side. Road excellent. Feed good; wood plenty. Prospected in several places along the river and found the "color" several times.

Afternoon's march 9 miles. Road good. Encamped for the night in the valley (now become one of the finest I ever saw). Wood, grass, and water plenty. Total distance made today, 17 miles.

Wednesday, Sept. 5. Broke camp at 8 o'clk. Marched 4 ¼ miles, and nooned. The Rocky Mountains, for many days distinctly seen, loom up in closer proximity than at any point yet. The boys "prospected" on a number of bars in the river and along

---

[23] The reference here and on September 3 and 11 is to the Mullan Road crossing of the Sun River.

[24] "Passengers" probably refers to the men who had paid the $100 fee to accompany the expedition. The Bassetts went on to Helena; it was apparently the O. B. Barber family who stayed with the prospecting party. See A. J. Fisk Diary, September 3, 1866.

the banks, but developed nothing more than the "color." The Sun river valley abounds in game to a greater extent than any we have passed through coming from the States — and our camp folks have been bountifully supplied with fresh game meats.

Afternoon's march, 8 miles. Encamped on the South branch of the Sun river, six miles from its confluence with the main stream, where we propose to establish our prospecting headquarters for the present. The valley here is from six to 8 miles wide, furnishing rich pasturage, and the abode of vast herds of antelope and deer. The stream is well timbered with cottonwood trees, many of them of respectable growth, and sufficient for the use of a numerous population for a number of years. The hunters today have brought in their usual supply of game meats, consisting of nine deer, four antelope, and a number of grouse and prairie chickens. Total distance made today, 12 ¼ miles.[25]

Thursday, Sept 6. The wagons having been so disposed as to form a close correl, as a precautionary measure against attack by Indians and a refuge for man and beast in case of emergency, preparations have thus early been instituted for sending out parties to prospect the headwaters of both the Sun river proper and its tributaries above and the South branch of the stream, which evidently penetrates into the mountain range some 15 or 20 miles from our present camp.

Capt Fisk, collecting his stores under canvass, opened his commissary at 1 o'clk, P.M., and issued to the men he had selected to form his party, consisting of 30 odd persons, such goods as they stood in need, (mostly in the provision line) giving the men trust for the same, to be promptly paid at the first opportunity. Weather warm and pleasant.[26]

Friday, Sept 7. Three prospecting parties, with 10 days rations, numbering 32 men in all, left camp during the forenoon. Two parties of eight men each, struck across the country in a northwesterly direction, intending to strike the main stream below the first range of upheavals; the third party, numbering 16 men, accompanied by brother Van, took a westerly direction from camp, their intention being to strike the South fork 8 or 10 miles up, and to follow the stream up into the mountains.

Those who have gone gold seeking and those who remain behind to care for the women folks and stock are hopeful but not over sanguine of success in developing a mine of riches at some point in this section of the Territory. A storm during the night covered the mountains with snow, and sprinkled the valley well with rain.[27]

Saturday, Sept 8. Capt Fisk, accompanied by Capt Ryan, and Mr. Frank Robinson, of Springfield, Mass., left camp for Helena City this morning on business. The Captain rode his celebrated mare "Beauty," and the two other gentlemen were well mounted on steeds that had carried them successfully over the journey of 1300 miles from St. Paul. The Capt is expected back in ten days.

Game is being brought so plentifully to camp that most of the party are engaged a portion of each day in cutting it up into slits or thin slips and drying it either in the

[25] The camp must have been somewhat south of present-day Augusta, Montana. See Harlan, in *Journal of the West*, 3:160.

[26] A. J. Fisk said they used a Sibley tent for their "sutler store" and had "a good assortment of mineing tools & 'Rations.' " Diary, September 6, 1866.

[27] For more details, see Harlan, in *Journal of the West*, 3:160; A. J. Fisk Diary, September 7, 1866.

sun or over slow fires. Deer and antelope furnish the major part of the game flesh prepared in this manner for winter consumption.

Sunday, Sept 9. All quiet to-day, the men remaining in camp, permitting the game, of which the valley is full, to feed in peace or rest undisturbed in the shade of the cottonwoods and in the green meadows. Nothing yet heard from the prospecting parties.

Monday, Sept 10. While driving the cattle down from the upper valley I killed a tremendous rattlesnake measuring 3½ feet, with nine (9) rattles.

Employed a portion of the day in repairing rents in clothing, (of which there seemed no end), and destroyed a hundred or more letters of old correspondence.

A man, taken sick with a billious attack, from one of the parties of 8 persons, came into camp about noon. He reports nothing favorable in reference to gold discoveries, and is inclined to the belief that none of the precious metal exists in any quantity along this portion of the Rocky Range. Allowance is made for the opinion held by this person in his present condition, and none in camp are discouraged by the predictions of one who naturally feels in a degree disheartened during temporary illness.[28]

Tuesday, Sept 11. Sent brother Jackey, with two of the boys [John Jackson, Nicholas Chemidlin], to the "Crossing," to bring up the 1500 lbs of flour left in the keeping of the Rancheroes there by Capt Fisk when we came up the Valley. Three yoke of cattle, attached to a heavy wagon, were sent along to haul the freight. The distance to the "Crossing," being only 42 miles, I directed Jackey to accomplish the round trip in four days.[29]

Wednesday, Sept 12. The prospecting party of 18, who have been absent since Friday of last week, returned to camp this P.M., reporting no success in the discovery of gold, on the South Fork of Sun River or any of its tributaries. Specimens of rock, containing copper ore, were brought in by several of the party, indicating the existence in considerable quan[ti]ties of copper in several prominent upheavals along the second range of mountains.

From the two other prospecting parties exploring the main stream have come to-day several men, all of whom report no discoveries of precious metals, in a search of 35 miles up the river from this point. The two parties are on their way in, and will reach camp during the forenoon tomorrow.

Thursday, Sept. 13. The remainder of the two prospecting parties from the headwaters of the Sun river proper arrived in camp at 10 o'clk a.m. One and all declared themselves of the opinion that no gold existed along that portion of the river they prospected, and were satisfied that further operations in that direction were useless.

The weather is pleasant, and many of the boys are out hunting elk, deer, and antelope. The feed in the valley is all that could be desired, and the stock are thriving daily on the rich grasses bordering either side of the river.

Friday, Sept 14. Put "Burma" in the buggy, and with Jack Hicks, (a noted hunter and trapper) drove 12 miles up the valley on a hunt.[30] Encamped at the base of "Hay Stack Peak," (a prominent mountain of the northern range), picketed the

[28] Andrew said that two men came in — Cornelius B. Adriance and J. T. Hostetler. Diary, September 10, 1866.
[29] For the journey, see A. J. Fisk Diary, September 11–14, 1866.
[30] On Jack Hicks, see p. 215n, below.

mare, and started on the chase for a deer. Both Jack and myself returned to camp at dusk without any game, much to our chagrin and disappointment.

Saturday, Sept 15. Took an early breakfast, and at 6 o'clk started from our temporary camp to scale the mountain looming up before me, to get a view of the surrounding country. "Jack" took off up the valley on the hunt.

On the way up the mountain saw and shot at a buck deer, without being permitted to lay my hunting knife to his throat. It was 9 ½ o'clk when I reached the extreme height of the bold peak, and seated myself, exhausted, on one of the numerous rocks covering the pinnacle. After a half hour's rest, — during which I had time to view the broad valley of the Sun river, lying before me, and stret[ch]ing out many miles to the North and East; the successive ranges of mountains west, north, and south, with lakes of pure water on their very tops, and rivers and streams flowing down from between a hundred buttes into the valleys below. — I left the lofty height on my way back to the valley, where I arrived a few minutes before 12 o'clk.

Jack having come in a little later without his usual success in hunting, it was proposed, after a hasty dinner, to return to camp, which we did killing a rattle snake and two prairie chickens on the way in.

Capt Ryan returned to headquarters camp from Helena to day, bringing with him the mail and word that Capt Fisk would not be back until Tuesday of next week. Among letters received, were two from "Elsie" [Elizabeth Chester] and one from brother Dan.[31]

Bro. Van headed a second prospecting party this morning, and left in the direction of the Sun river proper, intending to inspect that stream and its principal tributaries to their source, not being satisfied with investigations and representations made by the two parties who came into camp on Wednesday. The party numbers ten persons, and each man left supplied with 15 days' rations.

Sunday, Sept 16. Everything quiet in camp. Nothing of special importance to chronicle.

Monday, Sept 17. Twelve of our party, representing four wagons left this morning for Helena, not being satisfied to remain longer in the Sun river valley without the certainty of making a gold discovery this fall.

DIARY OF ANDREW J. FISK, 1866 [1]

TUESDAY, SEPTEMBER 18. It has snowed more or less all day — but the snow has melted as fast as it fell. The Mountains has not been visible all day — so foggy.

[Cornelius B.] Adriance got in [from a hunting trip] — with the buggy about

[31] Ryan reported that Helena was "a mighty rough 'hole.' Stores Pig pens — Stables &c all on the Main Street." Most of the emigrants found jobs of some kind there. See A. J. Fisk Diary, September 14, 1866.

[1] The section of Andrew's diary printed here takes up the story of the Fisk party at the point where Robert's diary ends. A few people remained at the prospecting camp on the Sun River, although most of the emigrants had gone on to Helena. Van Fisk and some companions were out on a second prospecting trip; James Fisk was in Helena transacting business.

The original diary is in the MoHS (photocopy in MiHS). Entries from September 18 through December 31, 1866, are reproduced here with the permission of the MoHS and Bruce M. Fisk, Seattle, Washington.

1 oclock P.M. He got lost yesterday afternoon & had to Camp out all night. This forenoon he wandered all arround on the pararie [*sic*] near here & finally came back just where he had started. Took a fresh start & got in. The Capts time is up — but he did not get in to night. The "Hicks" boys still catch a couple "Beaver" every day.[2] For supper we had the hind quarters of a large Beaver roasted or baked. I must say it is *good*. We had a shooting match this evening — 50 yds with rifles. I made the best shot — right through the "Bulls Eye."

Wednesday, September 19. On getting up this morning we found the ground covered with snow — about 1½ inches deep, but it was all off before noon.

About noon it cleared up and the "old Rocky" [Rocky Mountains] loomed up — all covered with snow. I tell you it looks mighty cool up that way. I should think this weather would be a damper on the prospecters in the Mountains. The Hunters got in to day — that went out a few days ago — the weather has been so unfavorable that they did not get any game. "My House" got destroyed by fire this evening. I have had a fire [in] front of it for the past few days — & this evening — I had just left for a few minutes — some sparks blew into the Hay — & in a moment the tent was all in a blaze. The tent was most all bur[n]t up but nothing inside was damaged.

Thursday, September 20. A couple Teams left to day for Halena [*sic*] City. There is only one Emmigrant team left here now — besides the Capts teams. Our Cattle are looking splendidly. We are now waiting — rather impatiently for Vans party of prospecters and the Capt from Halena. We are anxious — if Vans party discovers any thing, to go to putting up our winter quarters — or "dig out" for Halena City.

Jack Hicks brought in an Antelope this morning — He & Bob [Fisk] took the buggy & went up the River a few miles this afternoon — but they did not get any game. Weather has moderated a good deal — about noon it was quite warm. The wind is on a regular "rampage" this afternoon. It makes the old "Cottonwoods" on the river bend and sing like fun.

Friday, September 21. A windy cold day. Shouldnt wonder if this wind would blow up a rain.

Bro Bob has gone in parder-ship with the Hicks boys trapping. They sat about 40 traps for Beaver to day — some below here — but most all of them above on the Head waters of this River. Bob took Jack up the River in the buggy — and the traps. He is going to stop up there a few days. I shouldnt wonder if it would pay — if they could stay here this winter. No word from either the Capt or the prospecters.

Saturday, September 22. Commenced raining and snowing last night and it is still "continuing the struggle on that line." A most miserable — nasty day.

Mr [Orlando B.] Barber and [Stephen] Liberty — from the prospecting party got in this evening — very near played out. They say they have walked about 35 miles through the storm to day — & that the rest of the boys will get in tomorrow. They have found no gold — not even a color and they all say that there aint an ounce of gold on this side of the Range. Trappers got one Beaver.

Sunday, September 23. This morning at day lag [light] [Luke] Riley and

---

[2] The identity of the "Hicks boys" is uncertain. One was probably George P. Hicks, a farmer from St. Peter who was born in Vermont in 1808. He was accompanied by a Jack Hicks, who may have been his son or one of several other John Hickses living in Minnesota about this time. See MiHS Scrapbook, 69:37; *Methodist Herald*, 10:13 (June 10, 1896); United States Manuscript Census Schedules, 1860, Nicollet County, Minnesota, p. 79; Benton County, p. 89, 98.

[Edward] Overn got in from Halena City. They were lost all yesterday afternoon & last night. They brought a mail — I got a letter from Rob Anderson — a good long one.[3] Goodie [Mrs. James Fisk] got a letter from Capt. He will be home in a few days and a party of old miners — who have prospected here are coming out with him to show our men where the gold is so they say. He says he will be along in a few days — as soon as he could get his business settled. Frank Robi[n]son was with the party [Riley and Overn] last night and got lost — or rather they left him. Ryan & I started out as soon as we got breakfast — and rode all day. We found his trail about 17 miles from here — and found he had turned back & at sun down the trail was lost and we had to return to Camp — or rather [Thomas J. A.] Fletcher & Ryan lost it — I was off alone roaming arround the bluffs. I got in about 8 P.M. & Ryan about one hour later. I am afraid the poor boy [Robinson] is about gone up. He is sickly & not able to stand much. It has rained and snowed all day. Van — George [Burson] — and the rest of the prospecters got in to night — wet & hungry.

Monday, September 24. Capt Ryan — [I. N.] White and Harry Norton went out this morning to hunt for Robison. Ryan is to go to the Ranc[h]e on the Dearborn River [4] — and the other two are to go up to the head of the River and follow it down. It has finally quit storming — but the wind blows cold.

I have written a couple letters to day . . . I think I shall postpone writing any more letters till we get into winter quarters. I traded a large sized wesson revolver to Van — for his small "seven shooter" of the same make.

Bob brought in a couple large Beaver. Johney Jackson got in this afternoon from Halena. He couldent get any work so he had to come back.

Tuesday, September 25. [John] Lester — Closson [Timothy E. Clawson] and [Dan W.] Sprankle left for Halena City this morning. I sent a couple letters by them.

Capt Ryan got in at two oclock this morning — and White & Norton this afternoon — they were all unsuccessful in their search for Robison — but soon after the last party got in — Bob came down with the buggy from Jack Hicks Camp (about 9 miles up the River) bringing Robison with him. He ran across Jack Hicks yesterday — when he was just about completely played out. He has had a mighty hard time. He says the wolves were calling rather loudly for him. His feet are used up so bad that he can hardly step on them. Bob brought down six Beaver and a young Deer.

Wednesday, September 26. Quite warm to day — the moon is full now and I should not wonder if we should have some Indian summer. Capt Ryan and Liberty went out this morning to find Robisons horse — Saddle & Blankets.

Capt Fisk and [W. H.] Watson got in from Halena City this afternoon. They left Monday. The Capt has determined to pack up and move to Halena City — So we went to work with a will this afternoon — hauled the waggons up to the "old Sibley" [tent] and loaded up the waggons. Expect to get an early start tomorrow morning. This move has put a damper on Bro Bob and the Hicks boys & their trapping prospects. But I say "Bully for us."

[3] Hereafter most of the many references to letters written and received have been deleted and indicated by ellipsis marks. Andrew's correspondents seem to have been chiefly former army comrades and Minnesota friends.

[4] The terms "ranche" and "roadhouse" refer to frontier hotels or inns where travelers were able to obtain meals, lodging, or both. No information has been found about the unidentified ranches mentioned here and below.

Thursday, September 27. Camp on Bear Creek. Made about 18 miles. Got off this morning about 9 oclock and made about 8 miles to a small creek where nooned. The grass here is tolerable good — but there is no timber and but little water — but plenty for stock.

Road to day pretty rolling — and some Hills — had to double up on one. Mighty windy this afternoon but not very cool. We brought along one load of Hay to use tomorrow night at the ranche — where there is no Hay. Ryan and Liberty got in to night — after dark — hungry and tired. They did not succeed in finding Robisons horse.

Friday, September 28. Camp on the Dearborn River — Made about 15 miles. Broke Camp about seven and came right through without stopping at noon. About 10 of our Cattle got poisened last night by something they eat — and this afternoon they were pretty sick. This river is about the size of the Sun River where we were Camped — but there is very little valley on the River and very high bluffs on each side. We are camped about ½ mile below the crossing and the ranche. We leave the waggons at the ranche. Maj [William J.] Cullen passed here this afternoon enroute for the States. Large numbers are continually going down. A frieght train of some ten waggons — six yoke to a waggon — 6500 to each load — are camped a little above us. They have a quartz mill aboard. I sold my gun for $35 cash to a man bound for the States. A warm day.[5]

Saturday, September 29. Our Cattle strayed off last night — and we were compelled to lay over to day. The last of the Cattle were found this afternoon — over on "Bears Creek" — about 11 miles from here. I found the main herd this forenoon about 4 miles from here — on the bluffs — above the ranche. We have made a correll this evening so to be sure of an early start tomorrow morning. A nice warm Indian summer day. Several waggon loads of men — bound for the States passed Camp to day. This afternoon — having nothing in particular to do — I commenced reading the celebrated story — "Marrian Gray." Thanks due to Mrs Barber for the Book.[6]

Sunday, September 30. Camp on [Little] Prickly Pear River. Made 15 miles. Broke camp at Sunrise and moved out six miles & stopped for noon. After dinner — came a long hill very steep — which we had to "double up." From there Van and I came in by what is called the "cut off" 3 miles nearer but is a bad road for loaded teams. Several of the Cattle played out this afternoon — from the affects of the poison they got at Bears Creek.

This place is called "Canadas Ranche" & I vote him a gentleman for he sent us a mess of *Potatoes* — Lord — want they good. The grazing here is poor. The Missouri is two miles below here.

Monday, October 1. Camp on Prickly Pear. Made about 16 miles. Broke camp in good season and moved right up the Prickly Pear Valley — 4 miles up we came to

[5] William J. Cullen, a former superintendent of Indian affairs, went from Minnesota to Montana by steamboat in the spring of 1866, taking machinery for a quartz mill. His sons, Charles and Kimball, and his nephew, William E. Cullen, a St. Peter lawyer, accompanied Fisk. William E.'s account of the expedition appeared in the *St. Peter Tribune*, December 12, 19, 1866. For William J.'s experiences in Montana, see *Weekly Pioneer*, November 9, 1866.

[6] *Marian Grey, or The Heiress of Redstone Hall* was published in New York in 1863 by Mrs. Mary Jane Holmes, a popular novelist of the time.

the "Toll Gate" where they take $5.00 per team for toll — but Bro Jim has a pass for his Train. Here the road leads right into a canyon — where the bluffs are so high in some places that you can hardly see the Sky. Some of the most beautiful and romantic scenery I ever saw. The road was splended. We crossed the River 18 or 20 times — but it was bridged over part of the crossings. We nooned about half way up — it is about 8 miles long. At this end we come right out of the mountains — into a valley — at another toll gate — and [Malcolm] Clarks ranche which is about ½ mile below. A very warm Indian summer day.[7]

Tuesday, October 2. Cam[p] near small Spring. Made 13 miles. Warm day. We are Camped to night in sight of Halena City — that is if it was clear we could see it — away across the valley — about 13 miles from here.

This forenoon we came up a long hill — the steepest and hardest hill we have had on the trip — we crossed the divide and camped for noon down in the hollow — near a small Creek. This afternoon we crossed another small divide — Came down the hill a couple miles and Camped. There is a Ranche just oppisite with the sign up — "Best of Liquors." We had a grand and magnificent sight from the top of this hill.

Wednesday, October 3. Again we are compelled to lay over on acct of our Cattle. They were no where to be found this morning — and after hunting all day — they were found about 10 miles from here at "Bassets Ranche." It was dark when they got here so we cant move till tomorrow. A shower accompanied by a heavy gale of wind came up about sun down and for a few minutes made things fly arround.

Beaupre and Watson were out from the City to day — on a visit. Beaupre looks sickly. 12 "four mules" teams passed here this afternoon — from Benton. They took down passengers. Very warm and pleasant this forenoon. A Company of Soldiers passed here this afternoon — for Halena City. They are just from the "Big Horn." They report rich diggens there.[8]

Thursday, October 4. Camp on the "ten mile creek" or "Widow Dergans [Durgan's] Ranche" — 4 miles from Halena City. Made about 9 miles. Got here in Camp about noon. The road was down hill most all the way — it is the longest hill I ever saw — in all about ten miles from bottom to top.

We are camped here for a few days — until the Capt gets a place for his family — all of our teams went up to town and stored the goods in the Ware House. Part of the boys have left — & the rest go in the morning. Kim[ball] and Charlie Cullen came out here to meet us — they look *gay.* Mrs. Dergan sent us over some Butter & Cheese — *Thanks.* She is now worth about fifty thousand dollars — she came out with the Capt in 1862. She has a splended Ranche here.

Friday, October 5. Was up to Halena City to day. It is not so large a place as I thought it was — but it is the busiest place I ever saw. They have also got a good many fine buildings — and one splended Stone building is in course of construc-

[7] King and Gillette constructed an excellent toll road in the Little Prickly Pear Valley in 1866 at an estimated cost of from forty to fifty thousand dollars; the tolls were high and the builders were said to have cleared their costs in two years. Burlingame, *The Montana Frontier,* 146. On Clark, see p. 94n, above.

[8] An account of a prospecting trip to the Bighorn in the *Montana Post* of October 27, 1866, said that in an extensive exploration "not a respectable color of gold was obtained."

tion.[9] The streets are very narrow. There are a good many Chineese there and all of them (I guess) wash clothes for a living. I called on Mrs [Erwin] Sims & "Hannah." Also saw a good many of the Expeditionary fellows. Invested in several glasses of "Lager Beer" 25 cts per glass. In fact they dont look at a fellow for less than 25 cts apiece. Peaches are 50 cts apiece. The fruit came from Salt Lake. I saw good horses and saddles sold at auction for $40.00. Most all of our boys got pretty good places to work. Ed Overn has jumped a claim and I think of going in with him mining. Potatoes are 3 cents a pound — Green Apples are $1.00 per pound. Billiards 75 cts per game. Almost as warm as summer to day.

Saturday, October 6. On a claim in California Gulch — about two miles below the City.

Ed Overn — Luke Riley — George Burson — Van and I moved up on this Claim this morning — pitched our tents — got a load of Lumber from town — have got our "Sluice Boxes" most done — cleaned up some "Tailings" in the claim — and have gone to work in earnest. This is a deserted claim — has been worked about one month. We get a good prospect with the pan — but cant tell how much it will pay to work with sluices. Bros Bob and Jim are sinking a hole down at Widows Dergans Ranche to see what the prospects are. A "Jimme Cane" came up this afternoon — blew down our "A" tent — a little rain.

Sunday, October 7. This forenoon we finished our Sluice boxes and set them all ready to commence work tomorrow morning. We have about one hours work on the ditch yet.

This afternoon we went up town to see the sights. Sunday is the great day here. The town was thronged. Auction Store every ten feet — and every Auctioneer trying to call the loudest. Any amount of Miners drunk but must say they were very peacable. Played several games of Billiards — just to see how it would go. A good many of the Expedition boys were in town — some loafing but most all to work. In the evening I went arround to the several "hurdy girdys" or "dance houses" — where for the sum of $1.00 in funds you could have the pleasure of dancing with a girl and the whiskey thrown in. I did not invest. Also called arround to the Chineese quarters. Jim Overn has got back from "New York Gulch" and is going to work with us on the claim.

Met Dick [Richard] Hoback — Cady [George Caddy, Jr.?] & Rock — of Co "H" 2d Cavalry. Took supper where Charlie Trombly [Tromblie] is stopping.[10]

Monday, October 8. We were delayed about two hours this morning — our "Dam" broke away and we had to dig a ditch arround it. After that every thing went off lovely. Van and George cleaned up the "tailings" — Ed — Luke and Jim "Picked" and "Shoveled in" and I, picked part of the time — kept the Sluice Boxes clean with the "Sluice Fork" — and besides all that I am "Chief *Slush* and pastry cook." Ed cleaned out the Boxes to night but it was too late to "pan" out the dirt. So we cant tell how much we *made* to day. We are still having our splended "Indian Summer."

[9] This was probably the First National Bank on Wall and Main streets. See William C. Campbell, *From the Quarries of Last Chance Gulch*, op. 18 (Helena, 1951). The identity of "Hannah," mentioned below, is unknown.

[10] Most of the men mentioned by Andrew here and below were either former army acquaintances or members of the Fisk and Holmes trains. Known members of the expeditions are listed in the Appendix, below. The rosters of Company H, Second Minnesota Calvary, do not list a soldier named Rock. On New York Gulch, see note 29, below.

Our boys who are sinking a shaft down to Widow Dergan have struck water — and they have to get a pump before they can dig any more.

Tuesday, October 9. "Our Claim" dont pay "by a long Shot." This morning "Ed" washed out $2.25 from our yesterdays work. We concluded that we would try it an other day — but to days work was worse than yesterdays — only took out $2.00.

The dust is very fine — almost a[s] fine a[s] flour — but is the best looking dust I have seen in the place. There is a claim open above here about 300 yards and we think we will give that a trial for a couple days.

We get *lots* of Potatoes now — only 3 cents per pound — and fresh Beef for 15 cts. The Beef in this country is a great deal sweeter and more juicy than Minn Beef.

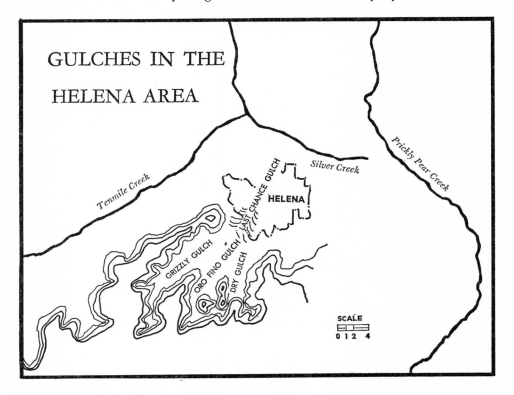

Wednesday, October 10. We moved our Sluice Boxes to the upper Claim this morning — got all ready to "run through" by noon.

Ed Avery [Overn?] then went up to "Dry Gulch" to see if he could not get us a good claim up there. He got back this evening — and says he thinks the prospects are good for getting a Claim. Van & him are going up tomorrow to see about it.[11]

George and I were down to the lower Camp to night — to see "Little Dell" [James Fisk's daughter] and get a few things. Bob was to work dressing his Beaver Skins. Bro Jim tells me that "P. B. is turning out to be a d———m S——— of ss[?]"

Thursday, October 11. We took out to night after a hard day and a half's work —

[11] Dry Gulch, east of Last Chance Gulch, was in the approximate location of present-day Davis Street, Helena. See Muriel S. Wolle, *Montana Pay Dirt: A Guide to the Mining Camps of the Treasure State*, 70, 82 (Denver, Colorado, 1963).

$10 — and although it pays better than the lower claim — it dont one quarter pay wages.

Van and Ed were up to "Dry Gulch" to day and bought a claim for $120.00 — pay part in labor at $5.00 per diem and the ballance in dust when we take it out — over and above our expenses. Ed thinks the claim will pay about $6 per day to the man. If it will pay that I will be satisfied for a while — till something turns up better. Our old Docter [Henry G. Weeden] who came over with us is sick down to Widow Dergan's.

Friday, October 12. Van and George moved up to "Dry Gulch" to day. We think we will try this claim a couple days longer — as we think we have got into a "pay streak." We went to work "Stripping" this morning and stripped about 12 by 16 feet — and this afternoon we run through some. I worked a couple blisters on my hands. Van and George are going to work tomorrow — for the man we bought our claim off.

A cold drizzling rain set in about dark and it is still raining quite hard. Our tent dont leak much — but it is getting mighty disagreeable — this Camping out.

Saturday, October 13. Rained all last night and all day to day — except this afternoon it has got cold and it has been snowing for several hours. It has been impossible to work in the claim. The Boys all went up town & left me to keep house and I went to bed to keep warm. Bro Jim was up town this evening and I expected a letter sure — but nary letter came.

The report is that there has been rich diggens struck over on the "Prickly Pear" but they will have no water to work there till spring.

Sunday, October 14. Widow Dergans Ranche. Got up this morning — found the [ground] covered with snow and concluded I would come down here and spend the Sabbath in Bro Jim's warm tent. Bro Jim was up town most of the day — overhauling his goods in the warehouse and getting us some provisions out. . . . Snowed some all day. This evening we spent over to Mrs. Dergans. She is a great talker. Goodie gave me a splendid dinner — oyster soup — Butter — cheese and *such* a piece of *Mince Pie. Lord* but twas good.

Monday, October 15. At Camp on Claim. Came up to day about noon and found nobody here — so I went up town and loafed arround all the afternoon. Times are getting quite dull in the City — to what they were a week ago. So many have left for the States — and still they are going.

It is still stormy — snow is a couple inches deep on the flat — and most as many feet on the mountains. Its mighty cold to night — coldest night of the season.

Paten [Isaac N. Payton] and [George H.] English are going back to the States. They are one of the "Danville Boys" & their motto on their waggon was "Montana or Bust" & now they ought to hang out "Busted by G—d." [12]

Tuesday, October 16. It cleared up this morning and we got to work at the Claim about ten oclock and we worked steadily and hard till almost Sun down. I "picked and Shovelled in the pit" all day — was a going to take the tailings but the pair of Rubber Boots tha[t] we got are too small for me — so Riley took his place there.

Van and George came down about noon — they say that they have got logs cut for our "Cabin" and one log arround — but cant do any more at it till we come up

[12] Fisk Roll, 1866, lists Payton, English, and Timothy Clawson as residents of Danville, Illinois; Payton's letter from the expedition was published in the *St. Cloud Democrat*, July 5, 1866.

— which will be in a few days if this thing dont pay — & I dont think it will. Freezing quite hard to night.

Wednesday, October 17. At Widow Dergans. We have finally proved our claim — dont amount to *shucks* — so tomorrow we move up to "Dry Gulch." Our claim payed us about $2 per day to the man — splended looking gold too.

Still storming — snowing a good part of the day. The sun came out bright for about half an hour this morning — looked as though it was going to be a splended day — but the next half hour it was snowing so that you couldent see the City. Bob and Ryan spent the evening over to the "widows" — nothing unusual though.

Thursday, October 18. Up in "Dry Gulch" about 2 miles above the City. Got one of the "widows" teams and moved up — bag & baggage this morning — got here about noon. The "Gulch" is quite narrow and a person has to look sharp in driving three yoke of oxen. Stumps evry few feet & shafts sunk all along at the sides of the roads. After dinner we went to work pulling down logs from away up the side hill and building our "Cabin." We got 4 logs up all arround. The snow on the side hills is about two feet deep — & we pull our logs down without much trouble.

Friday, October 19. Worked like "old ned" all day — and we have got our Cabin up — that is all the logs on — and some of the poles cut for the roof. Van has taken the job of building the "chimney" and has commenced to dig a hole to lay the "corner stone." We shall take dirt enough out of the inside to cover the roof. We first put on the poles — chink them — lay a lot of pine boughs on top & then pile on the dirt. Snowed by "jerks" all day.

Saturday, October 20. Dident get to work till late this morning — consequently dident do a very *large* days work. Van had the chimney about half done — but this evening one side of it caved in & he has to tear that side all down again. Rocks are mighty scarce and miserable ones at that — evry shape but square. It dident happen to snow to day — but the wind blew *some*.

Sunday, October 21. As "miners" dont work Sunday — we dident to day. The boys went away — Van to town and George down to widow Dergans — and left me to keep house. George says that Bro Jim & family are going to move up town tomorrow — pitch their tents on one of the lots and build a frame house.

It snowed a couple inches here last night & to day it is quite chilly — but down in the valley the dust is blowing — & it is quite warm — so the boys say. Jim Overn came up this evening — pretty *tight* — with a large pair of Rubber Boots on his back.

Monday, October 22. Quite a pleasant day — snow melted considerable. We have been to work digging the dirt out of our Cabin — covering the Roof and "chinking." Riley went up the bluff and "picked" out and rolled down a lot of Rocks — out of a ledge — for the Chimney.

George cut six logs for the Capt — three 30 feet & three 22 — for his house. Chmedlian [Chemidlin] got up here just at dark with a couple yoke of Cattle to haul them down. He brough[t] along hay & will stay till morning — for tis too late even to load up.

Tuesday, October 23. Bro Jims Camp — in Halena City. Got out of grub at our Camp & came down this forenoon to get some — sent it up by Bob & concluded I would stop all night. Was down town this afternoon and evening. Was into

"Fenton's" new saloon and reading rooms — he has got quite a cozy place. I Invested 50 cts in a *pie* — just for sake of old army times.[13]

Bro Jim is going to build in the upper part of town — just at the foot of this Gulch. Warm & thawing — a slight sprinkle of rain this evening.

Wednesday, October 24. At Home. Came up this afternoon — with a team — with lumber for Cabin and mess chest for ourselves. Found in said chest — a Box containing about 1 doz best Cigars — supposed to have belonged to Bro Jim — which I appropriated for *our* use. Cabin most done — Chimney up — Roof covered — & partly mudded — guess we will get it done tomorrow.

Has been quite warm — snow most all melted off. More than a "Sluice head" running down the gulch.

Thursday, October 25. In our Cabin. Finished our Cabin and this afternoon we moved in. Its mighty cozy. First night in a house since the sixth of June — the longest stretch — but one — in a tent. In 1864 we went into tent's on the 17 of May & got into quarters at Ft Ridgely on the 17 of October. I never care about taking an other summer's campaign in a tent.

Ed and I went to work this morning "sinking a shaft." We have got it 7 feet deep — pretty heavy shoveling. We threw out 175 cubic feet of dirt. Snow is melting fast — most all gone.

Friday, October 26. We sunk our shaft to day 2 feet farther and struck solid rock — so we had to give that shaft up. We have taken one of the old shafts that was sunk on the claim — it is already down about 20 feet. It needs cleaning out some. We have got our windlass up and all ready to go to work tomorrow. Van has gone to town this evening to get some rope & a few other articles. Bro Bob was up this morning — with Caps mare & buggy & brought us up some potatoes and fresh meat.

Saturday, October 27. Van got up with the Rope and some "Sundries" and the boys got to work at the Shaft. Ed was taken very sick this afternoon — cramps and pain in the Stomach and vomiting.

I worked with the Major [Francis(?) Blake] this afternoon down his shaft. It is about 28 feet deep — wet and muddy. I came out just at dark and [who] should I find at the Cabin but Eugene A. Erwin. Lord want I glad to see him. Never was so glad and surprised to see any one in my life. I supposed him in Minnesota. He came out with Holmes — & has been here six weeks. They are in McClellans Gulch — 10 miles from here — says they have got a pretty good claim. His brothers "Sid" and Dave are with him.[14]

Sunday, October 28. Gene and I had a good time this morning — reading over old letters and talking over old times. I went down town with him about noon — took lunch at Bros Jims — went arround town a little & he started for home.

I staid down town all afternoon — George [Burson] came down and we took supper at Jims. Jim gave me a couple letters just before we started back. . . . I wrote a long letter to Bob Anderson this evening. Send him a specimen of dust —

[13] The saloonkeeper was probably the John W. Fenton who joined Fisk's expedition in 1865 and spent the winter trapping on the plains with Van Fisk. See *Press*, September 6, 1865, and Fenton's pension record in file XC2666 108, NARG 15.

[14] The Erwin brothers — Eugene A., David, and Sydney H. — lived in Waseca, Minnesota, when they joined the Holmes train. Eugene served in the army with Andrew. See *Minnesota in the Civil and Indian Wars*, 1:553. McClellan Gulch (also called Pacific City) is northwest of Helena, between Wilborn and Lincoln. See Wolle, *Montana Pay Dirt*, 99, 111.

my first digging in "Last Chance." Th[e]re was several hundred Blackfeet Indians in town to day.

Monday, October 29. Worked all day with the Major — down the Shaft. Mighty cold — wet — muddy and disagreeable. He is down as far as he can go at present — the walls are so low that it is impossible to work. So he has to commence and cut the tunnel larger and prop it up. Our boys have had to quit the old shaft and start an other one. It was continually caving in.

Ed is still mighty sick. Has not eaten any thing since Sunday noon. He is taking a lot of medicine to night. . . .

Tuesday, October 30. George and I worked for the Major this forenoon getting out Timbers and this afternoon sinking a Shaft. The Maj has concluded to give up the old one — and sink a new one — in good shape. The finest day we have had since we got here. Our boys did not do much on our claim. They went off to town to see about a reported stampede — but couldent find out anything about it. Van is down town to night on business. George & I spent the evening up to Adriance's Cabin.

Wednesday, October 31. George & I worked on our shaft to day — & let *Luke* [Riley] and *Jim* [Overn] work for the Major. We sunk about 10 feet. To night we get a pretty good "prospect" and we are in hopes that we will be lucky enough to strike right on the "pay streak."

The Capt came up at noon. Little Dell was with him. She fell on the stove a couple days ago and burnt her cheek pretty badly. Jim brought us up some provision and me a pair of "Miners Boots." They look as if they would never wear out. Adriance and Hostetter [J. T. Hostetler] are spending the evening with us.

Thursday, November 1. We sunk the Shaft 8 or 10 feet deeper to day — it is about 21 feet deep. We have struck the rim rock running into the Gulch — and also water. We think we are now on the top of the "pay streak" and we intend drifting off to find the channel of the Gulch. We think the water will not bother us much — that we can bail it out easy. I find that tending the windlass is *some* on the *muscle*. . . . The weather still continues fine.

Friday, November 2. Sunk our Shaft about two feet deeper to day — and found that the Rim Rock came clear across the hole. Then we undertook to drift across — but the gravel was to loose — and we concluded it would be cheaper for us to sink a new shaft. So George and I commenced a new one — about three oclock and have got it about four feet down.

The "Major" — Adriance and Hostetter were here all the evening — playing "seven up" and having a jolly good time. The weather still continues fine.

Saturday, November 3. Have got our shaft done about 8 feet — the timbers up and evry thing ready for work Monday morning. Van found a little nugget — weighing about 20 cts to day — in the Sluice Boxes — when he had run through a few buckets of the bottom gravel of the old shaft. So we think the pay streak is there *sure*.

We played a game of seven up to night to see who would cook the next week — Jim was *salted*. . . . Van & George are up to Adriance's spending the evening.

Sunday, November 4. Was down town all day. George and I had a splended supper at Jims — "old peaches and cream." Ryan & Chmedlian were down at the

"Widows." They say that she is going to have a grand *hop* at her house when she gets it finished.

Met Dick Hoback in town and had a long talk with him — also Billy Merry and "Lou." No letters from home this week although I expected some *sure*. Bro Van and Lowery [Milner Lowry?] rode over to the "Prickly Pear" this morning. A splended day.

Monday, November 5. I worked for the Major to day — getting out timbers for the shaft — thought my hands had got a little tough — but I put three blisters on them.

Bro Van got back this afternoon — he brought up a good long letter . . . lots of news from home. Most evry body there seems to be joining the Church. Expect us *wild* boys wont stand much show when we get back there. Van brought up a *Cabbage* — paid 97 cts in dust for it.

Tuesday, November 6. Have got our shaft down to about 20 feet. We have struck the "pay streak" (we think) also the solid bed rock of old Granite. We got a good prospect — from 5 to 35 cts to the pan — coarse gold. We shall have to run a drift now.

Capt was up this afternoon — brought us up some provisions & a window sash for house — and Goodie sent us *boys* each a "fried Apple Turnover." *Lord* it was "old peaches and cream." Capt thinks we have got a "good thing" in our claims. "Seven up" for amusement this evening.

Wednesday, November 7. We started our drift across the Gulch to day. Ed was well enough to go down the shaft and superintend the job — while George did the work. We washed out what dirt we took out yesterday and to day — and cleaned up to night — only got about $2.75. So we aint on the pay streak yet. We think by drifting across the Gulch we will find it sure — if there is any in the Claim.

Rather cold and windy to day — am afraid this warm weather is about played out. But the Indian summer here dont begin to compare with our Minnesota Indian summers.

Thursday, November 8. Ed was well enough this morning to go down the shaft — so we couldent do much of any thing — so George & I went down to Bro Jims to grind the axe. They are busy on the house.

Bro Bob has got into a printing office — he is Editor & "Chief pusher" of the whole thing. The first issue will come out next week.[15]

This afternoon we worked at our shaft — have got in two set of Timbers & all "spiled" and all "O. K." Did some washing this evening and mended up old mining clothes.

Friday, November 9. A clear nice looking day — but cold. Have got our *drift* through, and into the shaft we last sank & washed all the dirt we took out and cleaned up to night *$1.50* — all in *dust*. We have found a crevice in the solid rock — in the middle of the channel — about two feet wide — and tomorrow we calculate to test that. And if the pay is not there — why I suppose we will have to drift in an other direction. I believe there is a pay streak there somewhere — *sure* — and if we persevere we will find it. Riley is cook for the next week.

[15] In October, 1866, Felix Poznansky and Edward House bought the press of the independent *Montana Radiator* and hired Robert Fisk to edit a Republican newspaper. See *Helena Herald,* December 27, 1902; *Helena Record,* July 13, 1907.

Saturday, November 10. At Bro Jim's In Helena City. Well I guess we finished up to day — that is for a spell — we cleaned out the crevice and it dident pay — not at all. So we think the claim is a *humbug*. A man came bye when we were working and he said that he worked the same claim last winter and dident make *grub*. So take it all arround I guess we wont do much more on the claim. Came down this afternoon and this evening I was down to Bobs "office." He is everlastingly "throwing his quill" for his first issue. Jo[seph] Delany is "picking type" for him. Got introduced to Mr [Edward] House the proprietor. Capt Ryan came near getting run over by a drunken horseman.

Sunday, November 11. Got Bro Jims horse this morning and rode over to "McClellan Gulch" — about 9 miles from here [Helena?] — to see Gene Erwin & Sid. I had a hard time to find them — first went to Montana City — (a small mining town on the "Prickly Pear") and then inquired the way to the Gulch.[16] I roamed arround the Mountains till about two oclock before I found them. Gene introduced me to *Sid* — who is a jovial — frank — warm hearted *boy* — and we had a couple hours pleasant and agreeable conversation. They wanted me to stay all night — but I couldent. Sid gave me his photograph. Got back here about an hour after dark. Went to bed and about half an hour after Van comes down and gets me out of bed to saddle the horse and go down to Widow Dergans after the buggy. He is going of[f] in the morning on a private stampede — him and the Major. It took me about two hours to get back from the widows — it was so dark that I could hardly find the road.

Monday, November 12. Van and the Major got off this forenoon. George was down from "our cabin" this forenoon. Think I shall stay down here for a few days. Helped do some work on the house. They would have it all done before now — but the lumber has not been sawed. . . . It snowed an inch last night — & it is cold to day & to night it is a "hummer."

Tuesday, November 13. At home up the [Dry] Gulch. Helped work some on the house. George came down this afternoon and I concluded I would come back with him.

The other boys in our Cabin are here yet — they have been down town all day — got back about dark. They are looking for a job — and I guess they have got one some where. Adriance was over this evening and we had a *jolly* game of pitch.

Wednesday, November 14. Thawing to day — but damp and windy. Looks like snow. Expect we will get plenty of it in a day or two. George is working with "Jo" down his shaft. He is not getting along very fast. He is blasting through solid rock. . . . Riley [Patrick Reilly] — of Adriance's party — is pretty sick with the chronic diarhea. Adriance and Hostetter were over this evening.[17]

Thursday, November 15. Bro Jims. Came down town this morning — worked all day banking up the house. Bro Van and Major Blake got back last night at midnight. They found things at "Lost Horse Gulch" just about as reported. Bro Van secured "Bar Claims" for himself — George & I, and Gulch Claims for Bob — Jim —

---

[16] The site of Montana City is identified by a marker near Highway 91, ten miles from Helena. A small settlement grew up in 1864, but it quickly declined as richer strikes were found elsewhere. It was probably the site of one of the camps of the 1862 Fisk expedition. See Wolle, *Montana Pay Dirt*, 68; Jean Davis, *Shallow Diggin's*, 137 (Caldwell, Idaho, 1962).

[17] Patrick Reilly of Toledo, Ohio, died two months later at Mrs. Durgan's ranch. A. J. Fisk Diary, January 17, 1867.

Chmedlian — Capt Ryan and Ed Overn. They think it is a big thing. The Gold is all coarse — one nugget was taken out that weighed $42.00. It is situated on the head waters of the "Prickly Pear" creek near the summet — but they say that the Gulch is so deep that it is never cold there. Van — George and Adriance are going to move over soon — for the winter.[18]

Friday, November 16. "The Helena Herald" — first issue — R. Emmett Fisk Editor — came out to day — printed on Brown paper — and it looked very well *concidering*. They expect thier paper from Salt Lake next week. They have heard from it — this side of "Bannock City." Capt Ryan is busy Soliciting for Subscribers & Advertisements.

Mrs Dergan & Hannah called on Mrs Fisk a few moments this evening. A terrible gale blew most all last night. It blew down one of our tents — & one of Bobs beaver skins has not been heard from since. *We boys* slept in the House. To night Capt & Goodie take the house & *we* thier tent.

Saturday, November 17. The forenoon I went up to the Cabin and brought down my "pie box" & clothes. I suppose I shall reside in Hellena City for a while now. George came down with me. Jim Overn has *Stampeded* to see if he cant get a claim in "Horse Shoe Gulch."

Mrs Sims made *us* a call this afternoon — that is she called on Mrs F — & I was there helping her fry Doughnuts & Pies — so I was included in the *us*.

Bro Bob had a regular row down town this evening — concerning a "local" in the paper. He cleaned out a couple of "roughs" han[d]somely. Bobs face is scratched up some.[19]

Sunday, November 18. Stormed a while this forenoon — snow and rain. The "peaks" over South are covered with snow.

Goodie movved into the house to day — and we boys take possession of thier tent. This afternoon we had a regular family dinner — Boiled beef and Cabbage — Pickeled beets — fried cak[e]s &c &c. George and Van were down. Van says that I am to go with them to "Lost Horse Gulch" to bring back the team.

Spent the evening in Bobs office and walking arround town. . . .

Monday, November 19. Van — George — Adriance Dan Sprankle & McCarthy got off this afternoon for "Lost Horse Gulch." Mac went to bring back the team — so I did not have to go.

Bro Bobs trial has been going on all day — will get through tomorrow. Sanders and Pemberton are his Lawyers — two of the smartest and best Lawyers in the Territory. If they dont get him clear in the Police Court — they will carry it up to District Court.[20]

[18] Lost Horse Gulch was located about twenty miles northwest of Helena. The *Montana Post*, November 24, 1866, reported that "some Minnesota boys" struck rich diggings there and that more than a hundred people, chiefly from Minnesota, left Helena on November 15 for the new discovery.

[19] According to the recollections of Felix Poznansky, Fisk "said something about a Mrs. Callahan being a loose character" in the first issue of the *Herald*. See *Helena Record*, July 13, 1907. The *Montana Post* of November 24, 1866, reported that the Callahans and a friend went to the *Herald* office and demanded a published apology. When Robert refused, Callahan attacked him and a fist fight ensued. Later the participants renewed the fight on the street until the police intervened.

[20] Wilbur F. Sanders was an able lawyer and one of the first United States senators from Montana. William Y. Pemberton later became a district judge and chief justice of the Montana Supreme Court. *Progressive Men of Montana*, 32–36, 88.

We had quite a little shower of rain this evening. Capt Ryan is boarding down at the "Crystal Palace Hotel." [21] One of the fancy houses was cleaned out this evening. They put some cotten saturated with cotten [*sic*] into the stove pipe — lit it — and raised the alarm of fire. The Hook and Ladder Company were present — and they busted up the house in grand style.

Tuesday, November 20. A fine day. Goodie received a letter from home — of the 20 ultimo. Bro Bobs trial was concluded at two oclock to day — the Judge found him guilty and fined him $20 and costs. Sanders & Pemberton immediately had it appealed to the District Court. They made some splended speeches. The Court Room was filled — and a good deal of anxiety was felt for the result.

The Dist Attorney (who is a Missouri Copperhead) made a regular *ass* of himself. He puffed — sweated — and blackguarded till I was afraid he would go into fits.[22] Bob has heard from their blank paper. It is out 15 miles from here.

Wednesday, November 21. Weather is still favorable — winter is holding off well. A man got back with the Capt Mare — from "Lost Horse" and reports favorably. He says that our "Bar Claims" are considered among the best thing there.

Mr House (pro of the Herald) and Capt Ryan went out to day to meet their paper — but could not find the waggons that had it on. So they will have to go to press with brown paper again. Was in the office this morning reading a book titled "The Vigalantes of Montana" — it is quite interesting.[23]

Thursday, November 22. The Herald came out this evening. Bob gives the district attorney fits — in a long article about the fight. . . .[24] Was down town a few minutes this evening — nothing particular going on. To day has been warm and hazy — similar to our Minnesota Indian Summer. Mrs Fisk is not very well this evening.

Friday, November 23. Bob and Capt Ryan were up to a party to day in "Grizzly Gulch" — at Whitlatch's celebrated quartz claim — Union Lode "No 2." [25] They say they had a fine time. Bobs office and bedroom is completed — and I took their bed clothes down this forenoon. He has a cozy place for winter. He recd a complimentary ticket this evening — to the Firemans grand ball — to be given on the 28th inst — Thanksgiving eve.

Took the buggy and hauled up a couple Hundred brick — to build the Chimney in the house. . . .

Saturday, November 24. Indian Summer still. Have been "sinking a shaft" to day — in Bro Jims yard — for the *capital* [outhouse?].

Was in Bobs office this evening — looking over the file of papers — cut ou[t] a

[21] On the Crystal Palace Hotel, see *Montana Radiator*, April 7, September 1, 1866; *Montana Post*, November 10, 1866.

[22] The district attorney was John H. Shober, who went to Montana from Dakota with the Holmes train of 1864. The *Montana Post* of November 24, 1866, was highly critical of his prosecution of Robert's case.

[23] The book was Thomas J. Dimsdale's *Vigilantes of Montana*, first published in Virginia City in 1866, after being serialized in the *Montana Post*.

[24] The November 22 issue of the *Helena Herald* is missing from the files of the MoHS and no copy has been found elsewhere.

[25] Whitlatch Union, the first quartz discovery of the region, was located by James Whitlatch in September, 1864, on the summit of a low divide between Grizzly and Oro Fino gulches, four miles south of Helena. The claim on Grizzly Gulch was an extension of the original discovery. See Bancroft, *Washington, Idaho, and Montana*, 723; Wolle, *Montana Pay Dirt*, 94–97; Davis, *Shallow Diggin's*, 121.

couple locals — about "Lost Horse Gulch." Report says that a Lieut has arrived in town from the mouth of the "Judith" with all of our mail which came up the Missouri this summer. Hope its so. . . . Our old expeditionary Doctor [Weeden] gave us a call to day. He is at present boarding at Mrs Dergan's.

Sunday, November 25. A little snow storm this morning — dident amount to much. Wind blew pretty hard all day. Look for cold weather now evry day.

Our large mail for the Expedition is at the Post Office — and is being distributed this evening. *Hope* I shall get a few letters. McCarthy got back with the waggon — from "Lost Horse" but I did not see him. Had some good maple syrup this evening — some that Goodie brought from home. Tasted like "old times." . . .

Monday, November 26. The large mail was distributed this morning. I recd nine letters . . . All old but welcome letters. Mrs Fisk got several from home.

Was down and inspected the large "bed rock flume" in Dry Gulch this afternoon. It has cost a good deal of time — labor and means and next summer they expect to get well paid for thier trouble. . . . We hear good reports from "lost Horse" Gulch.

Tuesday, November 27. MacCarthy and Pete Eckford started for "Lost Horse" this morning. We took quite a mail over for the boys. Mac has got a claim over there — and is going to "prospect" it this winter.

Bro Jim has been building his chim[ne]y to day. We did not have enough brick to finish — so I went after an other hundred but the *brick man* want at home.

A pleasant forenoon but cold and windy afternoon. On the Mountains on the oppesite side of the basin it has been snowing most all day. Wind blowing hard to night. . . .

Wednesday, November 28. A pleasant day — but a little windy. Brought up a load of Brick this forenoon and the chimney is near finished. Caleb Elphee [Elphie] was up here this forenoon a while — and we had a chat about old times. Gave him a letter I had for him.

The Fire Company have a grand Ball to night — at the "Young America" house. Expect it will be a grand affair. . . . Capt Ryan left for Virginia City to day — on business connected with the office. He will probably be gone several weeks.

Thursday, November 29. The Herald out again to day. Bro Bob gets it out in *style*. At the Firemans Ball last night he was toasted thus — "The Herald man — who fights his own battles and asks no odds of any one." To night he is at the Helena Club dance.

Hauled down enough lumber to day from yard to finish the office — and evry thing complete. . . . Bob Leach [Leech] is moving his goods over to "Lost Horse" to start a store. To day is Thanksgiving — but I dident se[e] the Turkey dinner.

Friday, November 30. We done a good days work on the office — boarded up two side — and have got the roof all most "sheeted" over. Saw three letters advertised in the Herald yesterday — for the Erwin boys — and to day I called and got them out. Will keep them till the boys come over — which I expect will be next Sunday. They are from Bob and Johny — judging from the writing.

Finished my letter to John Smith this evening — 12 pages of letter paper in all. Tis the first description of our trip I have written. Mailed the letter this evening & called arround to Bobs office & spent a couple hours looking over the file of papers.

Saturday, December 1. First day of winter — but a fine day — with the exception of a little "blow" just at dark — snow fell about ½ inch deep. Commenced Shingling the roof this afternoon. While handling my knife rather carlessly — I cut a *hunk* out of the end of my right forefinge[r] — which makes it very unhandy to write. Thanks to "Goodie" for a "buckskin cot" for the wounded finger.

My back has been troubling me — quite seriosly for the past week — & to night I got a fall — and it makes it very bad. It has not bothered me so bad before for over a year.

Sunday, December 2. "The Herald Office." A very windy day — a person had to hold on to his *hat* — while on the Streets.

George Burson got over this ev[en]ing. He has had a very bad tooth ache & Came over to get the tooth pulled. He stopped at Widows & the "old Doctor" soon had it out. George says that they have got them up a good Cabin 20 x 25. And they have taken the contract to build an other one — for $150.00.

Am stopping with Bob to night. Had a slight row in the Herdy house — under us — this evening. A knife drawn but nothing serious occured. . . .[26]

Monday, December 3. Brother Jims. Took breakfast with Bob at Resturant. Back feels some better to day. George was up Dry Gulch this forenoon to see Maj Blake. The Maj is taking out pretty good pay — out of the top pay streak. If He succeeds in striking any thing down his shaft — there is a man who wants to buy our claim.

The roof is nearly done. Mrs Fisk has been sick to day — and I — rather on the sick list — took care of the baby. The weather still fine.

Tuesday, December 4. Bro Jim and George left this forenoon for "Lost Horse" Gulch. There has been several new Gulchs struck in the vicinity of "Lost Horse" & Jim has gone over to look arround — see if there is a show for any thing *big*.

In finishing up my work this afternoon on the roof a slat gave way — and I came down rather suddenly to the ground — no bones broken. Mrs Dergan and "Hannah" were up this evening — on a call to Mrs Fisk. Chmidelin went down this afternoon and brought up the "Widows" cattle — to haul up some wood.

Invested in a plaster for my back — which seems to be slowly improving.

Wednesday, December 5. Weather moderate — a slight flurry of snow this forenoon. Finished the roof and battened up side of office. Chmedilin hauled up one load of wood — broke the wreach — "jumped the job" and took the cattle down home this evening. Put on his good clothes — expect he will court "Hannah" all the evening.

Adriance got in late this eving — from "Lost Horse." He says Jim came with him — as far as Silver City.[27] They were at a new gulch called "Cayuse" Gulch — & took some claims — will learn the particulars when Jim gets home.

Thursday, December 6. Adriance went back to "Lost Horse" to day — carried a cross gut [cut] saw over to the boys. Bro Jim says the new gulch is called "Trinity"

---

[26] The *Herald* office was located on the top floor of a large log building at the corner of State and West Main streets. The dance hall on the ground floor was a lively place on Saturday and Sunday nights. See *Helena Herald*, December 27, 1902.

[27] Silver City, some fourteen miles north of the Last Chance diggings, became a mining center in 1864. For a time it rivaled Helena for the county seat, but the mines soon played out. See Wolle, *Montana Pay Dirt*, 68, 99.

and he has got what he calls a good claim — if the Gulch is a[s] rich as it is reported to be. He says that I am to go over next sunday on business.[28]

The mail arrived from Salt Lake this forenoon — bringing me two letters . . . Have been taning a Beaver Skin & Cutting out a Cap & pair of Mittens. Bro Bob gave me a buckskin. His paper is out to day — on white paper & it looks first rate. He is trying to get the office in his own hands. To day was most as warm as summer. But to night is raining.

Friday, December 7. Snowed about 1½ inches last night. Sun came out warm this forenoon — but did not have much affect on the snow. Finished up my Beaver Cap — and to my eye tis about perfect. My Mits are about half done.

Was down town this afternoon — and coming up — Bob & I stopped at Post office. Found out that it takes 6 cents to send papers. So all we have sent with a three cent stamp on — only goes as far as Salt Lake.

Capt bought a stove for the office. They laid the floor to day.

Saturday, December 8. Tolerable cold to day. See by the papers that the Missouri River is frozen up — as far down as St Joe. But here up in the Mountains tis still open. I expect the upper Missippi all frozen up — ere this.

I was down to the Widow Dergan's this morning on an errand for Mrs F. I see that work in "Last Chance" is about suspended for the winter. Most of the sluice boxes are taken out and stacked up. The office was closed in to day and we moved in from the Tent. Tis warm and cozy — and when tis finished — twill be a comfortable room.

Sunday, December 9. Sun shone down as warm as summer all day — but about ½ inch of snow still remains. Twas a busy day in town for the Auctioneers and Merchants. I passed away an amusing half hour this forenoon — watching the half breeds and French man pack a Train of horses and mule. It was astonishing to see how quickly they could put on and fasten a large pack.

Bro Bob think of going over to New York Gulch tomorrow — and I am bound for "Lost Horse." . . .[29]

Monday, December 10. "Widow Dergans Ranche." Came down here early this morning — got a couple yoke of Cattle — took them up town — hitched on to one of the widows waggons — loaded up about eight hundred feet of Lumber and numerous other articles — and got back here — before Sundown. The widow & "Hannah" insisted on me taking tea with them and I *reluctantly* did so. After tea — we spent a couple very plasant hours chatting.

"Long John" and "Honest John" are with me — bound for Lost Horse. Chemidlin came down this eveing — with some more *traps* for the boys — and a note from Van — recd by the Capt this afternoon.

Tuesday, December 11. At the Mouth of "Trinity Gulch" Made about 18 miles. Left the Widows early — followed the Benton road till we crossed Silver Creek — & then followed up the Creek. We nooned on the Creek — passed Silver City — (a small min[in]g town) about 2 oclock P.M. and made Camp here — just at dark.

[28] Gold had been discovered in Trinity Gulch on December 1. Near Lost Horse, it was one of many gulches emptying into the basin at the head of the Little Prickly Pear. See *Montana Post*, December 15, 1866.

[29] York (New York) Gulch was east of Helena. Some quartz outcroppings were found but little was realized from them. See Davis, *Shallow Diggin's*, 234; Wolle, *Montana Pay Dirt*, 120.

Chained the Cattle to the waggon — & fed them some hay. After supper — I went up the Gulch a few hundred yards — to a Camp of Missouri boys — "All the way from Pike" & spent a pleasant hour chatting & telling yarns. They are prospecting a Bar. This is a newly discovered gulch.

Tis a beautiful moonlight eveing — so I say as I roll myself up in my blankets — my boots for a pillow & the Sky for a tent. This is life in the Mountains for me.

Wednesday, December 12. Lost Horse Gulch. This morning — when the Cattle were grazing — I went up to see the recorder of Trinity Gulch & pay him for recording our claims — but he said that I was to late — the Claims were all recorded. I guess he rather came the "gum game" on us. Nooned at a ranche — on the Prickly Pear — kept by some boys who came across with [Philip] Constans in 1864. They recognized me immediately. Here we left the road and struck up the Valley a couple miles — to an old Cabin. This was the end of the road — so I unyoked the Cattle — took our Blankets & started for this place — arrived at Van's Cabin just after dark and found him & Geo well and in good spirits & glad to see us. Thier Cabin is 25 by 22 in the cla[i]m — the largest one in town.

Thursday, December 13. The boys finished their first building to day — for which they will get $150.00.

This is a very lively little town — it is called Atlantic City — Bro Jim named it. It is laid off in Streets — lots 20 feet front. There are two Stores — Butcher Shop — Blacksmith Shop and a large Correll now building. Bob Leach ownes one of the Stores. He also "dishes out" *140 rod — fire proof tangle leg* — for 25 cts (greenbacks good) per drink. The Mountains are so steep on each side of the Gulch that the sun only shines about 2 hours each day. This bids fair to be a mighty lively Camp in the Spring.[30]

Friday, December 14. We were up this morning — and had breakfast and were off by day light to cut the road through and bring up the load of lumber — which we did. Part of the day we came along the side of the Mountain & the rest of the way up the Valley. I had the *honer* of driving the first waggon into Atlantic City. We only brought up about two thirds of the load. An old man (and he is a great blower) is down to the Cabin with a heavy load of lumber — & is now cutting the road clear up through the Valley.

The water being rather scar[c]e here — since it froze up — the citizens turned out and have got a good well dug.

Saturday, December 15. Van and "Honest" John went down this morning with the waggon to bring up the rest of the lumber — but as the road is not yet through the bottom — they concluded they would wait a few days. So they left the Cattle & waggon down to the Cabin.

I helped George dig the foundation of another Cabin the boys are going to put up for a Helena City man. Van is making furnitur this evening. Called in to Leaches [John and Robert Leech] this evening — they were having a jolly game of "seven up" for the Whiskey. The weather still continues splended — and may it still remain so — till I get back — at least.

Sunday, December 16. Camp at a Ranche, 1½ miles below Silver City. Big good bye to "Lost Horse" this morning. George came down to the Cabin with me —

---

[30] On Atlantic City, see *Montana Post,* March 2, 30, 1867.

helped me pack down my blankets & yoke up. It snowed about ten minutes this morning — but it has been warm & pleasant all day.

The Ranche — where I am stopping to night is kept by a New Yorker — and he is a good hospitable fellow. *This* is one of the best regulated Ranches I have seen in the Territory. He has a copy of the last "Gazette" — in which I see the account of a murder in Helena — and a Row in Cave Gulch — where three miners (Jumpers) were killed.[31]

Monday, December 17. At home — Helena City. Left the Ranche at day light — and got to the widows about 10 oclock. Left the Cattle & rode up with Bro Jim — in the buggy. He had just brought Goodie down on a visit. They have just returned from New York City — a mining town — 18 miles from here on the oppesite side of the river. He has commenced his business in negociating Quartz Property.[32]

I met young Robison down town this afternoon. He is just in from Sun River & is off for his home in Mass — in a couple days. His cough is mighty bad & I dont think he will live long. . . .

Tuesday, December 18. Snow fell a couple inches last night — and to day I saw a couple Sleighs out. But it is still warm.

Bob recd a letter from Ryan to day — from Virginia City. They have raised Bob $550. there towards buying out the Herald office. Bob thinks he will be able to get the office the last of the week or the first of next. He introduced me to Mr [James] Whitlatch last evening. Mr W. has made Bob a present of a Cabinet filled with specimen from the "Union" Lode.[33]

Jim & Bob are at a complimentary supper this evening — given to S. T. Hauser — president of the 1st National Bank — previous to his departure for the east. . . .[34]

Wednesday, December 19. A warm spring wind blowing to day — all the snow has disappeared. Our fri[en]ds got out their Sleighs to soon — it seems.

Bro Jim lost or rather had his large Cape stolen last night at the Supper — but he say[s] they had a jolly good time. I tried my engenuity Carpentering to day — making me a high stool to write on — and I succeeded beyond my highest expectations.

Was down to Bobs office this evening — and as us[u]al — he sat in his "easy chair" brow contracted — pencil in his hand — writing — writing — writing. His "negociating" for a hat — came out *lovely*. A fellow took the hint & made him a present of a splended one.[35]

---

[31] See the *Rocky Mountain Gazette* (Helena) for December 15, 1866. The shooting of the claim jumpers is also described in Davis, *Shallow Diggin's*, 234, and Wolle, *Montana Pay Dirt*, 122.

[32] James Fisk and W. A. C. Ryan were associated for a time in a quartz claim business of which no details are known. See *Helena City Directory*, 1868.

[33] The *Herald* was losing money at a rate of about one hundred dollars a week and the proprietors wanted to sell out. Andrew said that many merchants subscribed to the *Herald* fund receiving due bills for job printing and advertising. About $1,500 was raised in this way, and Whitlatch and Robert signed a note for $2,500, making the total amount necessary. The Fisks later bought out Whitlatch's interest. See *Helena Herald*, December 27, 1902; *Helena Record*, July 13, 1907.

[34] Samuel T. Hauser was a civil engineer who had worked in Missouri for a number of railroad companies before he went to Montana in 1862. He became a banker, an organizer of mining companies, and governor of Montana in 1885. See *Progressive Men of Montana*, 202. Comments on the dinner for Hauser are in the *Montana Post*, December 29, 1866.

[35] The *Herald* of December 6 mentioned that the editor was thinking of buying a hat.

Thursday, December 20. An other splended day to chronicle. This beats any thing for a winter that I ever saw. We all pray it may continue so.

The "Herald" is out to day & looks very neatly. Bros Jim & Bob were up to the "Whitlatch Union" to dinner. Mr. W. invited me — but I thought I hadent better go. By the way — he is a capital — jolly fellow — just makes the money fly. Bob this evening is off to some Ball — the way he gets invited to all good things is no bother at all. . . .

Went down to the "widows" this morning & brought up Hannah to help Mrs Goodie cl[e]an house. Met Lon Bootset [John Botset?] & had a chat with him this evening. Am stopping with Bob at the office this evening.

Friday, December 21. An other summer day. The moon is full to night — tis light as day out doors — clear and warm.

The Republicans are doing nobly for Bob. About $15,000.00 [*sic*] has been raised already — only wants $300 more. I am getting ready to come in the office and keep the Books.

Our folks at home are having a general cl[e]an up — scrubbing — washing &c. Before going in the house — we are inst[ru]cted to wipe our boots car[e]fully — & "tread lightly." About a dozen head of Beef Cattle — very fat — and gaily decorated with red & blue ribbons passed the office to day. Am stopping with Bob again to night.

Saturday, December 22. Have had a bad head ache all day — & to night I am nearly sick. Head jumps so that it seems as though twould burst. Chmedilin has taken Hannah home this evening. Got a table for Bobs office.

Some Soldiers were in the office — from the mouth of Judith River — & gave an account of some Indian depredations. Jo McKnight had a narrow escape.

Sunday, December 23. Bro Van — Sprankle and Adriance came in from Lost Horse to day. Van says a new gulch — Missouri has been discovered & he has got a claim — prospects good. Am about well again to day — bowels feel pretty sore. Looks like a Storm.

Monday, December 24. Whitlatch cleaned up $9,000 to day. largest cle[a]n up ever made in the territory. The propri[e]tor of the Herald is R. E. Fisk. A pretty good Christmas gift. Christmas is already commencing down town — every body appears to be getting drunk. Has been snowing most of the day — is about 3 inches deep now.

Tuesday, December 25. "Christmas." And most evry body seems "merry as a marriage bell." The City is full of miners on a drunk. Sleigh riding was the order of the day — two — four and Six horses on a Sleigh.

We *boys* all took dinner at home. It is the first Christmas for a good many years — that four of us brothers have spent a Christmas together. Van and Schmedilin have gone down the Valley to a dance this evening. Bob has gone out to visit several Ball's — Exhibitions &c. Personally — I amused myself playing a few games of billiards.

Have been several small rows arround town this evening — a good many revolvers drawn — but no one shot.

Wednesday, December 26. Have now taken up my place of "business" in the Herald office. Fixed up my table and desk to day, in style. We have not yet got our books from Gilpatrick & Bryant — our agents.[36] The "Herald" is out this evening. An editorial says that there will be issue next week. Bob was out sleigh riding this afternoon — with Travis & his 4 horse stylish "rig."

We have had no eastern mail for 8 or 10 days. The Stages are snowed in — near Virginia City — snow being 10 feet deep in the divide.

Thursday, December 27. It has been snowing for the past 24 hours — snow is now about 1 foot deep — & still snowing. All the stages that went out this morning — had to come back & get sleighs. There is 4 feet of snow in Deer Lodge valley. [A. J.] Oliver's Stage from Virginia had to turn back.[37]

I am spending my lesure minutes in learning to set type — get along capitally. The Vigalance Committee had a lot of bills struck off to day — warning evil doers — that will commence operations again — soon — if they dont keep quiet.

Friday, December 28. Quit snowing last evening — & tis now splended Sleighing. Bro Jim & Van made a "Jumper" — to day — to haul supplies over to Lost Horse with. Mail due to night — but did not arrive — expect they are snowed in.

Travis this afternoon went flying through the Streets — in a new fashioned Cutter — composed of a dried ox skin — with the whiffle tree hitched on one corner — & he standing up driving. . . .

Saturday, December 29. A large Eastern mail got in late last night. No letters for me.

Whitlatch got off on this morning — for the States. A pleasant trip to him. Van left this afternoon for Lost Horse — or Atlantic City — with a load of provisions & other necessaries. He took the new Cutter.

Bob has received his bills for paper sent from Salt Lake — & expects the paper by the next Stage. A pleasant day — but a little cool.

Sunday, December 30. . . . Cale[b] Elphee was in the office this afternoon. He is working for Whitlatch. He has applied for his extra $100. bounty.

Having nothing in particular to do this evening — I read a novel — Negro life on the Plantations. A very interesting Story. Snowing some this evening.

Monday, December 31. A cold day — by far the coldest we have seen this winter. George Burson got in this afternoon from Lost Horse. He says Van broke the Cutter all up & had to leave it — & his load of Provisions at Pagan Gulch [Piegan Gulch?]. Have been to work all day "setting up" & "distributing" type — think I shall learn the "biz" easily.

This evening — in company with Bob — I attended the "blow up" at the "Antelope" Saloon. Had a very good supper.

But I must bid the old year "good bye." I cannot help when looking over this book, to think of the good times — bad times — happy times & Sad time — I have had during the past year. How well I remember one short year ago to night — how *we* boys sat arround the warm stove at Ft Wadsworth, D. T. & smoked our pipes — saw the old year out & the new one in — how I thought & wondered then where I would be one year from that time. But my diary for 1866 is full — so old year — *farewell*.[38]

---

[36] Gilpatrick and Bryant had a bookstore and "news depot" on Wood Street. See *Montana Post*, December 1, 1866.

[37] On Oliver, see *Montana Post*, September 1, 1866, January 5, 1867.

[38] Additional diaries kept by Andrew are in the A. J. Fisk Papers, MoHS.

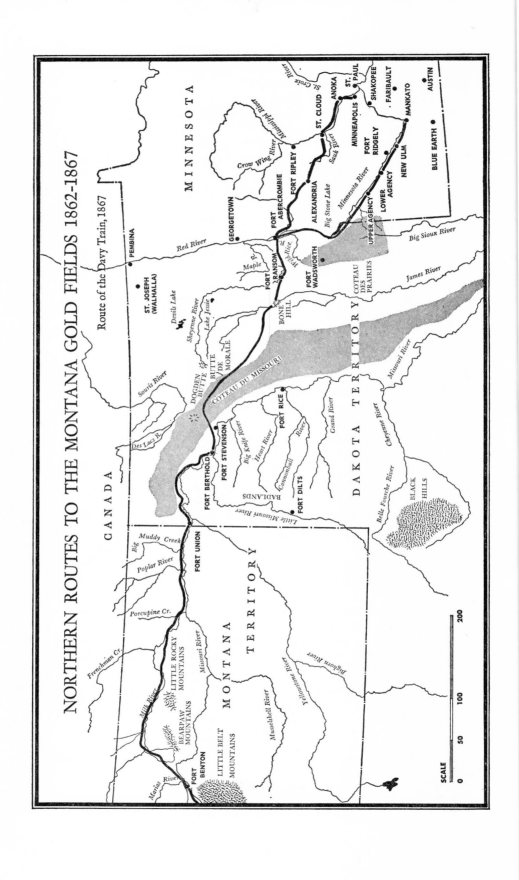

NORTHERN ROUTES TO THE MONTANA GOLD FIELDS 1862-1867

Route of the Davy Train, 1867

1867 ✿✿✿✿✿✿✿✿✿✿✿✿✿✿✿✿✿✿✿✿✿✿✿✿✿
THE DAVY EXPEDITION

1867 ✸✹✸✹✸✸✹✸✸✹✸✸✹✸✸✹✸✸

The Davy Expedition

THE LAST OVERLAND EXPEDITION from Minnesota to Montana was organized by Peter B. Davy in 1867. The short, dapper Davy was thirty-seven years old and a Canadian by birth. After attending Toronto Normal Academy, he taught school for several years before moving to the United States. In 1857 he settled at Blue Earth, a new village in southern Minnesota. There he bought a steam sawmill and for some years seems to have been a patent medicine salesman. At the time of the Sioux Uprising he enlisted in the army and served until 1866, becoming a captain in a Minnesota cavalry regiment. A veteran of the Sibley and Sully Indian campaigns, he was among the troops who went to the rescue of the Fisk expedition in 1864.[1]

Early in 1867, not long after his discharge, Davy announced that he planned to lead an expedition to Montana over the northern route. Associated with him in the project was James B. Wakefield, one of the founders of Blue Earth and a lawyer who held many county and state offices during his career. Wakefield's role seems to have been largely nominal, for Davy undertook most of the work of the enterprise. In February the latter made an eastern tour, presumably to gain support from investors and to attract prospective emigrants.[2]

Davy designated nine Minnesota towns as outfitting points for his expedition. For his southern Minnesota headquarters, he selected Mankato, a thriving little village strategically located at the bend of the Minnesota River and on a beeline between Chicago and Helena. Mankato citizens rallied to support his campaign and incidentally to promote their town as an attractive place for settlers. Boosters set forth Mankato's virtues, among them a population that could be "safely set down between three and four thousand souls," several fine stone and brick buildings, eight hotels, and sidewalks "twelve feet wide."[3]

As a promoter, Davy owed much to James Fisk, and his techniques clearly showed his mentor's influence. In response to many requests, his advertising cir-

[1] See Davy's compiled service record, Company K, First Minnesota Cavalry, and Company H, Second Minnesota Cavalry, NARG 94; his pension file, WC 259937, NARG 15; and Jacob A. Kiester, *The History of Faribault County, Minnesota, from its First Settlement to the Close of the Year 1879*, 282 (Minneapolis, 1896).

[2] *Press*, February 3, 1867; *Mankato Union*, February 15, 1867; Kiester, *Faribault County*, 578.

[3] *State Atlas*, February 6, 1867; *Mankato Union*, February 8, 22, March 15, 22, 29, April 5, 12 (quote), May 3, 1867.

cular stated, he had at length consented to take charge of an expedition to Montana. He proposed to follow the northern route, which he emphasized was five to eight hundred miles shorter than that over the central plains. His emigrants would travel along prairie paths blooming with flowers and feast on trout in luxuriant valleys of the Rockies. Fortune would smile on the emigrant, Davy promised, because boats laden with treasure from Montana were floating daily, even hourly, down the "turbid waters" of the Missouri.[4]

If, after this idyllic view, the prospective emigrant could bring himself to consider the humble arrangements for travel, he read the oft-repeated advice about teams, wagons, and supplies, and Davy's terms. The passage fee for one person and fifty pounds of baggage was $125. Families with their own wagons and outfits were charged ten dollars for each adult and five dollars per child. Men willing to drive wagons or perform other duties apparently could sign on to work for part of their passage fee. Davy clearly hoped to avoid some of the problems that had plagued earlier expeditions, for he stressed the mutual dependence of emigrants and the importance of a first-class outfit which would not break down and strand its owner along the trail.

Davy's announcements were received with little enthusiasm at St. Peter, Mankato's rival city on the Minnesota River. In the view of the *St. Peter Tribune,* the whole project was an outrageous form of exploitation. The editor disapproved of all the recent "Great Expeditions" to Montana, led by any "harpy or humbug" with a military prefix to his name who charged more than emigrants could afford to pay. He quoted Tom Holmes's opinion that "No man has a right to speculate on this travel over what is now a national highway, as *Plain and Easy* for one as for the other."[5]

It was not surprising that Davy raised no recruits in St. Peter, but his press campaign flourished elsewhere as spring came on. Davy was a gallant officer and an honorable gentleman, said the *St. Paul Weekly Pioneer* on February 8, and Wakefield a citizen of the highest standing. These testimonials undoubtedly impressed some possible emigrants, while others were intrigued by more unusual promotional techniques.

Davy announced that he had obtained the services of two eminent doctors to safeguard the health of those who went with him. Furthermore, he had secured an army printing press and two editors who were prepared to issue daily bulletins containing news of the expedition. In addition the march would be enlivened by a brass band under the direction of Benjamin M. Hazen, the proprietor of a St. Paul variety show. Musicians who wanted to go to Montana were urged to sign on with Hazen. The band, once organized, was a doubly useful device, for Davy sent it out on excursions to advertise the expedition.[6]

Another flood of letters to the press offered information, advice, and warnings to prospective gold seekers. Nathaniel Langford of the 1862 expedition notified emigrants of rumored Indian outbreaks along the way and advised them to follow Fisk's

[4] Davy's circular, *Ho! for the Gold Fields of Montana,* is in the MiHS library.
[5] *St. Peter Tribune,* February 27, May 1 (quotes), 1867.
[6] *Mankato Union,* February 15, March 15, June 7; *Press,* April 11, 14, May 30; *Minneapolis Tribune,* May 31, June 12 — all in 1867. Nothing more is known of either the doctors or the news bulletins.

1862 trail because it was the safest from ambush. W. A. C. Ryan and Andrew Fisk wrote of life in the gold country. Fisk urged friends to come to Montana for a few years. "Persevere," he advised, "be economical, industrious; keep away from the gambling hells with their enticing music and bewitching waiter girls . . . and sooner or later, fortune will surely smile on you."[7]

Letters from these and other Minnesotans were printed and reprinted in the newspapers, along with items from the *Montana Post* and the *Helena Herald.* Some writers, observing that the day of the pickax and shovel had already passed, urged emigrants to combine their resources and purchase machinery to work the rich quartz lodes.[8]

A more pessimistic note was struck by a former Minnesotan who signed himself "Mazaska Zi." To emigrants who planned to farm in Montana, he pointed out the necessity of building expensive irrigation ditches, hauling in wood for fences, and transporting crops fifty or a hundred miles to market. There were only two seasons in Montana, the writer continued, "late in fall and winter!" He thought the mineral resources sadly overrated, although there were many ragged persons about, he said, who still hoped to make fortunes.[9]

A useful summary of information on the gold fields was provided by the *St. Paul Pioneer* on March 2, 1867, when it printed excerpts from James W. Taylor's recently published report to the secretary of the treasury on gold mining in the territory east of the Rockies. Taylor reviewed the discoveries in Montana since 1862, gave figures on the annual production of gold, and estimated that the yield for 1866 alone would probably be worth twelve million dollars. Not forgetting the dreams of the decade, Taylor also spoke of the importance of developing transportation routes to the gold-bearing territories of the West.[10]

Meanwhile two imaginative schemes for achieving a permanent travel connection between Minnesota and Montana flourished briefly and died. One of them was a bill introduced by Ignatius Donnelly in the House of Representatives on January 15, which provided for the construction of a wagon road from Fort Abercrombie to Fort Benton for military and postal use. The road was to be financed by federal land grants. The bill was referred to the Committee on Public Lands and there died.[11]

A related project came to an equally disappointing climax in 1867. After years of memorializing and petitioning, in which Senator Ramsey played a key role, the Post Office Department was finally authorized to provide triweekly mail service to Helena over the northern route. Residents of St. Paul assumed that the contract would go to the Minnesota Stage Company, which already provided mail and stage service for a wide area in Minnesota. Early in 1867 Russell Blakeley of the company wrote to Fisk, asking to be "posted in detail, as to distances, wood, water and grass,

[7] *Press,* May 4 (quote), 17; *Pioneer,* March 30 — all in 1867.

[8] *Press,* May 4, 1867. See also, for example, *St. Peter Tribune,* January 9; *Pioneer,* January 26, March 1; *Stillwater Messenger,* March 13, May 22; *Winona Republican,* May 15; *Anoka Union,* May 23 — all in 1867.

[9] *Press,* May 2, 1867.

[10] Taylor's report was published in 39 Congress, 2 session, *House Executive Documents,* no. 92 (serial 1293).

[11] 39 Congress, 2 session, *House Journal,* 172 (serial 1280); the original bill, H. R. 996, may be found in the records of the Committee on Public Lands, NARG 233.

chances for stations, etc." Blakeley told Fisk that military protection had been promised and that mail service would be advertised soon.[12]

The Minnesota Stage Company made elaborate plans to use four-horse coaches, complete the trip in twelve days, and provide passenger and freight as well as mail service. Published reports do not indicate whether the firm intended to improve the roadway over the plains, or whether it expected this matter to be taken care of by the government under the terms of Donnelly's bill. In any case, St. Paul interests saw before them the inauguration of regular transportation and a golden opportunity for their city to become "the outfitting point and entrepot of this already great and rapidly expanding commerce of the Northwestern plains."[13]

Great was the consternation when St. Paul newspapers announced in April that the contract had been let to two relatively unknown men of limited financial resources.[14] It was reported that the contractors, whose names were Carlisle Doble and Charles E. Ruffee, intended to use ponies and half-breed riders and would make no attempt to do more than carry the mail — which was, of course, the object of the contract.

The *St. Paul Press* of April 11 prophesied disastrous results. Indians would attack solitary expressmen and failure to deliver the mail would prevent a renewal of the contract for another year. Without freight and express service there would be no chance to open a permanent road for commerce and emigrant travel; the state and St. Paul would lose millions of dollars in trade. The city's businessmen in a vain protest to the postmaster general, published in the *Pioneer* of June 5, noted gloomily that "any measure which will result in delaying the opening of this . . . route to Montana, must be regarded in the light of a calamity to the whole northwest."

As the critics predicted, the service was far from successful. Indians harassed the riders, mail was lost, and deliveries ran far behind schedule. The following year the mail contract was awarded to a Pennsylvania firm and, according to one former Minnesotan, Montana business went to Iowa instead of to Minnesota.[15]

Although the overriding concern of the St. Paul Chamber of Commerce was an acceptable mail contract, the organization took one action that proved to be of benefit to Davy. On January 22 the chamber appointed a committee to seek information from General Alfred H. Terry, commander of the Military District of Minnesota, about the protection that would be given to overland travel on the northern route. Terry promised to do everything in his power to safeguard emigration and listed a number of new forts which he expected the War Department to establish along the route.[16]

[12] *Weekly Pioneer*, May 8, 1866; *St. Cloud Democrat*, August 9, 1866; *Faribault Central Republican*, August 22, 1866. Blakeley's letter, dated January 1, was published in the *Pioneer*, March 7, 1867.

[13] *Weekly Press*, February 14, 1867 (quote); *Pioneer*, April 9, 1867.

[14] *Press* and *Pioneer*, April 9, 1867.

[15] *Press*, October 3, 1867; James H. Bradley, "Account of the Attempts to Build a Town at the Mouth of the Musselshell River," in *Montana Historical Contributions*, 2:305; *Reports of the Postmaster General*, 1867, p. 6 (40 Congress, 2 session, *House Executive Documents*, no. 1 — serial 1327), and 1868, p. 8 (40 Congress, 3 session, *House Executive Documents*, no. 1 — serial 1369). The Minnesotan's comments are in *Weekly Press*, February 20, 1868.

[16] *Pioneer*, January 23, 1867; *Press*, February 10, 1867. The latter report was copied by other newspapers; see, for example, *Stillwater Messenger*, February 13, 1867, and *Anoka Union*, February 14, 1867.

The construction of new forts was part of the army's larger strategy for guarding emigrant travel in the West. In other measures which affected the Davy expedition, the military again designated the northern trail for protection and planned to garrison forts in Dakota with enough troops to provide escort service. Except for a few minor changes, the army regulations of 1866 concerning organization and inspection of wagon trains remained in effect. Early in June, 1867, General Terry selected sites for the new posts, including three which became stopping points for the Davy train — Fort Ransom on the Sheyenne River, Fort Stevenson on the Missouri near old Fort Berthold, and Fort Shaw at the point where the Mullan Road crossed the Sun River.[17]

The correspondence with General Terry, initiated by the St. Paul chamber, received wide publicity in Minnesota newspapers and gave an assurance of military protection that indirectly assisted Davy's campaign for emigrants. Aside from this action the captain received little help from the St. Paul interests which had so enthusiastically supported Fisk in earlier years. Although capital city newspapers printed information about Davy's activities during the spring, the town was, the *Pioneer* reported on April 19, generally apathetic to the expedition. As St. Paul surrendered to indifference, Minneapolis, Mankato, and St. Cloud became the the chief points of rendezvous.[18]

Emigrants were slow to join up. A late spring, drenching rains, and flooding rivers dampened the spirits of would-be travelers. Roads were either under water or thick with mud. Highly exaggerated newspaper accounts of Indian attacks on the plains frightened some who had hoped to go west with Davy. In April a company of Canadians sent an agent to Mankato to investigate the possibility of joining the expedition; his report was probably adverse, for no further record of the group has been found.[19]

Davy's prospects brightened somewhat in May. Late in the month fifteen or twenty teams prepared to move out of the Mankato headquarters despite bad roads. Emigrants also began gathering at an expedition camp set up in Minneapolis under the direction of a Davy agent. The Minneapolis contingent was joined by a party of Civil War veterans from Hastings, traveling in ten wagons and armed with Spencer and Henry rifles. The *Minneapolis Tribune* of June 4 characterized them as men who would not grumble at the "wholesome discipline" of that "noble fellow," Captain Davy. The gold seekers camped near a brewery in north Minneapolis until a heavy rainstorm forced them to abandon their tents and take temporary refuge in a hotel. Meanwhile the brass band assembled in camp and paraded through the streets of Minneapolis to advertise the expedition.[20]

One of the men at the Minneapolis rendezvous was Samuel Anderson, a twenty-

[17] The army's strategy is described in William T. Sherman to George K. Leet, February 16, March 13, 1867, in Letters Received, Special File Indian War, 1867, Division of the Missouri, NARG 98. The new posts were provided for under Sherman's General Order 9, March 4, 1867, vol. 413C, NARG 94.

[18] On Davy's activities, see, for example, *Pioneer*, April 9, 17; *Press*, April 11, 14; *Weekly Pioneer*, April 19, May 3 — all in 1867.

[19] *Pioneer*, May 12, June 5; *Press*, May 24, 26; *Minneapolis Tribune*, June 16; *Winona Republican*, June 20; *Mankato Union*, April 5, 12 — all in 1867.

[20] *Pioneer*, June 5, 16, 18; *Mankato Union*, June 21; *Minneapolis Tribune*, May 31, June 12 — all in 1867. Davy's agent in Minneapolis may have been Jacob Emmett, Jr., in 1865–66 a member of a dry goods and grocery firm there. See his pension file, SC 263394, in NARG 15, and *Minneapolis City Directory*, 1865–66.

four-year-old Swedish immigrant who had worked on the railroads and in the Michigan copper mines before he set out for Minnesota to join the Davy expedition. While he waited for the expedition to get under way, he met Christina Lovisa Danielson, a Swedish girl who was doing housework in Minneapolis. She, too, wanted to make the trip, and she married Anderson when he agreed to pay her fare. In the same party were Anderson's brother, Gustaf, with his wife and their two young children. According to the *Minneapolis Tribune*, the expedition also included a gay divorcée who had joined up in order to escape a rejected lover. Unfortunately, the man in question also signed on with Davy, while a rival set out for Montana by a different route, intending to meet and "settle with" the first. Notwithstanding love triangles, Indian scares, and high water, great success was predicted for Davy's expedition. The main body of emigrants — about seventy men and twenty-two wagons — broke camp at Minneapolis on June 17 and started for St. Cloud.[21]

Waiting for the train at St. Cloud was another group of emigrants under the direction of Samuel E. Smith, a St. Paul mason and contractor who had been sent ahead by Davy to take charge at the central Minnesota outfitting point. The St. Cloud party included Henry Lueg, a German blacksmith and machinist whose diary of the journey, written in his native language, is the only known journal of the expedition. Lueg had come to the United States in 1861, served in the Civil War, and worked for the government in Washington, D.C., before moving to St. Paul. At St. Cloud he was assigned to a wagon which carried eight men and two women. Most of the passengers, he wrote, were Americans, but there were also Scandinavians, Germans, and Frenchmen.[22]

Some emigrants were said to have become discouraged and left the train at St. Cloud. The remainder traveled up the Sauk River Valley, following the route of the Fisk expedition of 1866. Fighting mosquitoes and picking their way through mudholes, the emigrants were encouraged on their way by the music of the brass band.[23]

Early in July the first teams of Davy's expedition began to reach Fort Abercrombie. A correspondent at the fort reported that the travelers had undergone a rough trip: "The children, poor little things, look worn out, also the female portion." Part of the Mankato group arrived after a journey up the Minnesota River Valley from Fort Ridgely. Also encamped at Abercrombie, waiting for military escort, was a large company of Germans from Stearns County who were bound for the Willamette Valley in Oregon. The temporary population at the fort celebrated Independence Day with a thirty-seven-gun salute, fireworks, and a balloon ascension.[24]

Davy's train eventually included sixty to seventy-five wagons and more than two hundred and twenty persons, half of them members of the German party bound

[21] Information about the Anderson family was obtained in an interview with Walter Dahl, St. Croix Falls, Wisconsin, in 1964. See also *Tribune*, May 29, June 1, June 30 (quote), 1867; *Pioneer*, June 18, 1867.

[22] On Smith, see *Minneapolis Tribune*, June 1, 1867; United States Manuscript Census Schedules, 1860, Ramsey County, Minnesota, p. 32; and his pension file, WC 427384, in NARG 15. On Lueg, see C. S. Kingston, "The Northern Overland Route in 1867: Journal of Henry Lueg," in *Pacific Northwest Quarterly*, 41:234–253 (July, 1950).

[23] *Minneapolis Tribune*, July 3, 1867.

[24] *Mankato Record*, July 13 (quote), 20, 1867; Kingston, in *Pacific Northwest Quarterly*, 41:236

for Oregon. At first, the Germans had been unwilling to join the expedition, convinced that their group was large enough to satisfy military regulations. Davy obviously wanted them, both in order to have a larger train and because he needed the nine-hundred-dollar fee he proposed to charge them. After some discussion a compromise was reached. The Germans agreed to travel with Davy, promising to pay three hundred dollars on the spot and an equal sum upon their safe arrival in the West.[25]

When this decision had been made, the train was organized into three companies. The expedition officers included William Cahill, adjutant; Jacob D. Rogers, in charge of ordnance and inspection; Charles H. Wagoner, aide-de-camp; and Samuel Smith, wagon master. Cahill was said to have been a major in the Fiftieth New York Volunteers. Rogers, twenty-six and born in Illinois, was a former St. Paul schoolteacher. Wagoner, a New Yorker by birth, was a clerk and southern Minnesota farmer. Both Rogers and Wagoner had served in Minnesota infantry companies and also commanded Negro troops during the war. The captains of the three divisions of the train were George H. Swartz, J. C. Rosseau, and Franz Nibler. Virtually nothing is known about Swartz and Rosseau. Nibler was one of five brothers in the German group. He was thirty-one, born in Bavaria, a farmer and millwright, and a veteran of the war.[26]

When Davy's train left Abercrombie on July 13, it started west in company with two other groups. Henry Gager, a government contractor, was conducting more than sixty wagonloads of medical and quartermaster stores to Fort Ransom, the new post on the Sheyenne River. Military escort was provided by a company of infantry commanded by Captain John L. Smyth, who was under orders to pick up a herd of beef cattle near Ransom and escort it to Fort Stevenson. Five miles along the trail the soldiers built a new bridge over the Wild Rice River, which had first been bridged by the Fisk emigrants of 1862. The Davy train followed Fisk's 1866 route, traveling the eighty miles to the Sheyenne River in five days. At Bears Den Hillock, two companies of infantry had begun construction of temporary quarters for Fort Ransom. The Davy train and the soldiers camped within half a mile of the post site until Smyth and his troops were ready to go on. The expedition band gave concerts on July 18 and 19, but apparently little but musical harmony existed in the emigrant camp.[27]

Murmurings of dissatisfaction with Davy's leadership which had been heard

[25] *Helena Weekly Herald*, October 3, 1867. For a roster of known members of the expedition, see Appendix, below. It was compiled from *Helena Weekly Herald*, September 26, 1867, and Kingston, in *Pacific Northwest Quarterly*, 41:251n.

[26] On Cahill, see *Helena Weekly Herald*, September 26, 1867. No service or pension records have been found. On Smith, see note 22, above. On Rogers, see his compiled service record, Company K, Eighth Minnesota Infantry, and 68 U. S. Colored Troops, NARG 94. On Wagoner, see service record, Company C, Third Minnesota Infantry, and 57 U. S. Colored Troops, NARG 94; pension file, XC 2683333, NARG 15. On Nibler, see service record, Company D, Fourth Minnesota Infantry, NARG 94; pension file, SC 121792, NARG 15; Kingston, in *Pacific Northwest Quarterly*, 41:251.

[27] Fort Ransom Records, 19:6, 7. Smyth's "Journal of the march . . . from Fort Abercrombie D. T. to Fort Stevenson D. T. and returning," in file 105S 1867, Letters Received, Department of Dakota, describes the route of the Davy train. For Smyth's orders, see Department of Dakota Special Orders 25–27, Department of the Northwest, 50:230, and William H. Sidell to assistant adjutant general, file 80S 1867, Letters Received, Department of Dakota. All these records are in NARG 98.

earlier on the trail broke into open rebellion during the week at Fort Ransom. On July 22 ten men, including three of the staff, petitioned Major George H. Crossman, the commanding officer at the fort, to investigate Davy's commissariat. They asserted that only "ten days' rations" remained on hand for some of the people whom Davy had contracted to subsist on the journey. Since the petitioners had supplied their own provisions, they feared that the others would be "quartered" on them, and they asked, if the supplies were found insufficient, to be allowed "to proceed without the incubus of these men."[28]

As dissension grew, the emigrants held a meeting on July 23 at which they proceeded to depose Davy and elect William Cahill as their new captain. Andrew Osland, a Norwegian "passenger," addressed a letter to Major Crossman, reciting his own grievances against Davy. Having paid the full $125 fee, Osland objected to performing any expedition duties. When he refused to work, he said, he had been roughly handled and tied behind one of the wagons. Other Scandinavians, it was later reported, felt that Davy was "brutal" and had discriminated against them. Lueg said that he was drunk and careless. Some passengers, under the impression that they had paid for transportation, objected to walking. Samuel Smith, the wagon master, was universally disliked, according to Rogers, because he was a "drunkard and blowhard" and "few if any of the train could endure his presence."[29]

Davy's problems were hopelessly complicated. He had apparently spent most of his money publicizing the expedition and was unable to buy an adequate supply of wagons, tents, and food. Far fewer emigrants bought passage than he had expected, and the supplies were inadequate even for them. Although most of the officers were capable, Smith was clearly no asset and Davy himself proved to be an inefficient manager. Whether his drinking interfered with his conduct of the train is not clear. Much of his trouble might have been avoided if he had been a more inspiring and sympathetic leader. No doubt part of the difficulty was caused by his inability to communicate effectively with the Germans and Scandinavians. All these factors reduced the expedition to utter confusion for several days.[30]

Somehow the situation was resolved, although details are lacking. A number of emigrants left the train after Major Crossman's inspection of Davy's commissary. Band-leader Ben Hazen took a job as a carpenter at the post. The unpopular Samuel Smith returned to St. Paul and publicized his own highly confused version of the expedition's affairs. Davy, reinstated as leader, was able to purchase sufficient supplies to carry the expedition through the next stage of the journey. For the moment peace reigned, and on July 25 the emigrants broke camp and fell in behind Captain Smyth's escort.[31]

[28] The petition is in "Papers connected with the Emigrant Train Commanded by (Capt.) P. B. Davy," in Letters Received, Fort Ransom Records, NARG 98.

[29] Statements of J. D. Rogers and Osland to Crossman, both dated July 23, 1867, in "Papers connected with the Emigrant Train," NARG 98; Dahl to the author, August 8, 1964; Kingston, in *Pacific Northwest Quarterly*, 41:236; *Helena Weekly Herald*, October 3, 1867 (quote). Osland's letter is printed on page 251, below.

[30] Davy was courtmartialed but found not guilty in 1865 on charges which included drunkenness. See his compiled service record, Company H, Second Minnesota Cavalry, NARG 94.

[31] *Pioneer*, August 25, 1867; *Helena Weekly Herald*, October 3, 1867; Fort Ransom Records, 19:7, NARG 98. Smith's version appeared in *Press*, August 10, and *Weekly Pioneer*, August 16, 1867; the former account is printed on page 253, below. Although the *Pioneer's* account reported that several men obtained work at Fort Ransom, the only civilian employee who can be con-

Guided by a scout from Fort Ransom, the expedition journeyed to the James River and followed it upstream for a time. After crossing the river the emigrants traveled in a northwesterly direction and on August 3 climbed onto the Coteau du Missouri near the headwaters of the Sheyenne. On August 6 the train camped on lakes five miles southwest of Dogden Butte. Little information is available about this part of the journey, but there are indications that it was not entirely pleasant. Somewhere on the plains Samuel Anderson, returning from a hunt, encountered Indians who tried to cut him off from the wagon train. Fortunately, he was able to elude them and reach camp safely. Somewhere a child died, a German woman "went crazy," two people were struck by lightning, and four dogs died of thirst and heat. On August 8 the expedition reached the Missouri.[32]

At Fort Stevenson, the new military post fifteen miles below old Fort Berthold, Davy's passengers were again short of food. Apparently the captain had to borrow money from the emigrants to pay for the supplies he purchased there. Some travelers heard unfavorable reports about the Montana gold mines and decided to obtain work at the fort. Captain Smyth, his military mission accomplished, started back across the plains for Fort Abercrombie. A new military guard was assigned to escort the beef cattle farther up the Missouri, and the Davy train tagged along behind.

Toward the end of August the emigrants reached Fort Buford, the army installation which had been started the year before a few miles below Fort Union. Here Davy faced another crisis when a number of his wagons broke down. After some argument the Germans agreed to carry the baggage and provisions of sixteen men who otherwise could not have continued the journey. At least four emigrants decided to remain at Buford.[33]

As in other years, the route beyond Fort Union was considered relatively safe from Indian attack and the train crossed Montana Territory without military escort. During this part of the journey the most exciting event of the whole summer occurred, according to the later recollections of young David Hilger. David was the eight-year-old son of Nicholas Hilger, who had gone to Montana with Holmes in 1864 and returned in 1867 for his family. Somewhere along the Milk River on September 3 the train, traveling cautiously in double column, passed a camp of about a hundred Indians. Suddenly a party of young warriors, brandishing their weapons, rode furiously toward the emigrants and ordered them to halt. In this crisis, David remembered, his father and the brass band saved the day. Captain Davy, "white as a sheet and trembling with fear," came to Nicholas Hilger and asked, "My God, what are we going to do?" The elder Hilger was equal to the occasion. "Captain," he replied, "order out the brass band at once and don't act like a cur." [34]

nected with the Davy train is Hazen. See Special Order 23, July 20, 1867, in Fort Ransom Records, vol. 41.

[32] Fort Ransom Records, 19:11, NARG 98; Smyth, "Journal of the march," July 25 to August 8, 1867, NARG 98; Dahl to the author, August 8, 1964; Kingston, in *Pacific Northwest Quarterly*, 41:236, 237; *St. Cloud Journal*, August 29, 1867.

[33] *Helena Weekly Herald*, October 3, 1867; Kingston, in *Pacific Northwest Quarterly*, 41:251n. For a conflicting version of this incident, see p. 259, below.

[34] David Hilger, "Overland Trail," in *Montana Historical Contributions*, 7:265–267 (Helena, 1910). For other versions of the affair, see *Helena Weekly Herald*, September 26, 1867, and Kingston, in *Pacific Northwest Quarterly*, 41:239. Davy's account appears on page 256, below.

Soon the astonished Indians heard the strains of "Yankee Doodle" performed by the members of the band with all the verve of a group playing for their lives. As David recalled the incident, his father then summoned the chiefs to a council, gave them trinkets, sugar, and coffee, and smoked a peace pipe with them. Other emigrants gave Davy full credit for bringing them safely through Indian country. Davy himself reported in the document printed in this text that "we dealt rigidly and fearlessly with" the Indians and "thrust them from our path."

Two weeks later, on September 16, the train camped on the Teton River near Fort Benton. Davy led the band into the bustling little village at the fort, where the inhabitants were "regaled" with "some very fine music." In spite of this pleasant interlude, the captain's relations with the German emigrants were again strained. Because their oxen were now in poor condition, they refused to carry any farther the heavy baggage of Davy's passengers, which they had taken on at Fort Buford. Davy, out of money again, wanted to sell one of the wagons and leave its passengers behind. Finally, amid much uproar and many threats of violence, a temporary agreement was reached and the train took the Mullan Road toward Helena.[35]

At Fort Shaw, where the road crossed the Sun River, a number of emigrants — Lueg says about two dozen — left the expedition to work for the government. At this point, too, Davy took a stagecoach into Helena and put his own version of the journey on the record. On September 26 the *Helena Weekly Herald* published a number of stories about the expedition. Besides Davy's account the issue contained a testimonial letter signed by William Cahill and other emigrants refuting the "slanderous" charges of Samuel Smith, which had been reprinted three weeks earlier from Minnesota papers.[36]

Davy was to need all the supporters he could get, for he had evidently determined to take legal action against the Germans in order to obtain his fees. When the train camped near Helena, Davy, accompanied by a sheriff, went out to meet it and demanded the remainder of his money from the German party. They refused to pay, protesting that in fact Davy owed them money for their services to the train. The sheriff and some twenty mounted men appeared later the same day to attach forty oxen belonging to the Germans. The case of Peter B. Davy *v.* Franz Nibler, *et al.* — heard before a jury in United States district court — was decided in favor of the Germans on October 9. Newspapers reported both sides of the affair, and the suit attracted considerable attention among the residents of Helena. After the verdict was announced Davy addressed a crowd outside the courtroom, "showing the justice of his cause, while other parties took up the defense of the emigrants." Two days later the German party, including Lueg and several Americans, prepared to go on to Oregon, free of Davy at last.[37]

Other members of the train settled permanently in the Helena area. Two Canadians, Alex and Angus Cameron, became miners and stock raisers. Louis Henry, a native of France who had lived in Hastings, Minnesota, became a pioneer

[35] *Helena Weekly Herald*, September 26, October 3, 1867; Kingston, in *Pacific Northwest Quarterly*, 41:240.
[36] See also Kingston, in *Pacific Northwest Quarterly*, 41:241. The *Helena Weekly Herald* of September 5 reprinted Smith's criticism.
[37] Brief reports of the case appear in the *Helena Weekly Herald*, October 10, 24, 1867; the original court records have not been found. See also *Weekly Herald*, October 3, 1867, and page 259, below.

in the boot and shoe business in Helena. After the first winter in Montana he went back to Hastings for his family and returned with them by steamboat. Some emigrants settled in the Gallatin Valley. Among them were the Jarvis Aikin family and Mrs. Aikin's parents, the James Aplins. Both Aikin and Aplin had gone to the Gallatin Valley from Wisconsin in 1864, farmed for two years, and then returned east for their families. Aikin established the first regular hotel in Gallatin City and the Aplins settled at Bozeman. Thomas C. Crane, a former resident of Wisconsin and Minnesota, lived at Spring Hill, Montana, for many years. There he established a water-powered blacksmith shop and invented an ingenious machine for boring fence posts which proved to be a great laborsaving device for farmers of the vicinity.[38]

Samuel Anderson went to Unionville, where he worked at the Whitlatch Mine and his wife cooked for the miners. In 1880 he took his family back to Minnesota. He and his brother Gustaf bought farms with their gold-field earnings and settled down, finally, in Lindstrom, a Swedish community in Chisago County.[39]

It is appropriate that a member of the last Minnesota overland expedition should have been one of the discoverers of a truly rich gold mine. Mose, or Moses, Manuel was a nineteen-year-old farm boy from Kelso, Minnesota, who traveled with Nicholas Hilger's party. He prospected in Montana for a year and spent nine more years searching for gold from the Mexican border to the Yukon. In 1876 he and a brother went to the Black Hills and discovered the Homestake Mine, at present-day Lead, South Dakota, the greatest body of gold ore in the world.[40]

All during the 1860s men in Minnesota and Dakota had been predicting rich gold discoveries in the Black Hills, and Peter Davy, his Montana expedition concluded, saw new fields to conquer. In the early months of 1868 citizens of southern Minnesota supported him in plans for a gold-seeking expedition to the hills that was touted as "an initiatory step towards opening a leading thoroughfare to the rich sections of Dakotah, Idaho, and Montana." The campaign was marked by public meetings, memorials to Congress, a promotional circular, and tours of other states to recruit emigrants and support. But all was lost in April when the government set aside the Black Hills as an Indian reservation and forbade the expedition to enter the area. Peter Davy made one last attempt to capitalize on his plains experiences. In 1869 he helped organize a touring expedition of Sioux Indians with their "lodges, ponies, carts, dogs, implements of war and the chase." Unfortunately, bad weather forced the promoters to abandon the enterprise after a few weeks, and Davy settled down to a quiet life in Blue Earth.[41]

[38] On the Camerons, see *Helena Independent*, April 19, 1909. On Henry, see *Helena Weekly Herald*, May 13, 1887; *Independent Record* (Helena), February 10, 1950. On the Aikins, see Leeson, ed., *Montana*, 631, 1096; *SMP Register*, 95. On Aplin, see *SMP Register*, 96; *Avant Courier*, June 30, 1887. On Crane, see Leeson, ed., *Montana*, 1302.

[39] Dahl to the author, August 8, 1964.

[40] See "The Discovery of the Homestake Mine" and "New Details on Trail of Hidden Gold," in *Southern Minnesotan*, 1:2, 23–26 (March, 1931), 2:16 (April, 1932); United States Manuscript Census Schedules, 1860, Sibley County, Minnesota, p. 27.

[41] Kiester, *Faribault County*, 246, 256, 281 (quote); *Mankato Union*, January 3, 1868; *Winona Weekly Republican*, February 15, March 11, May 16, 1868; George W. Kingsbury, *History of Dakota Territory*, 1:870 (Chicago, 1915). Files of the *Minnesota Southwest* (Blue Earth) from January 4 to May 16, 1868, also contain references to the Black Hill expedition. A copy of the promotional circular, *Captain P. B. Davy's Expedition*, is in the MiHS library.

Interest in travel across the plains continued in Minnesota, and scattered parties may have found their way overland by the northern routes after 1867. However, by 1868 travelers could reach Montana more easily by way of the Union Pacific Railroad and stage or freight branch lines. The Missouri River steamboat companies, reducing their fares, competed briskly for passengers and freight. As promoters of the northern Pacific railroad appealed to Congress for a cash subsidy to complete their line, hopes for a northern overland route now centered on various railroad projects.[42]

Meanwhile, Senator J. M. Howard of Michigan, chairman of the Committee on Pacific Railroads, summarized the aspirations of the upper Middle West for a northern railroad in words which echoed the rhetoric of the 1850s: "We, too, want our share of the benefits of intercourse with that wonderful coast and the rich and beautiful regions that intervene. . . . We want to reach the mines . . . to settle up those magnificent territories. We want quick and easy access to the East Indies and to see goods from China and Japan as well as the gold and silver of our northwestern mines passing down our long chain of lakes. In short, we want a fair chance to act our part and achieve honor and renown in the accomplishment of the great destinies of the American people held out in the future."[43]

The history of the northern overland expeditions to the Montana gold fields represents a brief chapter in man's long search for El Dorado and a prologue to the building of the northern Pacific railroads. It is a story of commercial ambition on a global scale, but it is also the story of restless Americans moving west, some knowing, some never comprehending, the broader significance of their journey. The following pages present the last episode in this story, told in the fragmentary and sometimes contradictory records of Peter Davy's expedition, the last to cross the northern plains.

[42] *Minneapolis Tribune,* February 22, 1868.
[43] *Press,* May 17, 1867.

1867 ✸✸✸✸✸✸✸✸✸✸✸✸✸✸✸✸

Letters from the Davy Expedition

"MONTANA" TO THE EDITOR OF THE ST. CLOUD JOURNAL[1]

Davy's Montana Expedition,
Ft. Ransom, D[akota] T[erritory], July 19th, 1867

EDITOR JOURNAL: Our march from St. Cloud to Fort Abercrombie was almost equal to General [Frederick] Steele's "mud march" through the black swamps of Florida and Alabama but, with a good stock of perseverance, we arrived at Fort Abercrombie on the 9th instant.[2] The expedition was then organized into companies, and a captain selected for each. Davy appointed his staff, and preparations were made for a speedy advance. The officers were as follows:

Capt. P. A. [*sic*] Davy, commanding; Bvt. Maj. Wm. Cahill, Adjutant; Capt. J. D. Rogers, Ordnance and inspecting officer; Capt. Chas. Wag[o]ner, A. D. C. [aide-de-camp]; Captain George Swartz, Co. A; Capt. [J. C.] Rosseau, Co. B; Capt. [Franz] Nibler, Co. C.

The train is composed of about one hundred and thirty men, and as many women and children. There is a good deal of dissatisfaction among Captain Davy's passengers, as they were promised a *ride* when they wished it, but the teams are so heavily loaded that they are obliged to walk all of the way. They think it rough to pay $125 for the privilege of *walking* to Montana. Who can blame them?[3]

We started from Fort Abercrombie on the 13th in company with a government train, and a detail of one hundred soldiers. We arrived here on the 17th, and are waiting now for the military to get ready for a forward movement. Yesterday some of us visited the place where an Indian was burned alive by his Indian captors, not long since. The carcass is still unburied. The limbs only were burned away. Indian rumors are abundant, but any one who is accustomed to the frontier and half-breeds knows how to take their reports. The latest is that there are five hundred

---

[1] The letter is reprinted from the *Montana Post*, August 31, 1867. It originally appeared in the *St. Cloud Journal*, August 10, 1867, but no copy of that issue has been found. The author's identity is unknown.

[2] Steele led a column of 13,000 men from Pensacola to Mobile during the Mobile campaign of 1865. Mark M. Boatner, *The Civil War Dictionary*, 559 (New York, 1959).

[3] Davy's circular stated that fifty pounds of baggage would be carried for each passenger, but did not promise transportation for the emigrant himself.

lodges two days drive ahead of us, and fifteen hundred lodges advancing on Fort Rice. These reports were brought in yesterday by scouts from Fort Sully.[4] We have plenty of buffalo beef, most of it obtained from hunters.

Since writing the above a scout has arrived from the James river. He states that there is an abundance of Indians on this side of the Missouri river, in consequence of the buffalo having come this way. He states that he saw five half-breed scalps and one white scalp and arm, which the Indians say they took from Ruffee's men who were carrying the mail, having killed the entire party.[5] They also had eight horses and five mules, which they found on the plains. This would give credence to a report that Gen. [Alfred H.] Terry had been attacked. The scouts from Fort Rice are due to-morrow morning. I give the reports as I get them from the scout.

Our men are splendidly armed. There are some thirty or forty Henry's sixteen shooters, besides various rifles, carbines, shot guns, etc., and scores of revolvers. The corral is composed of sixty wagons, and is large enough for all of our stock. The grass is splendid, and the stock all looks well.

The health of the party is good, there not being any sick in camp that I know of. One child died after we left Fort Abercrombie, having been previously injured by a shaft of lightning.

We think we will get through all right, by keeping a sharp lookout for our stock. Capt. Davy is as *spirited* as ever, but we are in hopes that his *spirits* will give way to his better judgment when we get out where there is danger. More anon,

MONTANA

ANDREW OSLAND TO GEORGE H. CROSSMAN[6]

At Fort Ransom D.T. July 23rd 1867

TO THE COMMANDING OFFICER OF FT. RANSOM, D.T.

SIR: I am a passenger of "Capt Davy's great expedition to Montana for health and wealth."

Mr. Davy told me that he would not take me with his said expedition for less than 125 doll[ar]s, as he had hired men enough for $50. I had 160 acres of land in Minnesota and, as he said he would take three persons through to Montana for the land, I handed him a deed for it, and thus paid him 375 dollars, which the land was worth and more too.

Davy never spoke to me that I had any thing or duty to do along the road. First at Fort Abercrombie he ordered me to work, and when I told him that I think he cannot command me to work, he became angry and said he would hand me the deed back, and that I and the two men I have paid for, had to leave the camp. I

[4] The writer may refer to an attack made several weeks earlier by a party of Sioux on a half-breed camp at Bears Den Hillock, in which several Sioux and some half-breeds were reportedly killed. For this incident and the reports of the scouts, see Fort Abercrombie Records, 3:65, 79, 116, NARG 98. Fort Sully, established in 1863, was situated on the Missouri about twenty-five miles above present-day Pierre, South Dakota.

[5] Charles Ruffee was one of the mail contractors for the northern route. See page 241, above, and *St. Cloud Democrat*, September 5, 1867.

[6] The original letter is in "Papers connected with the Emigrant Train," NARG 98. Osland has been identified as a Norwegian; see Dahl to the author, August 8, 1964. Although Osland claims below to have served in the Civil War, no military service or pension records have been found.

said that I was satisfied with his offer, but he has never handed me the deed back, and therefor I had to follow his expedition.

When we were some 50 miles west from Ft. Abercrombie Davy ordered me again for duty, and when I answered I would no extra work do except he pays me back $75, as I would not pay more than $50. as the rest of my countrymen, and as they had not done more than I. Thereupon he ordered his "Adjutant," or jackcatch,[7] to tie my hands together on my back, and put a halter round my neck, and thus tie me to the wagon, which was done of the so-called Capt [Samuel E.] Smith, and thus I had on that way to walk along, though I was some lame in my one leg, in consequence of that the guard first had dragged me along and hurted me. I was bound to the wagon from forenoon till late in the afternoon without dinner, as also I got no dinner some days, but had me under guard, and had to lay upon the ground without tent &c. Mr Davy ordered a court martial the other day before we arrived here. There was much of talking and motions in respect to what punishment I ought to get, but no sentence yet.[8]

When we (23 men), who have no other flower [flour] than the spoiled Red River meal, did complain for Davy about the said meal, as we can back [bake] neither bread nor pankake of it, he became angry, and said among other [things] that he should take the wagon from us, and that we ought to go along and pick turnips for food &c. I have walked the road all along except a couple miles. Davy has promised me tent, but none got. If I had had not by a chance a tent myself, I had had to sleep on the ground without tent. My clothes he took from me at St Cloud and sent them on another train to Ft. Abercrombie. When the clothes arrived there [they] were all spoiled as them had been wet a long while, and some of them were away, and lost for me.

I have no money here. If I had I had to buy provision like some others who have changed away their guns for milk which the Germans have to sell in camp.

My purpose is to write about Capt. Davy's treatment toward me, when in Montana, to my Government and also publish it through the press. Meanwhile I have here taken liberty to give you a statement of what has befallen me, and ask you, sir, if possible to order that I can be spared for a repetition of a such barbarous treatment as above told, and which I believe is in all regard without reason as it is unjust.

I remark that I told the whole crowd, before Capt Davy tied me up, that I shall do guard duty when all liable men in the camp also stand guard after tour, and that I have been on guard here and will continue if all stand as I. Besides I have to say that I have done about the same work along the road as them who have paid $50, and which my countrymen and others can say, too.

I beg you excuse me and my poor writing, which I cannot well do better here in this camp. I am yours respectfully

ANDREW OSLAND

I have been a soldier three years in the U.S. service the late war.

[7] A "Jack Ketch" is a public executioner or hangman, so named from a notorious seventeenth-century English executioner.

[8] According to one report, Davy ordered Osland to be hanged, but other emigrants opposed such an action. Dahl to the author, August 8, 1964.

NEWS FROM SAMUEL E. SMITH [9]

CAPT. S. E. SMITH, Adjutant General of Capt. P. B. Davy's great Montana Expedition, arrived in the city yesterday and brings late news from the expedition.

After leaving this vicinity, the company proceeded to Fort Abercrombie, where there was some trouble and delay in completing the organization. The expedition, when fully organized, consisted of two hundred and twenty-seven persons, men, women and children.

After leaving Fort Abercrombie all went well until they neared Fort Ransom, when a difficulty arose. Twenty-one German families, numbering 114 persons, were with the expedition.[10] They had provided themselves with provisions sufficient to supply them until they reached the end of their journey. As it appeared certain that the subsistence provided for the remainder of the company would prove entirely insufficient, these Germans became frightened lest the provisions of the others should fall short, and they would levy upon them, and thus starvation or great distress ensue.

A meeting for consultation was called at Fort Ransom, after which Capt. Davy's command of the expedition terminated.

At Fort Ransom thirty persons, comprising six families, left the expedition. Among them is Ben Hazen, who is working for the government at the Fort, at the carpenter's trade.[11]

Mr. Smith went on with the expedition until they reached Fort Berthold, on the Missouri river, when accompanied by an Indian guide and interpreter, he started on his return.[12]

About one hundred miles this side of the Missouri, and eighty miles beyond Fort Ransom, he saw in the distance about two hundred and fifty Indian tepees, comprising thirteen hundred and fifty Indians.

His Indian guide became frightened and tried to give Smith the slip, at one time taking to his heels, and flying like a deer. Smith, however, being on the watch, gave chase, lassoed the Indian and securing him to his horse, compelled him to keep in advance, letting him know that if he led him astray or tried to escape, he would kill him.

Smith was compelled to do this, as of course, without a guide and in a hostile region, escape would be next to impossible. As it was, he was compelled to travel at night, and rest during the day.

After reaching Fort Ransom, an escort and ambulance was provided by the Commandant there to convey Smith to Fort Abercrombie, from which point he

---

[9] This news story was printed in the *St. Paul Press*, August 10, 1867. Another account, varying in details, appeared in *Weekly Pioneer*, August 16, 1867.

[10] There were seventeen German families, according to Kingston, in *Pacific Northwest Quarterly*, 41:236.

[11] See p. 245n, above. Smith claimed that he succeeded Davy as leader of the train, but gave up the job in annoyance after a day or two. See *Weekly Pioneer*, August 16, 1867.

[12] In spite of this statement, Smith undoubtedly left the expedition at Fort Ransom. The train did not reach the vicinity of Fort Berthold until August 8; Smith was in St. Paul on August 9. Captain Smyth reported no concentration of Indians between Ransom and Berthold. See his "Journal of the march," July 25 to August 8, NARG 98.

came to Minneapolis, where he was confined to his bed for several days, and on arising from which, he came directly to this city.[13]

Capt. Smith thinks that upon reaching Fort Berthold, the expedition will be compelled to procure more provisions, or a large portion be obliged to stop there and work, to obtain the means of living or of going on to Montana.

We give the facts as narrated by our informant, as being of interest to those who may have friends in the company. Mr. Smith is stopping with H[enry] S. Temple, of this city, where he will give all the information in his power to any one desiring to hear more fully in regard to the expedition.

NEWS FROM PETER B. DAVY[14]

CAPT. P. B. DAVY, commanding the Minnesota emigrant expedition, arrived in this city yesterday morning. He left Sun river — at which point the rear guard of his train was encamped — on Friday, and came through to Helena by coach. The whole expeditionary force, numbering upwards of three hundred persons, (among whom are some forty families), are now probably across the Dearborne [Dearborn River], and a considerable portion of the number will be in camp near town by Tuesday next. The little Captain, — in whom we recognize an old Minnesota friend,[15] — expresses his satisfaction with the success attending his trip across the plains on the Northern route, and says the whole journey was performed without loss of life, Indian troubles, or accidents of moment occurring to any of his party. A number of the emigrants he brought out with him are bound through to Oregon, but the major portion of those having families with them are going into the Gallatin valley to settle. These sturdy yeomen of the North have brought with them, stock, farming implements, nails, window-sash, glass, and everything essential to opening up new homes in the rich and charming agricultural lands of the Gallatin.

Capt. Davy, who will spend some weeks in Helena and the mining districts hereabouts, will have ample opportunity afforded him of forming his own views of our mineral wealth, and the energetic people engaged here in developing the golden resources of the mountains. Just now, the sprightly Captain, with his short legs encased in top-boots, his compact body dressed in buckskin coat and jacket, his resolute visage adorned with a lusty growth of hirsute, and his top-knot unscathed by scalping knife, covered by a broad brimmed felt hat, is the centre of attraction for crowds of our people, who are attracted by something more than curiosity in beholding and having a "confab" with the "little man" who has safely brought from the Northland, through the whole length of the Indian country, a colony of permanent settlers for Montana. Captain Davy, who contemplates returning to Minnesota this Fall for the purpose of organizing another expedition next spring, gives us to understand that if our people properly encourage him in his efforts, he will pioneer through from the States another season a much larger body of emigrants than has

---

[13] The ambulance was sent, not primarily to convey Smith, but to pick up the quartermaster and his wife at Fort Abercrombie. See J. Chester White to post adjutant, Fort Abercrombie, July 27, 1867, in Fort Ransom Records, vol. 1, NARG 98.

[14] This account and Davy's letter, below, appeared in the *Helena Weekly Herald*, September 26, 1867.

[15] Davy had been Andrew Fisk's commanding officer in Company H, Second Minnesota Cavalry.

yet in any one year reached our enchanting and richly blessed Territory. Once known in the States that his expedition this year reached the land of golden promise in safety — all the predictions indulged in by thousands of Minnesotians to the contrary notwithstanding — Capt. Davy tells us what we have every reason to believe is true, that a host of the irrepressible Northmen will impatiently await his coming to enroll themselves under his leadership to be guided through to the mines and valleys of Montana next spring.

The Captain has placed in our possession a list of the names of his expeditionary force which will appear in the *Herald* of Tuesday.[16]

To the Editors of the Herald: Gentlemen: Agreeable to your request, I herewith transmit, together with a partial list of the members of the party composing my expedition, by the Northern route, just about closed, some few notes, which as data, may be of interest to the public.

In the matter of organizing and marshaling my party at the Fort Abercrombie rendezvous, I had, as you must be well aware, many adverse circumstances and the reports of threatened Indian difficulties to contend against; and while these things detracted largely from the number who had enrolled themselves to come, they also contributed to the delay of my starting until quite a late day in the season.

I may say, also, that the unusually wet season which prevailed during the spring throughout Minnesota and the Northwestern States rendered the first three hundred miles of our march from the central points in the State, west, somewhat tedious and slow. From this cause (the impassability of the roads), there were likewise very many teams that started from Wisconsin and southern Minnesota, actually compelled to lay up and abandon their journey, and give up their intention of joining me at the rendezvous.

However, by the 13th of July I had got together at Abercrombie, ready for the march to the plains, what I regarded as a party sufficiently strong and abundantly provided with means of protection, to render our journey across, secure and expeditious, and we moved out on that day as far as the Wild Rice river.

We found the plains covered with a most luxuriant growth of grasses, all the small lakes, ponds, streamlets and springs on our march to the Big Bend of the Sheyenne, (which we made over the trail established by Col. Fisk last year), bounteous in their supply of excellent pure water, plenty of wood at all camping places, and a sprinkling of small game spiced our larder acceptably. On reaching the Great Bend of the Sheyenne, known and christened by the Northern Sioux as "Bear's Den" — a favorite resort and camping place of the natives — we found here established a new military post, called Fort Ransom, and manned by two companies of the 10th Infantry, commanded by Major [George H.] Crossman. Learning at this point that Capt. Smith [John L. Smyth], with his company, "I," 10th Infantry, was soon to start for Fort Berthold, (or Stephenson [Stevenson], as the new post at that point is called), he having the duty of escorting 200 beef cattle across, we sojourned at Fort Ransom some eight days in order to avail ourselves of this addi-

---

[16] The list, which appeared in the issue of September 26, was used to compile the roster of the expedition in the Appendix, below. The names of those who went on to Oregon are given in Kingston, *Pacific Northwest Quarterly*, 41:251n.

tional protection, mutually, through the Coteaus, which was regarded as the most dangerous part of the route.

Leaving the Fort on the 24th of July, we enjoyed an uninterrupted and very pleasant journey — the whole route being literally alive with herds of buffalo and other game — to Fort Stephenson, where we arrived on the 9th of August, all well and the stock in fine condition. Here we again laid by several days to rest man and beast, and to give Lieut. [Cornelius C.] Cusick and escort, of the 31st U. S. Infantry, time to join us, which he did, and accompanied us as far as Fort Buford — adjacent to Fort Union. From Union to Benton (as had been the entire road over which we had traveled), I never saw or anticipated so desirable and delightful a natural route for travel. The published itinerary of distances, camping places, locality, quality and quantity of wood, water and grass, as published by Capt. Jas. L. Fisk from the records of his pioneer trip to and across the mountains over this route, I found to be in every way correct and reliable, and having a copy in my possession I felt it to be invaluable. This little book was, in fact, my sole guide, and it brought us through successfully.[17]

While on the march up Milk river, we met several tribes of Indians, among whom were Assiniboines, Yanktonais, Gros Ventres, etc. The Assiniboines and Yanktonais united in an effort to stop the progress of my train, and threatened us with war if we did not deal out to them the greater portion of our provisions and livestock. Not seeing it, however, in the same light as the savages viewed the matter, we dealt rigidly and fearlessly with them, thrust them from our path and moved on without experiencing further disturbance. Without suffering the loss of a single man, woman or child, (but on the contrary called upon to chronicle an increase to our numbers),[18] or sustaining any accident worthy of note on the entire journey, we arrived at Fort Benton on the 19th inst., feeling, in view of the fact that all other overland routes or thoroughfares from the East to Montana have been totally blockaded the whole season, and that no other train whatever had been able to get through, thankful indeed for our good fortune, and more than ever convinced of the many superior advantages which the Northern route possesses over the older and more Southern ones.

After reaching Sun river with my train, I took passage in the stage for this city, where I arrived on the 21 inst., and shall expect the main column into camp, near by, today. As you will perceive by the accompanying roster, there are a goodly number of families in the party — just such material as is most valuable in giving stability to society and in subduing the rough elements of your new and promising Territory.

Quite a number of these families are headed for the Gallatin valley, and are well provided for commencing life in their new homes to advantage.

It is now my purpose to return to Minnesota this fall, and prepare for entering upon this work on a grander scale, and to more account next season.

What Montana wants are actual settlers who will come here for permanent homes, and to practically develop her great mineral, agricultural and manufacturing resources, and if, as you have generously suggested, those who have at heart the

[17] Davy probably refers to Fisk's guidebook, *Idaho,* which would have been useful for the route beyond Fort Union.

[18] Nothing more is known of a child born during the journey.

future welfare of the Territory, should signify their willingness to render me some material encouragement and assistance in this work, I shall endeavor to render a full and entire equivalent therefor. As I have said, I go back to Minnesota to bring out next season my own family and as many neighbors as will join me; but I feel confident that by proper and judicious aid and encouragement I can as well bring a colony of three thousand as three hundred.

The following is a partial list of names of the party who left Minnesota with me, and who are now within a day's march of this city. My rolls not being at hand, accounts for the incompleteness of the list: [19]

JACOB D. ROGERS TO THE EDITOR OF THE ST. CLOUD JOURNAL [20]

Helena, Montana Territory. October 4th, 1867

EDITOR JOURNAL — I have delayed writing to you till I got settled, and could get some correct ideas of what Montana is but before saying anything about the country, I will occupy a few lines in sketching our journey across the plains, to the famous country of *dust*.

From Fort Ransom we took an entirely new road to Fort Stevenson, a new fort sixteen miles below old Fort Berthold — having a halfbreed guide, who understood the country perfectly. We arrived at that point August 8th, at Fort Buford on the 23d, and Fort Benton on the 17th of September. Between the last two named forts we had the finest hunting I ever saw. There was an abundance of buffalo, deer, elk, antelope &c., so that we had plenty of fresh meat, more particularly so, while on Milk River. We passed through a number of Indian camps all seemed friendly except one of the Yanktonais. They stopped the train and virtually forced us to give them some presents; we preferring that to a fight.

We arrived at Helena about the 25th of September, in good condition, having had no serious accidents, or bad luck. This has been a fine season for crossing the plains, as there was but little hot weather. The grass was good most of the way, but the stock was rather thin after so long a journey.

Capt. Davy filled the expectations of his friends after we left Fort Ransom. I think he is well qualified to bring a train over the plains. He certainly had a great deal to contend with. Minnesota was not anxious to lose any of her inhabitants, and consequently gave him no material assistance. The Indian reports were so unfavorable that hundreds gave up going after they had made preparations for the journey. He had expended a large sum of money in getting up the expedition, and when the time arrived for its departure there were only hundreds where he had been assured there would be thousands, and consequently a very small amount of money coming to him, besides men who had pledged him assistance abandoned him. Therefore he was without sufficient transportation or provisions for his passengers. This has caused a good deal of trouble, and his ability to command a train is very much doubted by some, but only by those I think, who are not aware of

---

[19] The names of the party are omitted here. See Appendix, below.

[20] The letter appeared in the *St. Cloud Journal*, November 7, 1867. On Rogers, see page 244, above. He wrote at least two other letters about the expedition. See *Press*, October 20, 1867, and *Helena Weekly Herald*, October 3, 1867.

the disadvantage he has been laboring under, or who have not appreciated the same. One thing is certain he brought the train safely through a hostile Indian country, and he surely managed the hostile Indians we encountered, splendidly. Had it not been for his good judgment and discretion I think we might have been robbed, if not massacred. "Honor to whom honor is due," is my motto. I opposed him strongly when I thought him wrong, and upheld him when I thought him right.[21]

Well I must pass to the subject, Montana. I should not have occupied so much space with the above, had it not been for reports that have been published which injure Capt. Davy and do him injustice.

Many of the men in the train who had no families, hired out at Benton and Fort Shaw — a new fort on Sun river — for wages ranging from $60 in dust to $125 in greenbacks, per month, and board. The former wages for teamsters, and the latter for brickmasons. Carpenters got $100 in currency from the Government. One hired as a baker and cook for $85 in dust. Helena is rather dull at this season of the year. Some of our party have gone into ranches, some to chopping wood, and some to prospecting. Wood pays about $2.25 in currency per cord for chopping. Board is from $8 to $15 per week in dust, but any one who wishes to can live cheaper, by boarding himself. There are plenty of houses to rent. From all I can see, there is a better chance here for men who are not doing very much in the States. But no one must expect luck here who is not a stirring, diligent person. I have met some of my acquaintances who came here last year, and they are all doing well, and speak well of the country. It is hard to tell much about it till one has been here during at least one summer. The winters are very dull.

I take great pleasure in acknowledging the receipt of a beautiful little flag, from St. Cloud, marked "From your lady friends," which was intended I presume for a Fourth of July present, as it was mailed in the latter part of June to my address at Fort Abercrombie. It was forwarded, and reached me on the fourth of October instead of July. "Sic transit gloria mundi." I trust I shall have the pleasure of wearing that same little flag in *St. Cloud,* some pleasant Fourth of July. All thanks to the fair donors.

I have written at such length that I fear I have wearied your patience. I will be more brief in the future, and hope I may have something to say about this country next time that will be more interesting to your readers. Yours,

J. D. ROGERS, JR.

P.S. Capt. Davy is going back to Minnesota across the plains, this fall, with a pony train. A number of men have already joined him.

A REPORT ON THE DAVY TRAIN [22]

CONSIDERABLE has been said and written about this individual and the train of emigrants which he has brought overland this season. It appears that the irrepressible Captain is to be the subject of still further interest, which at the present

---

[21] Rogers refers, no doubt, to his participation in the events at Fort Ransom, when he was a signer of the petition to Crossman and the secretary of the meeting that deposed Davy. See p. 245, above.

[22] This account appeared in the *Montana Post,* October 5, 1867.

writing it is not altogether assured will redound to his credit. As it is a matter that will come up for adjudication before the Courts, and the matter will then be thoroughly unraveled, we give both sides of the story as we can ascertain them from reliable sources, leaving our readers to form their own conclusions.

In the train which Davy brought over, or, more properly speaking, which brought over Davy, were a number of German emigrants whose destination was Oregon, and who, he claimed, owed him $600 as the price which they agreed to pay for the privilege of accompanying him overland. On last Friday the Germans started from their camp near Silver City on their way to Oregon, whereupon D. sued out a writ of attachment, and officer Alexander and another deputy Sheriff went out to serve it. On coming up with the train and making known their business, the Germans thought it was a "little joke" of their former quasi Captain's and politely told the officials they "couldn't see it," in fact that if an attempt was made to seize their cattle they would resist. Not being prepared for this kind of a demonstration, the officers came back and reported, when a posse of twenty-four mounted and well armed men was sent out, and the seizure was completed without any trouble.

This is the Captain's story, the Germans have another. It appears that an agreement was made at Fort Abercrombie between the Germans and Davy to the effect that in consideration of his taking them from that point to Walla Walla they were to pay him $600, one half of which was paid down, the balance to be given him at Walla Walla, or if it would not inconvenience the parties, at Helena. After considerable delay the train started, the Germans, as a general thing, traveling by themselves. Between Abercrombie and Union, Davy's train gave out and he was unable to haul the baggage and provisions of nearly sixty passengers whom he had contracted to take through at $125 per head, to Helena. He endeavored to obtain transportation in another train, but failed, and the Oregon party, whose teams were in better condition, took the freight of the whole party and provisions for eighteen men, some of the freight they took to Benton and some to Silver City.

Between Union and Benton Davy's party became short of provisions, and they mutinied, putting a rope around his neck and threatening to hang him. Wishing to save Davy's corpse from enhancing the beauties of the landscape in that section, the Germans told them they would furnish provisions until they arrived at Helena, which they did. At Benton, we believe an arbitration was had to make an estimation of the compensation the Oregonians were to receive for accommodating Davy in the manner they had, and the arbitrators decided that he owed them $440, which left a balance in their favor of $140. This they resolved to sacrifice rather than lose time in trying to collect it, and consequently started as previously mentioned. We understand an effort is being made to adjust the difficulty, but with what result we have not learned.

The train is mostly composed of families, and there are some forty children in it. The case cannot possibly come up at this term of court, and if they have to remain until the next term, untold suffering will be the consequence.[23] Much injury will also result to the Territory by the reports which these parties will send back to their friends.

[23] The suit was decided in favor of the Germans on October 9. See page 247, above.

1862-67 ❀❀❀❀❀❀❀❀❀❀❀❀❀❀❀❀
WAGON TRAIN ROSTERS

1862-67 ✸✸✸✸✸✸✸✸✸✸✸✸✸

Wagon Train Rosters

THE NAMES OF EMIGRANTS who are known to have traveled with each expedition have been compiled from rolls kept by the train leaders, newspaper references, diaries, letters, and reminiscences. Additional biographical material has been supplied from such sources as census schedules, military and pension records in the National Archives, personal interviews and correspondence with descendants of emigrants, and from genealogies, county histories, and other printed works. Specific sources for each roster are listed in the applicable textual footnotes above. For some expeditions — such as the 1862 Fisk train — the rosters are probably fairly complete. For others — like the 1866 Holmes train — the names of less than half the emigrants are known.

In the entries below, the emigrants for whom only a first or last name is known are listed at the beginning of each roster. Unless more reliable evidence for the name was found elsewhere, the form of the name as given on expedition rolls appears first. A question mark preceding a name indicates some doubt as to whether the person actually accompanied the train. Parentheses are used to indicate alternative names or spellings of names, and the first, maiden, or later married names of women. Brackets are used to enclose information which can be reasonably, but not certainly, associated with the person whose name appears on the roster. A few combined entries list a whole family, particularly when detailed data is available for the father only.

Any combination of the following known data about the emigrant appears after his name. The first item given is the emigrant's place of residence before he embarked on the western journey. The abbreviation "b.," for birth, precedes the place and date of birth. The place and date of the emigrant's death

follow the abbreviation "d." The symbol "r.," indicating residence, appears in many entries which give information — largely derived from census records or city directories — about places an emigrant lived at a given date. The abbreviation "ret." indicates that the emigrant is known to have returned East. The last item in the entry has to do with the occupation or profession of the person named. Town and county names not otherwise identified are located in Minnesota.

THE HOLMES TRAIN, 1862

The following emigrants are known only by a first or last name: Alec, Dutch Henry, Dutch Joe, John, Tom; Chambers, Corkergus, Danson, Gardner, Sherwood, Shoteau, Tracy, Whitcomb. Baptiste and Michelle were guides.

Beveridge, Francis. St. Paul. r. Nevada, 1863. lawyer

Bowers, Joseph. Le Sueur Co. b. 1828, Württemberg, Ger. r. Bannack, Mont., 1862. farmer

Brown, [George W. d. 1864, Madison Co., Mont. outlaw]

Butterfield, [David T. b. 1837, Me. r. Le Sueur Co., 1860. d. 1864, Memphis, Tenn. farm laborer]

Cady, Vallencourt H. Spring Lake Twp., Scott Co. b. 1810, Vt. r. Mont., 1862. real estate dealer

Calkins (Collins), W. H. [Henry]. Spring Lake Twp., Scott Co. [b. 1830, N.Y. r. Scott Co., 1860. farmer]

Chase, [Franklin], and nephew. Shakopee. [b. 1823, R.I. r. Shakopee, 1860. merchant]

Clark, ——. St. Paul d. 1863, Bannack, Mont.

Curtis, Francis E. St. Paul. b. 1833, De Ruyter, N.Y. d. 1900, Anaconda, Mont. carriage maker, butcher, stock raiser

Cuthbert, William

Flickner, T. [Thomas. Shakopee]. r. Virginia City, Mont., 1864

Francis, John. [b. 1826, Wales. r. Blue Earth Co., 1860. farmer]

French, Ernest M. Kasota. b. 1836, Ontario Co., N.Y. r. Divide, Mont., 1899. carpenter

French, Marcus L. Kasota. b. 1808, N.Y. r. Mont., 1864. farmer

French, Willard S. Kasota. b. 1843, Mich. r. Bannack, Mont., 1863. farmer

French, [Zelie. b. 1830, Eng. r. Waseca Co., 1860. ret. Stearns Co., 1866. farmer]

Grindell, John H. St. Paul. b. 1822, Md. ret. St. Paul, 1863. mechanic, carpenter

Hall, Amos W. St. Paul. b. 1824, Mass. ret. St. Paul, 1866. real estate dealer

Holmes, Thomas A. Shakopee. b. 1804, Bergerstown, Pa. d. 1888, Cullman, Ala. real estate dealer, townsite promoter, Indian trader

Hoyt, Freeborn F. Red Wing. b. 1833, Ohio. d. Red Wing. physician

Hoyt, John F. St. Paul. b. 1830, Ohio. d. 1905, Valley Co., Mont. lawyer, real estate dealer

Hutchinson, D. S. St. Paul. b. 1825, Pa. r. San Francisco, Calif., 1862. dentist

Ledbeater, Mark D. Breckenridge. b. 1830, Kent, Eng. d. 1911, Bozeman, Mont. hotelkeeper, merchant, farmer

Little, John [R.]. St. Peter. [b. 1835, N.C. r. Le Sueur Co., 1860. laborer]

Lovell, Philip. St. Paul. b. 1840, Yorkshire, Eng. r. Dillon, Mont., 1899. butcher, stock raiser

McDowell, Alex

Mahony, Richard

Milwaine, [John]. St. Paul. r. Calif., 1862. [b. 1820, N.Y. r. Ramsey Co., 1860. carpenter]

Miner, A. [Alonzo]. St. Peter. [b. 1838, Ill. r. Nicollet Co., 1860. farmer]

Moore, E. r. Bannack, Mont., 1864

Morrison, Wilson C. St. Paul. b. 1815, Whitehall, N.Y. d. 1892, St. Paul. farmer, merchant

Newhall, H. C. St. Paul. r. John Day River, Ore., 1863

Osier, Antoine. guide

Potter, John. Long Prairie. b. 1836, Athens, Me. d. 1915, Los Angeles, Calif. farmer, merchant

Potter, [Maurice. b. 1833, Vt. r. Long Prairie, 1860. laborer]

Potter, [Melville]

Salter, [Eugene]. Shakopee. [b. 1851, Iowa. r. Eagle Creek Twp., Scott Co., 1860]

Salter, F. Chase [Horace]. Shakopee. [b. 1823, N.Y. r. Eagle Creek Twp., Scott Co., 1860. farm laborer]

Seaburger [Seburger, Peter. b. *ca.* 1823, Prussia. r. St. Cloud, 1860. d. 1876, St. Cloud. brewer, hotelkeeper]

Smith, Lewis E. Le Sueur Co. b. 1812, Vt. r. Mont., 1862. farmer

Spencer, John B. St. Paul. b. 1820, Ky. d.

1904, Alameda, Calif. carpenter, builder, sawmill operator

Steele, Henry B. St. Cloud. r. Texas, 1875. merchant

Stockton, ——. r. Dalles, Ore., 1862. physician

Strickland, ——. [St. Paul] r. Hot Springs, Deer Lodge Valley, Mont., 1863

Terwilliger, N. Barney. St. Paul. b. 1835, N.Y. r. John Day River, Ore., 1862. painter

Turrell [Turrill, J. A.]. Le Sueur. r. Beaverhead, Mont., 1862. [b. 1830, Vt. r. Le Sueur, 1860]

Vandenburg, C. C. St. Paul. b. 1829, Mich. r. Pikes Peak Gulch, Mont., 1862. carpenter

Vater [Vaiter], James C. St. Paul. [b. 1832, Eng. r. St. Paul, 1860. butcher]

Wells, Albert. Shakopee. b. 1830, N.Y. hotel porter

Wyman, Charles. Hennepin Co. b. 1831, Me. r. Alder Gulch, Mont., 186–. lumberman

Wyman, Wooster. Hennepin Co. b. 1837, Me. r. Alder Gulch, Mont., 186–. lumberman

THE FISK TRAIN, 1862

?Aitkin, E. E. Detroit, Mich.

Arnell, A. L. (F.). Minneapolis. r. Prickly Pear, Mont., 1862. painter

Arnold, John M. Wabasha. r. Mont., 1874. teamster

Ault, John. Fort Ripley. b. 1819, N.Y. d. 1874, Bozeman, Mont. hotelkeeper, sawmill worker

Barrows, Isaac. St. Anthony. r. Walla Walla, Wash., 1862

Bartlett, William F. Minneapolis. b. 1823, Cortland, N.Y. d. 1921, Butte, Mont. hotelkeeper, merchant

Bentley, David. Otter Tail Co. b. 1828, Mass. r. Davenport, Iowa, 1875. farmer

Biddle, George W. St. Paul. r. Bannack, Mont., 1863. dentist

Biddle, Mrs. George W. (Emma). St. Paul. r. Bannack, Mont., 1863

Bond, Samuel R. St. Paul. b. 1832, Ipswich, Mass. d. 1922, D.C. lawyer

Bottineau, Daniel. Hennepin Co. b. 1846, Minn. guide

Bottineau, Pierre. Hennepin Co. b. 1810, Red River, Can. d. 1895, Red Lake Falls. guide

Boyd, William. St. Cloud. r. Prickly Pear, Mont., 1862

Boyden, E. R. Minneapolis. r. Prickly Pear, Mont., 1862

Bray, Cornelius. St. Paul. b. 1833, Clonmel, Ire. d. *ca.* 1908, Red Rock, Mont. tinsmith, hardware merchant

Bray, Patrick C. Sibley Co. b. 1829, Clonmel, Ire. d. 1893, Henderson. mill and lumber business

Brown, Joseph A. St. Anthony. d. 1863, Mont.

Brown, Richard T. Minneapolis. r. Prickly Pear, Mont., 1862

Burritt, Elihu H. St. Paul. r. St. Paul, 1870s. law clerk, stationer

Cardinell (Caldwell), Peter. Little Falls.

Carrick (Cormick), Theodore. St. Anthony. r. Walla Walla, Wash., 1862. teamster

Carrick, W. J. St. Anthony. r. Walla Walla, Wash., 1862

Castner, John M., St. Paul. b. 1815, Alderbaugh, Me. d. 1876, Bozeman, Mont. hotelkeeper, mayor, Virginia City, Mont.

Castner, Mrs. John M. (Henrietta). St. Paul. b. 1842, Pa. r. Bozeman, Mont., 1876

Charlton, David W. St. Anthony. b. 1829, N.Y. d. 1863, Mt. Pleasant, Martin Co., Ind. civil engineer, surveyor

Clark, Thomas H. St. Paul. b. 1820, Va. d. 1908, Townsend, Mont. gunsmith, farmer, freighter

Clement, Andrew A. St. Anthony. b. 1814, Clairmont, N.H. d. 1882, Minneapolis. hotelkeeper

Clifton, Thomas. St. Cloud. b. 1832, Eng. r. Prickly Pear, Mont., 1862. laborer

Cobb, Charles E. St. Paul. b. 1810, S.C. r. St. Paul, 1873. butcher, rancher

Cobb, George A. St. Paul. b. 1848, Ill. d. St. Paul, 1916. grocer

Conner (O'Connor), Thomas J. St. Paul. b. 1838, N.Y. r. Virginia City, Mont., 1864. tailor

Dalton, Alvin. Faribault. b. 1846, Wis. r. Virginia City, Mont., 1864

Dalton, Margaret. Faribault. b. 1859, Wis. r. Virginia City, Mont., 1864

Dalton, Matilda (Mrs. Z. B. Thibadeau). Faribault. b. 1843, Holton, Me. r. Anaconda, Mont., 1918

Dalton, Or(r)in. Faribault. b. 1849, Wis. r. Virginia City, Mont., 1864

Dalton, William P. Faribault. b. 1797, Me. d. 1864, Virginia City, Mont. farmer

Dalton, Mrs. William P. (Clara). Faribault. b. 1811, Can. d. 1864, Virginia City, Mont.

Davenport, Mr. and Mrs. L. W. St. Anthony. ret. 1863

Dibb, William D. St. Anthony. b. 1827, Eng. d. 1871, St. Anthony. physician

Dobbins, George. St. Paul

Dobbins, Mike J. St. Paul. r. Virginia City, Mont., 1863. miner

Doney, Enos. Wright Co. r. Prickly Pear, Mont., 1862

Donnelly (Donley), Mary A. G. (Mrs. Eugene Stickney). St. Paul. r. Virginia City, Mont., 1863

Donnelly, Scott. St. Paul. r. Prickly Pear, Mont., 1862

Dougherty, Patrick. Minnesota. b. 1837, Ire. d. 1920, St. Paul. farm laborer, stockman

Dow, James G. Henderson. b. 1809, N.H. d.

1881, Helena, Mont. grocer, restaurant operator

?Dudley, George W. Chicago, Ill.

Dunphy, Elijah M. St. Anthony. b. 1833, New Brunswick, Can. d. 1889, Helena, Mont. rancher, miner

Durgan, Mrs. Catherine A. (Mrs. Edward Whitcomb). St. Anthony. b. 1825, New Brunswick, Can. d. 1888, Tenmile Creek, Mont. hotelkeeper

Durgan, John H. St. Anthony. b. 1846, Me. r. Prickly Pear, Mont., 1862

Egnell, Albert. Ramsey Co. b. 1835, Sweden. r. Helena, Mont., 1860s. servant, stage-line operator

Ells, Robert S. Fort Ripley. b. 1835, Me. r. Cartersville, Mont., 1885. rancher, lumberman

Fenton, William A. St. Anthony. r. Prickly Pear, Mont., 1862

Fergus, James. Little Falls. b. 1813, Shawton, Glasford Parish, Lanarkshire, Scot. d. 1902, Lewiston, Mont. millwright, rancher

Fisk, James L. White Bear Lake. b. 1835, Royalton, N.Y. d. 1902, Minneapolis. promoter, expedition leader

Folsom, David E. Minneapolis. b. 1838, Epping, Rockingham Co., N.H. r. Palo Alto, Calif., 1916. teacher, rancher, banker, miner

Forbes, Hiram. Faribault. r. Prickly Pear, Mont., 1862

Forbes, Mrs. Hiram (Mary). Faribault. r. Prickly Pear, Mont., 1862

Gere, George. Fort Abercrombie, Dak. Ter. ret. 1862. Sioux interpreter

Gilham, Alonzo. Fort Benton, Mont. r. Prickly Pear, Mont., 1862

Godfrey, Ard. St. Anthony. b. 1813, Orono, Me. d. 1894, Minneapolis. millwright

Gould, Danville. St. Anthony. r. Prickly Pear, Mont., 1862

Graham, W. H. H. Faribault. b. 1817, N.Y. r. Bozeman, Mont., 1870. miner

Hacket(t), D. D. Troy, Winona Co. r. Prickly Pear, Mont., 1862

Haggerman, J. P. St. Anthony

?Hall, Benjamin. Chatfield

Hall, Francis. r. Walla Walla, Wash., 1862

Hall, William. London, Eng. r. Prickly Pear, Mont., 1862. butcher

Halliday, Robert. London, Eng. r. Bannack, Mont., 1863. artist

Hammond, C. H. St. Anthony. r. Prickly Pear, Mont., 1862

Hamper (Semper), William [J. W.]. Sauk Rapids. [b. 1833. d. 1878, Helena, Mont.]

Hanson, William. Minneapolis. r. Walla Walla, Wash., 1862. lumber dealer

Harrison, Henry C. Minneapolis. b. 1828, Wilmington, N.Y. d. 1895, Harrison, Mont. farmer, grocer, lumberman

Herrmann (Heman), Charles W. Mankato. r. Prickly Pear, Mont., 1862

Homer, John L. [Peter]. Chatfield. [b. 1847, Prussia] r. Prickly Pear, Mont., 1862

Iddings (Giddings, S.J.), Caleb W. St. Paul. d. 1876, Blackfoot, Mont. miner

Kinney, William. St. Anthony. r. Prickly Pear, Mont., 1862

Kirkpatrick, Thomas. St. Anthony. r. Prickly Pear, Mont., 1862

Klein, C. H. Fort Ripley. r. Prickly Pear, Mont., 1862

Knox, Robert C. St. Paul. b. 1823, Westmoreland Co., Pa. d. *ca.* 1888, Butte, Mont. merchant, probate judge, miner

Kruitz (Kritz, Browitz), John. St. Anthony. b. Ger. d. Helena, Mont. farm laborer, miner

Langford, Nathaniel P. St. Paul. b. 1832, Westmoreland, N.Y. d. 1911, St. Paul. banker, author

McIntyre, George. Sauk Rapids. r. Prickly Pear, Mont., 1862

McKenzie, B. F. St. Anthony. r. Walla Walla, Wash., 1862. laborer

McKenzie, J. O. St. Anthony. r. Walla Walla, Wash., 1862

McLellan, Alex. Can. r. Walla Walla, Wash., 1862

Mannheim (Manahan), John T. Chatfield. b. 1823, Prussia. d. 1879, Madison Co., Mont. brewer, baker

Marsden, James. Mounds View. b. 1843, Toronto, Can. r. St. Paul, 1902. farm laborer, miner, fruitgrower

Maxwell, Oliver H. St. Paul. b. 1815, N.Y. r. Virginia City, Mont., 1865. steamboat captain, mining speculator

Miles (Mills), Charles. St. Anthony, ret. Minn. 1863

Mitchell, William H. St. Anthony. d. 1863. outlaw

Moore, Hugh. St. Anthony. b. 1835, Ire. d. 1891, Helmville, Mont. herder, farmer

Moore(s), John D. St. Anthony. [b. 1835, Va.] r. Prickly Pear, Mont. 1862

Noyes, George Raymond. Hennepin Co. b. 1832, Chesterfield, Me. d. Butte, Mont. shipbuilder, blacksmith, rancher

Olin, Benjamin F. St. Anthony. b. 1845. d. 1929, Spokane, Wash. blacksmith, rancher

Olin, Giles S. St. Anthony. b. 1822. d. 1877, Butte, Mont. blacksmith, machinist

Olin, Mrs. Giles S. (Cornelia P.). St. Anthony. [b. 1834]. d. 1880, Deer Lodge, Mont.

?Owne, Caroline. St. Anthony

Putnam, Arthur. N.Y.

Rockwell, Orson J. Little Falls. r. Fairweather Gulch, Mont., 1863. miner

Rogers, Charles T. (G.). St. Anthony. r. Portland, Ore., 1862

Rowell, William A. St. Anthony. b. Me. ret. Minneapolis, 1862. teamster, merchant

St. Clair, Charles. St. Paul. b. 1823, Eng. d. 1873, Virginia City, Mont. clerk, miner, butcher

Shaw, Nathaniel L. Liverpool, Eng. r. Prickly Pear, Mont., 1862

Shepherd, J. H. St. Anthony. r. Prickly Pear, Mont., 1862

Silsby, I. C. St. Anthony. r. Walla Walla, Wash., 1862

Spencer, R. M. St. Paul. r. Rees River, Nev., 1863. [steamboat captain]

Spencer, William B. St. Paul. r. Prickly Pear, Mont., 1862

Stark, Josephus. Manchester, N.H. b. 1832, Manchester. d. 1905, Twin Bridges, Mont. soldier, hotelkeeper

Stark, Mrs. Josephus (Mary J.). Manchester, N.H. r. Twin Bridges, Mont. hotel, boardinghouse keeper

Stark, Julian Fisk. b. Dakota Ter., 1862. d. 1950, Kingman, Ariz. laborer, hotelkeeper

Strong, E. M. St. Cloud. ret. Minnesota, 1863

Sturgis, William. Little Falls. b. 1817, Can. d. 1901, New Smyrna, Fla. farmer, townsite proprietor, lumberman

Sutherland, David S. Stearns Co. r. Prickly Pear, Mont., 1862

Sutherland, William. Stearns Co. r. Prickly Pear, Mont., 1862

Tabour (Tabor, Saborn, L.I.) L. T. Minneapolis. ret. Minneapolis

Tyler, Joseph H. St. Anthony. b. 1834, Me. r. Prickly Pear, Mont., 1862. lumberman

Tyler, Mrs. Joseph H. (Caroline Abbott). St. Anthony. r. Prickly Pear, Mont., 1862

Tyson, E. J. Raymond. Staten Island, N.Y. ret. N.Y., 1862

Valentine, A. (L.) D. St. Anthony. r. Walla Walla, Wash., 1862

Whitman, Joseph P. (John). St. Louis, Mo. r. Prickly Pear, Mont., 1862

Wickham, George J. St. Anthony. [b. 1820, Ithaca, N.Y.] r. Virginia City, Mont., 1870. farmer

Wildman, John H. St. Anthony. b. 1835, Bangor, Me. d. 1909, Deer Lodge, Mont. saddler, hotel clerk, bailiff

Wright, William. Little Falls. r. Bannack, Mont., 1869

Young, James (M.). St. Anthony. r. Walla Walla, Wash., 1862. laborer

THE FISK TRAIN, 1863

Adams, Louis M. Fort Ripley. b. 1832, Mass. teamster

Anderson, J. [Joseph] R. [Skookum Joe, Richard Dick. b. Eng. d. 1898, Billings, Mont. prospector]

Balen, James

Bastien, Baptiste

Berg, Conrad

Bernardet, Felix

Brooks, John

Bruyère, Isidore

Campbell, Richard D. Pembina, Dak. Ter. deserted July 26, 1863

Clandening, William H. Wellington, Can. b. 1834, Walkerton, Can. d. 1914, Carman, Man. mining engineer, farmer, flour miller

Cobb, Charles E. See Fisk 1862 roster

Cochran, Charlton. Middleville, Wright Co. b. 1844, Iowa. farmer

Coulon, Emil

Crocker, B. F. Wis. r. Helena, Mont., 1868. prop. billiard hall

Dart, George W. St. Paul. b. 1837, Mt. Clemens, Mich. d. 1895, Dillon, Mont. tinsmith, hardware merchant

Denslow, Ellsworth H. N.Y.C. b. 1838, Enfield, Conn. d. 1913, Stockton Springs, Me. stockbroker, banker

Devereaux, Jeff

Dibb, John. Brooklyn Twp., Hennepin Co. b. 1830, Eng. farmer

Dibb, William D. See Fisk 1862 roster

Elliott, Leroy. Minn. r. Mont., 1863. teamster

Estes, Simeon. St. Paul. b. 1835, Lewiston, Me. d. 1909, Dillon, Mont. painter, freighter, rancher

Farmer, Louis

Favor, George E. b. 1845. r. Mont., 1863. teamster

Fisett, Peter

Fleuri, Firmin. [Dan Fleury. r. Helena, Mont., 1868. saloonkeeper]

Freniere, Antoine. Yellow Medicine. b. 1838, Minn. d. Dak. Ter., 1864. guide, interpreter

Gere, George. See Fisk 1862 roster

Glass, William. [Minneapolis. b. 1810, Scot. r. Minneapolis, 1860. carpenter, fur dealer]

Glover, Martin. Middleville, Wright Co. b. 1830, Scot. farmer

Gray, [Adjadews? name illegible]

Hamel, Jos. O.

Hannay, Peter. D.C. d. 1880, D.C. lawyer

Hesse, Frederick G. D.C. b. Prussia. r. D.C., 1863. professor of mathematics, U.S. Naval Observatory

Hingston, John G. St. Anthony. b. 1816, Ire. r. Minneapolis, 1860. ship's carpenter

Hiron, Léger

Holyoke, William H. St. Paul. b. Syracuse, N.Y. d. 1863, Mont. messenger, U.S. Indian office, St. Paul

Hooper, C. P.

Johnston, Samuel H. r. Fort Rice, Dak. Ter., 1865. journalist

Kendrick, J. [Joseph] H. [b. 1819, Ky. r. Winona Co., 1860. farmer]

McEwen? [name illegible], Andrew. [b. 1830, Scot. r. St. Anthony, 1860. laborer]

Major, John. D.C.

Marceau, Antoine. b. 1840, Quebec, Can. d. 1906, Butte, Mont. miner, wagonmaker

Marfield, Nicholas

Merrill, Thomas G. Taylors Falls. b. 1839, Comstock, Mich. r. Helena, Mont., 1885. teacher, surveyor, manager mining company

Miller, Hugh

Mohr, Joseph

Neudick, Louis. St. Anthony. b. 1820, Württemberg, Ger. d. 1864, Dak. Ter. butcher

Northup, George. b. 1841, Ohio. d. 1870, Duluth

Quigg[s], James. [b. 1832, New Brunswick, Can. r. St. Anthony, 1860. lumberman]

Rieth, Eugene. Benton Co. b. 1841, France. farm laborer

Rogers, John G.

Scherow, Albert

Scott, William C. [b. 1814, Pa. r. St. Paul, 1860. d. 1867, Helena, Mont. vegetable dealer]

Smith, Gurdon W. Taylors Falls. b. 1820, Ohio. r. Bitterroot Valley, Mont., 1863. lawyer

Stanley, Reginald. Minn. b. 1838, Hayle, Cornwall, Eng. d. 1914, Bexhall-on-Sea, Eng. businessman, industrialist

Torbet, Andrew M. Taylors Falls. b. 1813, Aberdeen, Scot. d. 1900, Boston, Mass. Baptist minister

Tucker, John

Voringer, Louis

Watson, J. C.

Younglove, Albert C. Cleveland, Ohio. r. Haiti, 1865. ornithologist

THE HOLMES TRAIN, 1864

The following emigrants are known only by a last name: Barney, Bartlett, Garner, Goodman, Grant, Merrit, Riley.

Allen, Joseph. Saratoga Springs, N.Y. [b. 1834, N.Y. r. Saratoga Springs, 1860. Negro, hack driver]

Babcock, Fred. Middletown, Conn.

Babcock, Henry. Middletown, Conn.

Bear, Benjamin. Eyota. b. 1821, Pa. r. Helena, Mont., 1864. farmer

Beckwith, Albert [Alfred J.]. Middletown, Conn. [b. 1829, R.I. r. Middletown, 1860, 1876. expressman]

Benedict, Gilbert. Glens Falls, N.Y. b. 1830, Glens Falls. d. 1920, Helena, Mont. harness maker, farmer

Benson, G. S. Monroe Co., N.Y. physician

Benson, L. W. Monroe Co., N.Y.

Blake, John M. Dak. Ter. b. 1840, Hope Center, N.Y. d. 1927, Helena, Mont. dentist, rancher, stock raiser

Brounworth, John. Shakopee. [b. 1823, Württemberg, Ger.] d. 1864, Mont. [farmer]

Bruce, Hezekiah. Goodhue Co. b. 1833, Vt. ret. Minn. 1865. farmer

Bushnell, G. W. Saratoga, N.Y.

Bycraft, John. Milwaukee, Wis.

Chamberlain(e), Collins [Colins S.]. Middletown, Conn. [b. 1831, Conn. r. Middletown, 1860, 1876. pewterer]

Clark, C. P. (P. T.). St. Anthony. b. Fair Haven, [Conn.] d. 1864, Fort Rice, Dak. Ter.

Cole, Harry. Eagle Creek. b. 1843, Baltimore, Md.

Constans, Philip. St. Paul. b. 1836, Deimeringen, Dept. du Bas Rhine, France. d. 1902, Unionville, Mont. saloonkeeper, merchant

Cooper, Thomas E. Pine Island. b. 1824, Ire. d. 1915, Grafton, N.D. farmer, supt. of schools, businessman

Crossman (Krossman), Mr. and Mrs. Adam and family. Adam, b. 1826, Ger. r. St. Paul, 1860. d. *ante* 1896, Helena, Mont. mason

Cutler, Charles. Pine Island. b. 1825, N.H. r. Eyota, 1860. ret. Minn. 1865. farmer, town commissioner, Last Chance Gulch

Cutler, Henry. Pine Island. b. 1824, N.H. r. Eyota, Minn., 1860. farmer

Dibb, Thomas. St. Cloud. b. 1825, Eng. r. Virginia City, Mont., 1864. farmer

Fay, James. Saratoga, N.Y.

Fenton, Henry. Glens Falls, N.Y.

Foote, George B. N.Y.C. b. 1838, Canton, N.Y. d. 1908, Helena, Mont. lawyer, civil engineer

Fountain, Henry. Middletown, Conn. r. Helena, Mont., 1865

Gleason, Jerimiah. Scott Co., Ohio

Gleason [Gleeson], John. Scott Co., Ohio. [d. 1866, Helena, Mont.]

Goodale, George. Middletown, Conn.

Grommisch, Nick. Chaska. b. 1841, Luxembourg. d. 1890, San Antonio, Tex. shoemaker

Hair, James. Shakopee. r. Mont., 1864

Hanchild (Handsheidt), George. Minn. b. 1863, Minn. r. Boulder, Mont., 1912

Hanchild, Hannah (Dakota). b. 1864, Dak. Ter. r. Helena, Mont., 1870

Hanchild, Henry A. Minn. b. Ger. d. *ante* 1896, Helena, Mont.

Hanchild, Mrs. Henry A. (Karline Hansen). Minn. b. *ca.* 1816, Den. d. 1881, Helena

Hanchild, John R. Minn. b. 1859, Nebraska (Utah). d. 1912, Boulder, Mont. deputy sheriff, policeman, bartender

Hartwell, Joseph W. St. Paul. b. 1834, Windham, Vt. d. 1899, Twin Bridges, Mont. miller, lumberman

Henry, Trume. Shakopee. r. Helena, Mont., 1864

Higginson, John. Middletown, Conn. [b. 1840, Ire. r. Middletown, 1860. laborer]

Higginson, William. Middletown, Conn. [b. 1840, Ire.] r. Helena, Mont., 1865. [laborer]

Hilger, Matthew. Henderson. b. 1834, Luxembourg. d. 1889, Helena, Mont. farmer, miner

Hilger, Nicholas. Henderson. b. 1831, Luxembourg. d. 1913, Helena, Mont. miner, stock raiser

Hopefield, P., and family. Minn. r. Helena, Mont., 1899 [Fred R. Hoffeldt. b. 1822, Hanover, Ger. r. Rice Co., 1860. farmer]

Howard, William. Middletown, Conn.

Howe (Hase, Haws), Edwin, N.Y. b. 1831, London, Eng. r. Helena, Mont., 1899. bank courier, grocer, hotelkeeper, stock raiser

Howe, Mrs. Edwin (Catherine Denn). N.Y. r. Helena, Mont., 1899

Ingham, Malcomb [Malcolm S.]. Middletown, Conn. [b. 1836, Conn. r. Middletown, 1860, 1876. mechanic, salesman]

Irving, Thomas W. Ashland, Dodge Co. b. 1830, Can. ret. Minn. 1867. farmer, miner

Jenjes, Paul

Jennings, H. S. Hastings. ret. from Fort Union, 1864. lawyer

Johnson, Buckley. Middletown, Conn. [b. Conn., 1833. r. Middletown, 1860. machinist]

Jurgens, John H. Shakopee. b. 1843, Hanover, Ger. d. 1922, Kalispell, Mont. blacksmith, merchant, miner

Keep, James H. Eagle Creek. b. 1848, De Kalb Co., Ind. r. Adrian, Mo., 1889

Keep, Oliver D. Eagle Creek. b. 1816, Painesville, Ohio. r. Cherryvale, Kan., 1889. steamboat captain, farmer

Kennedy, Ed. Shakopee. [b. 1832. d. 1877, Butte, Mont. livery business]

Kennedy, Frank. Shakopee.

King, Sidney. Saratoga, N.Y.

Kloeden, William. Yankton, Dak. Ter. b. 1829, Saxony, Ger. r. Helena, Mont., 1899. miner

Kopp, Xavier (Saffer, Sappher). Eagle Creek. b. 1839, Württemberg, Ger. d. 1864, Mont. farm laborer

Kratke (Kratkie), Paul. Kelso. b. 1838, Prussia. r. Helena, Mont., 1896. farmer

Kratke, Mrs. Paul (Darkus). Kelso. b. 1842, Ind. r. Helena, Mont., 1896

Krum (Crumb), Hiram. Glens Falls, N.Y. b. 1819, Middlebury, Schoharie Co., N.Y. d. 1904, Glens Falls. carpenter, building contractor

Landon, William. Middletown, Conn.

Le Brash, Mr. and Mrs. ——. Minn. r. Helena, Mont., 1896

Lemlein, Martin. Minn. d. *ca.* 1889, Helena, Mont. rancher

Lemlein, Mrs. Martin (Katharine). Minn. b. 1808. d. *ante* 1896, Helena, Mont.

Little, Daniel. Scott Co., Ohio

Lowry, Thomas J. Dodge Co. b. 1836, Crawford Co., Pa. d. Helena, Mont., 1886. lawyer

Marshall, Henry. Saratoga, N.Y. b. 1809. d. 1886, Red Mountain City, Mont. probate judge

Marvin, John B. St. Cloud. b. *ca.* 1845, N.Y. d. 1899, American Forks, Utah. tinner

Maxwell, A. [Amos] S. Saratoga, N.Y. ret.

1866 [b. 1822, N.Y. r. Saratoga Springs, 1860. d. *ante* 1872. lawyer]

Moore, William S. St. Cloud. ret. St. Cloud, 1865

Nichols, Benj(amin) D. Middletown, Conn.

Norris, D. G. Glens Falls, N.Y. ret N.Y., 1867. rancher, miner

Ramsdel (Ramsdale), Joe (l). Sauk Centre. b. 1837, Me. r. Deer Lodge, Mont. dairy farmer

Rep, S., and son. Saratoga, N.Y.

Rowland, E. S. Saratoga, N.Y.

Schnetz, Stephen. Minn. b. 1837, Switz. r. Rocker, Mont., 1899. merchant

Scott, W. Minn. ret. Minn., 1865

Selfridge, George. N.Y. b. 1826, N.Y. d. 1915, Butte, Mont. carpenter, contractor

Shannon, Capt. A. B. Lee, Mass.

Shober, John H. Bon Homme Co., Dak. Ter. b. 1832, Lovetsville, Va. d. 1925, Helena, Mont. lawyer

Smith, S. Minn. ret. Minn., 1865

Somerville, John C. Shakopee. b. 1810, Vt. d. 1889, St. Paul. ship's carpenter, lumberman, farmer, miner

Somerville, Mrs. John C. (Sophronia). Shakopee. b. 1822, N.Y. d. 1872, [Shakopee]

Stevens, Ed. Lee, Mass.

Strait, Trume [Freeman D.]. Shakopee. [b. 1843, Pa.] r. Prickly Pear, Mont., 1864. [farmer]

Tibbetts, John H. Shakopee. b. 1826, N.Y. ret. from Fort Union, 1864. jeweler

Van Sands, L. [Lucius] J. Middletown, Conn. [b. 1834, N.Y. r. Middletown City, 1860. bellhanger]

Walden, Joseph. Middletown, Conn.

Walworth, Ed. Eagle Creek. b. 184–, Mich.

Wells, B. Mich.

Wells, Frank. Weathersfield, Conn. b. 1828, Weathersfield. r. Radersburg, Mont., 1899. merchant, blacksmith, stock raiser

Weydert, Paul. Shakopee. d. 1901, Lewistown, Mont. wagonmaker, farmer, rancher

Weydert, Mrs. Paul (Mary A. Geyermann). Shakopee. b. 1836, Waldeck, Coblenz-on-Rhine, Ger. d. 1924, Lewistown, Mont.

Weydert, Peter C. Shakopee. b. 1864, Shakopee. r. Jacksonville, Fla., 1924. farmer, stock raiser

White, George W. (F.). Shakopee. b. *ca.* 1830. d. 1905, Helena, Mont. bricklayer, miner

THE FISK TRAIN, 1864

The following emigrants are known only by a last name: Daniel, Dresser, two Hawthorn families, Keem, Kenyon, McCarthy, Murphy family, Picott family, Walker.

Apgur [Apgar], Milo. Shakopee. [b. 1843, N.Y. r. Shakopee, 1860]

Bowles, William. St. Paul. [b. 1797, Mass. r. Fillmore Co., 1860.] livery business, bartender

Brumbaugh, Isaac. Anoka. b. 1827, Pa. r. St. Francis, 1860. teamster

Burson, George W. White Bear Lake. b. 1835, Kalamazoo Co., Mich. r. Thompson Falls, Mont. farmer, hotelkeeper

Chemidlin, August. Roseville. b. 1821, France. farmer

Chemidlin, Nicholas T. Roseville. b. 1843, N.Y.C. r. Fort Benton, Mont., 1899. newspaperman

Clark, Charles J. St. Cloud. [b. 1831, N.H. r. Anoka, 1860. painter]

Delany, Joseph. St. Cloud. r. Helena, Mont., 1866. printer

Dibb, William D. *See* Fisk 1862 roster

Dilts, Thomas Jefferson. Monticello. b. *ca.* 1825, Me. d. 1864, Dak. Ter. laborer

Dostaler, Louis

Dow, Henry S. [H.] St. Anthony. [b. 1834, Me. r. St. Anthony, 1860. millwright]

Dow, Lloyd. St. Anthony

Fewer, Walter. St. Anthony. b. 1832, Ire. d. 1864, Dak. Ter. lumberman, teamster

Fisk, Van Haden. White Bear Lake. b. 1840, Conneaut Harbor, Ohio. d. 1890, Helena, Mont. farmer, newspaperman

Fuller, [N. J. Anoka. b. 1823, Me. r. St. Francis, 1860. farmer]

Greaves (Grimes), Walter. White Bear Lake. d. 1864, Dak. Ter.

Harris, William E. [William A. b. 1842, Jerusalem, N.Y. d. *ca.* 1905, Melrose. farmer]

Johnson, James. Minneapolis. teamster. [b. 1825, Scot. r. Medina, 1860. ship's carpenter]

Johnston, Samuel H. *See* Fisk 1863 roster

Larned, Horatio H. Anoka. b. 1845, Hudson, Mich. r. Lansing, Mich., 1923. cattle herder, log driver, businessman, banker

Larned, William L. Anoka. b. 1817, Oxford, Mass. d. 1872, Lansing, Mich. mill operator, insurance company official

Larned, Mrs. William L. (Elizabeth J. Benson). Anoka. b. 1822, Groton, N.Y. d. 1892, Lansing, Mich.

Lennon, Isaac P. Anoka. teamster. [b. 1843, Me. r. St. Anthony, 1860. mill worker]

Libby, Charles L. Anoka. b. 1844, Limerick, Me. d. 1911, Redlands, Calif. teamster, Methodist minister

Libby, William W. Anoka. b. 1837, Me. d. 1892, Saco, Me. teamster, carpenter

Lovering [Loverin], Robert A. St. Anthony. [b. 1840, Wis. r. St. Anthony, 1860. teamster]

Marsh, George W. St. Paul. [b. 1837, Wis. r. Wabasha Co., 1860. printer]

Mitchell, Eugene F.

Neudick, Louis. *See* Fisk 1863 roster

Phebe, A. I.

Salmon, Billy. b. Pa. d. 1866, Dak. Ter.
Semper, Joseph H.
Shuler (Shular), Benjamin. Anoka. b. 1834, Pa. r. Anoka, 1860; [Mont., 1865]. millwright, teamster, carpenter
Shuler (Shular), Robert G. Anoka. b. 1832, Pa. r. Anoka, 1860; [Mont. 1865]. millwright
Sims, Charles F. St. Anthony. b. 1831, Jefferson Co., N.Y. r. Grand Forks, N. D., 1905. druggist, grain elevator manager
Sims, Erwin W. Anoka. b. 1837, N.Y. r. Helena, Mont., 1868. merchant
Smith, W. Ellis. engineer
Sykes, Harry N. Minn. b. 1830, Pendleton, N.Y. r. Mont., 1899. farmer
Wilson, George. Anoka. teamster

THE HOLMES TRAIN, 1866

The following emigrants are known only by a first or last name: Jo; Bruncer, Tillie, Williams.
Barron, [Norman. b. 1835, Vt. r. St. Mary, Waseca Co., 1860.] d. 1867, Cave Gulch, Mont. [farmer]
Beebe, Fred
Blackmore, Lew. trapper
Brown, Luther M. Shakopee. b. 1823, Rutland Co., Vt. d. 1886, Shakopee. lawyer
Cantankerous Jack. [b. ca. 1831, Eng.]
Christie, Hugh. Martintown, Can.
Davis, William. guide
Doyle, John. Prior Lake. ret. Prior Lake
Easterly, Allen M. Goodhue Co. b. 1843, Jackson Co., Mich. r. Radersburg, Mont., 1885. miner, sheriff
Erwin, David. Waseca. r. Waseca, 1924
Erwin, Eugene A. Waseca
Erwin, Sidney H. Waseca. b. 1847, West Constable, N.Y. d. 1924, Forsyth, Mont. miner, livery business
Freeman, Henry. ret. from Fort Union, 1866. herder
Fuller, Randall (Randolph). Faribault
Hare, James. Shakopee. *See also* James Hair, Holmes 1864 roster
Henderson, John. Pestigo, Wis. r. Virginia City, Mont., 1867. miner
Irving, Thomas W. Dodge Co. *See* Holmes 1864 roster
Johnstone, James. r. Virginia City, Mont., 1867. miner
Johnstone, William. Hamilton, Ont., Can. b. 1829, Axletrewell, Hodain, Scot. ret. Can., 1867
Kidd, Bill. Minn.
McAndrews, Mr. and Mrs. James
McCall, Neil. Prior Lake. b. 1841, Can. r. Prior Lake, 1869
McCall, Silas M. Prior Lake. b. 1843, Roxborough Twp., Can. r. Prior Lake, 1869
McGuire, Pat. 11 U.S. Inf.

McLoud, Donald. Roxborough Twp., Can.
?Manuel, Fred (Ferdinand). Kelso. b. 1846, Three Rivers, Quebec, Can. d. 1897, Los Angeles, Calif. miner, prospector
Medworth, [John. b. 1835, Eng. r. St. Mary, Waseca Co., 1860.] d. 1866, Cave Gulch, Mont. [farm laborer]
O'Brien, Richard. Faribault. b. 1848, N.Y. r. Faribault, 1867
?Palmer, Frank. Minn. r. Fort Benton, Mont., 1867
Parisian, Jean. Pembina, Dak. Ter. [Baptiste Parisan. b. 1828. r. Pembina, 1850. hunter]
Peck, Harrison J. Shakopee. b. 1838, Vt. d. 1913, Calif. lawyer.
Peck, Simon L. Ira, Vt. b. 1844, Vt. r. Ira, 1926. teacher
Pierce, Parker. Mankato. b. 1844, Me. r. Grantsville, Mont., 1867. farmer
Sears, Caleb. Minn. b. *ca.* 1834, N.Y. r. Helena, Mont., 1866. farmer
Sears, Mrs. Caleb (Mary A.). Minn. b. 1837, Ohio. r. Helena, Mont., 1866
Sears, Eugene C. Minn. [b. 1853, Faribault.] d. 1931, Chewelah, Wash.
Sears, Ida May. Minn. b. 1863, Minn. r. Helena, Mont., 1866
Warner, H. L., and family. St. Peter. lawyer. [Henry, b. 1845, Berkshire, Mass. r. Harrison, Mont., 1885. farmer]
White, Bob. Minn.
?Wickersham, M. R. Mankato. physician
?Wickersham, Price. Mankato. physician
Windslow [Winslow], James [M. b. 1812, Vt. r. St. Paul, 1860. building contractor]
Windslow [Winslow], Mrs. James [M. (Sarah A.). b. 1814, Vt. r. St. Paul, 1860]

THE FISK TRAIN, 1866

The following emigrants are known only by a first or last name: Antoine, the guide; Dozenberry, Gardner, Heinze, Hume, McCarthy, McCaully, Merneau family, Roberts, Mrs. Singer.

Adriance, Cornelius B. Buffalo, N.Y.
Ahne(r)man, Joseph. Pine Island. [b. 1839, Prussia. farmer]
Anderson, Joseph. Sauk Centre. [b. 1834. d. 1898, Coal Harbor, N.D. farmer]
Anseny, John. Jacobs Prairie, Stearns Co.
Barber, Charles. Fillmore Co. b. Pa. r. Sheridan, Mont., 1913. rancher
Barber, Helen E. (Mrs. Daniel W. Tilton). Fillmore Co. b. Pa. r. San Diego, Calif.
Barber, Orlando B. Fillmore Co. b. 1828, Hamburg, N.Y. d. 1913, Springbury, Pa. millwright, rancher
Barber, Mrs. Orlando B. (Samantha Gates). Fillmore Co. b. 1830, Dunkirk, N.Y. d. 1899, Sheridan, Mont.

Barker, H. [Hiram] E. Bangor, Me. [b. 1842, Corinth, Me. r. Lewiston, Idaho, 1896. farmer, sawmill operator]

Barker, T. R. Bangor, Me.

Barlow, G. Springfield, Mass.

Bassett, Francis. Fillmore Co. b. 1848, Iowa. d. 1874, Walla Walla, Wash.

Bassett, George W. Fillmore Co. b. 1846, Iowa. r. Washtucna, Wash., 19–

Bassett, Gilbert. Fillmore Co. b. 1851, Iowa. r. Helena, Mont., 19–

Bassett, Gilbert B. O. Fillmore Co. b. 1817, Middlebury, Vt. d. 1878, Carimona. printer, merchant, farmer

Bassett, Mrs. Gilbert B. O. (Mary Smith). Fillmore Co. b. 1816, Ancaster, Can. d. 1911, Washtucna, Wash.

Bassett, Mary (Mrs. William Harkness). Fillmore Co. b. 1857, Minn. d. 1900, Spokane, Wash.

Bassett, Samuel S. Fillmore Co. b. 1853, Iowa. r. Spokane, Wash., 19–

Bateman, Ira. Pine Island. b. 1811, Chenango, N.Y. d. 1884, Helena, Mont. carpenter, grocer

Bateman, Mrs. Ira (Eliza Hoffman). Pine Island. b. 1820, N.Y. d. 1900, San Francisco, Calif.

Bateman, James F. Pine Island. b. 1843, Chemung Co., N.Y. d. 1900, Butte, Mont. farmer, miner, carpenter

Bateman, Robert M. Spring Valley. b. 1843, Newbern, Va. d. 1925, Melrose, Mont. farmer

Beaudin, Narcisse. St. Arben, Dismore, Can.

Beaupre, Philip. Stearns Co. b. 1823, Can. d. 1906, Sauk Rapids. fur trader.

?Bennett, James. Nicollet Co.

Beyer, August. [St. Paul]

Bill, ——. Hartford, Conn. photographer. [George W. De Bill. b. 1840, Griswold, Conn. d. 1888, St. Cloud. tinsmith]

Blake, Major [Francis]

Briggs, Benjamin H. Little Spring Valley. b. 1837, Ohio. d. 1888, S.D. lumberman, farmer, merchant

Briggs, Mrs. Benjamin H. (Carmelia Bateman, Mrs. John H. Jurgens). Pine Island. b. 1844, N.Y. d. 1917, Kalispell, Mont.

Brown, D. [Daniel] P. Wright Co. [Carver Co. b. 1820, Sweden. r. Green Island, Nebr., 1878. Lutheran minister]

Brown, M. A. Fillmore Co.

Burson, George W. See Fisk 1864 roster

Bussell, J. [Jotham] S. Exeter, Me. [b. 1845, Cherryfield, Me. lumberman]

Butler, Benjamin F. Fair Haven. b. 1829, Cornville, Me. d. 1914, Minneapolis. farmer, millwright

Chapin, B. W. [Pine Island]

Chapin, Henry H. Spring Valley. b. 1841, Bloomfield, Wis. d. 1922, Rogers, Ark. farmer, blacksmith

Chapin, I. Fillmore Co.

Chemidlin, Nicholas T. See Fisk 1864 roster

Clark, Patrick. Woodstock, Can.

Clawson, Timothy E. Danville, Ill. b. 1839, Lake Co., Ill. d. 1904, Lake City, Colo. rancher, miner

Cobb, H. (Hiram) A. San Francisco, Calif.

Cook, Joe E. Portland, N.Y.

Cullen, Charles. St. Paul. b. 1848, Pa.

Cullen, Kimball. St. Paul. b. 1844, Pa. d. 1898, Los Angeles, Calif. businessman

Cullen, William E. St. Peter. b. 1837, Mansfield, Ohio. d. 1908, Spokane, Wash. lawyer

Cummings, Charles W. Springfield, Mass. [b. 1842, Plymouth, N.H. d. 1927, Napa, Calif. laborer, teamster, farmer]

Cunningham, Alex

Curtiss, (D.), Benjamin. Glastonbury, Conn. physician

Darret, Morice. Can.

Davis, John [H.]. Madison, Wis. [b. 1829, Sterling, Ky. d. 1895, Virginia City, Mont. miller, miner, farmer]

Davis, R. Exeter, Me.

Dedrick, William H. Springfield, Mass. b. 1836, Coxsackie, N.Y. r. Helena, Mont., 1870. armorer, blacksmith

Delany (Delaine), Andrew. Minneapolis. [b. 1848, Can. d. 1899, Chicago, Ill. printer, timekeeper]

Delany, Joseph. See Fisk 1864 roster

Dexter, Wheeler O. Pa. b. 1843, Steuben Co., N.Y. d. 1924, Fort Benton, Mont. oil driller, rancher, sawmill prop.

Dibb, Thomas. See Holmes 1864 roster

Diedrick, Philip. Jacobs Prairie, Stearns Co. b. 1831, Bavaria. farmer

Dodge, Joe

Doyle, James. St. Anthony

Durfee, James E. Esperance, N.Y. b. 1844, Schoharie Co., N.Y. d. 1907, Jamul, Calif.

Eckford, Peter. St. Paul. b. 1848, Scot.

Elmer, Peter. St. Paul. r. Butte, Mont., 1876

Elphie, Caleb, Jr. Chatfield. b. 1845, London, Eng. d. 1903, Elgin, Ill. blacksmith

English, George H. Danville, Ill. b. 1844, Perrysville, Ind. d. 1912, Danville

Erridge, H. Wis.

Evans, [John H. b. 1846. d. 1929, Chewelah, Wash. rancher, businessman]

Fadden, Joseph. St. Cloud. b. 1816, N.Y. farmer

Farrel, Dennis. Wis.

Farwell (Farewell), John. Maine Prairie. b. 1823, Can. farmer

Fenton, John W. Buffalo, N.Y. b. 1837, Buffalo. d. 1891, D.C. clerk

Fisk, Andrew Jackson. St. Paul. b. 1849, Cattaraugus Co., N.Y. d. 1910, Helena, Mont. newspaperman

Fisk, Dell (Mrs. Fred Staus). White Bear Lake. b. 1864, White Bear Lake. d. 1946, Pewaukee, Wis.

Fisk, Mrs. James L. (Lydia Burson). White Bear Lake. b. 1835, Prairie Ronde, Mich. d. 1876, D.C.

Fisk, John C. S. Port Gibson, N.Y. b. 1831, [N.Y.] d. 1915, Tina, Mo.

Fisk, Robert Emmet. Burlington, Iowa. b. 1837, Pierpont, Ohio. d. 1908, Berkeley, Calif. newspaperman, editor

Fisk, Van Haden. *See* Fisk 1864 roster

Fletcher, Thomas J. A. Marcellon, Wis. b. 1841, Can. d. 1895, Canton, Mont. harness maker

Fletcher, William H. Sauk Rapids. b. 1844, Ohio. d. 1928, Sauk Rapids. miller

Foh(e)r, William. St. Paul. b. 1830, Nassau. cigar manufacturer

French, H. M. Mass.

Fuller, Thomas P. Schenectady, N.Y. b. 1837, Schenectady. d. 1899, Mont. bookkeeper

Gammon, William. St. Anthony

Garlington, Edwin A. St. Cloud. b. 1837, Pa. d. 1901, St. Cloud. farmer

Garlington, James W. St. Cloud. b. 1843, Sharon, Ohio. d. 1932, Dayton, Ohio. laborer, farmer

Geer, Henry [C.] Pine Island. [b. 1816, Pa. r. Rochester, 1860]

Getchel, J. B. St. Cloud. r. Red Mountain City, Mont., 1867

Glidden, W. B. Old Town, Me.

Gordon, R. E.

Green, George. St. Anthony

Gustner, Joseph. Jacobs Prairie, Stearns Co.

Halloway, John. Pine Island. b. Eng. farmer

Ham, W. S. Bangor, Me.

Hampson, Eli. [Tarrytown], N.Y. [b. 1841, Eng. d. 1869, Bridgeport, Conn. hatter]

Hannum, A. C. Mass.

Hardy, Nathan. Van Buren Co., Iowa

Harlan, Wilson B. Red Wing. b. 1848, Columbiana Co., Ohio. d. 1935, Columbia Falls, Mont. clerk, fruitgrower

Harmon, James F. Gorham, Me. b. 1842, Portland, Me. d. 1909, Rialto, Calif. farmer, rancher

Harris, William. *See* Fisk 1864 roster

Harrison, W. A. Minn. b. 1836, Can. r. Sweet Grass, Mont., 1885. rancher

Hezekiah, John. Paris, Ohio. b. 1844, Harrison, Ohio. r. Fort Benton, Mont., 1880s. d. 1898. wagonmaker, hotelkeeper.

Hicks, George. Minn. [b. 1808, Vt. r. Nicollet Co., 1860. d. 1896, Minneapolis. farmer, storekeeper]

Hicks, Jack. Minn. hunter, trapper

Hoback, Richard. Minn. b. 1835, Ky. d. 1896, Calif. teacher, miner, real estate dealer

Hoback, Mrs. Richard (Mary Hays). b. 1849, Pa. r. Helena, Mont., 1885

Hoback, William. Minn. b. 1864, St. Peter. d. 1941, Helena, Mont. pressman

Holland, William. Conn.

Holmes, Charles. Minn. b. 1834, Sweden. d. 1905, Bozeman, Mont. farmer

Holt, Major [L. O. b. *ca.* 1836. d. 1876, Helena, Mont.]

Hostetler, J. T. (F.). Decatur, Ill.

Illingworth, William H. St. Paul. b. 1844, Eng. r. St. Paul, 1867. photographer

Jackson, John

Jacobs, Freedom. Chatfield. b. [1839], Ashtabula Co., Ohio. farmer

Jellison, Samuel B. Decatur, Ill. b. 1838.

Johnson, Andrew. Minneapolis

Johnson, Lixer. Minneapolis

Judd, *see* Lusk

Kemp, Jack. Pine Island

Kern, John. Little Spring Valley. b. 1846, Minn. d. 1923, Red Mountain City, Mont. miner

Kober, George C. Chicago, Ill. b. 1844, Chicago. d. 1902, Chicago. bank collector, hotel clerk, pension office examiner

Lane, ———. [A. S. Laine. r. Helena, Mont., 1867]

Larimer, Robert. Charleston, Ill.

Larkin, William T. [r. Butte, Mont.]

Lee, Mrs. Mary Jane Stanchfield (Mrs. Thomas H. Hamilton). Minn. r. Horse Prairie, Mont., 1868

Leech, John. St. Cloud. b. 1838, Ire. r. Helena, Mont., 1867. farmer

Leech, Robert. St. Cloud. r. Helena, Mont., 1867

Lester, John. Necedah, Wis. b. 1836, Ire. r. Little Blackfoot, Mont., 1867. laborer

Liberty, Stephen (Etienne E. Laliberte). St. Paul. b. 1843, Sorel, Can. d. 1911, Spokane, Wash. rancher

Lindahl, S., and family. St. Paul

Little, Oscar. Bloomington, Ill.

Long, Richard S. Mason City, Iowa. b. 1845, Wis. d. 1868, Fort Shaw, Mont.

Lowry, Milner R. Rochester. b. 1846, Meadville, Pa. d. 1900, Fergus Falls. feed store, bakery prop.

Lowry, Morrow P. Erie, Pa. b. *ca.* 1843, Pa. d. 1888, Helena, Mont. lawyer

Lusk, Judson D. (J. D. Judd, Daniel B. Jud, Wesson). St. Paul. [b. 1843, New Lynne, Ohio]. d. 1868, Virginia City, Mont. outlaw, [clerk, bookkeeper]

Maas [Maes], William. Pine Island. [b. 1830, Prussia. r. Pine Island, 1860. carpenter]

McCourt, John. Polk Co., Wis. b. 1840, Clinton, N.Y. d. 1901, Garneill, Mont. farmer, rancher

McCourt, Thomas. Polk Co., Wis. b. 1843, N.Y. d. 1910, Jennings, La. farmer, rancher

McCrai, Peter. Montreal, Can.

McIntyre, William H. Pa. [b. 1842, Indiana Co., Pa. d. 1905, Lincoln, Nebr. artist, photographer, carpenter]

McKnight, Jo [Joseph H. b. *ca.* 1845, Iowa. d. 1903, Havre, Mont. merchant]

McKusick, Freeman L. Stillwater. b. 1841, Baring, Me. d. 1912, Minneapolis. lumberman, city clerk

McLean, Isaac. Polk Co., Wis. b. 1836, N.Y. d. 1907, Osceola, Wis. farmer

McMillan, Angus. Can. b. 1843, Can. d. 1906, Beaver Creek, Fergus Co., Mont. rancher

Maginnis, Martin. Red Wing. b. 1841, N.Y. d. 1919, Los Angeles, Calif. newspaper publisher

Malben, Benjamin. Minn.

Marble, Henry. Bloomington, Ill. b. 1842, Harmony, Me.

Martin, David. [Masquilongé], Can.

May, B. W. [William B.]. Forestville, N.Y. [b. ca. 1837. d. 1882, West Gallatin, Mont.]

Mayhew, George V. Sauk Rapids. b. 1826, Herkimer Co., N.Y. d. 1899, Sauk Rapids. farmer

Metzelder, Derk (Dreschricht). Pine Island. b. 1832, Belg. d. 1903, Danville, Ill. grainer, farmer, peddler

Middleton, John. [San Francisco, Calif.]

Miller, M. H. St. Paul. [r. Helena, Mont., 1868. baker]

Millet[t], John W. [S.] Minn. [b. 1846, Dubuque, Iowa. r. St. Paul, 1864. farmer]

?Mills, John B. St. Cloud

Moore, John. St. Cloud

Mothey, Henry

Moulton, Ephraim F. Bloomington, Ill. b. 1845, Addison Co., Vt. clerk

Nevin, O. B. Chicago, Ill.

Newhall, A. Springfield, Mass. r. Helena, Mont., 1868. machinist

Nickels [Nichols], John. Pine Island. [b. 1827, Wales. r. Cherry Grove, Olmsted Co., 1860. farmer]

Norton (Morton), Harry

Noyes, Alva J. Minn. b. 1856, Minneapolis. d. 1917, Harlem, Mont. rancher

Noyes, Mrs. George R. (Amy Stanchfield). Minn. b. 1837. d. 1869, Silver Star, Mont.

Noyes, Maud (Mrs. Will A. Armitage). Minn. b. 1861, Minn. d. 1927, Dillon, Mont.

Olden, Elijah. Mass.

Olds, V. W. Minneapolis. b. Mass. r. Helena, Mont., 1868. carpenter

Overn, Edward. b. 1840, Ire. r. Pleasant Grove, Olmsted Co., 1860; Helena, Mont., 1867. farmer

?Paine, W. H. Montreal, Can.

Parkhurst, Rosswell. Red Wing. b. 1839. Potsdam, N.Y. r. Stevensville, Mont., 1885. fruitgrower

Payton, Isaac N. Danville, Ill. [b. ca. 1840, Ill. r. Danville, 1860. clerk]

Pease, Frank. Exeter, Me.

Reilly, Patrick. Toledo, Ohio. d. 1867, Prickly Pear, Mont.

Reynolds, L. [Lyman]. Stillwater. [b. 1825, N.Y. r. Lakeland, 1860. lumber merchant]

Riley, Luke

Robinson, [Curtis] B. (P.) St. Cloud. [b. 1842, Del.] d. 1867, Prickly Pear, Mont. [farmer]

Robi(n)son, Frank. Springfield, Mass. [d. 1877, Cow Creek, Mont.]

Robinson, Henry. N.Y.

Roesser (Roesier), Michael. St. Cloud. b. 1848. Holland. farm laborer

Rogers, John D. St. Cloud. r. Helena, Mont., 1867

Rollett(e), Joseph. "Indian Rice Village," Minn.

Rose, John. Houlton, Me.

Ryan, William A. C. Buffalo, N.Y. b. 1841, Toronto, Can. d. 1873, Havana, Cuba. clerk

Schibell, G. St. Cloud. [George Seible. b. 1832, Ger. r. St. Anthony, 1860. wagonmaker]

Shaw, William A. West Levant, Me.

Sims, Charles F. St. Cloud. See Fisk 1864 roster

Sims, Erwin W. Anoka. See Fisk 1864 roster

Sims, Mrs. Erwin W. [Anoka]

Sinclair, James. Houlton, Me. [b. 1823, Can. r. Portland, Me., 1865. tailor]

Spangler, Casper. Minn. d. 1890, Placer, Mont. hotelkeeper

Sperry, De Forrest. Throopsville, N.Y. b. ca. 1812, N.Y. laborer

Sperry, George W. Throopsville, N.Y. b. 1844, N.Y. laborer

Sprague, Mr. and Mrs. B. L., and family. Chippewa, Wis. [Benjamin, b. 1826, N.Y. r. Chippewa Co., Wis., 1860. farmer]

Sprague, V. B. r. Butte, Mont., 1866

Sprankle [Sprangle], Dan W. [d. 1906, Anaconda, Mont.] hotelkeeper

Stackpole, A. M. Cleveland, Ohio

Stackpole, Edward S. Cleveland, Ohio. b. 1834, Kenebec Co., Me. d. 1924. merchant, postmaster

Starbuck, Mr. and Mrs. M., and family. Ramsey Co.

Steele, Mr. and Mrs. Henry B., and two children. St. Cloud. See Holmes 1862 roster

Stuart, Charles R. St. Paul. b. ca. 1836, Detroit, Mich. d. 1885, Detroit. newspaperman, printer

Taillefer, Alfred. St. Martin, Can.

Terrell, Jack. [Terrill, J. M.]. Rochester. [b. 1829, N.Y. r. Rochester, 1860. painter]

Thomas, Charles. Old Town, Me.

Tibbetts [Tibbitts], George [W. b. 1845, Me. r. Wabasha Co., 1860. farm laborer]

Topping, Nathaniel B. Bath, N.Y. b. 1846, Bath

Trask, William C. Jefferson, Lincoln Co., Me.

Tromblie [Trombley], Charles. Redwood Falls. [b. 1845, Ill. r. 1860, St. Paul]

Tubbs, G. W. St. Cloud. r. Helena, Mont., 1869

Van Etten, Thomas M. St. Paul. b. 1836, N.Y. d. 1913, Sauk Rapids. lawyer

Wallace, C. H. Con. Wallace, Nova Scotia

Watson, W. H. St. Cloud. r. Helena, Mont., 1866

Weeden, Henry G. Viroqua, Wis. b. 1822, Vt. d. 1872, Blackfoot City, Mont. physician

White, I. N. Springfield, Mass.

Whitney, J. F. Exeter, Me.

Williams, Kate. St. Paul

Wilson, James. [St. Cloud.] r. Red Mountain City, Mont., 1868. carpenter

Winnet, Frederick S. St. Paul

Winney (Winnet), Charles. St. Paul. [Charles K. Winne. r. St. Paul, 1866]

Wise, George E. Minneota, Jackson Co.

Yost, Byron W. Bath, N.Y. b. 1846, Bath. clerk

Zitzman (Fitzman), Fred. Minneota, Jackson Co.

THE DAVY TRAIN, 1867

Ai(t)kin, Jarvis. Plover, Wis. r. Gallatin City, Mont., 1880. farmer, hotelkeeper

Ai(t)kin, Mrs. Jarvis (Louisa Jane Aplin). Plover, Wis. b. 1837, Taunton, Eng. d. 1874, Gallatin City, Mont.

Ai(t)kin, Nellie. Plover, Wis. b. 1862, [Wis.] d. 1873, Gallatin City, Mont.

Anderson, Alma A. (Mrs. —— Walley). Minn. b. 1860, Sweden. d. 1920, Lindstrom

Anderson, Charles. Minn. b. *ca.* 1866, Minn. d. *ca.* 1932, Clepper, Wash. farmer, rancher

Anderson, Gustave (Gustaf). Minn. b. *ca.* 1829, Sweden. d. 1912, Lindstrom. farmer

Anderson, Mrs. Gustave (Helena). b. *ca.* 1829, Sweden. d. 1912, Lindstrom

Anderson, Samuel. b. 1843, Sweden. d. 1915, Lindstrom. tinsmith, miner, farmer

Anderson, Mrs. Samuel (Christina L. Danielson). Minneapolis. b. 1847, Kalmar, Sweden. d. 1886, Lindstrom

Aplin, James. b. 1813, Somersetshire, Eng. d. 1887, Bozeman, Mont.

Aplin, Mrs. James. b. Eng. r. Gallatin City, Mont., 1874

Baker, Mr. and Mrs. O. C.

Beatty, Samuel

Benham, H. A. [Mrs. Isaac N. (Harriet). b. 1831, N.Y. r. Marine, 1860]

Benham, Isaac [N. b. 1827, N.Y. r. Marine, 1860. farmer. r. Spring Hill, Mont., 1874]

Benham, [William B. b. 1850, Pa. r. Marine, 1860]

Brewer, Thomas

Cadman, William

Cahill, William

Cahill, two sisters

Cameron, Alex. b. Can. r. Helena, Mont., 1909. farmer

Cameron, Angus. b. 1836, Can. d. 1909, Lincoln, Mont. miner, stock raiser

Choler, John

Crane, Thomas C. Rochester. b. 1836, Ire. r.

Spring Hill, Mont., 1885. blacksmith, inventor

Davy, Peter B. Blue Earth. b. 1830, Can. d. 1889, Blue Earth. teacher, salesman

Detrick, Ole

Dixon (Dickson), Charles. [b. 1827, New Brunswick, Can. r. Bethel, 1860]; Helena, Mont. [farmer]

Dixon, Mrs. Charles [Charlote]. [b. 1837, New Brunswick, Can. r. Bethel, 1860]; Helena, Mont.

Dixon, daughter. [(Mrs. Thomas Conlin). r. Helena, Mont., 1920]

Dixon, daughter. [(Mrs. Charlotte Tuohy). r. Helena, Mont., 1920]

Dixon, James W. b. 1860, Minn. d. 1920, Helena, Mont.

Donnel, James

Donnel, John

Dorrington, Thomas

Doty, C. T.

Dueber (Duba), Mr. and Mrs. Peter, and family, r. Portland, Ore., 1868

Dueber (Duba), Josephine. r. Helena, Mont., 1867

Dueber (Duba), son. r. Fort Buford, Dak. Ter., 1867

?Eckland, P.

Epp, Adam

Fenchmaker, J.

Fleischmann, ——, and children. [Peter Flesmann. b. 1800, Bavaria, Ger.] r. Walla Walla, Wash., 1868. [shoemaker]

Fleischmann, ——. [Mrs. Peter (Margret) Flesmann. b. 1818, Baden, Ger.] r. Walla Walla, Wash., 1868

Fountain, Edward

Gates, Charles, and children. [Charles, b. 1830, Bavaria, Ger. r. Hastings, 1866. d. 1907, Columbia Falls, Mont. farmer]

Gates, Mrs. Charles [(Regina Rappelcorn). b. 1826. r. Columbus, Wis., 1855]

Green, Wilbur [B. b. 1832, Wyoming, N.Y. farmer]

Harrison, George [S. b. 1843, Kalamazoo Co., Mich. r. Central Point, Goodhue Co., 1864. d. *ca.* 1900, Columbia Falls, Mont. farmer, musician]

Hastman, Mr. and Mrs. Peter, and family

Hazen, Benjamin M. St. Paul. b. 1840, Lewis Co., N.Y. r. St. Paul, 1869. musician, saloonkeeper

Henry, Louis. Hastings. b. 1834, France. d. 1887, Helena, Mont. musician, shoemaker

Hertzel, F. L.

Hertzel, Theodore

Hilger, David. Henderson. b. 1858, Minn. d. 1937, Helena, Mont. rancher, banker, hardware merchant

Hilger, Louisa (Mrs. —— Chandler). Henderson. b. 1863, Minn. d. Lewistown, Mont.

Hilger, Mary (Mrs. —— Dougherty). Henderson. b. 1861, Minn. d. San Francisco, Calif.

Hilger, Nicholas. *See* Holmes 1864 roster

Hilger, Mrs. Nicholas (Susannah). Henderson. b. 1830, Prussia. d. 1910, Alhambra, Mont.

Hilger, Regina. Henderson. b. 1865, Minn. d. *ca.* 1879, Ore.

Hilger, Susan (Mrs. —— Dougherty). Henderson. b. 1860, Minn. d. 189–, Boulder, Mont.

Hilger, Willie. Henderson. b. 1866, Minn. d. Lake Bennett, Alaska

Hoffman, H.

Holm, Andrew

Horner, J.

Jacobs, Katharina (daughter of Nicholas Jacobs). Stearns Co. r. Portland, Ore., 1868

Jacobs, Mr. and Mrs. Nicholas, and family. Stearns Co. ret. Minn.

Johnson, J.

Johnson, William

Kirchner (Kirchnor), Mr. and Mrs., and daughters. r. Walla Walla, Wash., 1868. [Michael Kriechner. b. 1810, Bavaria, Ger. farmer. Mrs. Michael Kriechner (Terassea). b. 1827, Bavaria. r. Richmond, 1860]

Krall, Mr. and Mrs. Michael, and family

Larsher, Mr. and Mrs. Alexis, and family

Larson, H.

Lewis, William

Lovering, Robert A. *See* Fisk 1864 roster

Lueg, Henry. St. Paul. b. 1830, Prussia. d. 1906, Portland, Ore. blacksmith, machinist

Lusk, William

McAlister, John

McDermot, John

McKillop, William

McLaughlin, Mr. and Mrs. E., and son. r. Waitsburg, Ore., 1867

Manuel, Mose(s). Kelso. b. 1848, Can. d. 1905, Helena, Mont. miner, prospector

Mariell, A.

Martin, Henry

Merrill, Nehemiah D. Buffalo. b. 1835, Me. d. Greenleaf, Meeker Co. farmer

Miller, Mr. and Mrs. Joseph, and family

Mills, Sanford

Nibler, Franz. Cold Spring. b. 1836, Bavaria, Ger. d. 1933, Gervais, Ore. farmer, millwright

Nibler, George. Stearns Co. b. 1829, Bavaria, Ger. r. Marion Co., Ore., 1868. farmer

Nibler, Mr. and Mrs. John, and family. Stearns Co. r. Gervais, Ore., 1887

Nibler, Joseph, and family. Cold Spring. Joseph b. 1826, Bavaria, Ger. r. Walla Walla, Wash., 1868. farmer

Nibler, Mrs. Joseph (Anna). Stearns Co. b. 1826, Bavaria, Ger. r. Walla Walla, Wash., 1868

Nibler, Mrs. Margaret. Stearns Co. b. 1792, Bavaria, Ger. r. Marion Co., Ore., 1868

Nibler, Michael, and family. Stearns Co. Michael, b. 1828, Bavaria, Ger. r. Marion Co., Ore., 1868

Nibler, Mrs. Michael (Terasea). Stearns Co. b. 1838, Bavaria, Ger. r. Marion Co., Ore., 1868

Olson, A.

Olson, O.

Olson, T.

Osland, Andrew (T. Oland)

Otto, Henry. r. Portland, Ore., 1868

Peel, W.

Peteran, Peter

Peterson, J.

Powers, T. B.

Rea, Benjamin

Ridgely, Mr. and Mrs. Joshua

Rishman, Mr. and Mrs. Andrew, and family

Rishman, Joseph

Roesmann, Mr. and Mrs. ——, and family. Minn. b. Bohemia, Ger. r. Helena, Mont., 1867

Rogers, Jacob D. St. Paul. b. 1841, Lee Co., Ill. teacher

Rosseau, J. C.

Sago, H.

Schaffner, Mr. and Mrs. Thomas, and family

Schoffen (Shoffen), Thomas. Stearns Co. b. 1821, Prussia. farmer

Schoffen, Mrs. Thomas (Susana). Stearns Co. b. 1825, Prussia

Schroner, Mr. and Mrs. John, and family. Minn. r. Portland, Ore., 1867

Schroner, Mike, and family

Schultheis, Mr. and Mrs. Michael, and family. Minn. r. Marion Co., Ore. [Michael Shouldise. b. 1838, Mo. r. Richmond, 1860. farmer]

Seaman, Samuel

Shapcott, Thomas

Smart, Dennis

Sperry, B. W. [Burdette M. b. 1837, Quincy, Ill. d. 1924, Sawtelle, Calif. carpenter, stonemason]

Sperry, M. H. [Miles H. d. 1889, Helena, Mont.]

Sperry, Nathaniel D. Rockford. b. 1835, Sullivan Co., N.H. d. 1889, Rockford. farmer, laborer

Stetson, L. W. [Lorenzo P. Cannon City. b. 1825, Androscoggin, Me. d. 1900, Greene, Me. farmer]

Stout, Tenbroeck. Lake City. b. 1838, N.J. d. 1883, Marshall. merchant, mining business

Stout, Mrs. Tenbroeck (Maggie Magee). Grant Co., Wis. b. 1844. d. 1902, Erick, Okla.

Swartz, Mr. and Mrs. George, and family

Swenson, C. O.

Temple, Moses

Tiffs, Franklin

Tollman, Mr. and Mrs. Robert, and family

Trumbull (Trimble), Mr. and Mrs. John, and two sons. r. near Walla Walla, Wash., 1867

Vamoigen, H.

Wagoner, Charles F. Trenton, Freeborn Co. b. 1844, Brown Co., N.Y. d. 1910, Eagle Lake. clerk, farmer

Wald, C. B.

Wardell, Mr. and Mrs. Franz, and family

Washburn, J. [James] B. [b. 1835, N.Y. r. Buffalo, 1860. laborer]

Waters, Isaac

Weber, Mrs. ——, and daughters. r. Fort Buford, Dak. Ter., 1867

Weber, Chathame, and family

Weber, John. b. 1850. r. Walla Walla, Wash., 1868

Wittmann (Whitman), Mr. and Mrs. Alex, and family

Wittmann, Mr. and Mrs. John, and family

Wittmann, Mr. and Mrs. Nickolas, and family. r. Marion Co., Ore., 1868. [Nicolas Witman. b. 1824, France. r. Cold Spring, 1860. farmer]

Wright, Edward

Young, W. P.

Zollner, Mr. and Mrs. ——, and children

INDEX

Index

ABBOTT, CAROLINE, wedding, 55n
Adriance, Cornelius B., 213n, 214, 224, 226, 227, 234
Advertising and publicity, Fisk, 8, 29, 35, 75–77, 101–107, 112, 137n, 138n, 163, 165, 167–169, 238, 256; Davy, 238, 239, 242, 245, 248, 250n
Aikin, Jarvis, family, 248
Alder Gulch, 18, 83, 96, 97. *See also* Virginia City
Aldrich, Cyrus W., congressman, 6, 26, 28, 76
Alexandria, described, 52
Alhambra Hot Springs, Mont., 130
American Fork, Mont., 33, 95n; described, 67
American Fur Co., 151; posts, 9, 129n; traders, 32, 94n, 173
Anderson, Gustaf, emigrant, 243, 248
Anderson, Joseph R. (Skookum Joe), miner, 84
Anderson, Mr. and Mrs. Samuel, emigrants, 242, 243, 246, 248
Anoka, 102, 114
Antelope, 70, 80, 87, 122, 140; hunting, 44, 56, 63, 65, 66, 67, 92, 123, 125, 172, 187, 198, 199, 200, 208, 209, 212, 213, 215, 257
Antelope Creek. *See* Big Muddy Creek
Antoine, guide, 197, 201
Aplin, Mr. and Mrs. James, emigrants, 248
Arikara Indians, 40, 203
Assiniboin Indians, 59; encountered by emigrants, 10, 49, 60, 81, 89, 90, 256; Broken Arm's band, 60, 81, 89
Atkinson, Dr. Monroe G., 65, 67; described, 32
Atlantic City, Mont., 235; named, 176, 232
Aurora borealis, described, 17

BADLANDS, Little Missouri River, 9, 17, 20, 109–111, 115, 126, 142, 151, 153, 161
Bancroft, H. H., quoted, 19
Bands. *See* Music
Bannack, Mont., 94n, 227; mining center, 17, 18, 19, 75, 93, 101, 130; emigrants at, 77, 82, 95, 96, 97, 101, 176; described, 83, 96

Bannock Indians, 10, 46, 47, 156n
Barber, Mr. and Mrs. Orlando B., emigrants, 211, 215, 217
Bartlett, Lt. Col. Edward M., 140
Bartlett, William L., Butte merchant, 34
Bass, W. E., 131
Bassett, Gilbert B. O., emigrant, 167, 174, 211
Bassett, Henry, 167
Battle Creek (Mont.), 93n
Bear, Benjamin, injured, 129
Bearpaw Mountains, 17, 63, 64, 91, 93, 129, 172, 208, 210; prospecting, 190, 192
Bears, grizzly, 57, 64, 65, 67, 80, 92, 172, 191
Bears Den Hillock, 174, 244, 251n, 255; described, 196. *See also* Fort Ransom
Beaupre, Philip, Fisk's assistant, 173, 203, 211, 218
Beaver, 63, 94, 95, 124, 215, 216
Beaverhead River, 46, 96n
Benedict, Gilbert, Helena pioneer, 111, 131n; journal, 107, 119–131
Benton City, Mont., described, 192, 210n, 247. *See also* Fort Benton
Betts, Corp. Marmaduke, 145, 150
Big Cheyenne wagon road, 160, 162n, 164, 165
Big Hole Basin, 82, 96; described, 95, 96; settlers, 176
Bighorn River, 113, 115, 142; prospecting, 83, 97, 103, 218
Big Knife River, 182
Big Muddy Creek, 61, 90, 128, 189, 206
Big Prickly Pear. *See* Prickly Pear Valley
Big Sandy Creek, 64, 93, 190, 210
Big Stone Lake, 114, 135, 136, 178, 179; proposed as rendezvous, 133, 137n, 161, 163; as army post site, 137, 157
Big Woods, 52n, 111
Bill, ——, photographer, 169, 196
Birch Coulee, battlefield described, 179
Birds, on trails, 52, 58, 62, 64, 66, 71, 80, 179, 195, 199, 200, 212, 214. *See also* Ducks, Geese, Grouse
Birdtail Butte, trail landmark, 65, 94, 129

279

Helen McCann White

began the preparation of this book for the Alvord Memorial Commission of the Mississippi Valley Historical Association in 1944. Since that time, because of her husband's government service, she carried the manuscript with her literally around the world. Frequently interrupted by family and community responsibilities, Mrs. White continued her work during the family's residence in five states and three foreign countries.

While she has contributed articles to such scholarly publications as *The American Archivist* and *Minnesota History*, this is Mrs. White's first book. She attended Hamline University in St. Paul and did graduate work in American history and literature at the University of Minnesota in Minneapolis. While abroad, she taught English and history in Tsuda Women's College and Jiyu Gakuen College in Tokyo, and at the American School in Manila.

From 1937 to 1941 Mrs. White was employed in the manuscripts department of the Minnesota Historical Society. Beginning in 1965, she returned to the society's staff as editor of the institution's National Historical Publications Commission project to microfilm the papers of Lawrence Taliaferro and Ignatius Donnelly and as historian for the long-range work of restoring historic old Fort Snelling. She is married, has three children, and resides in St. Paul.

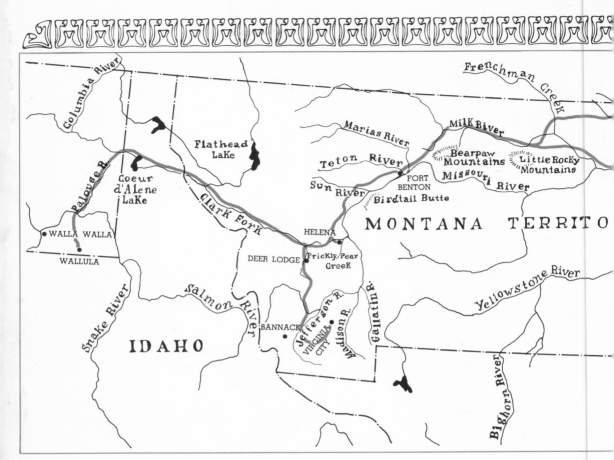

NORTHERN ROUTES TO MONTANA